# From Grammar to Meaning

## *The Spontaneous Logicality of Language*

In recent years, the study of formal semantics and formal pragmatics has grown tremendously showing that core aspects of language meaning can be explained by a few principles. These principles are grounded in the logic that is behind – and tightly intertwined with – the grammar of human language. In this book, some of the most prominent figures in linguistics, including Noam Chomsky and Barbara H. Partee, offer new insights into the nature of linguistic meaning and pave the way for the further development of formal semantics and formal pragmatics. Each chapter investigates various dimensions in which the logical nature of human language manifests itself *within* a language and/or *across* languages. Phenomena like bare plurals, free choice items, scalar implicatures, intervention effects, and logical operators are investigated in depth and at times cross-linguistically and/or experimentally. This volume will be of interest to scholars working within the fields of semantics, pragmatics, language acquisition, and psycholinguistics.

IVANO CAPONIGRO is an Associate Professor in the Department of Linguistics at the University of California, San Diego.

CARLO CECCHETTO is a Full Professor in the Department of Psychology at the University of Milan-Bicocca.

# From Grammar to Meaning

*The Spontaneous Logicality of Language*

*Edited by*

Ivano Caponigro

*University of California, San Diego*

Carlo Cecchetto

*University of Milan-Bicocca*

CAMBRIDGE
UNIVERSITY PRESS

**CAMBRIDGE**
**UNIVERSITY PRESS**

32 Avenue of the Americas, New York NY 10013-2473, USA

Cambridge University Press is part of the University of Cambridge.

It furthers the University's mission by disseminating knowledge in the pursuit of education, learning and research at the highest international levels of excellence.

www.cambridge.org
Information on this title: www.cambridge.org/9781107033108



First published 2013

*A catalogue record for this publication is available from the British Library*

*Library of Congress Cataloguing in Publication data*
From grammar to meaning : the spontaneous logicality of language / Edited by Ivano Caponigro, University of California, San Diego and Carlo Cecchetto, University of Milan-Bicocca.
pages cm
Includes bibliographical references and index.
ISBN 978-1-107-03310-8
1. Semantics. 2. Grammar, Comparative and general. 3. Meaning (Psychology) I. Caponigro, Ivano, 1970–editor of compilation. II. Cecchetto, Carlo, editor of compilation.
P325.F75 2013
415–dc23 2013000016

ISBN 978-1-107-03310-8 Hardback

Studies offered to Gennaro Chierchia

# Contents

# Contributors

MARIA ALONI
ILLC/Department of Philosophy
University of Amsterdam

ADRIANA BELLETTI
University of Siena

IVANO CAPONIGRO
Department of Linguistics
University of California, San Diego

CARLO CECCHETTO
Department of Psychology
University of Milan-Bicocca

NOAM CHOMSKY
Department of Linguistics and Philosophy
Massachusetts Institute of Technology

STEPHEN CRAIN
Department of Linguistics and ARC Centre of Excellence
in Cognition and its Disorders
Macquarie University

VENEETA DAYAL
Department of Linguistics
Rutgers University

ANAMARIA FĂLĂUŞ
Department of Linguistics and Basque Studies
University of the Basque Country (UPV/EHU)
and Linguistics Laboratory of Nantes (LLING)

FRANCESCA FOPPOLO
Department of Psychology
University of Milan-Bicocca

DANNY FOX
Department of Linguistics
Hebrew University of Jerusalem

MICHAEL FRANKE
ILLC/Department of Philosophy
University of Amsterdam

MARIA TERESA GUASTI
Department of Psychology
University of Milan-Bicocca

CHRISTOPHER KENNEDY
Department of Linguistics
University of Chicago

CLEMENS MAYR
Zentrum für Allgemeine Sprachwissenschaft
Center for General Linguistics
Berlin

FRANCESCA PANZERI
Department of Psychology
University of Milan-Bicocca

BARBARA H. PARTEE
Department of Linguistics
University of Massachusetts, Amherst

LUIGI RIZZI
University of Siena

ROSALIND THORNTON
Department of Linguistics and ARC Centre of Excellence
in Cognition and its Disorders
Macquarie University

Acknowledgments

We would like to thank our authors and reviewers for their willingness to help us in preparing the book, their extremely valuable feedback, and their cooperation with our strict time line. Our reviewers are: Flavia Adani, Maria Aloni, David Barner, Gregory Carlson, Jonathan Cohen, Luka Crnič, Veneeta Dayal, Edit Doron, Anamaria Fălăuş, Francesca Foppolo, Jon Gajewski, Maria Teresa Guasti, Christopher Kennedy, Giorgio Magri, Clemens Mayr, Isa Orvieto, Daniele Panizza, Francesca Panzeri, Jacopo Romoli, Uli Sauerland, and Benjamin Spector.

Thanks to Helen Barton, Helena Dowson, and all the other members of the CUP editorial team who supported the idea of this book from the very beginning and who have always been willing and ready to help us with our many questions and issues.

Thanks to Patrick Munoz for his extremely valuable help with formatting and editing and with the preparation of the bibliography and the indices.

Thanks to Daniel B. Kane for helping with editing the book proposal and the introduction.

Special thanks to Barbara H. Partee for her excellent feedback on the introduction and for bringing the play *Logic and Linguistics: A Marriage of Inconvenience* to our attention.

Thanks to Kathleen Adamczyk for finding an actual copy of the play, and to Kathleen Adamczyk and Raymond Turner for permission to publish it in this book as an appendix.

*Grazie di tutto cuore* to Isa Orvieto for her enthusiastic support of our plans for this book and for helping us in many ways, including making sure the project was kept hidden from Gennaro and providing us with a picture of Gennaro in collaboration with Marco Santambrogio, who we thank as well.

Veneeta Dayal deserves our highest gratitude. She was an extremely valuable consultant throughout the entire project; she was very generous in sharing her knowledge and wisdom; and, among many other things, she provided invaluable meticulous feedback on the introduction. *Dhanyavaad!*

# Abbreviations

| | |
|---|---|
| 1 | first person |
| 2 | second person |
| 3 | third person |
| ACC | accusative |
| ASP | aspect |
| CL | clitic |
| CONN | connective |
| DECL | declarative |
| IMP | imperative |
| MASC | masculine |
| NEG | negative |
| NOM | nominative |
| PAST | past tense |
| PL | plural |
| PROG | progressive |
| REFL | reflexive |
| SG | singular |
| SUBJ | subjunctive |
| TOP | topic |

# Introduction

*Ivano Caponigro and Carlo Cecchetto*

This book endorses and further develops a conception of human language that relies on two main ideas. The first idea is that core aspects of human language are determined by *grammar*, i.e., a set of features and principles that are specific to language, and that grammar determines fundamental components of language *meaning*, i.e., the informational content that language conveys. What is crucial is not just the two concepts of grammar and meaning and their close interaction, but also the direction of their interaction: *from* grammar *to* meaning. In other words, the phono-morpho-syntactic properties of a linguistic string systematically affect the content that the string conveys, and not the other way around.

The second main idea is that human language meaning can and must be studied by means of mathematical formal tools in order to unveil its *spontaneous logicality*, i.e., the deductive inferential system – the *logic* – that is tightly intertwined with human language and is responsible for a multiplicity of aspects of meaning.

These two main ideas about human language and meaning are fairly recent and far from being universally accepted. Only forty-three years ago, the logician Richard Montague still felt the need to make the claims and express the concerns below:

> There is in my opinion no important theoretical difference between natural language and the artificial languages of logicians; indeed, I consider it possible to comprehend the syntax and semantics of both kinds of languages within a single natural and mathematically precise theory. On this point I differ from a number of philosophers, but agree, I believe, with Chomsky and his associates. It is clear, however, that no adequate and comprehensive semantical theory has yet been constructed [footnote omitted, eds] and arguable that no comprehensive and semantically significant syntactical theory yet exists [footnote omitted, eds]. (Montague 1970: 373)

In the past four decades, the semantic and related syntactic landscape has changed substantially. Montague's research program on the semantics of natural language and the papers he wrote to implement it before his premature death in 1971 triggered the creation and rapid growth of the field of *formal semantics*, possibly in ways that Montague himself might not have expected or necessarily endorsed.

Formal semantics has borrowed and adapted formal tools from mathematical subfields like logic, set theory, model theory, type theory, and algebra (among others) and has created its own. It has also developed a very close connection with syntactic theory (both Chomskyan generative syntax and other varieties) with the so-called *syntax–semantics interface*, and, more recently, with some areas of pragmatics, with the so-called *semantics–pragmatics interface*. These developments have been crucial in describing the new data formal linguists have discovered, precisely formulating new generalizations, and providing fully explicit explanations and verifiable predictions.

Formal semanticists have paid increasing attention to the insights coming from semantic data from field work with understudied languages and cross-linguistic/typological data in order to substantiate broader generalizations (*cross-linguistic semantics*). Also, they have started to apply experimental techniques and developmental data (often in collaboration with psycholinguists, psychologists, and cognitive scientists) to further test the predictions their theories make (*experimental semantics*).

An overview of the main issues and a history of formal semantics fall largely beyond the purposes of this introduction. Among many useful resources, Chierchia and McConnell-Ginet's (1990) classic textbook provides a detailed introduction to most of the main formal tools and their application to a variety of linguistic constructions, together with an excellent overview of the empirical and theoretical foundations of semantic theory. Barbara H. Partee, one of the founders and protagonists of formal semantics, presents a fascinating and detailed historical reconstruction of the birth and development of the field in Partee (2011), while Partee (2005) contributes further with a more autobiographical approach and more personal details and insights.

The two ideas, that grammar affects meaning and that language is spontaneously logical, are at the core of formal semantics and are shared by all researchers in the field (with possible disagreement on specific details). A progressively larger number of linguists have endorsed them, also thanks to the developments and interaction we mentioned above. These ideas, though, are far from being widespread, commonly known, or accepted within the larger intellectual community that inquires about human language.

This book shows these ideas in action, and in doing so aims to broaden awareness of their force within the broader community of linguists and researchers working on language. Both its goal and its content owe a great deal to Gennaro Chierchia, who has been one of the protagonists of the development of these ideas and, more generally, formal semantics in all its aspects over the past three decades. This book has been deeply inspired by Chierchia's highly influential theoretical, cross-linguistic, and experimental work on semantics and its interfaces with syntax and pragmatics. The contributors to this book – from extremely promising young scholars to leading figures in linguistics – are all among Chierchia's intellectual mentors, former students, or collaborators. Their chapters range from broad foundational issues concerning the kind of data or principles semantic theory is based on to sophisticated and detailed theoretical analyses of complex data patterns, cross-linguistic generalizations, and new evidence coming from experimental and developmental investigations, often within the same chapter. Chierchia's assumptions, ideas, proposals, and findings are applied to new data, further developed, improved, and/or criticized. The variety of contributors and contributions further highlight the breadth, depth, and influence of his scholarship.

In the remainder of this introduction, we briefly touch on Chierchia's work, introduce the structure of the book and its chapters, and highlight connections among the chapters and with Chierchia's work.

Gennaro Chierchia received his Ph.D. in 1984 with Barbara H. Partee at the University of Massachusetts at Amherst. His dissertation committee also included Emmon Bach, F. Roger Higgins, and Edmund Gettier III. Nino Cocchiarella, Hans Kamp, and Edwin Williams played an important role as well. Chierchia was among the generation of scholars who played a pivotal role in the development of the field. He has held positions at Brown University, Cornell University, University of Milan, and University of Milan-Bicocca. He is currently Haas Foundations Professor of Linguistics at Harvard University.

Chierchia is one of the foremost philosophical linguistic semanticists of the past thirty years and his research has spanned all the main aspects of formal semantics and formal pragmatics (see his list of publications in Appendix A). He has worked on foundational issues concerning the formal nature of semantic theory through his work on Property Theory. He has developed existing theoretical proposals and improved their empirical coverage with his work on Dynamic Semantics, Type-Shifting, and Alternative Semantics. He has investigated major syntax–semantics interface issues like control, anaphora, binding, quantification in questions, and bare plurals. He has proposed highly influential new solutions for classical (and puzzling) distinctions like mass vs. count nouns and kind-denoting vs. individual-denoting expressions that he has grounded on cross-linguistic data and generalizations. He has elaborated the new notion of *semantic parameter* in addition to the already familiar Chomskyan notion of syntactic parameter in order to handle cross-linguistic variability. He has changed the conception of the semantics–pragmatics interface by providing a radically new analysis of what used to be considered a core pragmatic phenomenon: scalar implicatures. He has argued, instead, that scalar implicatures depend on a logically based, grammatically driven mechanism, which manifests what he has called the *spontaneous logicality of language*. He has shown that the very same mechanism that is responsible for scalar implicatures can also handle what looks like a completely different phenomenon on the surface:

polarity items, for which he has also provided a detailed cross-linguistic investigation of their distribution and semantic behavior. Chierchia's seminal work on the semantics-pragmatics interface has been fundamental for the recent birth and fast growth of the new field of formal pragmatics. Chierchia has also been among the first semanticists to closely collaborate in psycholinguistic, neurolinguistic, and language acquisition research. When he joined the University of Milan-Bicocca, he was a faculty member in the Psychology Department where he created a Linguistics Lab. Chierchia's work and his ideas continue to inspire new and exciting research in theoretical as well as experimental domains.

The FIRST PART of the book contains chapters by Barbara H. Partee and Noam Chomsky, who address historical and foundational issues concerning formal semantics and philosophy of language, and help trace the development of Chierchia's work and his thinking about the relationship between grammar and meaning and the spontaneous logicality of language.

In **Chapter 1**, Barbara H. Partee portrays her former advisee's early years from the late 1970s to the late 1980s: first as a brilliant graduate student at the University of Massachusetts at Amherst, and then as one of the leading young scholars at Brown University and later at Cornell University. In addition to the (auto)biographical details (see also the play in Appendix B), Partee reconstructs the vibrant intellectual climate of the early years of formal semantics and Chierchia's central role in it: the discussion about the best formal apparatus for the theory, the division of labor and the interaction between syntax and semantics, the exchange and collaboration among linguists, logicians, computer scientists, mathematicians, philosophers, and psychologists.

In **Chapter 2**, Noam Chomsky, the founding figure of modern linguistics and a point of intellectual reference for Chierchia (and many others), questions the notion of denotation, which is at the core of formal semantics together with the two ideas that grammar affects meaning and that language is spontaneously logical. The importance of the concept of denotation in the theory of meaning has been argued for in the philosophical tradition stemming from Frege. Denotation is at the root of the so-called *aboutness* of human language, i.e., the idea that human language is *about* something else and meaning is the bridge between language and this something else. Although Chomsky does not deny that we can use language to convey information about the external world, he strongly objects to the view that the notion of denotation is solid enough to play a critical role in the scientific investigation of language. In his opinion, formal semantics, including model-theoretic semantics, should be viewed as a form of symbol manipulation, much like syntax.

The SECOND PART of the book is devoted to studies that exemplify how formal semanticists proceed from grammar to meaning and, in doing so, how they develop semantic theory, discover novel data and generalizations, and raise new issues and challenges. All the studies contribute to topics that Chierchia has brought to the center of the debate as quintessential instantiations of the spontaneous logicality of language: bare nominals, polarity sensitivity, scalar implicatures, and presupposition projection.

Bare plurals are plural nominal expressions without a determiner, like *dogs* or *young men*. They constitute an intriguing puzzle for formal semanticists (and anybody who is interested in natural language) because they are widespread across languages and their interpretation within the same language varies in a similarly systematic way, despite the lack of any overt change in their morpho-syntactic shape. For instance, *dogs* can be close in meaning to the nominal expression *some dogs* with the overt existential quantifier *some* as in episodic sentences *Dogs are barking* and *Some dogs are barking*. On the other hand, the very same bare plural form *dogs* can be better paraphrased with a nominal with an overt universal quantifier *every* like in the generic sentences *Dogs bark* and *Every (standard) dog barks*. Since no specific lexical item in the nominal *dogs* can be responsible for its change in meaning and since the change in meaning is systematic across languages with bare plurals, it follows that bare plural interpretation must depend on general principles that regulate language meaning. In other words, bare plurals are a special window on the spontaneous logicality of language.

Chierchia's (1998) paper on bare plurals has been extremely influential and pivotal in the development of cross-linguistic semantics. Building on Carlson's (1977) seminal work, Chierchia highlights regularities and generalizations in the behavior of bare plurals across languages and advances a proposal that appeals to a relatively small conceptual apparatus. Adopting a view that bare plurals are always kind terms, Chierchia accounts for the complex cross-linguistic data pattern by means of three fundamental type-shifting operations that have been independently argued for, a ranking according to which those operations apply, a principle that favors semantic operations triggered by overt determiners over type-shifting, and a rule that existentially quantifies over instantiations of a kind when a kind-denoting term combines with a predicate that doesn't select for kinds.

In **Chapter 3** of this book, Veneeta Dayal first introduces Chierchia's system and discusses its main features and problems, then proposes a major simplification of this system by pushing it to its logical limits. She only assumes Chierchia's two type-shifting operations that are meaning preserving (i.e., they don't introduce any kind of quantification) without the need to rank them and with a slight but crucial modification for one of them having to do with variation in size (of the set of instantiations of a kind over situations). She also reformulates the combinatorial rules to eliminate quantification over instantiations and appeals to domain widening to get the relevant effects. Dayal supports her proposal with previously unnoticed data from English and Hindi and new tests to detect them. Overall, the picture that emerges unveils an even simpler and more elegant spontaneous logicality behind language.

In the last decade, Chierchia has worked on a major investigation of the large family of polarity items (negative polarity items, free choice items, epistemic indefinites, etc.) and scalar implicatures, two broad phenomena that were considered completely unrelated (a.o. Chierchia 2004, 2006, to appear a). Chierchia, instead, has argued that their interpretation is regulated by a single mechanism, the same mechanism that has been suggested for handling the interpretation of focused material. Roughly put, Chierchia's main idea is that all these phenomena involve an enrichment of the basic propositional meaning of the sentence they occur in by means of extra inferences that are due to a systematic activation of a set of alternatives, i.e., a set of propositions that are closely related to the basic propositional content of the sentence. Once alternatives are activated, the grammar together with its logic provides a precise procedure for dealing with them, combining the result with the basic propositional content of the sentence. Polarity items, scalar implicatures, and focus differ along three parameters only: optionality vs. obligatoriness of the activation of alternatives, the kind of alternatives they activate, and the operator that is responsible for eliminating alternatives within a very limited set of grammatically determined options.

Free choice polarity items are the focus of Chapters 4 and 5, while Chapters 6 and 7 are about scalar implicatures in numerals. Finally, Chapter 8 deals with the related semantics–pragmatics topic of how presupposition triggers interact with quantifiers.

In **Chapter 4**, Anamaria Fălăuş investigates epistemic indefinites, a kind of polarity item, across several languages by studying how they behave when they are focused. Epistemic indefinites are nominal expressions introduced by a restricted class of determiners that license so-called "free-choice" inferences conveying some form of ignorance (or indifference) with respect to the entire set of individuals their noun refers to (e.g., German *irgendein* NP, Italian *un qualche* NP and *un* NP *qualunque*, Romanian *vreun* NP and *un* NP *oarecare*, and Spanish *algún* NP). For some of them, the ignorance/indifference extends to the entire set (total variation), while for others just to a subset (partial variation). Also, some epistemic indefinites can behave as negative polarity items as well. By looking at this cross-linguistic pattern, Fălăuş provides preliminary evidence in favor of a new generalization about the strength of the free choice inferences epistemic indefinites license and their ability to bear focal stress: total variation epistemic indefinites can be focused (and give rise to a 'not just any' reading in downward-entailing contexts), while partial variation epistemic indefinites disallow focus. After reviewing Chierchia's alternative-based framework for polarity, she applies it to account for the cross-linguistic pattern of epistemic indefinites.

In **Chapter 5**, Maria Aloni and Michael Franke examine the distribution and interpretation of three elements in three languages and compare how the inferences they trigger vary depending on whether those elements are under the scope of an epistemic or deontic modal: the German indefinite determiner *irgendein* gives rise to different inferences under the two kinds of modals, the Romanian determiner *vreun* is licensed under epistemic modals, but not under deontic modals (Fălăuş 2009), and concessive scalar particles like Slovenian *magari* are licensed under deontic modals but not under epistemic ones (e.g. Crnič 2011b). Though exhibiting different restrictions, all these items license similar "free-choice" inferences, which Chierchia considers to be all slightly different instantiations of free-choice polarity (to appear a). Aloni and Franke notice that the explanations that have been proposed so far for these items share a common feature, which they call the *Modal Variability Hypothesis*: all proposals assume that deontic and epistemic modals differ in the way they license free-choice inferences. In particular, deontic modals trigger free-choice inferences that seem to enter into the recursive computation of compositional semantic values, whereas epistemic modals do not. Aloni and Franke acknowledge the possibility, explored in great depth by Chierchia (2006, to appear a) and others, of (quasi-)pragmatic inferences taking effect "locally" during the composition of semantic meaning; but they still argue for a purely pragmatic perspective on the distribution of such local pragmatic effects and propose a pragmatic explanation for the Modal Variability Hypothesis based on the notion of *pragmatic fossilization*.

Chapters 6 and 7 focus on scalar implicatures in numerals. Numerals have been central in the debate about contextual information and grammatical meaning since the interpretations of sentences containing numerals crucially seem to involve pragmatic enrichment of a more basic meaning.

In **Chapter 6**, Clemens Mayr investigates the pragmatic behavior of nominals containing a less studied kind of numeral, i.e., modified numerals like *at least three boys* and *more than three boys*. Previously, it has been noticed that modified numerals don't trigger scalar implicatures in the same way as unmodified numerals like *three boys*, though the two kinds of modified numerals had not yet been studied in parallel. Mayr brings strong evidence showing that both kinds of numeral modification behave in the same way as far as scalar implicature triggering is concerned and proposes a new generalization to capture this pattern. He then carefully reviews existing proposals that deal with just a subset of the data like the "density" approach by Fox and Hackl (2006) and shows that they cannot be easily extended to cover the entire empirical range of the new generalization. Finally, Mayr considers two alternative approaches to scalar implicatures, the neo-Gricean approach and Chierchia's grammatical view of scalar implicatures, and shows that neither can provide a straightforward account for the new generalization, including a development of Chierchia's approach that relies on non-monotonic alternatives for modified numerals. Overall, this chapter reshapes the empirical landscape of scalar implicatures with modified numerals and prepares the ground for those who want to take on the challenge of accounting for Mayr's new generalization.

In **Chapter 7**, Christopher Kennedy deals with scalar inferences in numerals as well, but he focuses on unmodified numerals. It is well-known that unmodified numerals like *three boys* allow for an "exact quantity" interpretation ('exactly three boys') in many environments, but also for a lower-bounded interpretation ('at least three boys') in others. The standard pragmatic account, which Kennedy calls the *Classic Analysis*, assumes the lower-bounded interpretation of unmodified numerals as basic, combines it with the scalar implicatures triggered by the numeric scale, and in this way derives the exact quantity interpretation (Horn 1972). Kennedy challenges this account and its possible developments within the neo-Gricean framework (Horn 1992, a.o.) and Chierchia's grammatical theory of scalar implicatures (Chierchia 2004, 2006; Chierchia et al. 2012; Mayr this volume, a.o.). He shows that all these approaches fail to account for the interaction of numerals with negation, quantifiers, and modals. In particular, they incorrectly predict, among other things, that sentences with numerals should exhibit the same inferential pattern as sentences with other scalar items such as quantifiers like *some*, *many*, *most* as well as modals, aspectual verbs, and so forth. Finally, Kennedy argues for a new purely semantic analysis of numerals as generalized quantifiers over degrees, true of a property of degrees D just in case the maximal degree that satisfies D is equal to a specific numeric value. Language acquisition findings are discussed to further support the proposal.

In **Chapter 8**, Danny Fox studies the way quantifier phrases project the presuppositions of their arguments. While in a simple sentence like *John drives both of his cars to school* one can say that the word *both* introduces the presupposition that a particular person (John) has exactly two cars, a similar treatment is not possible if the sentence contains a quantificational subject, as in *No boy drives both of his cars to school*. Furthermore, as Fox shows, the way presuppositions are projected in these quantificational contexts depends on a variety of factors like the type of the quantificational determiner, the type of presupposition triggers, and individual speakers' preferences. Despite this variability, Fox argues that at least one fact seems to be constant, namely the acceptability of the relevant sentences in specific contexts that Fox describes and exemplifies. Fox develops his account within a trivalent approach to presupposition projection, coupled with two independently needed mechanisms: one which strengthens presuppositions, and another which incorporates presuppositions into truth conditions at various scope positions.

The THIRD PART of the book deals with experimental studies and how they inform and are informed by semantic theory. Chierchia has participated in studies on language acquisition, language processing, and neurolinguistics in collaboration with psycholinguists and psychologists. His theoretical work has also been influential, directly and indirectly, in inspiring other scholars to engage in experimental research into formal semantics and pragmatics. The three chapters in the third and last part of the book are examples of this influence.

In **Chapter 9**, Stephen Crain and Rosalind Thornton address the issue of a nativist approach versus a usage-based approach to language development by examining cross-linguistic acquisition work in semantics and pragmatics. They present and discuss a series of experimental studies that are inspired in large part by Chierchia's ideas about human language (see especially Chierchia 2004). The studies investigate children's and adults' knowledge of polarity items, scalar implicatures, and logical operators like disjunction in upward-entailing and downward-entailing contexts in languages like English, Japanese, Mandarin Chinese, and others. Crain and Thornton point out that their findings are highly problematic for a usage-based approach because the phenomena that exhibit the same patterns are very different on the surface and the language input children are exposed to is often insufficient or points in the opposite direction. On the other hand, they argue that their findings strongly support a unified view of polarity items, scalar implicatures, and logical operators, along the line of Chierchia's unified proposal and his idea of the logicality of language.

In **Chapter 10**, Francesca Panzeri, Francesca Foppolo, and Maria Teresa Guasti report novel experimental data on the acquisition of gradable adjectives, like *tall*, and suggest that children initially interpret these adjectives categorically, i.e., as referring to sets of objects, and only at a later stage switch to the adult comparative-like interpretation. They claim that their findings are more easily explained within a framework that assumes that gradable adjectives denote a partial function from individuals to truth-values, rather than in the alternative framework in which gradable adjectives correspond to a function that attributes to an individual the possession of the relevant property to a certain degree. They further suggest a parallelism with the phenomenon of scalar implicature computation in children. Children stick to the categorical interpretation of the adjective when they do not have enough resources to retrieve the standard of comparison, much as they stick to the logical (but uninformative) reading of *some* in sentences like "Some Ss are P" in situations in which the sentence "All Ss are P" would be more appropriate.

In **Chapter 11**, Adriana Belletti and Luigi Rizzi deal with the classical issue of intervention effects, which also play a role in the explanation of semantic phenomena like scalar implicatures and licensing of negative polarity items, as recently shown by Chierchia and others. Belletti and Rizzi's starting point is a parallelism concerning A-bar dependencies between psycholinguistic evidence and acquisition data. In experimental tasks adults show difficulties with configurations in which a category which is similar to the target intervenes between the two links of an A-bar dependency. This difficulty takes a more extreme form in children who, for a long phase, do not comprehend sentences displaying the relevant configuration. Belletti and Rizzi propose a particular implementation of the Relativized Minimality principle according to which intervention effects are triggered only if the morphosyntactic features of the intervener fully match the morphosyntactic features of the target. Young children, they claim, show more severe intervention effects because they cannot compute a relation of proper inclusion in the relevant configurations.

All these chapters crucially rely on the two main ideas about human language we started with: that grammar affects meaning and that language is built on an intrinsic logic. Although in different ways, all chapters contribute to the development of a precise theory of human language and meaning according to these ideas. In doing so, they also highlight the crucial role that Chierchia, his work, and his scholarship have played in developing those ideas as an intellectual guide and source of inspiration not just for this book, but for an entire field and research community that investigates human language meaning.

We decided to work on this book for two reasons. The official reason is to honor Gennaro Chierchia, the scholar, the mentor, the friend, and to surprise him on his 60th birthday. The more secret reason is the same that has led us the editors, Gennaro, and all other linguists to choose this field for a living: to be rich and famous.

*Part I*

# From grammar to meaning: foundational issues

# 1 Portrait of a semanticist as a young man: Gennaro Chierchia 1979–1988

*Barbara H. Partee*

## 1. Chierchia's Ph.D.-student years: 1979–1983

Gennaro Chierchia's application to enter the Ph.D. program in Linguistics at UMass Amherst in Fall 1979 reached us through the Institute for International Education, which handled all Fulbright applications. We had no writing sample to look at and no correspondence with the applicant. We saw that his background was entirely in philosophy at the University of Rome, and I don't think we even knew the title of his diploma thesis, *Da Carnap a Montague: Rilevanza Linguistica della Semantica dei Mondi Possibili*, "From Carnap to Montague: Linguistic relevance of possible worlds semantics." And we had not heard of the professors who wrote letters for him. Altogether the application looked quite "risky." But he would have a Fulbright fellowship for the first year; so we decided to admit him for the M.A./Ph.D. sequence, with the understanding that there was no guarantee that he could stay beyond the first year. So he came.

He arrived with his wife Isa Orvieto at the end of August, and after they had spent a few days in the Campus Center without much contact, Emmon and I found them and brought them to live with us while they hunted for an apartment and things to furnish it with.[1] That was a week that we and they look back on as the beginning of a lifelong friendship.

And we very quickly understood how very wonderfully suited he was for our Ph.D. program. In his first semester, he was exempted from Linguistics 610, our first-semester introduction to semantics, and took instead the normally third-semester Linguistics 753, Montague Grammar. And he got the only A+ in the class on his term paper, "On Carlson's treatment of bare plurals." Already in his second semester, Spring 1980, he started thinking about doing a generals paper on kinds. At that time our Ph.D. program required two generals papers, one in syntax and/or semantics and one in phonology and/or historical linguistics, to be written in the fourth and fifth semesters, so Gennaro was off to an unusually fast start. He was worried about phonology and doing a phonology generals paper – if he had had his way, he would have done only semantics and syntax with some philosophy on the side. But he discovered to his surprise that he enjoyed phonology with Lisa Selkirk and Alan Prince, and he wrote his second generals paper on "raddoppiamento sintatico" in Italian. That paper turned into a NELS paper published in 1982, and later, in 1986, he published an article on length, syllabification, and the phonological cycle in Italian in the *Journal of Italian Linguistics*. He also found his way into psycholinguistics courses in our program and took a serious interest in psycholinguistics and cognitive science more generally, driven by hard questions about mental models, mental representations, and human competence in the domains of semantics and logic.

Gennaro's years in our Ph.D. program, from 1979 to 1983, came right at the time of our interdisciplinary Sloan Grants in Cognitive Science. The first was a collaborative project between Linguistics and Computer & Information Science (COINS) from 1978–1980. One of the most successful results of that grant was the hiring of Lyn Frazier in 1978 in a new position in psycholinguistics whose first two years were funded by the grant. Lyn soon became actively engaged in joint research with Charles Clifton and with Keith Rayner, both in Psychology, and those collaborations greatly strengthened our ties with the Psychology Department. Lyn had been at UMass for just a year when Gennaro arrived; his work with Lyn is mentioned below. The second Sloan grant was a five-year grant from 1980 to 1985, with four participating departments, Linguistics, COINS, Psychology, and Philosophy, and at that same time we instituted a Cognitive Science Program, with provisions for specializations in Cognitive Science within the Ph.D. programs in each of the four cooperating departments. In Linguistics it was agreed that the normal four-year Ph.D. program would be extended to a five-year program for students doing a Cognitive Science specialization, implying an additional year of funding. The Sloan grants were a very big help for research activities and especially for the support of students as Research Assistants in relatively 'poor' departments like Linguistics and Philosophy in the years that we had them.

In Spring 1980 Gennaro took a very "Sloany"[2] interdisciplinary Linguistics-Philosophy-COINS seminar on Formal Semantics and Computational Semantics that I co-taught with Elliot Soloway of our COINS department and a Sloan-funded visitor, Douglas Moran, who had worked with Joyce Friedman on computer models of Montague grammar. Topics included computer implementations of model-theoretic semantics (Friedman *et al.* 1978a, 1978b), AI approaches to semantics, problems of integrating model-theoretic semantics with linguistic theory and processing models (including issues I had been wrestling with in Partee 1979), dynamic partial models, non-monotonic logics, and models of belief and inconsistency. Gennaro was one of three students in the seminar for credit, and his participation greatly raised the level of the class. He wrote a nice term paper on the problems of the semantics of belief sentences and hyperintensionality, a topic to which he indirectly returned in his explorations of property theory and alternatives to Montague's intensional logic.

In his second year, 1980–81, Gennaro was in my very lively Fall seminar on anaphora, cross-listed with COINS and Philosophy but very linguistic in content; others in that seminar included Yasuaki Abe, Dorit Abusch (Philosophy), Dan Finer, James Pustejovsky, and Mats Rooth. The seminar included presentations by Edwin Williams and me on our debates (started the previous spring in an introductory semantics class) on formal semantics versus Chomskyan "logical form," and presentations by Mats Rooth on VP-deletion, by Emmon and me on our new joint work on pronouns and reflexives in Montague grammar, by Irene Heim on *donkey*-sentences, by Jonathan Mitchell on Castañeda's quasi-indexical *he**, known since David Lewis's work (Lewis 1979a) as a *de se* pronoun, and much more. And in Spring 1981 he participated in a Linguistics and Philosophy seminar that Emmon and I led on tense and aspect and anaphora. Mats Rooth was in that one too; he had started just a year before Gennaro, and they were often in seminars together; other participants included Jonathan Mitchell, Dan Finer, Yasuaki Abe, Peter Sells, James Pustejovsky, and auditors Dorit Abusch, Murray Kiteley, Barry Richards, and Wynn Chao. Toward the end of the semester a major focus of the seminar was trying to better understand the new work of Hans Kamp on Discourse Representation Theory (DRT), particularly Kamp's work on how DRT might help some problems about aspect and temporal anaphora, and the equally new work of Barwise and Perry (Barwise and Perry 1981), including Barwise's work on events (Barwise 1981).

Spring of 1981 was when Irene Heim was finishing her dissertation, which she defended in the fall (while starting a postdoc at Stanford.) Irene and Gennaro overlapped during Gennaro's first two years – she had started in 1977, and had nearly stopped taking courses when Gennaro arrived in 1979. My interdisciplinary Sloan-funded workshop on "indefinite reference" which gave Irene her dissertation topic (she found the problems non-trivial and interesting, and realized that no one really had a good semantic account of them) had been in the year before Gennaro arrived, with its first part in Fall 1978 and its second part in Spring 1979. My memories of Gennaro and Irene carrying on long intense debates off in some corner during conferences must come mainly from the years after they had both finished.

Also in the Spring of 1981, Gennaro took a psycholinguistics seminar with Lyn Frazier. Gennaro was one of the first of many students to work with Lyn on problems of semantic processing, and he has gone on to become one of the leaders in the growing fields of semantic processing and semantic acquisition, as discussed in other chapters in this volume. In that seminar, he wrote a paper suggesting potential ways of testing Greg Carlson's hypothesis about bare plurals not being quantifier phrases by means of experiments related to Philip Johnson-Laird's work on mental models. And he participated in some of our Thursday evening Cognitive Science Program interdisciplinary meetings, including one in February featuring mostly philosophers discussing issues in the foundations of cognitive science (Gary Matthews on children and philosophy, plus short talks by Jay Garfield, Elliot Soloway, and others), and one in March on semantics, which featured a presentation by Gennaro on Hans Kamp's new Discourse Representation Theory and its relation to issues of logical form, compositionality, and model-theoretic semantics, as well as presentations by Emmon Bach and by Irene Heim. I have a copy of Gennaro's handout from his presentation, where he managed to pack into one page the basic issue of Discourse Representation Structure (DRS) as an intermediate level of representation, the DRS handling of possible and impossible donkey-sentences, and something that looks like it might be the beginnings of the argument that he and Mats Rooth developed in their paper for the 1983 NELS at UMass (Chierchia and Rooth 1984) against some of Kamp's claims about the indispensability of the intermediate DRS level in accounting for anaphora.

And that spring he wrote his semantics generals paper. I haven't found a record of the title of Gennaro's semantics generals paper, but I know that it further developed his work on an alternative approach to Carlson's theory of bare plurals, using a Cocchiarella-influenced foundation instead of Montague's intensional type theory. So I think it is probably the paper he refers to in several places as his 1981 manuscript "English bare plurals, mass nouns, and the structure of the world," a version of which was later published (Chierchia 1983a). And very soon after that he had two papers published developing those themes, his 1982 WCCFL paper, "Bare plurals, mass nouns, and nominalization" (Chierchia 1982a), and his 1982 paper in *Linguistics and Philosophy*, "Nominalization and Montague Grammar. A semantics without types for natural languages" (Chierchia 1982b). Those two papers brought his work to the wider attention of the semantics and philosophy of language communities. That work, and Heim's dissertation, and Rooth's work on a two-dimensional semantics for focus constructions not long after, were a major step forward in foundational semantic research. They represented some of the first work anywhere by linguists with enough formal facility to propose serious changes to the metatheory we worked in.[3] Up until then, "we linguists" had been largely dependent on philosophers and logicians to provide the theoretical tools for us to work with. When philosophers asked me why I was working with a typed rather than an untyped logic, I could only reply that that's what Montague had provided, and I had no competence to try to judge or change that logic. Linguists have always been open to theoretical innovations from philosophers and logicians – David Kaplan once remarked that linguists seemed like vacuum cleaners, though Emmon Bach noted wryly that he hoped we weren't just taking in dust and dirt. But in semantics, linguists had been more or less relying on first-order predicate logic until Montague's work, and through the 1970s most of the Montague-influenced work by linguists adopted Montague's formal framework without serious modification and focused on extending empirical coverage, exploring alternative approaches to the syntax–semantics interface, looking for possible constraints to make the theory more "linguistic," and sometimes worrying about how to integrate a Chomskyan perspective on language "in the head" and the Frege–Montague approach to semantics in terms of mind-external truth-conditions. Gennaro was the first *linguist*, I am pretty sure, to challenge both Montague's type theory and his possible-worlds-based account of intensionality. The transition from "Montague grammar" as the name of the field to the now-standard "formal semantics" had several causes; one of the most important was the kinds of challenges to the foundations that Gennaro, Irene, and Mats (and Angelika) raised.

Gennaro's background in philosophy and logic was clearly part of what made him able to propose foundational changes, but his argumentation was strongly grounded in empirical linguistic phenomena. His acquaintance with Nino Cocchiarella's work played a big role. He writes in the introduction to his dissertation (Chierchia 1984a), as a preamble to his acknowledgment to Cocchiarella:

> Before getting into linguistics I studied philosophy in Italy. On the plane during my first trip to the States, I decided to say goodbye to hard-core philosophy by reading a paper by Cocchiarella which [then] sat in the back of my mind for a while to pop out again when I began to think about G. Carlson's beautiful theory of bare plurals. (pp. iv–v)

Starting with his first-semester work on Carlson's treatment of bare plurals, he came to view that construction as one instance of a process of nominalizing predicates, other instances being the formation of mass terms, infinitives, and gerunds, as well as the nominal use of color terms like *blue*, and to see Montague's rigid adherence to type theory as an obstacle to achieving an explanatory account of such processes. In his *L&P* paper, he showed how one could adapt one of Cocchiarella's non-standard second-order logics (HST*) to construct a non-typed variant of Montague's intensional logic (IL*) and use it to obtain an improved account of bare plurals as part of a general account of nominalizations extending also to infinitives and gerunds. The paper is quite long and contains difficult material (I depended on my philosophy colleagues to help evaluate technical parts that were over my head); but it is lucidly and beautifully written. It includes along the way the most interesting arguments I had seen up to that point within the model-theoretic tradition for the inclusion of a separate level of logical form within a grammar, arguments related to those of Cresswell (1973) for structured meanings, building on earlier arguments by Carnap for his notion of "intensional isomorphism" and David Lewis's proposals for structured meanings in Lewis (1970). There were two big changes from Montague's intensional logic. One of the most radical was the abandonment of the type theory, so that a function could apply to an argument 'of the same type'; this was motivated by appeal to an important pattern of behavior of predicate expressions and their nominalizations, illustrated by examples like the following from Chierchia (1982b).

(1) a. My pen is blue.
b. Blue is a nice color.

(2) a. John is running for president.
b. To run for president is interesting.
c. Running for president is interesting.

(3) a. My ring is gold.
b. Gold is an element.

(4) a. Fido and Templeton are dogs.
b. Dogs are mammals.

(5) a. John is honest.
b. Honesty is a virtue.

Chierchia argued that the subjects of the *b* sentences and of (2c) should be regarded as individual-denoting nominalizations of the predicates seen in the *a* sentences. He showed how an elegant account could be gotten by seeing property expressions as having two 'faces': they can be used as predicates, as in the *a* sentences, but they can be nominalized when we want to be able to predicate something of those properties in turn. Cresswell (1973) had argued that the e-type domain should contain correlates of the kinds of things found in all the other semantic domains – propositions, properties, etc. Within a type theory this cannot be done uniformly without paradox. Cresswell avoided paradox by letting the mapping from other domains into the entity domain be partial. Chierchia followed Cocchiarella in doing away with the typing and moving to a property theory instead, with basically just two types – individuals and relations. This is not the place to try to fill in the details, but these issues were central in his dissertation and continued to recur in Gennaro's work over the next years, resulting in some of his most well-known early contributions to the field.

By the end of the Spring of 1981, it was known that Emmon and I would be away at the Max Planck Institute in Nijmegen during 1982–83, and since I would be his dissertation chair and Emmon would be on the committee, it seemed that it might be difficult for Gennaro to write his dissertation that year, his fourth year in our program, as would be normal. And since he had already completed his Generals Papers, he strongly considered trying to finish in just three years, something that had been done only once in our Ph.D. program, by Greg Carlson. But I have a copy of a letter I wrote to him in June to Italy, where he and Isa had returned for the summer, in which I report that the faculty strongly advised that he take advantage of being a Ph.D. student for the full four years for which financial support was more or less guaranteed, with the suggestion that a fifth year of support could very well be approved if necessary. (He agreed, and in the end he did finish in four years, defending his dissertation in August 1983 shortly after our return, filing it in November and getting his degree in February 1984.)

Our second Sloan grant, 1980–85, had added the Psychology and Philosophy Departments to the collaboration with Linguistics and COINS; Psychology had become a strong partner through Lyn Frazier's collaborations, and we already had strong connections with Philosophy through semantics and philosophy of language. That second Sloan grant gave us funds to bring in three postdocs each year, aiming for people whose research spanned two or more of our fields. My own interests continued to most strongly include philosophy, as did Gennaro's. And by lucky coincidence, Hans Kamp had just introduced me to the work of Ray Turner, a theoretical computer scientist at the University of Essex, whose first Ph.D. had been in mathematics and whose second Ph.D. was in philosophy with Kamp, with a dissertation on how to use finite approximations to model the semantics of counterfactual conditionals without possible worlds. Turner's main research interests were the mathematical foundations of denotational semantics for programming languages and in varieties of logics. I got in contact with Turner, and told him I would love to have a chance to learn enough algebra and model theory sometime to be able to understand his dissertation, since I was quite excited about what it seemed to be about. I asked him if he would like to apply for one of our postdocs. He did, and his work was deemed of interest to the computer scientists, the philosophers, and the linguists, and we got him here for a year in 1981–82, Gennaro's third year.

So in 1981–82 Ray Turner was here for the year, and Gennaro had finished his Generals Papers, had some publications in progress, and was starting to plan his dissertation. In both 1980–81 and 1981–82 Gennaro was my Research Assistant on the Sloan grant, with his own research as his main task. I happened to have a "Conti Fellowship" in 1981–82 from the Graduate Dean, which reduced my teaching load and left me more time for graduate teaching and research. So with Gennaro's help, Ray and I organized an informal "Monday evening model theory seminar" within the Sloan-supported Cognitive Science program, with a couple dozen participants from Linguistics, Philosophy, COINS, Mathematics, and Psychology – faculty, graduate students, postdocs, and visitors, including our graduate students Gennaro, Mats Rooth, Craige Roberts, Nirit Kadmon; Charles Clifton from Psychology, Frank Wattenberg from Mathematics, Michael Arbib from COINS (he and I were co-directors of our Cognitive Science program in those years), Michael Jubien and Ed Gettier from Philosophy, and several Linguistics faculty. One of my goals was to learn a little bit of classical model theory, but I mostly worked on that on my own. In the seminar we focused more, with Ray's help, on the kinds of tools that allow for finite (approximate) modeling of various sorts of infinite phenomena, which I hoped could help in the search for theories of human semantic competence, where we are up against the problem of finite brains and the plausibly non-denumerable cardinality of the sets of possible semantic values in possible-worlds semantics.

In the Fall 1981 Monday evening model theory seminar, one of the first topics Ray proceeded to teach us about was Dana Scott's semantics for the lambda-calculus, related to Scott-Strachey semantics for programming languages (Stoy 1977), and how notions like continuity of functions could be defined on finite domains with Scott's techniques. When Ray gave his first lecture, a couple of our linguistics graduate students told me afterwards that they hadn't understood a word. One problem was that Ray was not accustomed to lecturing to people who knew as little mathematics as many in the audience did; another was that he had a constitutional aversion to giving examples.[4] So since I had some freed-up time that semester and knew that the best way to learn something is to teach it, I took it upon myself to spend the week before the next Monday to prepare to retell what Ray had just taught us, with examples; and I had a chance to check it all with Ray in advance. We went through about half the semester that way, with it often taking me two or three hours to retell what Ray had told in one. Later our mathematician colleague Frank Wattenberg explained the basics of non-standard calculus with infinitesimals, and showed how it has a similar motivation, though different techniques.

By the end of the Fall semester of 1981, Gennaro's dissertation prospectus had been approved, with the title "Syntax and semantics of infinitives and gerunds in English and Italian," and a committee consisting of me as chair, Emmon Bach, Roger Higgins, and Ed Gettier from Philosophy. In the Spring of 1982 the dissertation was in progress, and Gennaro and Ray also audited the Tense and Aspect seminar that Emmon and I taught as a cross-listed Linguistics/Philosophy seminar. Students in the seminar for credit included Nirit Kadmon, Dorit Abusch, Charlie Jones, Bipin Indurkhya (from Computer Science), and David Lebeaux. Auditors besides Gennaro and Ray included Lyn Frazier, Mats Rooth, Murray Kiteley, Toshi Nishigauchi, and Dan Finer. Ray gave a talk on counterfactuals in that seminar, based on his dissertation. He related possible-worlds semantics approaches like Stalnaker's and Lewis's to metalinguistic approaches like Goodman's and Rescher's, and wanted to find a way to make use of the best features of each; one of his main ideas concerned ways to approach the idea of comparative similarity between "worlds" via successively refined approximations.

And the Monday night model theory seminar continued through Spring 1982, with Ray and Gennaro both playing an active role. One topic for the model theory seminar was property theory and what it could be good for in linguistic semantics. Gennaro made some presentations in which he introduced the mathematicians to the problems posed for Montague's type theory by the semantics of nominalizations. He presented the basic ideas of property theory, and explained Cocchiarella's approach and how he was using it to solve the problems of nominalization in his dissertation work. Michael Jubien of the Philosophy Department was working on his own approach to property theory

(Jubien 1989), and he gave some presentations about that. We also had more discussion of Barwise and Perry's newly developed Situation Semantics, particularly the role that properties played in that approach.

Ray and Gennaro got well acquainted that year, and Ray was one of the few people around who could discuss Cocchiarella's work with Gennaro; Ray had some objections to Cocchiarella's approach. Gennaro and Ray had many discussions of Scott's type-free semantics for the lambda-calculus and its potential application to natural language syntax and semantics. Gennaro mentions that and some other alternatives to Cochiarella's system in his papers and dissertation, but stayed with his IL* based on Cochiarella's HST* for the purposes of the dissertation, and the two of them didn't start to work seriously together on alternatives until after the dissertation had been completed.

One big event of the Spring 1982 semester was a Sloan-grant-funded semantics conference that I organized featuring Hans Kamp presenting his new Discourse Representation Theory (Kamp 1981) and Barwise and Perry presenting their new Situation Semantics. The official title was "Propositional Attitudes, Situation Semantics, and Mental Models," but I might as well have called it "Discourse Representation Theory and Situation Semantics," since giving those two new approaches a critical hearing was the main purpose of the conference.[5] Other participants from outside the Five College community (UMass Amherst plus Amherst, Hampshire, Mt. Holyoke, and Smith Colleges) included Manfred Bierwisch, Tyler Burge, Ewan Klein, Michael Dummett, Bas van Fraassen, David Lewis, David Dowty, Aravind Joshi, Dana Scott, Sylvain Bromberger, Joseph Almog, Richmond Thomason, Philip Johnson-Laird, W. V. O. Quine, Daniel Dennett, William Lycan, Jerry Fodor, Janet Fodor, and Robert Stalnaker. One nice fringe benefit of those Sloan grant conferences for the hosting university was how they gave students like Gennaro a chance to hear and meet such a stellar array of scholars.

Gennaro's research was well underway by the time Emmon and I left for the Netherlands in the summer of 1982. And Gennaro and Isa's first son Gabriele was born in June 1982 – something else to keep them both busy. Gennaro was supported by another semester of Sloan grant Research Assistantship in Fall 1982, and a Teaching Assistantship in Spring 1983. We corresponded and he sent me drafts of chapters, and he even managed to come visit us in Nijmegen from November 22 to December 4. In addition to intense discussion of his dissertation, he came with us to semantics seminars in Amsterdam and Groningen (which we attended regularly all year), and got acquainted with many of the scholars who made the Dutch semantics scene so lively and productive. We went together to Groningen to an all-day workshop on interrogative quantifiers November 26, and on December 2 Gennaro was one of two invited speakers (the other was Henk Zeevat) at the regular Groningen semantics seminar, where he presented his revision of Montague's Intensional Logic.

In the Amsterdam seminar we heard Johan van Benthem one week, and Fred Landman the next week. And around the New Year our family (including my three sons and Emmon's son and daughter) visited him and four generations of his family in Rome, where they graciously found room for all seven of us to stay in one of the family apartments, and where we played some wonderful Italian card game together on New Year's Eve.[6]

During the spring semester Gennaro mailed chapters from Amherst to Emmon and me in Nijmegen and we continued to correspond back and forth. He accomplished a great amount of what he set out to do; he only regretted not being able to include as much about Italian in the dissertation as he had hoped to. The title he had proposed in his prospectus had explicitly mentioned "English and Italian"; since he couldn't include very much about Italian, but did have some interesting sections on Italian and didn't want it to seem to be just about English, he changed the title to "Topics in the syntax and semantics of gerunds and infinitives."

Back in Amherst, Gennaro was having a busy Spring 1983 semester, teaching an introductory linguistics course, applying for jobs, and finishing his dissertation. He gave a talk at WCCFL II in February on the theory of control that he worked out in Chapter 4 of the dissertation, published as Chierchia (1983b).

Since we communicated by writing letters to each other the year I was in Nijmegen, there are records of some of our conversations. A letter from Gennaro June 1, 1983 mentions getting good comments from Hans Kamp, which makes me remember that we had succeeded in getting Hans Kamp to join our Philosophy Department starting in Fall 1982, although he stayed only two years before moving to the University of Texas, so we were there together only one year, 1983–84. But he was there long enough for a number of our students to benefit from his teaching and advising, including Gennaro and especially Nirit Kadmon and Craige Roberts.

When Gennaro wrote from Amherst on June 1, he sent a draft of Chapter 5, the fourth complete chapter draft that I had received. Chapter 1, "Theories of Properties and Natural Language Semantics," laid out his preferred logic IL* based on Cocchiarella's HST*, with motivations and discussion, and comparison with four other approaches including Cresswell's, Parsons's 'floating types approach,' and Scott's semantics for the untyped λ-calculus. Chapter 2, "Locally Configurational Grammar," spelled out his approach to syntax, the syntax-semantics map, sortal distinctions to replace the missing "types," and a substantial theory of features and morphological operations. Chapter 4, "Control and Semantic Structure," gave his theory of control as semantic entailment and an account of the differences among obligatory control, "semi-obligatory control," and prominence control, plus a novel account of control vs. raising. Chapter 5, "Infinitives, Gerunds, and Anaphora," included accounts of $\mathrm{PRO}_{\mathrm{ARB}}$, strict and sloppy anaphora, reflexives, and control. All that remained

to draft was Chapter 3, on infinitives and gerunds in English and Italian, and in the end that chapter was mostly about English.
An excerpt from the accompanying letter:

> I've got good comments from Hans on Ch. 1. Also Cocchiarella has announced me [sic] that he'll let me have his comments soon. After that I'll revise it. I guess it won't happen too often to get 2 students of Montague's to comment on the same stuff. Meanwhile, I'll get to chapter 3, that looks pretty tough. Then I'll try to show that everything follows from everything else.

During the summer Gennaro was working intensely on finishing his dissertation. He had gotten a job at Brown to start in the fall, but getting a proper visa was a problem involving a painful amount of uncertainty and bureaucratic hassle, since his Fulbright scholarship had come with a stipulation that he return to his home country for two years before reapplying for a US visa. Isa and baby Gabriele had gone back to Italy for the summer; Isa was not totally overjoyed with the decision to stay in the US after Gennaro completed his Ph.D., and took the summer to be back in Italy while she could. Gennaro reports that he was working intensely but it was lonely, and the uncertainties and difficulties about whether he was going to be able to get the visa added to his preoccupations.

On June 20, he sent a complete draft of Chapter 3. Chapter 3, "Distributional Properties of Predicative Expressions and the Semantics of Nominalization," contains a substantial theory of infinitivals and gerunds as a species of nominalization, arguments about the constituency of infinitives and gerunds, and a typology of clausal constructions and the notion of finiteness. Instead of a complete treatment of Italian infinitivals and gerunds, he included a substantial case study of lexical subjects in Italian infinitives, contrasting his semantic account with Rizzi's syntactic account. Early in the chapter he presents his account of Chomsky's so-called "PRO theorem": the "PRO theorem" had purported to derive the fact that PRO must be ungoverned, but Bresnan had shown that since one of the premises on which it was based was false, it actually ended up being a stipulation. One of Chierchia's basic claims is that a finite VP like *runs* denotes a propositional function, while *to run* denotes an individual, the result of nominalizing the propositional function. Since only a propositional function can take an argument, it follows that **John to run* as a sentence is semantically ill-formed. And conversely, *to run* but not *runs* can be an argument of *tries* (*tries to run* vs. **tries runs*). Using such basic aspects of his proposed semantics, Gennaro offered a semantic explanation of the fact that verbs may take both finite (*that S*) and non-finite (*for NP to VP*) sentential complements, but only non-finite VP complements, never finite ones (**tries runs*). His account went farther in explaining a range of facts about the distribution of "PRO" and about control in general on the basis of general semantic principles plus some plausible assumptions about English syntax and morphology. (Needless to say, it was not the last word – his later work on attitudes and *de se* anaphora (Chierchia 1989) was one of the subsequent major advances in work on control and anaphora.)

On July 13, shortly before our return, I sent Gennaro several pages of comments and questions, also some comments from Ray Turner, who had visited for a few days the week before and read Chapter 1, and had some general observations concerning the relations among Scott's techniques and Cocchiarella's property theory. His advice was that Gennaro might say that probably all the issues he's concerned with are independent of the choice of *how* you avoid paradox while allowing self-application of properties; Cocchiarella's "homogeneous stratification technique" is one way, Scott's construction is another.

We returned a little later that July. He and I had many meetings in August, and he successfully defended his dissertation August 26. Then he went to Brown to start his first job. I still have a note from him from September 8, 1983, written in haste and beginning with "I got my visa!!" So he could be legal for the rest of that year, and "even can get paid." At Brown he had Polly Jacobson as a valued colleague, and they soon were at work designing joint research projects at the intersection of their interests.

The specifically linguistic interest of Gennaro's dissertation lies in the rich payoff that his innovations in the treatment of model-theoretic semantics produced for the description of such central linguistic concerns as control, thematic relations, and predication. He also took a major step forward in bringing empirical linguistic argumentation to bear on the choice among alternatives to Montague's type theory, arguing that a second-order theory offers greater explanatory power for natural language semantics than either a first-order theory or a full type theory like Montague's. One of many lasting contributions from the dissertation is his contention that the only semantic types for which there is a full range of anaphora and quantification in natural language – i.e., for which there are something like real variables and variable-binding phenomena – are first-order or second-order: entities or properties. This interesting generalization, which has held up well over the decades, has had important consequences of several sorts. An example concerning the analysis of particular phenomena is the treatment of degree modification, where his hypothesis suggests that "degrees" are to be seen as a subclass of entities. A more general consequence comes in language acquisition, where he predicts a big difference between the acquisition of first- or second-order vocabulary, where the whole logical space is available for potential meanings, and higher-order vocabulary, which is generally restricted to a small number of lexical items. There his prediction is that the only higher-order lexical items that languages exploit come from a small set of potentially universal and innate possible meanings, so that the learner does not have to make arbitrary discriminations within higher-order meaning spaces.

That work required a combined depth of understanding and creative intellectual power in all three areas of linguistics, logic, and philosophy. Already then he combined in one person to a remarkable degree the interests and abilities of the ideal linguist and the ideal philosopher–logician, including being highly independent and undogmatic. With his willingness to consider and draw upon work from highly diverse frameworks and his ability to integrate and modify, he was able to have a strong positive influence in helping to see beyond battles between "schools" in working toward larger shared goals, as well as being a major contributor to research of importance for both linguistics and philosophy. In the dissertation, his treatment of non-overt subjects and control structures was novel and elegant: without positing null subjects at either a syntactic or semantic level of representation, he treated control relations as semantic entailments of predicates, ultimately as restrictions on admissible model structures. The formal innovations in the treatment included the beginnings of a formal theory of thematic relations in which they are viewed as higher-order relations between n-place predicates and individuals, and play a role in the formulation of constraints on the possible interpretations of natural language predicates. (In a sense part of this work could be viewed as the beginnings of a linguistically motivated theory of "meaning postulates," or of constraints on lexical meaning and lexical entailments.) Using this "directly semantic" approach, he achieved an account of Visser's and Bach's generalizations that built on but improved upon both Bresnan's and Bach's treatments, and provided an integrated account of the distribution of intensional argument positions, non-thematic argument positions, and the distinction between Equi and Raising.

## 2. The assistant professor years: 1983–1988

Gennaro's first position was at Brown University, starting in Fall 1983, where Polly Jacobson was his closest colleague. Gennaro was busy revising his dissertation to submit in late fall, and settling in to teaching.

In November Gennaro and Mats Rooth, who was still at UMass, presented a joint paper, "Configurational notions in Discourse Representation Theory" at NELS 14 at UMass,[7] published in 1984 (Chierchia and Rooth 1984). This was an interesting and carefully argued paper that challenged a fundamental anti-compositionality claim in Kamp's seminal DRT paper (Kamp 1981). It was well-known that in a theory that adheres to the principles of Montague (1970), the use of an intermediate logical representation language (such as Montague's IL) must strictly be dispensable: there must be a direct compositional model-theoretic interpretation, obtainable as the composition of the translation function from the object language to the logical representation language and the interpretation function that gives a model-theoretic interpretation of the logical representation language. Kamp claimed that his intermediate representation language, the language of "DRS boxes," was not dispensable, because a geometrical notion of "accessibility" was said to be needed for characterizing possible anaphoric relations. As Gennaro and Mats write, if this is the best possible theory of anaphora, then the internal geometry of DRSs would have to be regarded as a crucial and indispensable component of natural language semantics, contrary to Montague's general view.

What they show in their paper is that accessibility can be dispensed with in Kamp's theory, and that binding possibilities (i.e. bound anaphora, the only anaphora treated in Kamp (1981) or in Montague's work) follow from the properties of the model-theoretic interpretation – in Kamp's case, from embedding conditions for embedding a DRS into a model. As a byproduct, they show that there is no theoretical or empirical difference between Kamp's notion of discourse referents and the notion of variable familiar from Tarskian satisfaction-based semantics. This was an important result, and the first of several works that showed how one can relate DRT notation and interpretation to more familiar kinds of logics, especially Zeevat (1989) and Muskens (1994).

Gennaro and Polly soon applied for a joint NSF grant for research on syntax and semantics, which they eventually got, and which resulted among other things in their exciting joint paper about two kinds of control (Chierchia and Jacobson 1986), which I return to below.

In Spring 1984 he was one of just three or four invited speakers at a Tarski Memorial Symposium at Ohio State University in March. His talk, based on his dissertation, was "A Fregean approach to predication in English," an early version of Chierchia (1985). Another part of his dissertation was developed into a talk on anaphoric properties of infinitives and gerunds at WCCFL 3 in April, published as Chierchia (1984b).

In the meantime, the System Development Foundation had come into existence as a deliberately short-lived entity, created as a non-profit entity in 1969 when the non-profit System Development Corporation became a for-profit corporation, and functioning as a grant-giving foundation from 1980, when SDC was sold to Burroughs, until it had disbursed all of its funds in 1988.[8] By far the biggest grant from SDF was the $15 million grant in 1983 to Stanford University together with SRI International and Xerox PARC to found CSLI, the Center for the Study of Language and Information, a research center involving linguists, philosophers, logicians, mathematicians, and later also psychologists. I was asked to serve on the Advisory Board, and at one of the first meetings I attended, in November 1983, it was strongly hinted that I should get acquainted with the chief program officer, Charlie Smith, and put in an application for a grant of our own for semantic research at UMass, ideally in some sort of collaborative arrangement with CSLI, and perhaps getting and using some of the same kind of "Dandelion" computers that CSLI had just acquired. (The Dandelions were among the first machines with 'windows' and 'mice'.[9]

Exciting and powerful but reportedly very temperamental.) So I invited Charlie Smith to come pay a visit to UMass in February 1984. I took him around to meet colleagues in linguistics, philosophy, and computer science and to give him an overview of the kinds of research we wanted to pursue as a follow-up to our Sloan grants. Charlie Smith was a strange character; he managed to look as though he was sleeping through a lot of the brief presentations we were giving for him, but would occasionally ask some sharp question or say something almost hostile; he seemed to enjoy making people uncomfortable. When he was meeting with a group from the Philosophy department, Michael Jubien described the work he was doing on property theory, and his hopes to get a book written on it. Charlie Smith asked how long it would take to write the book. Michael estimated that with his teaching load it would probably take a few years. Charlie asked how much money it would take to buy out enough teaching time to get it done in a year. Michael, surprised, managed to make an estimate (I no longer remember the numbers involved; it was basically a semester's teaching time plus a summer), and Charlie basically offered him a grant for that much on the spot, telling him to please write up the proposal and send it in and get to work writing. By the end of his visit he also encouraged me to submit a proposal; those were the only two he encouraged from UMass. I mention all this because what I was most anxious to do with the grant was to get Ray Turner back to UMass again and try to continue promoting interaction between him and Gennaro on property theory and related topics.

One sticking point was that Charlie Smith seemed to very strongly suggest that if I wanted a grant, it should include a request for some Dandelion computers. My colleagues and I were not so sure. So with helpful advice from my colleagues and close consultation with Ray Turner, I wrote up a proposal for a 3-year grant asking for funds for several Research Assistants, a visiting faculty position for Ray for three years and a post-doc or two, some summer salary, and a visit out to CSLI in the summer of 1984 accompanied by Ray, Gennaro, Emmon, three linguistics Research Assistants, and a Computer Science Research Assistant, for the purpose of acquaintance by immersion with the research going on at CSLI and with the computer environment there, promising that I would submit a separate equipment grant after I better understood our computational needs and what a Dandelion environment had to offer.

I got the grant, with most of what I wanted – tiny in comparison to CSLI's funding, but very large for me; I had asked for a million dollars and got about $750,000, and the project did begin with just such a visit to CSLI that summer, from late June to early August, with Emmon (only for two weeks, after his trip to China for the lecture series which led to his book (Bach 1989)), Ray, and Gennaro, and Computer Science student Bipin Indurkhya, and three linguistics graduate students, Craige Roberts, Karina Wilkinson, and Nina Dabek. A lot of quick planning was involved; the students and I would arrive just in time for a

COLING conference that included some tutorials the week before, starting June 25, and the linguistics students decided to take advantage of Brian Smith's LISP course and Bipin and I took Fernando Pereira's very wonderful PROLOG course – both courses designed specifically for linguistic and computational linguistic applications. (The PROLOG course turned out to use as examples the parsing and interpretation of Montague grammar constructions augmented by Robin Cooper's quantifier storage mechanisms, so with that and Pereira's great clarity, I was able to follow well and could spend some of the homework time on the local computers experimenting with things like possible quantifier scopes for NPs embedded in PPs inside other NPs.) Ray and Gennaro arrived July 2; Emmon came later for just two weeks. I had some good email conversations in advance with Jose Meseguer about formal properties of PROLOG, unification, and the relation between algebraic semantics and model-theoretic semantics. Email was brand new to me then; Stanford and SRI were on the ARPAnet and UMass was on cs-net, and at UMass I composed messages via a terminal connecting me to a VAX in the COINS department, with the EMACS editing program as a primitive "word processor" (designed for editing programs, not text; it was great for making sure that parentheses matched), and then over in the COINS department I could print out long folded pages of files of saved mail. One of Jose Meseguer's replies to a big pile of questions in April begins, "Barbara, Isn't it neat, the way that we can communicate with each other using these electronic networks?" And as primitive as they look now, it really was.

We rented two houses and rented a car; CSLI helped with some of our expenses, and gave us a computer terminal for one of the houses and shared offices at CSLI. The graduate students explored the computational environment, learned LISP and/or PROLOG, got acquainted with some of the work that was going on at CSLI on anaphora and other topics, and worked on their current research projects. Ray and Bipin especially helped us figure out that there would be no way we could have Dandelions in the Linguistics Department without a full-time expert to take care of them. We did see some impressive Dandelion demos at Xerox PARC, where Chris Halvorsen showed us how syntactic analyses of LFG derivations in Bresnan and Kaplan's system could be displayed – you could see a whole tree on a screen, but "click" on a node of the tree and you would get a window showing the full feature analysis at that node, and I think the nesting of displays of layers of structure was recursive. Really nice, and potentially very useful. But the machines needed constant expert maintenance. So when I did later put in an equipment request, it was for some much more mundane desktop computers that would be valuable for the department's phonological and phonetic research. The original grant included a simple desktop computer for me – that was my first.

Ray, Gennaro, and Bipin lived in one of the houses and the rest of us lived in another. We frequently invited two or three Stanford (or visiting) colleagues over to dinners with all of us at the bigger house; on those evenings one or two or a team of us would cook for the whole gang; our guests included Joan Bresnan and Marilyn Ford and their daughter Alexandra; Fernando Pereira and Jose Meseguer; Ewan Klein and Mary Tait; Robin Cooper and Elisabet Engdahl; Joyce Friedman, Jane Robinson, and Eva Hajičová; Peter Sells and Gerald Gazdar; and Jon Barwise and Brian Smith.

All of that interaction and talking with people was good but much of it was slightly superficial. The main work involved a few key projects. I had a chance to work a bit with Hans Kamp on our project on prototype theory and compositionality, which took years of infrequent interaction to finish (Kamp and Partee 1995). And I made some breakthroughs in my work on type shifting, thanks in part to very valuable feedback, especially from Joe Goguen and Jose Meseguer,[10] when I presented it at CSLI (Partee 1986a, 1986b). Ray and Gennaro were interacting intensely all the time they were there, and they also had some meetings with the mathematician Solomon Feferman, a student of Tarski's and a collaborator with Montague on a never-completed book on topics in the foundations of set theory. Feferman's work, like Ray's, concerns the relation between logic and computation, and he has done a lot of work on constructive mathematics, and "proofs as programs, programs as proofs" (Feferman 1985).

Ray and Gennaro gave a well-received CSLI colloquium talk in July, "Property theory and the foundations of semantics." Their collaboration had the nature of a long-running argument that became steadily richer.[11] Ray thought a non-constructive consistency proof that didn't show you how to build a model was not good enough for a logic that was supposed to be an underpinning of natural language semantics; that was his complaint against Cocchiarella's system, if I understand it correctly. Ray and Gennaro both understood that there were many challenges to developing a theory that had the properties they considered necessary for a successful account of intensionality and nominalizations, and many different choices that could be made at various choice points. The lasting value of much of their work, I believe, lies in laying out so clearly what the desiderata are, what the theoretical and descriptive choices are, what challenges face each choice, which choices may be independent of which others and which are crucially interconnected, and what kinds of motivations may lead researchers to prefer one line of development over another. And in the joint paper which grew out of their interaction (Chierchia and Turner 1988), they arrived at a fully worked out account of property theory which they claimed could support the semantics of natural language, driven by Gennaro's guiding intuition that properties are the semantic counterparts of natural language predicative expressions. On their joint theory, English is a multi-sorted first-order language, rather than the second-order language argued for in Chierchia's earlier Cocchiarella-inspired work; they show how everything captured with the help of Montague's type theory can be captured in their system as well, sometimes even better, as in their variant of the treatment of generalized conjunction and disjunction of Partee and Rooth (1983). And they illustrate the kinds of natural language phenomena for which property theory seems most necessary with examples that involve reference to and quantification over properties, property anaphora, predicates like *is fun* which can take both individual-denoting DPs and property-denoting infinitival expressions as subject.

Gennaro and Ray continued their collaborative work into the 1986–87 year, partly through visits to UMass supported by the SDF grant. Ray could not stay for the three full years 1984–87 as we had hoped, because he obtained a chair at Essex that required him to spend most of his time there; good news overall, though a disappointment for my plans, and I did not learn as much about property theory and alternative logics as I had hoped; by 1987 my own energy had turned instead to collaboration with Emmon and Angelika Kratzer on our big NSF-sponsored cross-linguistic study of the typology of quantification – possibly my first-ever non-interdisciplinary grant!

But in 1984–85 the SDF project had a good first full year. Ray visited for two months in the fall and a month in the spring, the mathematician Bill Marsh from Hampshire College was able to spend two months of the fall semester with us, and Fred Landman came from Amsterdam for the full fall semester. Hans Kamp visited in September, and Gennaro made several short visits up from Brown. We resumed an informal evening seminar on Model Theory and Foundations of Semantics, with linguists, philosophers, mathematicians, and computer scientists. The principal participants included Emmon and me, Fred Landman, and Ray Turner, and Gennaro when he could come. Central issues included the semantics of variables (a topic that Fred and I both had a long-standing interest in, and on which Fred was doing important original work (Landman 1986)), type theory, and theories of partial information (Fred and Ray).[12]

In December of 1984 Gennaro and Polly Jacobson were awarded their NSF grant for joint research on syntax and semantics. Plans were then made for Gennaro to spend the first half of summer 1985 working with Polly at Brown on their grant and the second half working with Ray and me here on mine. Gennaro was in fact at Brown just from 1983 to 1985, and then accepted an offer from Cornell. But Gennaro and Polly continued their collaborative project, which ran through 1987 and resulted in their valuable paper (Chierchia and Jacobson 1986). Up until then, semanticists had been debating three different approaches to controlled subjects of infinitivals like *to leave* in *John tried to leave* or *Mary persuaded John to leave*: (i) many followed traditional transformational grammar analyses and posited a null PRO subject in the syntax, interpreted as a bound variable in the semantics; (ii) some followed Montague in treating infinitivals simply as *to* plus a VP, which required finding a way to derive passive VPs like *to be fed properly*, for which there were various proposals like my early "Derived VP rule" (Partee 1973) or the meta-rules of GPSG (Gazdar 1982, Gazdar *et al.* 1985); Chierchia in his dissertation and related articles argued explicitly for such an approach, with no null subject in either the syntax or the semantics. And (iii) some argued for having no null subject in the syntax, but introducing a (bound variable) subject in the semantics (LFG, some Montague grammar analyses such as Bach and Partee (1980)). What was new in Chierchia and Jacobson's work was the marshaling of evidence to show that the best analysis was not the same in all cases: that "local" control works as Chierchia proposed, via semantic entailments that determine what, if anything, the property denoted by an infinitival VP is to be predicated of, whereas "long distance" control involves determining the interpretation of a null PRO subject. Their work enriched the control literature by providing a rich new set of diagnostics for discriminating the different kinds of control.

So in the summer of 1985, as planned, Gennaro spent the first part of the summer working with Polly at Brown on that grant project, and the last part at UMass on the SDF project.

During the summer he made two trips to give invited talks. The first was "Aspects of a categorial theory of Binding" at a Categorial Grammar conference in Tucson in June organized by Emmon Bach, Dick Oehrle, and Deirdre Wheeler (Chierchia 1988a), a new topic not at all connected with his dissertation. There he argued against the purely semantic approach to binding argued for in Bach and Partee (1980) and in favor of a theory combining the Bach and Partee semantics with a syntactic counterpart, involving coindexing on a categorial structure and using a theory of predication inspired by work of Edwin Williams (Williams 1980). He made use of Gazdar's approach to binding, arguing that *all* binding phenomena should be treated in terms of syntactic binding features analogous to Gazdar's slashes. This gave him a way to handle case-marking phenomena that purely semantic approaches could not; and he resolved problems that Bach and Partee had left open about the status of indices or the individuation of variables. He also drew interesting consequences for across-the-board phenomena, a topic he had not ventured into earlier, and for control, which he had already studied deeply, and where he was able to maintain his position that (local) control does not involve any covert subject, and where control could be viewed as an instance of subject-predicate agreement, a single assumption that offered a great simplification over the then-current GB assumptions about control.

And in July 1985, Gennaro, Ray Turner, and I spent two weeks at CSLI. Gennaro and Ray gave an invited and well-received presentation of their ongoing research at a CSLI-hosted meeting of the Association for Symbolic Logic, "Semantics and Property Theory," an early version of the work they published together in 1988. I also gave an invited talk there, "Syntactic

Categories and Semantic Types" on types and type-shifting. The meeting was preceded by an interesting set of one-week courses, of which I particularly remember Yiannis Moschovakis's course on the theory of algorithms, in which he reported on his efforts to find a suitably 'intensional' notion of "function," more discriminating than the standard set-theoretic extensional notion, but not as excessively fine-grained as some notions of algorithm. There was a great density of logicians with an interest in language, in keeping with the mission of CSLI; other short courses were offered by Barwise, Thomason, Plotkin, Meseguer, Moss, and Maarten van Emden, and it was a very lively atmosphere.

Then in August we had an informal but intensive research gathering of participants in my SDF grant in Amherst, including Partee, Bach, Chierchia, Turner, Hans Kamp, seven research assistants, and other informal participants. Topics included Ray and Gennaro's work, the work that Craige Roberts and Nirit Kadmon had begun with Hans Kamp while he was on our faculty concerning modal subordination (Craige) and distributivity (Nirit), and I recall a great deal of discussion of alternative approaches to the semantics of plurality and distributivity.

At the end of the summer of 1985, Gennaro and his family moved to Ithaca, where Gennaro began teaching at Cornell. That fall he and Polly Jacobson presented their joint paper at the NELS conference at McGill in November, and in January he gave an invited talk on "The Logic of Control" at the University of Geneva.

During 1985–86 Gennaro was at Cornell, but made several visits to UMass. Ray Turner was here part of the time in 1985–86 as well.

Our main collective SDF-project event in 1985–86 was a conference in March 1986 that Gennaro, Ray, and I organized on Properties, Types, and Meaning, bringing logicians, philosophers, and linguists together to address some of the foundational issues central to our grant project and linguistic problems involving them. The conference took place at Hampshire College through the kindness of our Hampshire colleagues, especially Jay Garfield, and many of the participants were housed in a quaint dormitory there which also held our meeting room. The conference is described in the two-volume collection based on it that the three of us edited (Chierchia *et al.* 1989b). The presenters were Ray, Gennaro, Peter Aczel, Rich Thomason, Nick Asher and Hans Kamp, Michael Jubien, George Bealer, Johan van Benthem, Jeroen Groenendijk and Martin Stokhof, David Dowty, Greg Carlson, Lenhart Schubert and Jeff Pelletier, Henk Zeevat, Solomon Feferman, Ewan Klein, and Gordon Plotkin. There was a good group of invited discussants as well, including Emmon, Janet Fodor, Erhard Hinrichs, Angelika, Fred Landman, Richard Larson, Godehard Link, Chris Menzel, Uwe Mönnich, and Carl Pollard. Gennaro's paper in that volume argues in favor of structured meanings, on the basis of arguments concerning thematic roles and control, independent of propositional attitudes, and staying neutral concerning property theory. Ray's paper (Turner 1989) succinctly lays out the difficult problems of intensionality and nominalization, and how the problems require a theoretical framework permitting properties to be regarded as individuals, as spelled out in his joint work with Gennaro. Using work further described in Chierchia and Turner (1988), he shows a way of achieving this with a rather weak logic and property theory using "close variants of models of the λ-calculus" (Chierchia *et al.* 1989a: 7) and contrasts it with other approaches, including that of Gennaro's dissertation.

That conference was in a sense the peak of our joint collaboration. Ray and Gennaro both visited UMass some more in the following year, and there was a lot of work to do on the editing of the two volumes, most of which fell on Gennaro. By earlier agreement, I did very little work on the editing. In fact almost all of the editing work fell on Gennaro, and he was the sole author of the introduction to Volume 2. Ray helped with some specific advice on some of the technical papers in Volume 1. Gennaro read every article with care, and corresponded extensively with the authors about suggested revisions, and endured all the editorial headaches. The introductions to both volumes are important works in themselves, one solely by Gennaro and the other largely by Gennaro; they not only give very good summaries of the main ideas of the papers, but they insightfully place them in the context of the larger linguistic, logical, and philosophical issues to which the conference was dedicated. The conference and the book represented a rare confluence of ideas and approaches from logic, philosophy, foundations of computer science, and linguistics, and I believe the book has been a useful resource for anyone interested in approaches to and linguistic uses of property theory or type theory.

In the summer of 1986, Gennaro and I both gave talks (at different times) in July at the Workshop on Logical Form organized by Irene Heim, Howard Lasnik, and Bob May at the LSA Linguistic Institute at CUNY. My summer 1986 in Amherst involved working with a number of students on their research, several of them supported on the SDF grant while working on their dissertations; Craige Roberts and Arnold Chien defended their dissertations that August. Emmon and Angelika and I spent a lot of time reworking the NSF grant proposal on cross-linguistic quantification that we had submitted unsuccessfully the year before. (This time it was successful.) I don't have any record of any visits to CSLI that summer or any summer visits from Ray or Gennaro.

But then during 1986–87 Gennaro spent much of the time in the spring semester, from January to June, at UMass as a Research Associate on the SDF project. That spring Nirit Kadmon, Jae-Woong Choe, Sandro Zucchi, Karina Wilkinson, and Mark Aronszajn (Philosophy) were all working on their dissertations – there were a record number of semantics dissertations right around then, perhaps partly because of the unusually high amount of funding and semantics research activity the grants of that period made possible. During that spring while Gennaro was here, Emmon, Angelika, and I gave our first joint seminar, on the semantics of events. Gennaro had much to contribute from his work on infinitives and gerunds, and Sandro Zucchi followed up on some of the seminar topics for his later dissertation work. Gennaro was still managing to be active back at Cornell at the same time, and in May was co-organizer with Fred Landman of a conference on "Events and Thematic Structure" at Cornell.

In April 1987 Gennaro gave a talk "Anaphora and attitudes *de se*" at the Amsterdam Colloquium (Chierchia 1989). This paper, a new direction for Gennaro then, was another great combination of philosophical and linguistic insight, bringing badly needed clarity to the old and vexing questions of how to treat Castañeda's "quasi-indicator" pronouns, how they relate to the understood subjects of infinitives, and how they relate to ordinary bound variable pronouns. These were puzzles that linguists of many different schools had found themselves embroiled in willy-nilly, and Gennaro is one of the few linguists (Fred Landman is another) who managed to turn these questions into an area of fruitful research rather than a pit of quicksand. David Lewis had laid a good bit of groundwork (Lewis 1979a), but I believe that Gennaro was the first to find a successful way to make use of Lewis's ideas for linguistic analysis.

In the summer of 1987 Gennaro and I were both at Stanford, at the 1987 LSA Linguistic Institute. Gennaro was invited to give the basic Semantics course, and it was one of the half-dozen lectures chosen to be videotaped and offered for sale. He also "taught" in Linguistics 230, the Workshop on Generics, sponsored by Ivan Sag's NSF grant, where many of the contributors to the long-in-gestation Generic Book (Carlson and Pelletier 1995) started the project with much lively discussion and debate. I met Gennaro's first Ph.D. student Veneeta Srivastav (Veneeta Dayal) in my semantics seminar there, and she was one of the top students in my big class, already showing many of the qualities that have made her one of the leaders in the field. The heavy teaching schedule kept us very busy there, but Isa has some nice photos of a poolside afternoon when Solomon and Anita Feferman had invited Gennaro and Isa and their boys (two then, I believe – Gabriele and Tommaso) and me for lunch at the faculty club swimming pool on August 1.

By the fall of 1988, when he was up for tenure, the very nice semantics textbook that he and Sally McConnell-Ginet published in 1990 was well under way. That textbook is still an ideal choice to use with students who are not necessarily going to become formal semanticists themselves but to whom you want to convey some of the most important and beautiful ideas of contemporary pragmatics and formal semantics, and it furthermore gives a very sound foundation for any who do decide to pursue semantics or pragmatics further.

Also by the fall of 1988, Gennaro had been appointed to the editorial boards of *Linguistics and Philosophy* and of *Linguistic Inquiry*, was co-editor of the *Linguistic Inquiry* Squibs and Discussion Department, and had taken on the managing editorship of Kluwer's book series *Studies in Linguistics and Philosophy.* His joint paper with Ray Turner was about to appear, and he had a paper in press in the proceedings of Krifka's 1988 conference on Genericity (Chierchia 1988b).

Gennaro was by then a recognized star in semantics. His dissertation was published in the Garland Outstanding Dissertations series in 1988, the same year our co-edited conference volumes came out. His work on his own and with Ray Turner on property theory and its linguistic applications was understood to be extremely important foundational work with important consequences for both the philosophy of language and the linguistic practice of semantics. I have always regarded that work, like much of his work, as important steps in "vindicating" natural language by showing that one can make good sense of the observable syntax of natural languages if one can find the right sort of semantics (and pragmatics) to use in compositionally interpreting it. That has always been Gennaro's strength; it's nice to see that he has found and uses a phrase that encapsulates that vindication, "the spontaneous logicality of language." Perhaps we can characterize Gennaro himself as manifesting in the highest degree a similar property, "the spontaneous insightfulness of the ideal philosopher-linguist."

## Acknowledgments

My thanks to Ivano Caponigro for valuable advice, feedback, and editorial assistance with this chapter. Special thanks to Kathleen Adamczyk for unearthing a copy of the 1984 play that Raymond Turner and she wrote about the property-theory debates that consumed Ray and Gennaro during that summer, which is now being published as an appendix to the present volume; and to Raymond Turner and Bipin Indurkhya for feedback on my description of that summer. All errors or lapses of memory are my own.

NOTES

1. In the fall of 2011, when Gennaro and Isa were coming to visit Amherst and would stay here at 50 Hobart Lane for the second time, Gennaro reminisced in an email about the first time he and Isa had stayed here: "On August 28, 1979 (nearly 31 years ago) we landed at the campus center. Nobody was around. The first person we met in the Dept. was Toni Borowsky; and shortly thereafter, Janet Randall. We spent 3 nights at the campus center hotel. After that Barbara [and Emmon – BHP] came back to the rescue and we moved into Hobart Lane, where we stayed for over a week. Among

many other things she did, Barbara drove us to Paul's Old Time furniture, where we got our first bed and living room set. The rest is history, as they say . . ." According to my own little black book, it was August 28 that they moved into our house, so they would have arrived a few days before that. But Gennaro may be right.

2. The Sloan grants, which were held by quite a number of universities in the first two phases of the program, in 1978–80 and 1980–85, led to various "Sloan" terminology; since interdisciplinary Cognitive Science conferences and interdisciplinary postdocs were strongly encouraged parts of the programs for all, such phrases as "Sloaning around" and "becoming all Sloaned out" became common.
3. Most of the "foundational" work of the late 1970s and early 1980s in formal semantics came from philosophers and logicians like Hans Kamp and the Amsterdam and Groningen groups (Groenendijk and Stokhof, van Benthem, and colleagues). I should mention that two notable instances of linguists contributing to foundational developments include Arnim von Stechow and his student Angelika Kratzer.
4. I've discovered that he is not the only mathematician to feel that way. As he explained to me, any example will have a number of inessential properties that may be misleading, so it's safer to stay on the level of pure abstractions. And I've discovered that I'm not the only linguist who needs examples to help me grasp abstractions; I try to get around the 'misleading' problem by trying to find several dissimilar examples. Doing that was part of what made my retellings of Ray's lectures longer, but the linguistics students (other than Gennaro and Mats) and I needed it.
5. During the 1982–83 year I received a copy of the manuscript of Barwise and Perry's book *Situations and Attitudes* (Barwise and Perry 1983), and my early enthusiasm was replaced by disappointment in the gulf between the early promise of Barwise (1981) and what they did in that book (even though they did make many revisions from the initial manuscript), for reasons recounted in Partee (2005). Situation semantics seemed to gradually languish, despite some interesting work by Robin Cooper and others, until reintroduced in a very different framework by Angelika Kratzer, where possible situations are parts of possible worlds. Kratzer's version has proved far more successful and influential. See overview in Kratzer (2011).
6. I think the game may have been "Scopa"; it used beautiful Italian playing cards that we had never seen before. (My sons bought decks of those beautiful cards and took them back to Nijmegen, where they made the game popular among their Dutch schoolmates.) The game was delicately rigged to make sure that Gennaro's grandmother would win, which she did. Both Gennaro's grandmother and 6-month-old son Gabriele were the objects of great demonstrative affection – Gabriele was never allowed to cry for a moment. I loved what I saw there of Italian family life!
7. That was the NELS organized by Charlie Jones and Peter Sells and their team of fellow graduate students, featuring a memorable disco party at a fraternity house where Toni Borowsky was house mother. That was very different from the 1972 NELS where the slightly formal party was held in Alumni Hall (those first NELSes were organized by faculty, that one by Don Freeman as part of his successful campaign to put the brand-new UMass program on the map as quickly as possible), and from the 1977 NELS organized by Mark Stein and fellow students, where the party was a laid-back indoor-outdoor affair in the since torn-down Fairley Lodge.
8. See http://en.wikipedia.org/wiki/System_Development_Corporation and www.oac.cdlib.org/findaid/ark:/13030/tf429003m4/.

9. There were famous fights later on about whether Apple, and also Microsoft had "stolen" the windows idea from Xerox, or whether Xerox had in effect given it away, but there seems to be no dispute over the fact that the researchers at Xerox PARC had developed it first. (Fisher, Lawrence. "Xerox Sues Apple Computer Over Macintosh Copyright," *The New York Times*, December 15, 1989.)
10. In fact, what is sometimes called the "Partee triangle" in my type-shifting paper wouldn't have been a triangle, but just a list, without the category-theory-related suggestions from Goguen and Meseguer.
11. After the end of the summer, a play (Turner and Adamczyk 1984) about their long debate was created for one of our evening model theory seminars, co-authored by Ray and our inimitable secretary Kathy Adamczyk, who was then still on soft money funded first by the Sloan Grant and then by a combination of Lyn Frazier's and my grants. Ray's recollection (p.c.) is "that I wrote it with the wonderful Kathy typing it, adding prose, jokes and the hilarious stage directions. I recall that Kathy wrote the very funny penultimate line where B[ipin] asks: *Can I go into the bathroom now*? Kathy and I should share authorship. Gennaro gave his own paper and mine was written as a surprise for him. He knew I was up to something, but did not know what. He became suspicious because Kathy and I were huddled in the office writing and laughing, but he never knew what was going on until the morning of the talks." Kathy's interpolations include uncannily accurate indications of Ray's and Gennaro's body language. She beautifully evokes Gennaro's manner of pacing while he talks, pausing with outstretched arms to beg for his interlocutor's agreement. Kathy has found a copy of the play, and it's included as an appendix.
12. The plans for the fall seminar were somewhat curtailed after the sudden tragic death of Emmon's daughter on November 2, 1984; in fact I believe that we were at Gennaro and Isa's house in Providence, during the NELS conference at Brown, when we got the news from Texas, and their presence was a great comfort.

# 2 Notes on denotation and denoting

*Noam Chomsky*

In their now classic introduction to the foundations of semantic theory, Chierchia and McConnell-Ginet (1990) observe that "denotation might constitute the fundamental semantic relation" if it is possible, as they argue, to extend the elementary case of a proper name to other expressions, perhaps "to expressions of any kind whatsoever." In the elementary case, a name like *Pavarotti* "refers to or denotes its bearer (the popular singer)"; and generally, "from a denotational point of view, symbols stand for objects."

This core notion – the *referentialist doctrine* – is standard, as indicated even in the titles of some of the founding works on these topics in the early days of contemporary linguistic semantics over half a century ago: *Words and Things* (Brown 1958) and *Word and Object* (Quine 1960). And of course the referentialist doctrine has much deeper roots. Chierchia and McConnell-Ginet argue that it should serve a dual function, leading to explanation of the two fundamental questions of semantics: the link between symbols and their information content, the "aboutness of language," its connection to the external world; and "language as a social activity."

To illustrate the critical role of denotation beyond the elementary case, Chierchia and McConnell-Ginet provide examples of language use in which noun phrases "besides proper names seem to derive their significance or semantic power from their reference." In these cases, "an act or demonstration" individuates the reference of the expression "in our perceptual space" – e.g., the expression "this" in an utterance of "this is yellow." And we would not "understand the meaning of the NPs in these [cases] if we didn't know what they referred to." Accordingly, "the notion of reference appears to be a fundamental component of what the NPs in question mean."

As indicated by the illustrative examples, the relation of reference derives from acts of referring (an act or demonstration according to Strawson 1950). The name *Pavarotti* refers to Pavarotti insofar as we refer to him by using the name. In much the same way, we say "the key opens the door," presupposing an agent who opens the door with a key, the latter being the basic notion (to borrow an analogy of Richard Larson's). Distinguishing denoting (an action) from denotation (a mind–world relation[1]), it would seem more appropriate to take the notion of referring, not reference, "to be a fundamental component of what NPs mean." That acts of referring take place is uncontroversial, but it does not follow so easily that the derivative relation of denotation holding between *Pavarotti* and the bearer of the name is any more significant or substantive than the derivative relation of *opening* holding between the key and the door. The examples provided by Chierchia and McConnell-Ginet illustrate the act of denoting (referring). But the examples leave open the status of the relation of denotation; that is, the question whether there is a relevant relation between the internal symbol used to refer and some mind-independent entity that is picked out by the expression that is used to denote: an object, a thing, individuated without recourse to mental acts. Or even whether such an object or thing exists, except in the circumstance-dependent sense in which a particular sound exists when we pronounce the name (for a lucid discussion of some of these issues in a more general context, see Elbourne 2011).

We can perhaps clarify what is at stake by considering this latter aspect of mind–world relations in the case of human language, the case of Word-and-Sound, that is, the ways internal symbols are externalized by the sensorimotor system SM. Take the word *kitten* and the corresponding phonetic symbol [kɪ'n], the latter an internal object, an element of I-language, in the mind. We can carry out actions in which we use [kɪ'n] to produce a sound S (or counterparts in other modalities), the act of pronunciation. The sound S is a specific event in the mind-independent world, and there is a derivative relation between the internal symbol [kɪ'n] and S insofar as we use [kɪ'n] to pronounce S. There is however no relevant direct relation between [kɪ'n] and S, and it would be idle to try to construct some mind-independent entity to which [kɪ'n] corresponds even for a single individual, let alone a community of users. Acoustic and articulatory phonetics are devoted to discovering how internal symbols provide ways to produce and interpret sounds, no simple task as we all know. And there is no reason to suspect that it would be an easier task to discover how internal systems are used to talk or think about aspects of the world. Quite the contrary.

Returning to the denotational aspect of the relation of internal symbols (say, *Pavarotti* or *this* or *kitten*) to the external world, suppose we take the fundamental component of what NPs mean to be the action of referring, as seems reasonable. We use the internal symbol to refer to/denote some aspect of the mind-independent world, which we take to be a specific instance of an object or a thing (not innocent notions), much as we use the internal symbol [kɪ'n] to produce (or interpret) a specific mind-independent event S. In the latter case, we do not go on to posit a relation between [kɪ'n] and S (or some construction from possible S's). Should we depart from this practice in the former case, postulating a relation between *Pavarotti* or *this* or *kitten* and a mind-independent object or thing, in accordance with the referentialist doctrine? That would require an argument, and it is not clear that there is one that carries any weight.

Furthermore, there is good reason to believe that it would be a mistake and that the referentialist doctrine is untenable. If so, the meaning of *Pavarotti* is not an object that a physicist could identify without reference to the mind, but rather an array of perspectives for referring to the world – rather as [kɪ'n] provides "instructions" to the SM system for the acts of pronouncing and interpretation.

A familiar objection, going back at least to Frege, is that meanings in this sense are individual, internal properties, and as such would interfere with use of language as a social activity, for communication in particular. The objection is correct, but it is hard to see why it should be considered to have any force, any more than it does with regard to externalization as sound. Communication and other forms of social interaction with language are not Yes-or-No affairs; rather More-or-Less. The hearer seeks to determine the expression that the speaker is using, often not an easy task; and beyond that to determine what the speaker has in mind, perhaps dismissing linguistic evidence in the process (typically without awareness).

Let's turn to the objects and things to which a speaker refers. What qualifies? Quine was much concerned with this topic in his influential *Word and Object*.[2] He observed that in some cases an NP may not be "a compelling candidate – on the surface, anyway – for thinghood," as Dennett (2012) puts the matter in discussing the issues Quine raised. We say "for Pete's sake" or "for the sake of," but would be hard put to answer questions about sakes or about Pete that are appropriate for things, for example, what are the identity conditions for sakes, how many are there, how tall is Pete, etc.? Similarly, Dennett observes, "Paris and London plainly exist, but do the *miles* that separate them also exist?" Quine's answer is that a noun of this kind is "*defective*, and its putative reference need not be taken seriously from an ontological point of view."

Often there is direct linguistic evidence of deficiency of "thinghood." Consider the nouns *flaw* and *fly*. In some constructions they function in similar ways: *there is (believed to be) a fly in the bottle – a flaw in the argument*. In others not: *there is a fly believed to be in the bottle (*a flaw believed to be in the argument)*; *a fly is in the bottle (*a flaw is in the argument)*. Some constructions carry a form of existential import that others lack, a matter that falls within an explanatory framework with a variety of consequences (and, as usual, interesting open problems, cf. Chomsky 2001).

There do seem to be distinctions among "candidates for thinghood," but questions soon arise. Presumably the word "thing" should be a compelling candidate for thinghood. So what are the identity conditions for things and how many are there? Suppose we see some branches strewn on the ground. If they fell from a tree after a storm, they are not a thing. But if they were carefully placed there by an artist as a work of conceptual art, even given a name, then they are a thing (and might win an award). A little thought will show that many complex factors determine whether some part of the world constitutes a thing, including human intention and design, which are not properties that can be detected by study of the mind-independent world. If *thing* does not qualify for *thinghood*, then what does?

What about Dennett's examples Paris and London? Surely we can refer to them, as if I were to say that I visited London the year before it was destroyed by a great fire and then rebuilt with entirely different materials and design 50 miles up the Thames, where I intend to re-visit it next year. Does the extra-mental world contain an entity with such properties, an entity that a physicist could in principle discover? Surely not. How then can we truly refer to London, either by using the expression *London* or a pronoun linked to it (or some more complex phrase, say, "Ken Livingstone's favorite city")? Assuming the referentialist doctrine, we cannot, even though we clearly can. It seems then that we must abandon it in this case. If we do, the problem dissolves. In my I-language there is an internal entity *London* (or the *meaning of London*) – not necessarily matching exactly for you and me – which provides perspectives for referring to aspects of the world, much as the internal entity [kɪ'n] (or the configuration of its component properties) – also not necessarily matching exactly for you and me – provides means to pronounce and interpret certain events in the world. This is only one of a host of similar problems discussed in the literature, including the simplest words that are used to refer to things in the world.[3]

The difficulties posed by the referentialist doctrine extend to other proper names, like *Pavarotti.* Adapting Saul Kripke's Paderewski paradox (Kripke 1979), suppose that Pavarotti happens to be an anarchist, and Pierre, who is perfectly rational, knows him as a singer and as an anarchist but is unaware that it is the same person. Suppose that attending an opera, Pierre says sincerely that Pavarotti is tall, and at a street rally sincerely denies that he is tall. Thus a rational person can sincerely hold contradictory beliefs, which makes no sense. The paradox presupposes the referentialist doctrine, and dissolves when we abandon it. There is nothing puzzling about the possibility that Pierre has two lexical entries, with different meanings (arrays of perspectives for use), which happen to be pronounced the same way and when used by Pierre to refer, happen to pick out the same person – whatever a person is, again not a simple matter.[4]

There are many traditional paradoxes of a similar nature. Consider the famous puzzle of the ship of Theseus, tracing to Plutarch. Suppose that the ship is in the Athens museum, a board falls off and is replaced by another one, etc., until every board has been replaced. It is still plainly the ship of Theseus. Suppose further that the boards have been collected and used to reconstruct the ship of Theseus out of its original materials. That is also the ship of Theseus. But now there are two ships, each the ship of Theseus, which cannot be. A paradox, if the referentialist doctrine holds, and the NP *ship of Theseus* picks out an entity in the mind-independent world; but no paradox if the internal entity *ship of Theseus* provides perspectives that do not happen to provide a clear answer for every situation that can be conjured up. As Wittgenstein observed, we use language against a background of beliefs, and if these do not hold, we may have no answers to questions about referring and much else.

Science fiction often plays with such examples, and often the answers are obscure. To mention an experiment (with a ludicrously small sample), my grandchildren sometimes corralled me into watching a TV series featuring a space ship equipped with a box that a person can enter and be transported to some distant planet – but remaining the same person. I once asked them what would happen if the person who was transported also remained in the box. Which would be the original person (essentially the ship of Theseus)? Mostly puzzlement, no clear answers, nor should that be surprising.

Many other cases are considered in classical philosophy. Aristotle (*Metaphysics* VIII.3; *De Anima* I.1) concluded that we can "define a house as stones, bricks and timbers," in terms of material constitution, but also as "a receptacle to shelter chattels and living beings," in terms of function and design; and we should combine both parts of the definition, integrating matter and form, since the "essence of a house" involves the "purpose and end" of the material constitution. Hence a house is not a mind-independent object. That becomes still clearer when we investigate further, and discover that the concept *house* has far more intricate properties, an observation that generalizes far beyond (see references of note 3). In his development of the Aristotelian theory of language, Moravcsik (1975) suggests that "there are no expressions that perform solely the task of referring," which we can revise as the suggestion that the referentialist doctrine is radically false: there are no expressions that pick out objects or things that are mind-independent. That seems accurate for natural language. Many inquiries illustrate that even the simplest expressions have intricate meanings; it is doubtful that any satisfy the referentialist doctrine.[5]

The referentialist doctrine has a role elsewhere. In mathematics, for example – though exactly what numerals refer to (if they do at all) is not a trivial question. In the sciences, one goal is to adhere as closely as possible to the referentialist doctrine. Thus in devising technical notions like *electron* or *phoneme*, researchers hope to be identifying entities that exist in the world, and seek to adhere to the referentialist doctrine in using these notions. It is common to speak of "the language of mathematics/science," but these constructs should not of course be confused with natural language – more technically, with the linguist's I-language. Further confusions can arise if these different systems are intermingled. Thus chemists freely use the term "water" in informal discourse, but not in the sense of the word of natural language. There is much discussion in the literature of the status of the expression "water is $H_2O$," a question that cannot even be posed unless it is determined what language the expression is in (it's accepted that the meaning of a sentence depends on the language to which it belongs). It is not the "language of chemistry," which does not have the term *water* (though it is used informally). It is not the natural language English, which does not have the term $H_2O$, at least if we take enough care to distinguish the sharply different ways in which expressions that enter into thought and interchange are acquired and used. If we consider the mixed system in which the expression appears, its status will depend on whether *water* is used in the sense of normal English (in which case the expression is false) or in the sense of chemistry (in which case it is true by definition, putting aside some technicalities, and irrelevant to the topics for which it is invoked).

Note that Aristotle was defining the entity *house*, an exercise in metaphysics, not the word *house*. The entity in his terms is a combination of matter and form. In the course of the cognitive revolution of the seventeenth century, the general point of view shifted towards seeking the "innate cognoscitive powers" that enter into our understanding of experience, expressions of language in particular – interpretive principles that "derive from the original hand of nature," in Hume's phrase; genetic endowment, in contemporary terms. Summarizing many years of discussion of such topics, Hume concluded that "the identity we ascribe" to minds, vegetables, animal bodies, and other entities is "only a fictitious one" established by the imagination, not a "peculiar nature belonging to this form," a conclusion that appears to be basically correct (cf. references of note 3 for discussion and sources).

One classical illustration of the deficiencies of the referentialist doctrine is the concept *person*. Thus when we say that the name *Pavarotti* denotes its bearer, what exactly is the bearer? It cannot be simply the material body. As Locke observes in *Essay Concerning Human Understanding* (Book II, chap. XXVII), there is no absurdity in thinking that the same person might have two different bodies: if the same consciousness (which individuates a person) "can be transferred from one thinking substance to another, it will be possible that two thinking substances may make up one person." And there are many variants. Personal identity thus consists (at least) in "identity of consciousness," in psychic continuity. Locke adds that the term *person* (or *self*, or *soul*) is, furthermore, "a forensic term, appropriating actions and their merit; and so belongs only to intelligent agents, capable of a law, and happiness, and misery."

The roots of the conception are classical (for a lucid review of the history of the topic, see Goetz and Taliaferro 2011). For Plato, it is accidental that Pavarotti has this particular body (and reincarnated, he will have a different one). Aristotle too takes a person to be a composite of form and matter (rather like a house), where the form is the *soul*, a type of soul that differs from those shared with other organic entities in that it provides for the possibility of thought.

Similar notions appear throughout the history of thought, along with the conception that actions of humans are explained irreducibly by purposes and reasons. The notions are explored in science fiction – transporting one person's thought into another body, etc. – and are perfectly natural for young children. In a typical fairy story, the wicked witch turns the handsome prince into a frog, and so he remains until the frog is kissed by the beautiful princess – but he was the prince all along, though he had the physical properties of a frog. The same extends easily to animals, and further investigation reveals that psychic continuity as a condition (or even the criterion) for personhood presumably falls together with the manner in which organization of parts and common end are taken to determine what counts as the same tree or river, or any other entity of the natural world that enters into our thought and reflection, also topics investigated in the philosophical tradition, suggestively if inadequately (again, see references of note 3).

Recent studies of language acquisition (Gleitman and Landau 2012, Landau and Gleitman 1985, Medina *et al.* 2011) have shown that meanings of even the most elementary linguistic expressions are acquired from very restricted evidence, and very rapidly during the early years of life, even under severe sensory constraints. It is difficult to see how one can avoid the conclusion that these intricate structures depend on "innate cognoscitive powers" of the kinds explored in interesting ways in the "first cognitive revolution" of the seventeenth century. Intricacies mount rapidly when we proceed beyond the simple elements used to refer, reinforcing the conclusion that innate properties of the mind play a critical role in their acquisition and use. Such considerations seem impossible to reconcile with traditional views of language acquisition as based on ostention, instruction, and habit formation; in particular, with what Føllesdal (1990), in his penetrating study of Quine's theory of meaning, calls the "MMM thesis": *The meaning of a linguistic expression is the joint product of all the evidence that helps learners and users of the language determine that meaning.*[6] Analogous theses are untenable for phonology and syntax, and are even more remote from reality in the case of the meanings of expressions.

The conclusions pose very serious problems for any potential theory of evolution of language – more properly, evolution of language users, since languages do not evolve (in the biological sense of the term). It appears to be the case that animal communication systems are based on a one-one relation between mind/brain processes and "an aspect of the environment to which these processes adapt the animal's behavior" (Gallistell 1990). If so, the gap between human language is as dramatic as what we find in other domains of language structure, acquisition, and use.

If such conclusions as those discussed here do indeed generalize, then it would follow that natural language has no semantics in the sense of relations between symbols and mind-independent entities. Rather, it has syntax (symbol manipulation) and pragmatics (modes of use of language).[7] And at least in this respect, the two interface systems have significant common properties. These are all matters that seem to me to deserve considerably more attention and concern than they have received.

NOTES

1. I will keep to the relations between linguistic symbols and extra-mental entities that could in principle be identified by a natural scientist without attending to the mind of the speaker. Essentially the same questions arise, along with others, in the case of denotation of mental states and events.
2. Quine's concern was in part natural language, in part "regimented" language designed for science and a minimal ontology, two different enterprises, not always clearly distinguished.
3. See among others Chomsky (1966), including James McGilvray's introduction to the third (e-) edition of this book (McGilvray 2003); Chomsky (1996); Chomsky (2000b) and my comments on Peter Ludlow's essay included in Antony and Hornstein (2003).
4. Kripke's puzzle about belief also presupposes the referentialist doctrine, in some form, and does not arise if it is abandoned.
5. For discussion in the context of consideration of Saul Kripke's theory of names, see Chomsky (1975) and references of note 3.
6. In an appreciative comment, Quine (cf. Barrett and Gibson 1990: 110) endorses Føllesdal's interpretation, but with a crucial modification, stating that "What matters is just that linguistic meaning is a function of observable behavior in observable circumstances" which would be true no matter how rich the crucial innate endowment, just as the visual system is a function of observable visual input.
7. Formal semantics, including model-theoretic semantics, fall under syntax in this categorization. Though motivated by external world considerations, the results do not fall with metaphysics ("what there is," in Quine's formulation).

*Part II*

# From grammar to meaning: formal developments, new findings, and challenges

# 3 On the existential force of bare plurals across languages

*Veneeta Dayal*

## 1. Introduction

Bare plurals across languages can be associated with existential quantificational force. In the neo-Carlsonian account of Chierchia (1998), there are two distinct sources for this. One is the low ranked ∃-type shift of Partee (1986b), which comes into play when the higher ranked *nom* and *iota* are unavailable. The other is the basic kind-level meaning for bare plurals, where ∃ force comes into existence as a result of sort-adjustment by the rule of Derived Kind Predication (DKP), in the spirit of Carlson (1977). Noun phrases shifted by ∃ are marked by the ability to take scope over other operators. Noun phrases that tap into DKP are characterized by obligatory narrow scope with respect to other operators. This chapter re-examines both sources of existential force and presents a new perspective on them.

Canonically, bare plurals allow reference to kinds but there are some that do not. ∃-type shift is posited by Chierchia for bare plurals that are not kind denoting. In this chapter, a hitherto overlooked distinction among such bare purals is noted. It is shown that while one set indeed shows scopal flexibility, as expected under Chierchia's analysis, the other set does not. It is argued that allowing ∃-type shift for even the first set is not viable when a larger set of facts is taken into account. Alternative ways of achieving the same effects are proposed, to compensate for eliminating ∃-type shift from the set of covert options available to bare plurals.

The chapter then turns to the more familiar class of bare plurals, those for which Chierchia maintains a kind-based approach and uses DKP to obtain existential readings. New diagnostics are presented to show that the narrow scope existential readings imputed to bare plurals are not sufficient to capture the full range of their behavior. In order to accommodate these new facts, ∃ quantification is eliminated from DKP. Bare plurals in episodic contexts are argued to refer to a unique maximal entity, defined over a widened domain. The so-called ∃ readings are claimed to be "representative group readings" of such maximal entities.

The end result of the investigation, then, is to do away with both sources of ∃ force for bare plurals. Doing away with ∃-type shift pushes Chierchia's original formulation of the hierarchy of covert type shifts to its logical limits, where only the two operations that he classifies as meaning preserving are available in natural language. Doing away with ∃ quantification in DKP further delinks the alignment between bare plurals and indefinites in favor of aligning bare plurals with definites, pushing forward a view proposed in Dayal (2004). Treating bare plurals as involving no quantification of any kind, as de facto definites, appears quite radical. But I build up to this conclusion incrementally, inviting the reader to go along with me as far as they can. The hope is that even if no part of the new proposal proves persuasive, the empirical motivations behind it will re-energize the bearers of the standard view to look at an old problem from a new angle.

I introduce in Section 2 the theoretical framework of Chierchia (1998), within which I develop my account of bare plurals. In Section 3, I draw attention to a distinction among bare plurals that do not denote kinds, and show why they are problematic for current accounts. In Section 4, I capture the distinction by modifying the presuppositions associated with kind formation and by eliminating ∃-type shift from the grammar. In Section 5, I look at kind denoting bare plurals and, on the basis of new data, argue against incorporating ∃ in DKP and in favor of treating bare plurals as definites over a widened domain. In Section 6, I consider some issues raised by the shift in perspective argued for and suggest lines for further inquiry.

## 2. Bare plurals in Chierchia's neo-Carlsonian approach

Chierchia (1998) put on the research agenda the goal of developing a theory of cross-linguistic variation in the domain of noun phrases. The impact of this paper has been phenomenal and the response to it has transformed the empirical landscape, informing and deepening our understanding of the interpretive possibilities available across languages. In this section I will present the key ingredients of his theory, making explicit the background against which I will undertake the reanalysis of bare plurals.

The basic premise of the neo-Carlsonian position is that bare plurals refer to kinds, not only in the case of kind-level predication but also in the case of object-level predication, as originally proposed in Carlson (1977). Their quantificational force, however, is governed by the same principles that Lewis (1975), Kamp (1981), and Heim (1982) demonstrated govern the quantificational force of regular indefinites.[1] In a generic statement, for example, a bare plural can have either (quasi) ∀ force or ∃ force, depending on whether it is interpreted in the restrictor or the nuclear scope. In an episodic statement, which does not have a tripartite logical structure, bare plurals are necessarily mapped into the nuclear scope and so have ∃ force.

Chierchia takes this general approach a step further and proposes a cross-linguistic theory of noun phrase variation. Within the general perspective of flexible types (Partee 1986b), he admits three basic operations for turning an NP with a predicative meaning (type <e,t>) into an argument (type <e> or <<e,t>t>), *nom*, *iota* and ∃:

(1) a. **iota**: $\lambda P\ \iota P_s$, if there exists a unique maximal entity in P, undefined otherwise. (Chierchia 1998: 346)

b. **nom**: For any property P and world/situation s,
$^{\cap}P = \lambda s\ \iota P_s$, if $\lambda s\ \iota P_s$ is in K, undefined otherwise
where $P_s$ is the extension of P in s and K is the set of kinds. (Chierchia 1998: 350–351)

c. ∃: $\lambda P\ \lambda Q\ \exists x\ [P(x) \wedge Q(x)]$ (Chierchia 1998: 359)

Of these, Chierchia considers the first two meaning preserving, in the sense that they map a predicate into an entity without introducing quantificational complexity. The first is *iota* which picks out the unique maximal entity in the extension of the predicate at the relevant situation, if there is one, and is undefined otherwise (Sharvy 1980). In English, this shift has a lexical exponent *the*, but in many languages it is a covert type shift. *Nom*, the kind forming operator of Chierchia (1984a), is a function from indices to the maximal entity that is in the extension of the predicate at that index – that is, it yields the unique maximal entity that instantiates the kind at the index. *Nom* is defined to yield falsity rather than presupposition failure at indices where the extension of the predicate is empty. It is, however, a partial function because it is undefined for predicates that do not fit the concept of a kind: "not all individual concepts are going to be kinds. Only those that identify classes of objects with a sufficiently regular function and/or behavior will qualify. Moreover, kinds . . . will generally have a plurality of instances (even though sometimes they may have just one or none). But something that is necessarily instantiated by just one individual (e.g., the individual concept or transworld line associated with Gennaro Chierchia) would *not* qualify as a kind" (Chierchia 1998: 350). The third type-shift ∃, from Partee (1986), not only turns a predicative expression into an argument, it also introduces ∃ quantificational force. Since this yields an expression of the generalized quantifier type, it can interact scopally with other scopal expressions. Unlike the first two operations, ∃ is a total function.

In Chierchia's system these possibilities are constrained by two principles specific to type shifts (2a,b) and a third general constraint of economy in grammar (2c).[2]

(2) a. ***Ranking***: nom > {iota, ∃} *to be revised (cf. 13)*

b. ***Blocking Principle***: ('Type Shifting as Last Resort'):
For any type shifting operation τ and any X:
*τ(X)

if there is a determiner D such that for any set X in its domain,
$D(X) = \tau(X)$.

(Chierchia 1998: 360)

c. ***Avoid structure***: Apply SHIFT at the earliest possible level.

(Chierchia 1998: 393)

Finally, there is the rule of DKP which mediates between a kind denoting term and a predicate of objects, a repair operation of sorts (3). It first takes the extension of the kind at an index defined as in (4), converts it into a predicate of objects, and $\exists$ binds into this predicate (3). Since this $\exists$ is introduced at the point where the sort adjustment is required, it ensures obligatory narrow scope for its operand:

(3) Derived Kind Predication Rule (DKP):
If P applies to objects and k denotes a kind,
then $P(k) = \exists x\, [^{\cup}k(x) \wedge P(x)]$

(Chierchia 1998: 364)

(4) PRED ($^{\cup}$):
$^{\cup}k = \{\lambda x\, [x \leq k_s]$ if $k_s$ is defined, $\lambda x[\text{FALSE}]$ otherwise$\}$,
where $k_s$ is the plural individual that comprises all of the atomic members of the kind k.

(Chierchia 1998: 350)

With this much background, we can demonstrate how the theory captures the core facts related to bare plurals in two languages, English and Hindi. These two languages share the property of encoding number sensitivity in the nominal system while differing on the existence of determiners.[3] Let us start with English, and consider bare plurals that are conceptually kinds:

(5) a. Dogs have evolved from wolves.
b. Typhoons arise in this part of the Pacific.
c. Dogs are barking.

(6) a. evolve-from($^{\cap}$dogs, $^{\cap}$wolves)
b. GEN s x [$^{\cup\cap}$typhoons(s)(x) $\wedge$ C(s)] [arise(s)(x) $\wedge$ (in-this-part-of-the-P)(s)(x)]
b′. GEN s x [this-part-of-the-P(s)(x) $\wedge$ C(s)] [arise-in-x(s)($^{\cap}$typhoons)]
= *DKP* $\Rightarrow$
GEN s x [this-part-of-the-P(s)(x) $\wedge$ C(s)] $\exists$y [$^{\cup\cap}$typhoons(s)(y) $\wedge$ arise-in-x(s)(y)]
c. $\exists$ [are-barking (s) ($^{\cap}$dogs)] = *DKP* $\Rightarrow$ $\exists$x [$^{\cup\cap}$dogs(s)(x) $\wedge$ are-barking (s)(x)][4]

Since *evolve* is a kind-level predicate, and the predicates *dogs* and *wolves* have the requisite intensionality, *nom* turns them into arguments which can be fed into the verb meaning directly. In the case of *arise*, which is an object-level predicate in a characterizing sentence, we have a tripartite structure and depending on what goes into the restrictor of the GEN operator, we get distinct truth conditions for the sentence. (6b) uses PRED to shift the type of the bare plural from kind to predicate and generically bind it. It says of typhoons in general that they arise in this part of the Pacific. In (6b′) the bare plural is mapped into the nuclear scope and serves as the argument of the verb *arise*. Since *arise* cannot hold of the kind, only of instantiations of the kind, DKP comes into play. (6b′) says that it is generally true of all contextually relevant situations involving this part of the Pacific, situations in which the climatic conditions are conducive, that there are typhoons that arise. Similarly, in the case of the episodic statement in (5c), DKP negotiates the relationship between an object-level predicate and a kind-level argument, as shown in (6c).

Since we will be focusing on episodic contexts in this chapter, it is worth noting that the truth conditions associated with (6c) are the same as those of a corresponding statement with an overt indefinite. However, a difference shows up in scopal contexts. Take, for example, the negative statements in (7), under the LF where the bare plural/indefinite outscopes negation:

(7) a. Dogs are not barking.
    b. Some dogs are not barking.

(8) a. [dogs$_i$ [not [t$_i$ are barking] ]]
    b. $\lambda x_i$ ⟦[not [t$_i$ are barking]]⟧ (⟦dogs⟧)
    $\Rightarrow \neg$are-barking (s) ($^\cap$dogs)
    = *DKP* $\Rightarrow \neg\, \exists x[^{\cup\cap}$dogs(s)(x) $\wedge$ are-barking(s)(x)]

(9) a. [Some dogs$_i$ [ not [ t$_i$ are barking]]]
    b. ⟦some dogs⟧($\lambda x_i$ ⟦[not[ t$_i$ are barking]]⟧)
    $\Rightarrow \lambda Q\, \exists x$ [dogs(s)(x) $\wedge$ Q(x)] ($\lambda x_i$ [$\neg$ are-barking(s)(x$_i$)])
    $\Rightarrow \exists x$ [dogs(s)(x) $\wedge \neg$ are-barking(s)(x)])

Since the bare plural is individual denoting (type <s, e>), it gets lowered into the argument position of the negative predicate. When DKP adjusts the mismatch between *barking* and $^\cap$*dogs*, $\exists$ enters into the derivation, necessarily below negation. The regular indefinite, on the other hand, is a generalized quantifier, which means that it enters into an operator-variable relation with its trace and therefore has scope over negation. Appealing to reference to kinds for bare plurals and to a generalized quantifier meaning for indefinites thus yields the radically different truth conditions observed in such cases.

We see, then, that Chierchia's basic system preserves the original insights of Carlson's account, accommodating for advances in our understanding of external sources of quantificational force for indefinites (see also Carlson 1989 on this). Briefly put, the key insight is that the semantic *type* of the bare plural ensures that it will always be interpreted closest to the verb, but its *sort* forces $\exists$ to be introduced at the level of the mismatch, i.e. at V, below any other operator.

We now turn to those aspects of interpretation that are specific to Chierchia's system: namely the *blocking principle*, *ranking*, and *economy* (cf. 2). We start with the fact that bare plurals in English do not admit definite readings (10a), while those in Hindi do (10b):

(10) a. Some $children_i$ came in. $Children_{*i}$ sat down.
b. kuch $bacce_i$ andar aaye. $bacce_i$ baiTh gaye.[5]
Some children inside came children sit went
'Some children came in. The children sat down.'

The explanation for this difference follows straightforwardly from *blocking*. Since *iota* is lexicalized in English, the definite plural must be used in this context and covert type shift for the bare plural via *iota* is ruled out. Since Hindi does not have a lexical determiner, the bare plural is free to shift via *iota*. This seems to be generally representative of languages with and without determiners and thus seems to be a welcome prediction of the theory (but see Dayal in prep).

The ranking of type shifts becomes important when we turn to English bare plurals that do not denote kinds. They differ from kind terms in allowing wide scope over negation:

(11) a. Parts of this machine are not new.
b. $\exists x$ [parts-of-this-machine(s)(x) $\wedge \neg$ new(s)(x)]

Of such NPs, Carlson (1977) notes that they refer "to a FINITE set of things, things that must exist at a certain time in a given world" (*emphasis his* – p. 196). As such, they do not display the kind of intensionality associated with kind terms. For Chierchia, this means that such bare plurals are not in the domain of *nom*. Since *iota* is lexically blocked by *the*, the bare plural now shifts via the low-ranked $\exists$ type shift and predictably displays the same scopal flexibility that characterizes regular indefinites.[6]

As pointed out in Dayal (1999, 2004), the ranking proposed by Chierchia requires revision since it does not capture the facts that he wants to capture. For example, it is predicted by the ranking in (2a) that the definite reading of bare plurals in languages like Hindi would not be available because of the availability of the higher ranked *nom*. But the ground reality is that *nom* and *iota* do not compete – Hindi bare plurals are acceptable with kind-level predicates, in addition to having definite readings.[7] There is a further problem noted there with respect to the indefinite readings of bare plurals in languages without determiners. The scopal properties of such bare plurals are precisely those of English bare plurals – they obligatorily take narrowest scope. In other words, bare plurals can have definite readings or DKP-based narrow scope $\exists$ readings, but they do not have the wide scope readings associated with $\exists$ type shift:[8]

(12) vahaaN bacce nahiiN haiN[9]
There children not be
'There are no children there.' or 'The children are not there.'
NOT 'Some children are not there.'

This point is worth emphasizing. The popular view that bare plurals in languages without determiners can be definite or indefinite is simply not supported empirically. What this means for the theory is that we do not want bare plurals in such languages to be able to access ∃ type shift. This is accomplished by revising the ranking in the following way:

(13) {nom, iota} > ∃

(Dayal 2004: 419)

I consider this a friendly amendment to Chierchia's system and will adopt it as part of the baseline theory in the rest of this chapter.

In this section I have presented the details of Chierchia's system at work, in preparation for the discussion to follow. I now turn to the task of establishing that ∃ type shift is not required in some cases and leads to incorrect predictions in others. This will be followed by arguments for dispensing with the ∃ force built into DKP. While I motivate the revisions on empirical grounds, the revisions themselves bear on the specifics of the theory presented above.

## 3. Indexical bare plurals

In this section I will take a closer look at non kind denoting terms, which had received little attention since Carlson's original discussion. They remain under-examined even in the literature that has emerged in response to Chierchia's proposal regarding cross-linguistic variation in the interpretation of noun phrases. I would like to begin though by introducing a terminological change. I will refer to such bare plurals from here on as indexical bare plurals since they typically include some indexical expression. I will continue to refer to standard bare plurals as kind denoting, reminding the reader that Carlson included in the set not only natural/well-established kinds such as *dogs* and *wolves*, but also novel kinds such as *houses with red roofs and yellow windows* or *dogs with three legs*.

### *3.1 Two types of indexical bare plurals*

As mentioned in connection with (11), Carlson (1977) notes that some bare plurals, typically those modified by relative clauses or PP's with an indexical expression, behave differently from standard bare plurals. The following are some canonical examples of indexical bare plurals:

(14) a. Parts of that machine
b. People in the next room
c. Books that John lost yesterday
d. Bears that are eating now

Indexical bare plurals do not lend themselves to kind-level predication (15a) or to binding by adverbs of quantification (15b). They are also not very good with individual level predicates (15b).

(15) a. ?Parts of that machine are widespread.
b. ?Dogs in the next cage are (usually) intelligent.

He notes that such bare plurals can be ambiguous between opaque and transparent readings. The following can be read in a way that the content of the description is not included in Bill's belief worlds or in Sue's search:[10]

(16) a. Bill believes that people in the next room are about to leave.
b. Sue is looking for books Bill lost yesterday.

Recall that Chierchia's account, as summarized in Section 2, is that such bare plurals are ∃ generalized quantifiers because they are shifted to argument type by the low ranked ∃ type shift. It therefore predicts full convergence between indexical bare plurals and indefinites, but this has been challenged by Van Geenhoven (1999). One point of difference between the two positions is empirical. While Chierchia argues that such NPs can take wide scope with respect to negation, Van Geenhoven claims wide scope readings to be unavailable. The source of this disagreement, I believe, is due to a distinction in the class of indexical bare plurals that has so far escaped notice.

The examples in (17) show that indexical bare plurals are not a homogeneous class. Some of them, those in partitive constructions, indeed allow wide scope over negation, and this can be made explicit. This scopal flexibility, however, does not hold generally:

(17) a. Parts of this machine are not new, but parts of it definitely are.
b. # Light bulbs for this lamp I sell but light bulbs for this lamp I don't sell.

While (17a) behaves as predicted by Chierchia, (17b) from Van Geenhoven (1999), is contradictory. This buttresses Van Geenhoven's arguments against Chierchia. Of course, the acceptability of (17a) does not support Van Geenhoven's view that these bare plurals are semantically incorporated indefinites.[11]

We can abstract away from scope interactions, and note that there remains a distinction between the two types when we try to use them in statements with incompatible predicates.[12] In (18a)–(18c) there are no other operators, so distinctions having to do with kind terms vs. semantically incorporated indefinites are irrelevant. However, there is a contrast between (18a) and (18b)–(18c). We understand the first clause in (18a) to apply to some parts and the second clause to apply to other parts. The same option is clearly not available to (18b) and (18c), where we apparently interpret all the people/light bulbs to have the first property so that applying the second property leads to contradiction:

(18) a. Parts of this machine are old but parts of it are new.
b. # People in the next room are tired but people in the next room are full of energy.
c. # Light bulbs for this lamp were bought at Home Depot but light bulbs for this lamp were bought at Lowe's.

Given that scopal effects are at the heart of the distinction between type shift by *nom* and type shift by ∃, this distinction clearly merits further attention. I should note in closing that these facts are equally problematic for both approaches to bare plurals, the neo-Carlsonian approaches that treat such bare plurals as kinds and the ambiguity approaches that treat them as object-level indefinites.

### 3.2 *Infelicitous indexical bare plurals*

There is a further problem with taking indexical bare plurals to tap into ∃ type shift. Not all bare plurals that are conceptually incompatible with kinds are, in fact, acceptable. The crucial data rests on contrasts in contextually anchored bare plurals of the kind discussed by Condoravdi (1997), those she terms "functional" bare plurals. In addition to her example (19a), I include two others:

(19) a. There was a ghost on campus. Students/The students were afraid.
b. My garden is in shambles. Groundhogs/ The groundhogs eat up whatever I plant.
c. The bus stopped. Passengers/The passengers quickly got off the bus.

I will not be concerned with the particulars of Condoravdi's approach but rather with what her data implies for Chierchia's theory.[13] The bare plurals in (19) pose a challenge because they seem to suggest the operation of *iota*, rather than ∃. The real problem, however, is that there are structurally parallel sentences such as the ones in (20) where the bare plural appears infelicitous. That this is not an effect restricted to bridging contexts but is more generally true of indexical bare plurals can be seen in (21), where the contextual grounding is lexically encoded in expressions inside the noun phrase:[14]

(20) a. I bought a car. The wheels/ *Wheels need to be replaced.
b. John has a rope. The fibers/ *Fibers are made of nylon.
c. Sue visited the ancient monument. She found the stones/ *stones impressive.

(21) a. The wheels/ *Wheels of my car need to be replaced.
b. The fibers/ *Fibers of this rope are made of nylon.
c. Sue found the stones/ *stones of the monument impressive.

One might, of course, appeal to *the blocking principle* to explain this effect, but we would then have a problem showing why the same does not apply to (19). In addition, it would not explain why the ∃ type shift, which does not have any presuppositions associated with it, does not become available once *iota* is lexically blocked. Once again, it bears emphasizing that the data in (19) to (21) pose a challenge not only for Chierchia's theory but for all current theories of bare plurals.

## 4. A proposal: *nom* and ∃ in a system of ranked type shifts

In this section I will lay out my solution to the problems regarding indexical bare plurals discussed in Section 3. The solution turns on two changes that I propose to Chierchia's theory: one, I extend the scope of Chierchia's kind forming operator *nom* to include some indexical bare plurals; two, I do away with ∃ as a covert type shift.

### *4.1 Extending the scope of* Nom

I will take as my starting point the surprising infelicity of certain bare plurals discussed above. The obvious conclusion to draw from the facts is that there are only two covert type shifts in natural language, *nom* and *iota*. In languages with definite determiners *iota* is indeed lexically blocked, as claimed by Chierchia. This entails that if for any reason a bare plural cannot undergo *nom*, it will simply be unacceptable. We now have to figure out the reason why some indexical bare plurals in English undergo *nom*, while others do not and are therefore infelicitous.

I start by delinking *nom* from kind terms. Instead, I build partiality into the function in a somewhat different way. That is, instead of an appeal to the concept of kinds in Chierchia's (1a), repeated here as (22a), I appeal to a notion of proper variation in size, as shown in (22b):

(22) a. **nom** (Chierchia 1998: 350–351):
For any property P and world/situation s,
$^{\cap}P = \lambda s\ \iota P_s$, if $\lambda s\ \iota P_s$ is in K, undefined otherwise
where $P_s$ is the extension of P in s and K is the set of kinds.

b. **nom** (revised):
For any property P and world/situation s,
$P = \lambda s\ \iota P_s$, if $\exists s\ \exists s'\ |P_s| \neq |P_{s'}|$, undefined otherwise
where $P_s$ & $P_{s'}$ are the extensions of P in s and s′.

Let us see how this helps us deal with indexical terms. Recall that Chierchia takes kinds to be individual concepts that live in the domain of quantification U, if and only if, they "identify classes of objects with a sufficiently regular function and/or behavior" and "generally have a plurality of instances (even though sometimes they may have just one or none)" (Chierchia 1998: 350). As we can see, there is both an appeal to intensionality and an appeal to variation in size in defining the notion of kinds here.

My revision of *nom* in (22b) preserves the notion of variation in size as integral to *nom* but it lets in a certain amount of extensionality. Let us consider the requirement of variation in size first. The idea that number morphology plays a role in licensing kind formation goes back to differences I noted in Dayal (1992) between bare plurals/mass terms and definite singular generics in English and between bare plurals/mass terms and bare singulars in Hindi. There were two conclusions I drew from these comparisons. I located number morphology, rather than definiteness marking, as the locus of the differences since they were maintained across languages with and without determiners. A second conclusion I drew there was that singular morphology would constrain the resulting kind term to singleton instantiation sets. I argued that there were fundamentally two types of operations involved in kind formation: a "plural" kind formation and a "singular" kind formation. The former is what we have been discussing here: *nom* is defined on predicates whose extensions vary in size from index to index; it is undefined for singular terms "because the number feature clashes with the presuppositions associated with a kind term" (Dayal 1992: 48).[15] This point is highlighted by Chierchia. His definition of *nom* in (1b) builds in the uniqueness associated with *iota* and effectively rules out *nom(dog)*, as clashing with the notion of kind. The semantics of plural morphology allows *nom(dogs)* because now plural individuals of different sizes can be denoted at different indices. The proposed revision in (22b) takes things a bit further. It not only prevents *nom* from applying to singular terms, it also blocks it from applying to plural predicates if their extension remains constant in size across indices. Let us see what this buys us.

I repeat the crucial contrasts from Section 3:

(23) a. There was a ghost on campus. Students (on campus) were afraid.
b. My garden is in shambles. Groundhogs (in my garden) eat up whatever I plant.
c. The bus stopped. Passengers (on the bus) quickly got off the bus.

(24) a. I bought a car. *Wheels (of my car) need to be replaced.
b. This rope is very strong. *Fibers (of this rope) are made of nylon.
c. Sue visited the monument. She found *stones (of the monument) impressive.

A crucial difference between (23) and (24) is in the relationship of the bare plural with the noun it is associated with. Take a given campus. While it is readily possible to accommodate a set of students by the mention of a campus, it is not strictly speaking necessary that there be students for a campus to be considered a campus. Similar considerations apply to buses and passengers or gardens and groundhogs. In each case, if we define a function from a given campus/garden/bus to students/groundhogs/passengers in it, we are likely to end up with different sets at different times, and most likely these sets will be of different sizes.

Turning to (24), we see that the connection between the two nouns is much tighter. A car cannot be considered a (complete) car if it does not have wheels. Similarly, while monuments do not, in and of themselves, entail the existence of stones, a given monument made of stone does: the monument cannot exist if the stones are removed. It is the same with a rope, which cannot exist without its fibers. Another way to express this is to say that the noun which provides the functional pivot (e.g., *car*, *rope*, *monument*) and the bare plural it is functionally related to (e.g., *wheels*, *fibers*, *stones*) are co-extensional. If the function is restricted to indices in which the pivot exists, the cardinality of the predicate denoted by the bare plural will remains constant across all of them.

I am suggesting that the infelicity of the bare plurals in (24) is due to this requirement of variation in size but I am aware that this particular implementation of the intuition may not be precise enough. Ivano Caponigro (p.c.) correctly points out that one can conceive of a given rope as having fewer fibers in one world than in another. If the two ropes count as the "same" rope, (22b) fails in its job (see Heller and Wolter 2011 for relevant discussion). There is, of course, a simple way to take care of this problem. We can tap into the intuition that there is a minimum limit on size. There is no world in which we can conceive of the rope without any fibers, so the presupposition on *nom* could conceivably be stated as: $\exists s\ P_s = \emptyset$. I do not pursue this line here since it does not rule out unacceptable bare singulars, such as the ones in (25a). There are many situations in which the same country does not have a president/monarch so the requirement that there be an index at which the extension of the nominal is empty would be insufficient. It would have to be combined with the requirement of variation in size:

(25) a. The country is flourishing. #President/#Monarch is very popular.
b. The platoon is under attack. Soldiers are being killed.

Another alternative to (22b), suggested by an anonymous reviewer, is to have variation in the instantiation set itself instead of in its size: $\exists s\ \exists s'\ P_s \neq P_{s'}$. This would work as well for the contrast we are interested in, since it would rule out the set in (24) where the bare plurals are co-extensional with the pivot of the function. It would also explain cases like (25b) where one might imagine a context in which a platoon is defined in terms of a fixed number of soldiers, but the actual soldiers in a given platoon could change from time to time. The reason I have not adopted this suggestion is that it is not clear to me that the same reasoning would not apply to cars and wheels. After all, the wheels on a typical car get changed several times and yet (24a) is clearly unacceptable, unlike (25b). Furthermore, eliminating reference to size would require a separate explanation for cases like (25a). The function from a given country to its president/monarch yields different (atomic) individuals at different times, but bare singulars are unacceptable. The fact that bare singulars do not seem to undergo *nom* suggests that rigidity vs. flexibility in size is critical.

For the moment, then, I will continue to take (22b) as the appropriate way of constraining *nom*, though I will return to this question briefly in Section 6 (see Dayal in prep for further discussion of the alternatives considered here). To sum up, (22b) allows *nom* to apply to predicates that do not include a deictic term, i.e., standard kind denoting bare plurals, as in Chierchia's original formulation. It privileges bare plurals over bare singulars which are restricted by number morphology to invariably denote an atomic individual. In the case of indexical bare plurals, it makes a crucial distinction. The deictic expression restricts variation to situations with the contextually salient entity in it, in the actual world or in worlds with counterparts of it. The presupposition of variation makes *nom* undefined for predicative terms where co-extensionality with the deictic term leads to invariance in size. With *iota* being lexically blocked, such terms are correctly predicted to be infelicitous if ∃ type shift is not in the set of covert shifts. It should be obvious that even if some variant of (22b), such as the ones we have considered above, were to be adopted instead of (22b), the conclusion would remain valid that the infelicity of indexical bare plurals can only be explained if ∃ type shift is removed from the equation.

### 4.2 Partition-inducing bare plurals

In the last section I argued for expanding the domain of *nom* to include those indexical bare plurals that meet a reduced bar for intensionality. The fact that such bare plurals show the same scopal behavior as canonical kind denoting bare plurals is no longer surprising. We expect DKP to apply equally to both and yield narrow scope ∃ readings. The question we must now address is the behavior of those indexical bare plurals for which Chierchia's ∃ type shift seemed to capture the scope facts correctly: *parts/slices/pieces of NP.* Given that ∃ type shift is no longer among the set of covert options, we need an alternative account of the ability of such bare plurals to take scope over other operators.

Drawing on the discussion of *part-of* in Chierchia (2010), we can take it to be a function from an entity to sets of entities. Extending the account of *part* to include *pieces, slices*, etc., we can treat all of them as subdividing the entity denoted by the inner NP into non-overlapping i-parts. Their role, roughly speaking, is akin to that of classifiers, in that they create properties that have the appropriate structure for counting. Phrases headed by such partition inducing nouns can therefore serve as arguments for cardinal expressions or determiners, as shown in (26a):

(26) a. Every part /Three parts /The (three) parts/ No part of the machine
b. Parts of this machine are not new, but parts are.

The question that concerns us here is how to interpret such phrases when there is no cardinal or determiner in the structure. As we know from examples like (26b) they display the scopal properties that ∃ generalized quantifiers have.

In order to address this question, let us consider cardinal phrases which show a similar pattern of behavior. They can be arguments of determiners (27a) or function by themselves as ∃ generalized quantifiers (27b):

(27) a. The three students are standing.
b. Three students are not standing but three are.

A standard view of cardinal expressions in work stemming from Link (1983) is that they are predicate modifiers. This allows them to serve as arguments of determiners. When there is no determiner they are taken to shift to a generalized quantifier meaning by a default ∃ type shift (Landman 2004, Ionin and Matushansky 2006, Chierchia 2010, among others). We have argued in the previous section, however, against the possibility of such an option, in order to explain the infelicity of some indexical bare plurals. A further argument for an alternative explanation comes from cross-linguistic considerations. We know that in languages without definite determiners, such as Hindi, Russian, or Chinese, bare plurals cannot interact scopally with other operators. We have captured this fact by allowing them to shift to argumental meaning via *iota* as well as *nom*. Interestingly, cardinal expressions in these languages behave like cardinal expressions in English in allowing scope interaction with other operators. That is, they behave like regular indefinites, rather than definites. If we were to allow phrases headed by cardinal expressions to be covertly type-shifted into argumental meaning, we would predict incorrectly that in these languages they would make use of *iota*, just like bare plurals.[16] An alternative in which covert type shifts do not come into play for cardinal expressions is clearly preferable.

I suggest that cardinal expressions, universally, are ambiguous between predicative and ∃ generalized quantifier meanings. Thus there are two options for their interpretation. (28a) involves a predicative meaning for the cardinal. (28b) involves the existential generalized quantifier meaning. What is ruled out is the derivation in (28c), where the cardinal has a predicative meaning and undergoes ∃ type shift covertly.[17]

(28) a. $[_{DP}\ \text{the}_{<<et>e>}\ [_{CardP}\ \text{three}_{<et>}\ [_{NP}\ \text{boys}_{<et>}]]] = \iota x\ [3(x) \wedge \text{boys}(x)]$
b. $[_{DP}\ \text{three}_{<<et><<et>t>>}\ [_{NP}\ \text{boys}_{<et>}]] = \lambda P\ \exists x\ [3(x) \wedge \text{boys}(x) \wedge P(x)]$
c. $[_{CardP}\ \text{three}_{<et>}\ [_{NP}\ \text{boys}_{<et>}]] = \lambda x\ [3(x) \wedge \text{boys}(x)]$
$= {*}\exists \Rightarrow \lambda P\ \exists x\ [3(x) \wedge \text{boys}(x) \wedge P(x)]$

There remains one final issue to settle. Assuming that cardinal phrases are not in the domain of *nom*, a derivation like (29a) will be ruled out in languages with determiners due to *blocking* by the lexical definite. In languages without determiners, however, they are predicted, incorrectly, to be possible under a definite reading due to a covert application of *iota*, as shown for Hindi in (29b):

(29) a. $[_{CardP}$ three$_{<<et><et>>}$ $[_{NP}$ boys$_{<et>}]] = \lambda x\ [3(x) \wedge boys(x)]$
= *blocked by 'the'* $\Rightarrow \iota x[3(x) \wedge boys(x)]$
b. $[_{CardP}$ tiin$_{<<et><et>>}$ $[_{NP}$ laRke$_{<et>}]] = \lambda x\ [3(x) \wedge boys(x)]$ = **iota* $\Rightarrow \iota x[3(x) \wedge boys(x)]$
three boys

In order to rule out the derivation in (29b), we may consider the primary meaning of cardinals to be that of a generalized quantifier. However, in structures where a predicative meaning is required they shift by a covert application of BE (Partee 1986).[18] Assuming that such shifts are repair operations, there is no motivation for a predicative meaning for the cardinal expression in a structure like (29b). Without a determiner above, it is predicted that phrases headed by cardinal expressions will necessarily denote generalized quantifiers and show scope interaction with negation and other operators cross-linguistically. Back to indexical bare plurals, I suggest the same holds for partition-inducing expressions like *part-of/slices-of*, etc.

### 4.3 *Some predictions for indexical bare plurals*

The proposal I am advancing makes an essential distinction within the class of indexical bare plurals. The first type, those that shift via *nom*, are predicted to undergo DKP in episodic contexts and display obligatory narrow scope, just like kind denoting bare plurals. The second type, those with partition-inducing head nouns, are predicted to behave like regular indefinites in being able to take scope over other operators. However, there are two properties noted by Carlson that apply equally to both types of indexical bare plurals. One is the ability to take narrowest scope in contexts where indefinites cannot take such scope, the other is the ability to have *de re* readings of the sort that kind denoting bare plurals do not have. Since I am aligning one kind of bare plural with kind terms and another with indefinites, these shared properties call for some further discussion.

Carlson (1977) notes that the following have differentiated scope readings. That is, they allow different books/puzzles to participate in different sub-events of destruction/discovery. Overt indefinites do not display similar effects. These data are particularly important because they show that the ∃ readings of bare plurals are not a subset of the ∃ readings of indefinites:

(30) a. Fred repeatedly destroyed books I lost yesterday.
b. Max discovered pieces from that puzzle for three hours.

(31) a. #Fred repeatedly destroyed some books I lost yesterday.
b. #Max discovered some pieces from that puzzle for three hours.

Under the present account, (30a) is unproblematic since the bare plural denotes a kind and is subject to DKP. The challenge is to explain (30b). If these bare plurals are like indefinites, (30b) should pattern with the examples in (31), where the generalized existential quantifier takes scope over the adverb and leads to the implausible readings in which the same set of entities is destroyed/discovered multiple times.

So far I have argued that *pieces of that puzzle* or *parts of this machine* can have the same semantics as regular indefinites. However, this does not preclude the possibility that they can also be analyzed as simple predicative terms. If so, they would be able to undergo *nom* as long as they satisfy the presupposition of variation in size.[19] It seems to me that they do. It is possible for there to be different partitions of the same entity at different indices: a puzzle can be made into a 50-piece puzzle in one world and into a 100-piece puzzle in another; a cake can be cut into 6 slices in some world and into 8 slices in another. If so, then it should come as no surprise that they would have the option of aligning with other kind terms in taking lower scope than indefinites that function unambiguously in argument position as generalized quantifiers.

The second property that the two types of indexical bare plurals have in common is the potential for *de re* readings. Carlson (1977) notes, albeit somewhat tentatively, that (32a) seems to be ambiguous in the relevant way, while (32b) clearly is not:[20]

(32) a. Bill believes that people in the next room are about to leave.
b. Bill believes that people are about to leave.

(32a), under the present account, is predicted to have the interpretation in (33a), after the application of DKP. This can be compared to (33b), the representation of (32b):

(33) a. believes (s) (b, $\lambda s'\exists \underline{x}[^{\cup\cap}\underline{\text{people-in-room-next-to-}y_i(s')(x)}$ & about-to-leave $(s')(x)])$
b. believes (s) (b, $\lambda s'\exists \underline{x}[^{\cup\cap}\underline{\text{people}(s')(x)}$ & about-to-leave $(s')(x)])$

I assume that the situation index on a bare plural, shifted via *nom*, must be identified with the situation index at the lowest point in the tree where one becomes available. In an intensional context, this necessarily yields an opaque reading. An indexical expression inside the bare plural (e.g., *next* and its logical translation 'next-to-$y_i$'), however, anchors the interpretation of the bare plural to a set of finite entities of whom the attitude holder could potentially have direct knowledge. This is what I claim is the source of the *de re* feel of these examples. In other words, the apparent *de re* reading is a piggy-back effect based on the contextual anchoring provided by the deictic expression. When the bare plural is unmodified or when the modification does not contextually anchor the interpretation, the effect cannot arise. The effect is also unlikely to arise if the anchoring is to a set that is potentially too large for an attitude holder to have direct knowledge of its members. I think the following would not be characterized as allowing a *de re* construal:[21]

(34) a. Bill believes that people on this earth are about to perish.
b. Bill believes that victims of the earthquake in Turkey will be adequately compensated.

No doubt this issue needs further thought, both in terms of the generalizations as well as implementation (see Dayal in prep), but I hope that the remarks here suggest a way of reconciling the fact that interpreting such indexical bare plurals via *nom* still leaves room for distinctions between indexical bare plurals and canonical kind terms.

Before ending this section, I would like to acknowledge that the issue of scope interaction with negation for *nom* shifted indexical bare plurals remains somewhat debatable. Gennaro Chierchia (p.c.) points out that (35a)–(35b) are accepted by speakers in situations where only some of the books were bought or read. The point I would like to emphasize, though, is that this cannot be made explicit, as shown in (36a)–(36b):

(35) a. I didn't buy books I wanted to buy.
b. I didn't read books suggested by you.

(36) a. #I didn't buy books I wanted to buy but I bought books I wanted to buy.
b. #I didn't read books suggested by you but I read books suggested by you.

The data seems a bit puzzling at first glance but I suggest that the wide scope effect we get for (35a) and (35b) is due to the possibility of a contrastive reading. Take a context in which I bought almost all the things I had intended to buy, including perhaps some books that I wanted to buy. I can utter (35a) to convey that among the things that got left out were books I wanted to buy. Similarly, if I read almost everything I was supposed to read including some books suggested by you, I can say (35b) to convey that among the things I didn't read were books suggested by you. In fact, as pointed out by an anonymous reviewer, even (36a)–(36b) become acceptable if the verbal constituents are contrastively stressed (and *but* is changed to *and*). The point worth emphasizing is that these are not the standard wide scope readings of indefinites. It is only bare plurals that can plausibly be analyzed as having partition inducing head nouns that allow for true wide scope, where conjunctions with affirmative and negative counterparts do not result in contradiction. The case of indexical bare plurals that do not countenance conjunction of incompatible predicates but nevertheless seem to allow a ∃¬ reading no doubt merits further attention. But I would like to suggest that the locus of this inquiry should be the role of modification, not the possibility of the ∃ type-shift.

## 5. A more radical proposal: DKP modified

In Section 4 I made two modifications to Chierchia's system that only affected indexical bare plurals but left untouched his account of kind denoting bare plurals. In this section, I would like to make two further modifications that are somewhat more significant in that they impact on our general understanding of bare plurals. I claim that in episodic statements, the extension of the kind is accessed, i.e., that reference is made to the maximal entity that instantiates the kind at that index. I also argue that the interpretation involves a widened domain, in the sense of Kadmon and Landman (1993). The so-called ∃ force typically associated with bare plurals in such contexts is re-analyzed as a representative group reading of the maximal entity in the widened domain.

### *5.1 Arguments against ∃ force for kind denoting bare plurals*

I start with two facts that argue against the ∃ force associated with bare plurals. I give in each case the logical representation that would be derived under Chierchia's neo-Carlsonian approach as well as under the ambiguity approach. I do this to highlight the fact that the problems are not specific to the neo-Carlsonian position:

(37) a. Dogs, (#namely Spotty and Rover), are barking.
b. $\exists x\, [^{\cup\cap}dogs(x) \wedge x{=}Spotty{+}Rover \wedge barking(x)]$
c. $\exists x\, [dogs(x) \wedge x{=}Spotty{+}Rover \wedge barking(x)]$

(38) a. #Dogs are barking and dogs are sleeping.
b. $\exists x\, [^{\cup\cap}dogs(x) \wedge barking(x)] \wedge \exists x[^{\cup\cap}dogs(x) \wedge sleeping(x)]$
c. $\exists x\, [dogs(x) \wedge barking(x)] \wedge \exists x[dogs(x) \wedge sleeping(x)]$

(39) Dogs are barking and dogs are running around.

(37a) shows that the referents of a bare plural cannot be listed. If all that is involved in interpreting bare plurals in episodic contexts is some form of existential quantification over (instances of) dogs, as shown in (37b)–(37c), there is no reason why they should resist specification via a list. The data in (38) is the problem of incompatible predicates we had encountered earlier in connection with indexical bare plurals. As shown in (38b) and (38c), standard approaches do not have a way of accounting for the oddness of (38a). Since there is no issue of scope interaction and each conjunct would normally be acceptable on its own, their conjunction should be as well. Note that switching to compatible predicates has an ameliorating effect, as shown in (39). I should note that it is important in applying this diagnostic to keep the interpretation of both conjuncts fixed to a single spatio-temporal location.[22]

These facts are replicated cross-linguistically. Consider the following Korean paradigm.[23] In the first case, we have a nominative marked bare nominal, in the second a nominative marked bare nominal with the overt plural morpheme. Both are judged unacceptable:

(40) a. # ai-ka camtul-eiss-ko ai-ka wancenhi kkay-eiss-ta.
child-NOM asleep-be.PROG-and child-NOM completely awake-be.PROG-DECL
('A child is asleep and a child is wide awake.')
b. # ai- tul-i camtul-eiss-ko ai- tul-i wancenhi kkay-eiss-ta.
child-PL-NOM asleep-be.PROG-and child-PL-NOM completely awake-be.PROG-DECL
('Children are asleep and children are wide awake.)

Switching to compatible predicates leads to improvement in the basic version and full acceptability in the plural-marked version.

(41) a. ? ai- ka noraeha-ko iss-ko ai-ka chwumchwu-ko iss ta.
child-NOM sing-CONN be.PROG-and child-NOM dance- CONN be.PROG-DECL
'A child is singing and a child is dancing.'
b. ai-tul-i noraeha-ko iss-ko ai-tul-i chwumchwu-ko iss-ta.
child-PL-NOM sing-CONN be.PROG-and child-PL-NOM dance-CONN be.PROG-DECL
'Children are singing and children are dancing.'

To sum up, specification is resisted in languages with definite articles. In languages without definite articles, specification is possible under a definite reading of the bare plural, but not under an indefinite reading. Bare plurals seem to resist the conjunction of incompatible predicates universally. In addition to English and Korean, I have tested the data in Hindi and Japanese as well. As already shown, these facts are as problematic for the neo-Carlsonian account which always refers to kinds in the interpretation of bare plurals, as they are for the alternative ambiguity-based accounts that interpret them as object-level indefinites. Since my focus here is on Chierchia's theory, I will pitch my solution to the problem posed by these facts in relation to the rule of DKP, which is responsible for deriving the existential readings of bare plurals in his theory. However, there are obvious implications for the ambiguity approach as well.

## 5.2 *Bare plurals as definites over a widened domain*

There are two modifications I will propose to DKP. The first is to remove existential quantification from it, and simply have the sort mismatch between the predicate and the kind term repaired by taking the extension of the kind, i.e., the maximal entity that instantiates the kind at the relevant index (see also Dayal

2011a for discussion of this way of deriving definiteness in Chierchia's system). The second is to require the domain of quantification for a bare plural to be wider (cf. Kadmon and Landman 1993). Furthermore, I impose a requirement of proper widening where the instantiations of the kind in the widened domain must properly include the instantiations in the base situation:

(42) a. **DKP-Modification 1 (Maximality):**
If P(s) applies to objects and k is a kind, then $P(s)(k) = P(s)(k_s)$,
where $k_s$ is the extension of the kind at s.
b. **DKP-Modification 2 (Maximality + Proper Widening):**
If P(s) applies to objects and k is a kind,
then $[\![P(s)(k)]\!] = 1/0$ if $[\![\exists s'\ s < s' \wedge P(s)(k_{s'})\ ]\!] = 1/0$,
where $\exists x[x \leq k_{s'} \wedge \neg\text{in-s}(x)]$ and is undefined otherwise.

The claim of widening immediately accounts for the impossibility of specification, demonstrated in (37). If the instantiation set extends beyond the contextually salient set, it follows that it would not be possible to specify through a list the entities denoted by the bare plural. The explanation for the impossibility of conjoining incompatible predicates, demonstrated in (38), becomes tractable under the claim of maximality. It is parallel to the explanation for the oddness of conjoining incompatible predicates with definites, shown in (43). The same individual cannot have conflicting properties simultaneously (Löbner 1985):

(43) a. # The dogs are barking and the dogs are sleeping.
b. $\text{barking}(s)(\iota x[\text{dogs}(s)(x)]) \wedge \text{sleeping}(s)(\iota x[\text{dogs}(s)(x)])$

This line of argumentation, however, begs the question of how to derive the intuition that bare plurals seem to have indefinite readings. In the next section I show that in accounting for the facts in (37) and (38) we haven't thrown away the baby with the bathwater. The solution rests on both aspects of the proposed modification: maximality and widening.

## 5.3 *Representative group readings*

The challenge, in brief, is to reconcile the maximality that clearly helps rule out the conjunction of incompatible predicates with the perception that bare plurals in episodic contexts allow predication to a subset of relevant entities. In order to show that maximality need not be anti-thetical to our intuitive understanding of bare plurals, I will begin with definite determiners which canonically are thought to encode maximality. An interesting fact about them is that although they refer to maximal entities, they can actually allow a weaker reading in which the predication, strictly speaking, only holds of a subset of the group. It is easy to see this when definites are contrasted with universal terms:

(44) a. Every reporter asked questions at the press conference.
b. The reporters asked questions at the press conference.
c. $\forall x[\text{reporter(s)}(x) \rightarrow \text{ask-question(s)}(x)]$
d. $\text{ask-question(s)}(\iota x[\text{reporters(s)}(x)])$

In a situation where 3 out of 10 reporters asked questions, (44a) would be false but (44b) may well be accepted. Note that this is independent of the domain restriction for which resource domain variables have been proposed. In both (44a) and (44b) the resource domain variable may restrict the evaluation to reporters at a press conference in the White House on a particular day. The difference between universals and definites remains unaffected even when the common noun has this restricted interpretation.

This phenomenon, known as representative group readings or pragmatically weakened readings, has been studied by Dowty (1987), Taub (1989), Brisson (1998), and Lasersohn (1999), among others. Lasersohn (1999) discusses these facts within a more general perspective on various items that countenance and regulate such effects.[24] His main point with regard to data such as (44b) is that statements with definites can be evaluated with respect to subsets of the full set of entities, *pragmatic halos* in his terms, as long as the gap between the halo and the actual denotation is irrelevant in the utterance situation.

Let us work through a concrete case to see how the account works. Consider a situation in which there are four reporters, a, b, c, and d. Of these a, b, and c ask questions at the news conference. In this scenario, the halos for the definite plural would be the set in (46a), with the halos ordered from tightest on the left to loosest on the right. Assuming the compositional semantics in Lasersohn, the halo of a complex expression is derived by applying normal semantic rules to all possible combinations of elements drawn from the halos of its immediate parts. Under this view a sentence like (46b) may be judged true in virtue of a proposition like (46c), where a particular halo of the definite functions as the argument. That is, a loose halo with only three of the four reporters suffices for truth, as long as the context supports treating them as representative of their group $\iota x[reporters(s)(x)]$:

(46) a. Halos for the definite plural: {a+b+c+d, a+b+c, a+b, a+c, b+c, a, b, c}
b. The reporters asked questions at the press conference.
c. $[\![\text{ask-questions(s)}(a+b+c)]\!] = 1$

My claim is that bare plurals present a parallel situation. In the same situation as above, the halos of the bare plural would include larger entities, as represented on the left in (47a). A statement like (47b) is verified on the basis of a loose halo such as the one we see in (47c), as long as the context supports treating them as representatives of their group. This is parallel to what we saw in (46), except that the group represented happens to include other possible reporters:

(47) a. Halos for the bare plural: {a+b+c+d+e+f. . ., a+b+c+d, a+b+c, a+b, a+c, b+c, a, b, c }
b. Reporters asked questions at the press conference.
c. $[\![\text{ask-questions}(s)(a+b+c)]\!] = 1$

This is represented diagrammatically in (48):

(48)

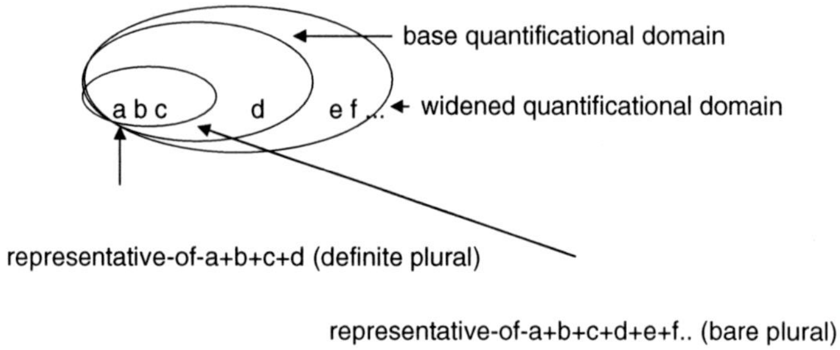


With this in mind, let us take a closer look at the "indefinite" reading of bare plurals. A canonical context for such readings might be something like (49). You are looking out of the window, you see dogs, none of them known to you, running around the garden. Your friend asks you the question in (49a). You might respond with (49b):

(49) a. What's happening outside?
b. Not much, dogs are running around.
c. $[\![\text{running}(s)({}^{\cap}\text{dogs})]\!] = DKP \Rightarrow$
$\Rightarrow [\![\text{running}(s)({}^{\cap}\text{dogs}_s)]\!] = 1$ iff $[\![\exists s' [s < s' \wedge \text{running}(s)({}^{\cap}\text{dogs}_{s'})]]\!] = 1$

You know that the dogs you see could not possibly be all the dogs in the world, possibly not even in the neighborhood. You use the bare plural to refer to this larger entity, though the truth of the statement is based on the halo that refers only to the dogs in the base situation. The intuitive characterization of this reading may be that it is an indefinite because world knowledge tells us that only a subset of the dogs in the wider set are involved. The point I am making is that such a reading technically does not involve ∃ quantification over dogs in the way that an actual indefinite like *some dogs* does. One way to think of this is to say that by choosing a kind term, the speaker signals that the truth of the statement will be verified with respect to a loose halo that refers to a group larger than the contextually salient one. This puts, if you will, empirical bite into the claim of reference to kinds in episodic contexts.

There is an interesting consequence of the account I am proposing. Consider what happens if you utter (49b) when there are no dogs outside. There will not be a halo for ${}^{\cap}dogs_{s'}$ that will make the sentence true, but the term itself will not be undefined because the presupposition of existence can be satisfied on the widened domain. In the case of a plural definite on the other hand, the term itself, *ιx [dogs(s)(x)]*, is undefined. We can capture, without stipulation, a difference between definites and bare plurals by appealing to different domains of quantification for presupposition satisfaction.

Another welcome consequence is that it provides a straightforward account of the problem of incompatible predicates. Consider the following paradigm, due originally to Kroch (1974):

(50) a. Some of the townspeople are awake.
b. The townspeople are asleep.
c. # Although the townspeople are asleep, some of them are awake.

Assume a context in which (50b) will be judged true under a pragmatically weakened reading. That is, a context in which *asleep(the townspeople)* is true only of a proper subset of the townspeople. The question is why in (50c) those members who are awake cannot make the second conjunct true. The reason, according to Lasersohn, is that the choice of a halo is context sensitive. If their being awake is relevant enough to justify the assertion in the second conjunct, a halo that leaves those people out cannot be supported to make the assertion in the first conjunct.

The same obviously applies to conjunctions with plural definites. Two conjuncts which have incompatible predicates cannot be remedied by applying the predicates to different halos since a subset that is deemed irrelevant to the truth of the first conjunct cannot then be resurrected as relevant in the next conjunct. In this respect, definites differ from indefinites, whose semantics has predication to subsets built into it and need not rely on halos for the relevant reading:

(51) a. # The reporters asked questions while/but/and the reporters kept quiet.
b. Some reporters asked questions while/but/and some reporters kept quiet.

Under the view that a bare plural is a type of definite, the solution to the problem of incompatible predicates with bare plurals follows from our assumptions about maximality and representative group readings. To go back to our White House press conference scenario, whether the plural individual a+b+c represents the contextually salient set of reporters (for the definite) or reporters more generally (for the bare plural), we cannot predicate *kept quiet* or *did not ask questions* in the same context by referring to those that are set aside by the halo deemed appropriate for *asked questions*. Lasersohn's account, though it incorporates the notion of halos into compositional semantics, leaves to pragmatics the choice of halo appropriate for an assertion. While the semantics proper allows for conjunction of incompatible predicates, the pragmatics of assertion, which regulates the choice of halos, militates against it.

## 6. Taking stock

In the previous sections I have presented arguments against having a covert ∃ type shift as well as against the ∃ force introduced by DKP. I have provided alternative explanations for the effects previously attributed to these sources. Instead of ∃ type shift for partition inducing bare plurals, I have posited a lexical ambiguity where one of the meanings of these phrases is that of the ∃ generalized quantifier. I have re-analyzed the indefinite feel of *nom*-shifted bare plurals as a representative group reading of a definite, interpreted over a widened domain. This new angle obviously raises a host of questions requiring revision of previously accepted explanations for the behavior of bare plurals. Considerations of space prevent me from addressing all the ones I am aware of but I will briefly touch upon a few, indicating the directions of research I hope to pursue in the future.

### *6.1 Scope matters*

An important aspect of the semantics of bare plurals has always been the propensity for narrow scope. Let us see if the revisions I have proposed capture this aspect of their behavior, starting with negation:

(52) a. Dogs are not barking.
b. $\text{barking(s)}({}^{\cap}\text{dogs}) = DKP \Rightarrow \text{barking(s)}({}^{\cap}\text{dogs}_s)$
c. $[\![\text{barking(s)}({}^{\cap}\text{dogs}_s)]\!] = 1 \text{ iff } [\![\exists s' \, [s < s' \wedge \text{barking}({}^{\cap}\text{dogs}_{s'})]\!] = 1$

I believe the facts follow from what we have said so far. Since we are taking bare plurals to be definites, the presupposition of existence will project above negation. If there are no dogs in the base situation, it does not matter. The presupposition can be satisfied in a larger situation. With the presupposition satisfied, DKP comes into play in the computation of the sentence at the level of the predicate *bark*. If there are no barking dogs in the base situation, either because there are no dogs or because no dog is barking, there will be no halo of the extension of the kind to make it true. (52c) will be false, so (52a), the negative statement will be true, as desired. But now suppose there is one sole dog barking. In a particular context, that one dog may be enough to make (52c) true and, in that case, (52a) will be false, as desired. Instead suppose that the one barking dog for some reason doesn't count as particularly relevant. In such a situation we can ignore that dog and choose a halo without it, making (52c) false and consequently (52a) true.

This last fact goes against the received wisdom about bare plurals and negation but I think it better captures the reality. Consider the White House press conference scenario and assume only one reporter got to ask a question. It may be possible to say in this context either (53a) or (53b), depending on how easy it is for us to treat the sole reporter that asked a question as an outlier:

(53) a. The reporters did not get to ask questions.
b. Reporters did not get to ask questions.

Finally, we might wonder about cases in which the presupposition of existence cannot be met, as shown in (54):

(54) I didn't see dinosaurs, because there are no dinosaurs.

What seems to be going on is that the first part of the sentence is uttered in a context where the presupposition that dinosaurs exist is entertained, but is subsequently abandoned (see Chierchia and McConnell-Ginet 2000: 384–386 for discussion of apparent cases of presupposition cancellation). But this is not how bare plurals under negation typically behave. Typically, the presupposition of existence is accommodated and the negative sentence evaluated as true either because there are no relevant entities in the base situation, or it is evaluated as true/false depending on whether there is a halo that makes the embedded sentence true. I have suggested that the diagnostic of narrow scope be tweaked to allow for some pragmatic weakening but the rest follows from what we know about negation, definites, and halos. Thus the present account maintains the results of the standard neo-Carlsonian account.

Let us now consider the fact that bare plurals show differentiated scope. These are sentences where they take scope below a temporal adverbial, at a point where indefinites cannot:

(55) a. Leaves kept falling all morning.
b. $\forall s[s < S \rightarrow \text{fall}(s)({}^{\cap}\text{leaves})] = DKP \Rightarrow \forall s\ [s < S \rightarrow \text{fall}(s)({}^{\cap}\text{leaves}_s)]$

There are many issues that come up in relation to such sentences but an intuitively adequate way of characterizing them is to take them as involving quantification over times within a temporal interval. Just to keep things simple, I have taken the quantification to be over sub-situations s of a contextually salient situation S. After the intervention of DKP, we look for a halo of leaves at each s to see if *fall* can be truthfully predicated of it. Since this is a once-only predicate, we take each sub-situation to license access to a distinct halo for the kind term. This seems reasonable enough but requires further thought when we consider definites in such structures. A variant of (55a) with a definite is also acceptable, as we might expect given the kinship we are claiming between bare plurals and definites. However, we need to be cautious in drawing parallels because the alignment is not perfect.

In contrast to the periphrastic construction, a low pluractional adverbial such as *twice* yields a more nuanced comparison. With a small time interval like *this morning* the definite has the implausible reading but with a larger time interval like *last year* the differentiated scope reading re-emerges:

(56) a. Leaves/ #The leaves fell twice this morning.
b. Leaves/The leaves fell twice last year.

Descriptively, it is clear what is happening in (56). One can imagine one set of leaves falling and then a new set sprouting subsequently and falling later in the year, but not within a single morning.[25]

We know that the reason indefinites do not show differentiated scope is because their type does not allow them to be interpreted low enough in the structure, but this does not hold true of definites. Carlson did not compare bare plurals with definites and the literature since then has also not done so systematically. The data discussed here argue for a systematic investigation into the differences between bare plurals and definites, both of which have the same type and can therefore occur as direct arguments of the verb. But clearly bare plurals have more flexibility than definites in allowing reference to distinct individuals within short intervals, thus allowing for distinct halos.

## 6.2 *Bare plurals and discourse*

Since I have extended the scope of *nom* and therefore of the modified DKP to indexical bare plurals, we need to see how proper widening plays out in these cases:

(57) a. In 1995, there was a ghost on campus. Students on the campus were afraid.
b. $[\![\text{afraid(s)}(^{\cap}(\lambda s \lambda x(\text{students(s)(x)} \wedge \text{on-the-campus(s)(x)})))]\!] = DKP \Rightarrow$
c. $[\![\exists s' \, [s < s' \wedge \text{afraid(s)}(^{\cap}\text{students-on-the-campus}_{s'})]]\!]$

Given the restriction imposed by the modifier to a specific time and place, the requirement of proper widening cannot be satisfied if both properties are involved in the comparison. Because of the anchoring to a particular campus at a particular time, the set of students is fixed regardless of how much we widen the domain of quantification. However, because we are dealing with a complex noun phrase, I suggest that it is possible to satisfy widening with reference to the head noun alone. We can see this graphically:

(58)
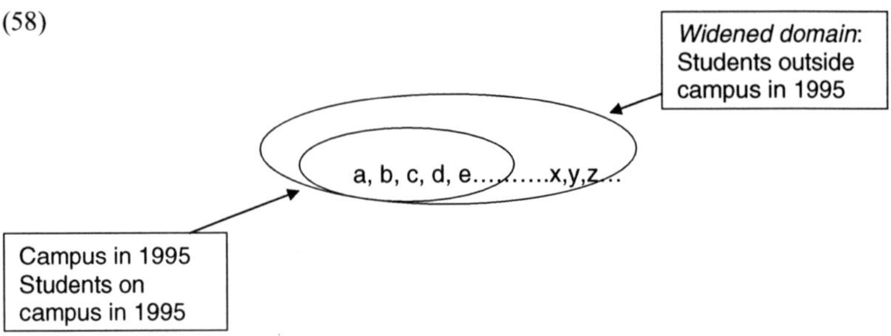


The bare plural is felicitous because even though $\neg\exists x \, [x \leq k(s') \wedge \neg \text{ in-s}(x)]$, when $k = \lambda s \, \iota x[\text{students(s)(x)} \wedge \text{on-the-campus(s)(x)}]$ , it is the case that $\exists x \, [x \leq$

$k(s') \wedge \neg$ in-s(x)] iff $k = \lambda s\ \iota x$[students(s)(x)]. The head noun alone satisfies the presupposition of proper widening so widening can technically be satisfied. The implicit (or explicit) restriction by the indexical effectively blocks reference to a plurality beyond the base situation. The "indefinite" feel of the bare plural is predictably missing because the students on campus cannot represent a larger plurality of students on campus. We thus derive Condoravdi's "functional" readings, which align bare plurals with definites rather than indefinites. Note that we needed to block *nom* from applying to *wheels on the car*, because if it were admitted as a kind term the same reasoning that we have applied to (57a) would apply to it and yield the unavailable reading.

Continuing further with the general issue of relation to discourse, let us move away from functional contexts to contexts in which there is an explicit antecedent. There are two possibilities to consider: an anaphoric link between the antecedent and the bare plural, and a partitive connection. I repeat English and Hindi (10) here to illustrate:

(59) a. Some children$_i$ came in. Children$_{*i}$ sat down.
b. kuch bacce$_i$ andar aaye. bacce$_i$ baiTh gaye.
Some children inside came children sit went
'Some children came in. The children sat down.'

In a language like English the bare plural is unacceptable. In a language like Hindi it is acceptable, but only if anaphorically linked to the children in the first sentence. As far as I know, it is not possible for bare plurals to refer to a subset of a previously mentioned set in any language. This follows under the present account since bare plurals are never interpreted with $\exists$ force, neither through $\exists$ type shift, nor through DKP. The only possible reading is an anaphoric one, and that is dependent on whether the language has a lexical definite or not. This is, I believe, an important advantage of treating bare plurals as definites.

### 6.3 *Proper widening and variation in size*

Finally, I would like to consider whether we really need to constrain *nom* by requiring predicates to vary in size across indices and have a requirement of proper widening when bare plurals are used in object-level statements. In order to do so, I will first look at how predicate selection can affect the felicity of bare plurals. I start by noting some predictions of the view that the indefinite feel of bare plurals is due to representative group readings of a definite, interpreted over a widened domain.

It has been claimed that the choice of predicates can influence the availability of pragmatically weakened readings (see Dowty 1987; Taub 1989; Brisson 1998):

(60) a. The senators are a large group.
b. The senators have elected a speaker.
c. The senators are meeting in the next room.
d. The senators have finished voting.

(60a)–(60b) can only be verified with respect to a tight halo. That is, the totality of senators must be taken into account. (60c)–(60d), on the other hand, admit loose halos. Not all senators need be involved in the relevant activity.

It is predicted that if a predicate requires a tight halo a bare plural will be inadmissible because it will run afoul of proper widening: if all the senators are already in the base situation, widening cannot add more senators. This prediction is borne out:

(61) a. # Senators are a large group.
b. # Senators have elected a speaker.
c. Senators are meeting in the next room.
d. Senators have finished voting.

Crucially, what we get is infelicity of the otherwise acceptable bare plural *senators*. This is explained under the view that bare plurals have a presupposition of proper widening but not under a simple view of bare plurals as indefinite.

Coming now from the opposite angle, consider some potential counterexamples to the claim that bare plurals do not tolerate conjunction of incompatible predicates, a feature crucially explained by their being definites. (62a) is a context provided by an anonymous reviewer but other such examples are easy to construct:

(62) a. Context: live report from a disaster scene.
"People are screaming, people are jumping out of windows, people are trying to force the doors open . . ."
b. Context: teacher describing her classroom.
"What a peaceful day it is. Children are playing happily, children are reading quietly, children are doing their homework. I wish everyday were like this."

An interesting fact about such cases is that there is typically a framing sentence that describes the overall situation, after which follows an elaboration. (62a) most likely follows upon a statement like "There is complete chaos here. People are screaming . . ." The elaboration seems to pick out sub-situations from a partition of the overall situation. Under these circumstances, it appears possible to use different halos for each sub-situation. In the examples I had used to make the case for bare plurals being definites, the situation was held constant and the judgment was that conjoining incompatible predicates led to contradiction. The point was that holding the situation constant precludes a switch in halos for a bare plural. This would not be an obstacle if the bare plural were an indefinite because an ∃ quantifier could still make reference to different subsets.

In a twist on the same theme, certain infelicitous bare plurals seem to improve when they are part of a list. (63b), due to Omer Preminger (p.c.), contrasts with our previous example, repeated here as (63a):

(63) a. This is a very strong rope. #Fibers are made of nylon.
b. This rope needs to be replaced. Fibers are sticking out and the edges are frayed.

This is a bit of a puzzle but here is how one might try to make sense of it. Suppose, contrary to what we had assumed in Section 3, that *fibers* even in the context of an indexical is a kind term. Suppose further that in interpreting the phrase *fibers are sticking out* in (63b), we focus only on a part of the rope, that part where we see some fibers sticking out. Then, we can satisfy proper widening by considering the whole rope which has fibers that are not sticking out. Not only do we get a felicitous bare plural, we also capture the intuition that only some of the fibers in the rope are sticking out. But if we are talking about what those fibers are made of, as in (63a), we look at the whole rope and now proper widening is not possible and the bare plural is ruled out.

The explanation I am giving for (63b) brings us back to the question we had started with: can an appropriate understanding of how proper widening interacts with predicate selection make it possible to eliminate the constraint of variation in size on kind formation? I am clearly not in a position to answer this question in this chapter though the theoretical appeal of such a streamlining is obvious.

## 7. Conclusion

I have taken a rather unorthodox view of the core data regarding bare plurals, and by extension, mass terms since the two generally align together. Although I believe I have motivated it on sound empirical grounds, I recognize that further buttressing may be needed to convince the skeptic of the need for such unorthodoxy. In the previous section I indicated some issues that remain open in my mind. It is quite possible that more sophisticated ways of treating discourse and (in)definiteness may reveal a way to reconcile the facts which have formed the basis of my proposal with a treatment of bare plurals as encoding $\exists$ force after all.

I would like to end this chapter by noting my intellectual debt to Gennaro Chierchia. Here, as always, I have tried to follow his lead in making explicit and testable claims about linguistic phenomena. I have also tried to indicate, in appropriate places, what the implications of my investigation would be for other languages. I can only hope that the revisions to his theory that I have proposed here meet the bar he has set for the cross-linguistic adequacy of semantic theory.

**Acknowledgments**

This chapter has benefitted from comments from audiences at SURGE (the Semantics Research Group at Rutgers) and Harvard University, as well as from participants in the course on *(In)definiteness and Genericity*, taught at Jawaharlal Nehru University (Delhi) in Spring 2010 and at Rutgers in Spring 2011. Special thanks to Ivano Caponigro, Gennaro Chierchia, Ayesha Kidwai, Roger Schwarzschild, and three anonymous reviewers for probing questions, comments, and suggestions. Usual disclaimers apply.

NOTES

1. Proponents of the ambiguity approach (Wilkinson 1991, Gerstner-Link and Krifka 1993, Kratzer 1995 and Diesing 1992, among others) take bare plurals to refer to kinds when they serve as arguments of kind-level predicates and to ordinary individuals when they serve as arguments of object-level predicates. The ambiguity approach and the neo-Carlsonian approach converge, however, on the need for a flexible mapping of noun phrases into the logical structure. For a comparison of the two approaches, see Krifka *et al.* (1995) and Dayal (2011a), in addition to the references mentioned here.
2. Chierchia's stance on the ranking of covert type shifts has to be gleaned from two separate discussions. The distinction between languages with and without determiners leads him to rank *iota* and ∃ at par (Chierchia 1998: 360–361). The distinction between English kind denoting and non-kind denoting bare plurals leads him to rank *nom* above ∃ (Chierchia 1998: 374). The two positions are actually inconsistent, as pointed out in Dayal (1999, 2004). Some of the arguments from there are used to motivate the revision of (2a) in (13).
3. I am leaving out of this discussion an important aspect of Chierchia's proposal, the *Nominal Mapping Parameter.* Hindi and English have the same parameter setting [+arg, +pred], unlike Chinese which has the [+arg, –pred] setting and French which has [–arg, +pred] setting. These distinctions do not directly bear on the issues this chapter focuses on.
4. I assume that the situation variable in episodic statements is indexical, rather than existentially bound, though nothing of relevance to the issues discussed here rides on this.
5. *T* is a retroflex voiceless stop, *d* is a dental stop, *h* following a stop indicates aspiration.
6. Chierchia argues that *some* is not a lexical exponent of ∃, unlike *a*, which is. Thus it does not block the application of ∃ here. Bare singulars are ruled out because they are not in the domain of *nom* and *iota* and ∃ are lexically blocked. Crucial to the distinction between *some* and *a* is that only the latter lends itself to binding by a generic operator.
7. The idea that Hindi bare nominals are ambiguous between kind terms and definites, not true indefinites, was first proposed in a joint paper (Porterfield and Srivastav 1988). The facts generalize beyond Hindi to other typologically unrelated languages such as Russian and Chinese. On the latter, see also Yang (2001).
8. The two available readings may have different intonational contours and might need different contexts to make them salient. Neither intonation nor context can make

available a wide scope ∃ reading, a reading in which the predication only applies to some of the relevant individuals. An overt indefinite *kuch bacce* 'some kids' or *ek baccaa* 'one kid' would have to be used to convey the intended meaning.

9. *N* indicates nasalization of the immediately preceding vowel.
10. Carlson notes certain respects in which these bare plurals align with kind denoting bare plurals (see Section 4.3).
11. Van Geenhoven (1998) posits a rule of semantic incorporation where bare plurals are predicative expressions bound by an ∃ introduced by the lexical rule. Hers is, in effect, a translation of Carlson's account of the scope properties of bare plurals, minus reference to kinds.
12. This is an important new diagnostic that I use in this chapter. I elaborate on it in Section 5.
13. According to Condoravdi, bare plurals are indefinites that are ambiguous between being weakly and strongly novel. She defines a weakly novel NP as requiring its index to be novel, while presupposing its descriptive content. A strongly novel NP places a requirement that the index be novel, but imposes no conditions on its descriptive content. Her claim is that the novelty condition on the index of bare plurals rules out anaphoric readings for them in contexts such as those in (19), but because they have only a requirement of weak novelty, the descriptive content can be entailed by the context. This results in the observed functional readings. For more details, the reader is referred to Condoravdi's work.
14. I owe (21b) to Ayesha Kidwai (p.c.).
15. Singular terms, of course, can be interpreted as taxonomic kind terms. Crucially, taxonomic kinds do not allow access to individual members in the way that DKP does for kind terms formed by *nom*. Since we are focusing on bare plurals in this chapter, I will not go into details of singular kind formation, referring the reader to Dayal (1992) and the development of those ideas in Dayal (2004).
16. By and large cardinal phrases allow wide scope indefinite readings and disallow definite readings. Trinh (2011) notes that Vietnamese cardinal phrases also have definite readings. I focus here on the indefinite readings which seem to be universally available, leaving discussion of definite readings which are possible in some languages to Dayal (in prep).
17. Ionin and Matushansky (2006) argue against a generalized quantifier meaning for cardinal expressions. The semantics they give for complex cardinals like *twenty-two N* or *two hundred and three N* requires a predicate modifier meaning for the lower cardinal. Note that their argument is not inconsistent with an ambiguity analysis of the kind I am positing. Well-formed cardinal phrases will all require the lower cardinals to be predicate modifiers in order to avoid a type-clash. The option of utilizing a generalized quantifier meaning will only meet type matching requirements for the cardinal which is the highest expression in the phrase. I have not followed the specifics of Ionin and Matushansky's account of numerals though I consider it correct, since the precise choice of a predicate modifier semantics for cardinals is orthogonal to the point under discussion. The reader is referred to the original article for details.
18. BE is defined as: $\lambda P_{<<e,t>,t>}\ \lambda x\ [P(\lambda y[y=x])]$ in Partee (1986).
19. Zucchi and White (2001), in fact, admit to the possibility of treating such noun phrases as kind denoting but do not elaborate on it. See also Lasersohn (1995), Van

Geenhoven (2004), and more recently, Dayal (2011b) where this phenomenon is discussed at more length.

20. An anonymous reviewer asks what the facts would be if *in the next room* were changed to *on Mars* in (32a). The judgments are subtle, but briefly put, they turn on whether the extension of the term varies from index to index within a given world (the familiar kind denoting bare plural) or whether the extension of the term is fixed in a given world to a finite set of entities though allowing for variation across worlds. For present purposes, if it is possible to think of *people on Mars* in the first sense, it would behave like (32b) in resisting *de re* readings; if it is possible to think of it in the second sense, it would behave like (32a) in allowing it. I refer the reader to an illuminating discussion of the distinction between kind denoting and indexical readings of *alligators in the New York sewer system* (Carlson 1977: 197), and to Dayal (in prep).
21. Thanks to Matt Barros for confirming these judgments.
22. See Dayal (2004) for a similar diagnostic in the characterization of bare singulars.
23. I thank Hyunjoo Kim for consulting a large number of Korean speakers in eliciting this data.
24. Lasersohn discusses *all*, *exactly*, *precisely*, as expressions which regulate such weakened readings. See also Brisson (1998).
25. See references cited in note 19 for relevant discussion about the scope properties of bare nominals and such adverbs.

# 4 Broaden your views, but try to stay focused: a missing piece in the polarity system

*Anamaria Fălăuş*

## 1. Introduction

Epistemic indefinites (henceforth EIs) are existential elements that convey some form of ignorance (or indifference) with respect to the referent of the indefinite phrase, as in (2) below:

(1) I have to read the biography of **an** Italian composer.

(2) a. Tengo que leer la biografía de **algún** compositor italiano. Spanish
have.1SG that read the biography of *algun* composer Italian
b. Je dois lire la biographie d'**un** compositeur italien **quelconque**. French
I must.1SG read the biography of-a composer Italian *quelconque*
'I have to read the biography of some Italian composer.'

For the sentences in (2) to be felicitous, there has to be more than one Italian composer that could satisfy the modal claim. Whereas the sentence in (1), with a simple indefinite, admits a continuation like *namely Rossini*, this is not possible in the examples in (2), with the Spanish EI *algún* or the French EI *un quelconque*.[1] This much is common to all EIs (sometimes also called *modal* or *anti-specific* indefinites), and in fact characterizes a wider class of 'polarity sensitive' determiners, i.e. expressions which have a restricted distribution, such as negative polarity items (NPIs) like Italian *alcuno* (3a), free choice items (FCIs) like French *n'importe quel* (3b), or items that have both free choice and negative polarity uses, like *any* (3c):

(3) a. Ascolta molta musica, ma non suona **alcuno** strumento musicale, Italian
listens_to much music but not plays *alcuno* instrument musical
#cioè il violino.
namely the violin
'He listens to a lot of music, but doesn't play any musical instrument, #namely the violin.'
b. Choisissez **n'importe quel** instrument, # notamment le violon. French
choose.IMP.2PL *no-matter which* instrument namely the violin
'Choose any instrument, #namely the violin.'
c. You (don't) like **any** Italian composer, #namely Rossini.

Ever since Haspelmath's (1997) typological survey, where many of these elements are discussed, EIs have received an increasing amount of attention in the literature (e.g., Aloni and Port 2010; Aloni and Rooij 2004; Alonso-Ovalle and Menéndez-Benito 2008, 2010; Chierchia 2006, to appear a; Farkas 2002, 2006; Fălăuş 2009, 2011; Giannakidou and Quer 2011; Jayez and Tovena 2006, 2008; Kratzer 2005; Kratzer and Shimoyama 2002; Zamparelli 2007, among many others). These studies reveal a heterogeneous class of elements across languages, but more interestingly they also indicate that the attested diversity is amenable to a fairly small number of dimensions of variation. Distribution-wise, EIs vary with respect to their ability to occur in (i) episodic, (ii) modal, and (iii) negative polarity contexts. Meaning-wise, EIs have been shown to differ in terms of the free choice inference they trigger (which can be weaker or stronger, depending on whether it involves partial or total variation in the quantificational domain). These empirical findings led to a research agenda that aims not only to identify and explain the possible parameters of variation, but also to determine how they interact, a goal to which many of the above-mentioned studies subscribe.

This chapter deals with a hitherto unexplored parameter of variation among EIs, namely their interaction with focus. The goal of this investigation is twofold. On the one hand, I put together novel and existing empirical observations, and identify a correlation between the free choice inference triggered by an EI (more precisely, its ability to convey total variation) and the possibility to associate with focus. On the other hand, I explore an alternative-based account of these facts, couched in the framework developed in Chierchia (to appear a). The main hypothesis put forth is that the observed patterns can be derived from the interaction between lexically activated and focally activated alternatives. The relation between EIs and focus is a complex matter, and the preliminary discussion in this chapter addresses only a small subset of the empirical and theoretical issues it raises. But I hope to provide useful insights that can foster research in this area and contribute to a better understanding of EIs.

The discussion proceeds as follows: Section 2 provides a brief overview of the alternative-based approach to EIs due to Chierchia (to appear a), and the micro-variation we find in this area, by focusing on two parameters: (i) strength of the free choice inference and (ii) NPI use. Section 3 tackles the interaction with focus, and introduces evidence in favor of a correlation between the inference triggered by the EI and the possibility to associate with focus. To account for the observed patterns, it is argued that focus affects lexically activated domain alternatives. Section 4 concludes and discusses some open issues.

## 2. Epistemic indefinites in the polarity system: the role of alternatives

In this section, I briefly lay out the main assumptions underlying the approach to EIs developed in Chierchia (to appear a). I start by introducing the alternative-based framework in which this proposal is couched (Section 2.1), and follow by considering two parameters of variation that will turn out to be relevant for their association with focus – the free choice inference EIs give rise to (Section 2.2) and the possibility to be used as NPIs (Section 2.3). I limit myself here to an outline of the theory, referring the reader to Chierchia's work for detailed discussion and argumentation. The only aspect that is relevant for our present purposes concerns the role of alternatives in deriving the distribution and interpretation of EIs. This will provide the basis for the interaction with focus alternatives.

## 2.1 *Alternatives and exhaustification*

Chierchia (to appear a) extensively argues that the properties of EIs are best understood within a more general theory of polarity and free choice phenomena, implemented in an alternative-based semantics. The core hypothesis underlying this strongly unitary program is that all kinds of polarity sensitive items (e.g., NPIs and FCIs like those in (3) above, or the EIs under consideration here) are (weak) indefinites (i.e., existentially quantified elements) that activate sets of alternatives. Once they are active, alternatives must be factored into meaning (just like alternatives activated through focus). One way to do this is via the insertion of covert exhaustification operators, whose semantics is roughly akin to *only* and *even*. Exhaustification through a silent *only* has been argued to be at work when calculating scalar implicatures (cf. Chierchia, Fox, and Spector 2012; Chierchia to appear b), but there is evidence that such covert operators can be found in a wider variety of instances:

(4) a. A: Who did you see?
B: Paul and Sue.
**O** (I saw [Paul and Sue]$_F$)

b. A: Did many people come to the party?
B: Yes. Imagine – [my ex]$_F$ was there.
**E** ([My ex]$_F$ was at the party)

In (4a), we normally interpret B's answer as conveying that the speaker only saw Paul and Sue, i.e., he did not see any other individual(s) that might have also been contextually relevant. The positive answer in (4b) indicates that such an exhaustive meaning can also come about via an *even*-like operator, whereby we get the interpretation that B's ex came to the party, and B's ex was the least likely person to do that (plus an additional inference that someone else was there too, an additive component which is not relevant here). The semantics of these alternative-sensitive operators is as in (5) below:

(5) a. *Only*-EXHAUSTIFICATION:
$O_C(p) = p \wedge \forall q \in C\ [q \rightarrow p \subseteq q]$
where $p \subseteq q$ means $p$ entails $q$

b. *Even*-EXHAUSTIFICATION:
$E_C(p) = p \wedge \forall q \in C\ [p <_C q]$
where '$p <_C q$' means $p$ is less likely than a contextually relevant alternative $q$

O and E are binary operators that combine with a set of propositional alternatives (here represented by the subscript C) and a proposition $p$ (the prejacent). According to the definitions in (5), the application of O says that $p$ (and its entailments) is the only true member of the set of alternatives C, and the application of E conveys that $p$ is the least likely among the relevant set of alternatives C. This mechanism is assumed to enrich meaning whenever alternatives are activated, regardless of whether they come about through focus, contextual factors, or are lexically determined. To understand the alternative-based treatment of polarity sensitive items, let us briefly go through an example:

(6) a. *I teach **any** class (this semester).
b. I do**n't** teach **any** class (this semester).

The assertion in (6a) is identical to what we would have with a plain indefinite *a class*, i.e., an existential statement, made with respect to a contextually relevant domain of quantification D. For simplicity, assume D is a set consisting of only two elements, a semantics class and a pragmatics class. The presence of the polarity sensitive element *any* leads to the consideration of subdomain alternatives, i.e., subsets of the relevant contextual domain. Active alternatives compose via pointwise functional application, so at the sentential level we have alternatives that look as in (7b):

(7) a. ASSERTION:
$\exists x \in D\,[\text{class}(x) \wedge \text{teach}(I, x)]$, where D = {semantics, pragmatics}
b. ALTERNATIVES:
$C = \{\exists x \in D'[\text{class}(x) \wedge \text{teach}(I, x)],\ D' \subseteq D\}$ =
{I teach a semantics class, I teach a pragmatics class}
c. $O_C$[I teach any class] =
$O_C[\exists x \in \{\text{semantics, pragmatics}\}\ [\text{class}(x) \wedge \text{teach}(I, x)]]$ =
$\exists x \in \{\text{semantics, pragmatics}\}\ [\text{class}(x) \wedge \text{teach}(I, x)] \wedge$
$\neg\exists x \in \{\text{semantics}\}[\text{class}(x) \wedge \text{teach}(I, x)] \wedge$
$\neg\exists x \in \{\text{pragmatics}\}\ [\text{class}(x) \wedge \text{teach}(I, x)] = \bot$
d. $O_C$[I don't teach any class] =
$O_C[\neg\exists x \in \{\text{semantics, pragmatics}\}\ [\text{class}(x) \wedge \text{teach}(I, x)]]$ =
$\neg\exists x \in \{\text{semantics, pragmatics}\}[\text{class}(x) \wedge \text{teach}(I, x)]$

The alternatives introduced by the NPI must be exhaustified, i.e., require the presence of an appropriate alternative-sensitive operator in the structure, O in (7c). As defined in (5a) above, the application of the operator O says that the assertion is true and all non-entailed alternatives (in C) are false. Therefore, once we apply O to the assertion in (7a), we get a contradictory meaning: I teach a class chosen from the set {semantics, pragmatics}, but I do not teach a semantics class and I do not teach a pragmatics class. Whence its deviance.[2] Things are different in a negative statement like (6b), where the presence of negation (or any other downward-entailing operator) renders the exhaustified meaning non-contradictory. Since all alternatives are entailed by the assertion, there are no stronger alternatives, and therefore nothing gets eliminated via exhaustification (7d). Put another way, exhaustification in this configuration is vacuous – it simply amounts to the initial assertion *I do not teach a class in D.*

Let us now turn to EIs, which in this framework are characterized as alternative bearing existentials, on a par with the other members of the polarity system. To understand how their interpretation comes about, it is best to consider the following set of modal sentences:

(8) a. You may play the guitar or the violin.
b. You may play the guitar and you may play the violin.

(9) Tu peux étudier **un** instrument musical **quelconque**. French
you can study a instrument musical *quelconque*
'You may study a musical instrument, any musical instrument.'

The disjunction in (8) and the EI *un quelconque* in (9) – both existential elements under the scope of an existential modal – end up having a conjunctive interpretation, where each of the relevant alternatives (guitar or violin in (8) or any musical instrument in (9)) constitutes a legitimate choice. On the present alternative-based account, the observed free choice effects uniformly arise via recursive application of O, the exhaustification operator defined in (5a).[3] More specifically, it is assumed that the alternatives activated in both cases are identical, and come in two varieties: scalar alternatives (SC-ALT), which are stronger alternatives on a numerical scale *two*, *three*, etc. (10b), and subdomain alternatives (D-ALT), which consist of subdomains of the relevant set of musical instruments (10c).

(10) a. ASSERTION: $\Diamond\exists x \in \mathrm{D}\,[\mathrm{one}(x) \wedge \mathrm{instrument}(x) \wedge \mathrm{study}(\mathrm{you},x)]$
b. SC-ALT = $\{\Diamond\exists x \in \mathrm{D}\,[n(x) \wedge \mathrm{instrument}(x) \wedge \mathrm{study}(\mathrm{you},x)]: \mathrm{one} < n\}$
c. D-ALT = $\{\Diamond\exists x \in \mathrm{D}'[\mathrm{one}(x) \wedge \mathrm{instrument}(x) \wedge \mathrm{study}(\mathrm{you},x)]: \mathrm{D}' \subseteq \mathrm{D}\}$

To emphasize the parallel with disjunction, let us assume that the EI in (9) existentially quantifies over a domain with only two elements, i.e., guitar and violin. If D = {guitar, violin}, then the assertion and the alternatives can be represented as follows:[4]

(11) a. $\Diamond$ (guitar $\vee$ violin) ASSERTION
b. $\Diamond$ (guitar $\wedge$ violin) SC-ALT
c. $\Diamond$ guitar $\Diamond$ violin D-ALT

Exhaustification with respect to this set of alternatives leads to a contradiction (e.g., Sauerland 2004). The solution, extensively discussed in Fox (2007a) and Chierchia (to appear b) to whom I refer for details, is to allow for recursive exhaustification, i.e., the consideration of 'pre-exhaustified' domain alternatives.[5] Roughly speaking, exhaustified domain alternatives (EXH D-ALT) are obtained by applying O to each one of the alternatives in (11c), as shown in (12a,b). For an alternative like "you may study the guitar," the exhaustified meaning is equivalent to "you may only study the guitar," i.e., "you may study the guitar and you may not study the violin" (12a), and similarly for the other active alternative (12b).

(12) a. $O \Diamond \text{guitar} = \Diamond \text{guitar} \wedge \neg \Diamond \text{violin}$ EXH D-ALT
b. $O \Diamond \text{violin} = \Diamond \text{violin} \wedge \neg \Diamond \text{guitar}$ EXH D-ALT

Exhaustification relative to this set leads to the enriched meaning in (13):

(13) $O \Diamond (\text{guitar} \vee \text{violin}) =$
$\Diamond (\text{guitar} \vee \text{violin}) \wedge \neg \Diamond (\text{guitar} \wedge \text{violin}) \wedge \neg O \Diamond \text{guitar} \wedge \neg O \Diamond \text{violin} =$
$\Diamond (\text{guitar} \vee \text{violin}) \wedge \neg \Diamond (\text{guitar} \wedge \text{violin}) \wedge \neg (\Diamond \text{guitar} \wedge \neg \Diamond \text{violin}) \wedge$
$\neg (\Diamond \text{violin} \wedge \neg \Diamond \text{guitar}) =$
$\Diamond \text{guitar} \wedge \Diamond \text{violin} \wedge \neg \Diamond (\text{guitar} \wedge \text{violin})$[6]

Once we put together the assertion with the derived implicatures, the enriched meaning of the sentence in (9) expresses that every musical instrument in D (i.e. both the guitar and the violin) is a possible option. The assumption that EIs activate scalar and (pre-exhaustified) domain alternatives, just like disjunction or other scalar terms, thus derives the free choice inference observed in (9).

These considerations suffice to illustrate the alternative-based analysis of EIs adopted in this chapter. The account just sketched relies on obligatory activation of alternatives, a property EIs share with polarity sensitive elements. The idea that polarity or free choice indefinites activate alternatives of some kind is not new, and various aspects of the theory defended by Chierchia have been proposed in previous literature (cf. Kadmon and Landman 1993; Krifka 1995; Lahiri 1998; Kratzer and Shimoyama 2002; Aloni and van Rooij 2004, among others). The novelty lies in the execution of this proposal in a framework which deals uniformly with ordinary scalar implicatures (cf. Chierchia, Fox, and Spector 2012 and references therein) and a wide variety of polarity sensitive phenomena. The result is a conceptually unitary system, with a broad empirical coverage, where the interplay between alternatives and exhaustification generates the various patterns of polarity attested across languages. On this view, the main difference between scalar terms (e.g., disjunction, simple indefinites) and polarity sensitive indefinites is that alternatives associated with the former are only *optionally* active, whereas those associated with the latter are *obligatorily* active. As briefly illustrated for NPIs and EIs above, the narrower distribution of polarity sensitive items falls out from their conjectured lexical semantics (active alternatives and constraints on exhaustification) and the way it interacts with the operators in their context of occurrence (e.g., downward-entailing or modal operators). Variation in the polarity system is captured through a restricted number of parametrical choices, along two interconnected dimensions: (i) types of active alternatives and (ii) modes of exhaustification. A closer look at variation among EIs offers the opportunity to illustrate both.

## *2.2 Variation among EIs: free choice inference*

It has been recently shown that the free choice inference triggered by EIs can be of two kinds, depending on whether it concerns the entire domain of quantification or only a part of it (e.g., Jayez and Tovena 2008; Alonso-Ovalle and Menéndez-Benito 2008, 2010; Fălăuş 2009, 2012; Aloni and Port 2010). In the examples in (14), the EI conveys that the speaker is ignorant/indifferent with respect to the referent of the indefinite and *all* alternatives in the relevant domain qualify as possible options. Following Chierchia (to appear a), I refer to this inference as *total variation*:

(14) a. Tu peux étudier **un** instrument musical **quelconque**. French
you can study a instrument musical *quelconque*
'You may study a musical instrument, any musical instrument.'
b. Dovrei imparare a suonare **uno** strumento musicale **qualsiasi**. Italian
should.1SG learn to play a instrument musical *qualsiasi*
'You should learn how to play a musical instrument, any musical instrument.'

In contrast to this total freedom of choice among relevant alternatives, certain EIs convey a weaker free choice effect, called *partial variation*: *some, but not necessarily all* alternatives qualify as possible options. The difference is most readily seen in the following hide-and-seek scenario (due to Alonso-Ovalle and Menéndez-Benito 2010):

(15) CONTEXT: Maria, Juan, and Pedro are playing hide-and-seek in their country house. Juan is hiding. Pedro believes that Juan is inside the house, but not in the bathroom or in the bedroom.
a. Juan tiene que estar en **alguna** habitación de la casa. Spanish
Juan must be in *algun* room of the house
'Juan must be in a room of the house.'
b. Juan trebuie să fie în **vreo** cameră la etaj. Romanian
Juan must SUBJ be in *vreun* room on floor
'Juan must be in some room upstairs.'

The context makes it clear that not all rooms of the house are possible choices, and as such the variation associated with the EI is limited to a subset of elements in the relevant domain. While the use of *algún* or *vreun* is perfectly acceptable in this scenario, a total variation item like *un NP quelconque* or *qualsiasi* would be infelicitous.

On the alternative-based approach to EIs, the total vs. partial variation difference is argued to stem from a different choice of domain alternatives. More precisely, if the active domain alternatives are non-minimal, i.e., include any subset of the relevant D, we get the usual free choice, i.e., total variation, meaning effect. If on the other hand, domain alternatives are restricted to singletons, once we exhaustify over these alternatives, we obtain the partial variation inference. To demonstrate how this difference derives the desired interpretation, let us look at two EIs in Romanian in the scope of a possibility modal, the total variation EI *un NP oarecare* (16a) and the partial variation *vreun* (16b):

(16) a. Luca poate cânta la **un** instrument muzical **oarecare** (e foarte talentat). Romanian
Luca can play at a instrument musical *oarecare* is very talented
'Luca can play a musical instrument, any musical instrument (he is very talented).'
b. A: I would like to learn how to read musical notes.
B: Poate cântă Luca la **vreun** instrument muzical (şi te poate ajuta). Roman.
maybe play.3SG Luca at *vreun* instrument musical and you can.3SG help
'Maybe Luca plays some musical instrument (and he can help you).'

Assuming a domain of quantification with three elements, the assertion and the scalar alternatives are as in (17):

(17) a. ASSERTION: $\Diamond \exists x \in D[\text{one}(x) \wedge \text{instrument}(x) \wedge \text{play}(\text{Luca},x)]$
b. SC-ALT = $\{\Diamond\ \exists x \in D[n(x) \wedge \text{instrument}(x) \wedge \text{play}(\text{Luca},x)]: \text{one} < n\}$
c. $\Diamond$ (guitar $\vee$ violin $\vee$ cello) ASSERTION
d. $\Diamond$ (guitar $\wedge$ violin) $\Diamond$ (guitar $\wedge$ cello) $\Diamond$ (violin $\wedge$ cello) SC-ALT
$\Diamond$ (guitar $\wedge$ violin $\wedge$ cello)

More relevant for our present purposes are domain alternatives, plain and exhaustified, in (18):

(18) a. Domain alternatives activated by *un instrument oarecare*
$\Diamond$ (guitar $\vee$ violin) $\Diamond$ (guitar $\vee$ cello) $\Diamond$ (violin $\vee$ cello) D-ALT
$\Diamond$ guitar $\Diamond$ violin $\Diamond$ cello
b. Exhaustified domain alternatives for *un instrument oarecare*
$\Diamond$ (guitar $\vee$ violin) $\wedge \neg \Diamond$ cello $\Diamond$ guitar $\wedge \neg \Diamond$ violin $\wedge \neg \Diamond$ cello EXH D-ALT
$\Diamond$ (guitar $\vee$ cello) $\wedge \neg \Diamond$ violin $\Diamond$ violin $\wedge \neg \Diamond$ guitar $\wedge \neg \Diamond$ cello
$\Diamond$ (violin $\vee$ cello) $\wedge \neg \Diamond$ guitar $\Diamond$ cello $\wedge \neg \Diamond$ guitar $\wedge \neg \Diamond$ violin
c. Domain alternatives activated by *vreun instrument*
$\Diamond$ guitar $\Diamond$ violin $\Diamond$ cello D-ALT
d. Exhaustified domain alternatives for *vreun instrument*
$\Diamond$ guitar $\wedge \neg \Diamond$ violin $\wedge \neg \Diamond$ cello $\Diamond$ violin $\wedge \neg \Diamond$ guitar $\wedge \neg \Diamond$ cello EXH D-ALT
$\Diamond$ cello $\wedge \neg \Diamond$ guitar $\wedge \neg \Diamond$ violin

After exhaustification, the enriched meaning of (16a) amounts to the free choice inference familiar from (9) above: Luca can play a single instrument chosen among the guitar, the violin, and the cello, and each one of them is a possible choice. This is the total variation implicature given in (19).

(19) a. $O \Diamond (\text{guitar} \vee \text{violin} \vee \text{cello}) = \Diamond (\text{guitar} \vee \text{violin} \vee \text{cello}) \wedge$
$\neg \Diamond (\text{guitar} \wedge \text{violin}) \wedge \neg \Diamond (\text{guitar} \wedge \text{cello}) \wedge \neg \Diamond (\text{violin} \wedge \text{cello}) \wedge$
i. $\Diamond (\text{guitar} \vee \text{violin}) \rightarrow \Diamond \text{cello} \wedge$ iv. $\Diamond \text{guitar} \rightarrow (\Diamond \text{violin} \vee \Diamond \text{cello}) \wedge$
ii. $\Diamond (\text{guitar} \vee \text{cello}) \rightarrow \Diamond \text{violin} \wedge$ v. $\Diamond \text{violin} \rightarrow (\Diamond \text{guitar} \vee \Diamond \text{cello}) \wedge$
iii. $\Diamond (\text{violin} \vee \text{cello}) \rightarrow \Diamond \text{guitar} \wedge$ vi. $\Diamond \text{cello} \rightarrow (\Diamond \text{guitar} \vee \Diamond \text{violin})$
b. $O \Diamond (\text{guitar} \vee \text{violin} \vee \text{cello}) = \Diamond (\text{guitar} \vee \text{violin} \vee \text{cello}) \wedge$ (= Assertion)
$\neg\Diamond(\text{guitar} \wedge \text{violin}) \wedge \neg\Diamond (\text{guitar} \wedge \text{cello}) \wedge \neg\Diamond (\text{violin} \wedge \text{cello}) \wedge$ (= Scalar Implicature)
$\Diamond \text{guitar} \wedge \Diamond \text{violin} \wedge \Diamond \text{cello}$ (= Total Variation)

If on the other hand, exhaustification applies to the singleton domain alternatives activated by *vreun* (18c–d), the enriched meaning winds up looking as in (20):

(20) $O \Diamond (\text{guitar} \vee \text{violin} \vee \text{cello}) = \Diamond (\text{guitar} \vee \text{violin} \vee \text{cello}) \wedge$ (= Assertion)
$\neg\Diamond (\text{guitar} \wedge \text{violin}) \wedge \neg\Diamond (\text{guitar} \wedge \text{cello}) \wedge \neg\Diamond (\text{violin} \wedge \text{cello}) \wedge$ (= Scalar Implicature)
i. $\Diamond \text{guitar} \rightarrow (\Diamond \text{violin} \vee \Diamond \text{cello}) \wedge$ (= Partial Variation)
ii. $\Diamond \text{violin} \rightarrow (\Diamond \text{guitar} \vee \Diamond \text{cello}) \wedge$
iii. $\Diamond \text{cello} \rightarrow (\Diamond \text{guitar} \vee \Diamond \text{violin})$
(i) + (ii) + (iii) = $(\Diamond \text{guitar} \wedge \Diamond \text{violin}) \vee (\Diamond \text{guitar} \wedge \Diamond \text{cello}) \vee (\Diamond \text{violin} \wedge \Diamond \text{cello})$

According to the meaning derived in (20), Luca can play one of the three instruments in D, and if he can play one of them, he can also play some other one (i.e., not necessarily all of them). This is the weaker partial variation inference, satisfied in scenarios like (15) above.

This briefly illustrates how a different choice of alternatives (singleton vs. non-singleton subdomains) determines the two meaning effects triggered by EIs. The total *versus* partial variation distinction thus appears to be wholly derivable from a constraint on domain alternatives, a matter of lexical choice.

Across languages, we find EIs that only sustain total variation (Romanian *un NP oarecare*, Italian *un NP qualsiasi*, or French *un NP quelconque*) and EIs that only sustain partial variation (Romanian *vreun*, Spanish *algún*, Italian *un qualche*). In addition, it has been recently pointed out (mainly in work by Aloni and Port) that certain EIs can trigger both kinds of inferences, depending on the context of occurrence. More precisely, German *irgendein* gives rise to a total variation implicature under a deontic modal, as in (21a), but can also be used in a partial variation scenario analogous to (15) above, as attested by the example in (21b):

(21) a. Maria muss **irgendeinen** Arzt heiraten. German
Maria must *irgendein* doctor marry
'Maria must marry a doctor, any doctor.'
b. Juan muss in **irgendeinem** Zimmer im Haus sein.
Juan must in *irgendein* room in-the house be
'Juan must be in some room of the house.'

In Chierchia (to appear a), the behavior of *irgendein* is suggested to be the result of an ambiguity: *irgendein* can activate both minimal and 'larger' (i.e., non-singleton) subdomains, but the large alternatives are optional. Such an EI can then go both ways depending on the properties of the operators with which it interacts: deontic modalities typically force a total variation implicature, whereas partial variation is satisfied in epistemic modal contexts (for an extensive discussion of this difference between modalities see Fălăuş 2012, and Aloni and Franke, this volume). We come back to this ambiguity hypothesis in Section 3.3, where we consider the interaction between *irgendein* and focus.

### 2.3 *Variation among EIs: NPI use*

A second parameter of variation among EIs, which will turn out to be relevant for the possibility to associate with focus, concerns the use as a negative polarity item. Some EIs can be freely used in downward-entailing contexts, where they behave as regular NPIs and have narrow scope existential readings:

(22) a. Nimeni nu are **vreo** informaţie despre concert. Romanian
Nobody NEG have.3SG *vreun* information about concert
'Nobody has any information about the concert.'
b. Niemand hat **irgendein** Buch mitgebracht. German
No_one had *irgendein* book brought_along
'No one has brought along any book.'

The disappearance of the scalar and the free choice implicature in downward-entailing contexts is fully expected on the present approach. To see this in slightly more detail, assume that the domain relevant for the interpretation of *irgendein* in (22b) contains three books {a,b,c}. The assertion to which exhaustification applies looks as in (23a) (assuming for simplicity that *niemand* translates as sentential negation), and the alternatives as in (23b):

| | | | | |
|---|---|---|---|---|
| (23) | a. $\neg(a \vee b \vee c)$ | | | ASSERTION |
| | b. $\neg(a \wedge b)$ | $\neg(b \wedge c)$<br>$\neg(a \wedge b \wedge c)$ | $\neg(a \wedge c)$ | SC-ALT |
| | c. $\neg(a \vee b)$<br>$\neg a$ | $\neg(b \vee c)$<br>$\neg b$ | $\neg(a \vee c)$<br>$\neg c$ | D-ALT |
| | d. $\neg(a \vee b) \wedge c$<br>$\neg a \wedge (b \vee c)$ | $\neg(b \vee c) \wedge a$<br>$\neg b \wedge (a \vee c)$ | $\neg(a \vee c) \wedge b$<br>$\neg c \wedge (a \vee b)$ | EXH D-ALT |

It is clear that both the scalar alternatives and the negation of the exhaustified domain alternatives are entailed by the assertion.[7] As a result, no scalar or free choice inference arises and the EI is interpreted as an existential, i.e., it acquires an NPI-reading.

In contrast to this, some other EIs do not have NPI uses: if they occur under a downward-entailing operator, they can only acquire a "not just any" reading (in the presence of focus or contextual bias), illustrated in (24b) and (25b):

(24) Dubito che Luca abbia visto **un** concerto **qualunque**. Italian
doubt.1SG that Luca has seen a concert *qualunque*
a. *'I doubt Luca has seen any concert.'
b. ✓ 'I doubt that Luca has seen just any concert (he only attends classical music concerts).'

(25) Nimeni nu a vizitat **un** muzeu **oarecare**. Romanian
Nobody NEG has visited a museum *oarecare*
a. *'Nobody has visited any museum.'
b. ✓ 'Nobody has visited just any museum (everyone picked their favorite one).'

On the present account, this difference among EIs is captured by assuming a restriction on exhaustification. More precisely, certain EIs (and more generally free choice indefinites) require that the result of exhaustification be properly stronger than the assertion. This requirement cannot be satisfied in downward-entailing contexts, where the assertion entails all alternatives, and hence, exhaustification simply returns the assertion. Formally, this is cashed out by defining $O_{PS}$, a presuppositional operator selected by certain EIs:

(26) *The Proper Strengthening (PS) parameter* (Chierchia to appear a: Ch. 5)
$O_{PS}(p) = O(p)$, if $[O(p) \subset p]$; $\bot$, otherwise
(where $O(p) = p \wedge \forall q \in C\, [q \rightarrow p \subseteq q]$)

$O_{PS}$ functions like the usual exhaustification operator O (i.e., eliminates stronger alternatives), but is defined only if the result of exhaustification properly entails the assertion. In modal contexts, the derived free choice interpretation is clearly stronger than the assertion, and thus EIs that select for $O_{PS}$, e.g., *un NP qualunque* or *oarecare*, can be felicitously used. On the other hand, in downward-entailing contexts, the presuppositional exhaustification does not work, and the EIs that select for it are therefore ruled out.

This brief overview demonstrates how differences among EIs are captured on an alternative-based framework. Just like everywhere else in the polarity system, variation stems from constraints on lexically determined sets of alternatives (e.g., minimal vs. non-minimal subdomains lead to partial and total variation inferences) or on exhaustification (the proper strengthening requirement precludes an NPI use). With this background in mind, we now turn to a further parameter of variation, namely the interaction with focus.

## 3. Epistemic indefinites and focus: facts and issues

On the alternative-based approach pursued here, it is clear how EIs relate to other types of (polarity sensitive) indefinites. Just like simple indefinites (and disjunction), universal free choice indefinites (*any*, *qualsiasi*) and basic NPIs (*alcuno*, *ever*), they activate (scalar and subdomain) alternatives, and may allow for pre-exhaustified alternatives. All these three categories can associate with focus (at least contrastively), as illustrated in the following examples:

(27) a. Paul doesn't buy me A flower a day, he buys me THREE flowers a day.
b. Verdi didn't compose *La Traviata* OR *Aida*, he composed both.
c. A: Do you like Lisa's cat?
B: I don't like ANY cat, I'm allergic to cats.
d. A: Can the queen move sideways?
B: The queen can move in ANY direction, it's the most powerful piece in the game.

The presence of focal stress on these elements has different effects: in the case of a scalar element (indefinite or disjunction), focus signals the fact that the item receives an enriched interpretation under negation, e.g., the sentence in (27b) receives a coherent interpretation only if disjunction is construed as exclusive. Emphatic *any*, both in its NPI and FCI use, has often been claimed to signal the consideration of a quantificational domain wider than the one it contrasts with, the so-called "domain widening" effect discussed in Kadmon and Landman (1993) and Krifka (1995), among many others.

We now set to examine the interaction between EIs and focus, a parameter of variation that to my knowledge hasn't been explored in previous literature. For the purposes of this chapter, I limit myself to the subset of EIs in Table 4.1, which summarizes their relevant empirical properties:

Putting together novel and previous observations, I will provide preliminary evidence in favor of a correlation between the type of modal inference triggered by the EI and the possibility to associate with focus. More precisely, it will be shown that items that sustain total variation can bear focal stress, whereas items that convey partial variation (only) cannot. This interesting restriction will be argued to follow from the interaction between lexically determined and focally activated alternatives. I will focus on data from Romanian, dealing primarily with the total variation EI *un NP oarecare* (Section 3.1), and partial variation *vreun* (Section 3.2), but I will mention parallel facts from other Romance

Table 4.1. *(Some) Properties of (some) EIs*

| Epistemic indefinite | NPI use | Total variation | Partial variation |
|---|---|---|---|
| German *irgendein* | yes | yes | yes |
| Romanian *vreun* | yes | no | yes |
| Italian *un qualche* / Spanish *algún* | no | no(/yes)[22] | yes |
| Romanian *un NP oarecare* / Italian *un NP qualunque* | no | yes | no |

languages along the way. Finally, I will have some remarks on German *irgendein* (Section 3.3), which triggers both partial and total variation, but can associate with focus only in the latter case.

### 3.1 *Total variation and focus in downward-entailing contexts*

It has often been observed that certain EIs can acquire a "not just any" reading in downward-entailing (DE) contexts, if they are used in a denial context or if focused. The following Italian examples (from Chierchia to appear a) and Romanian sentences (due to Săvescu-Ciucivara 2007) illustrate this behavior:[8]

(28) a. Nessuno ha letto **un** libro **QUALUNQUE**. Italian
Nobody has read a book QUALUNQUE
'No one has read just any book.'
b. Dubito che Gianni abbia visto **uno** studente **QUALUNQUE**.
I doubt that Gianni has seen a student QUALUNQUE
'I doubt that Gianni has seen just any student.'

(29) a. Puţini copii au rezolvat **o** problemă **OARECARE** din manual. Romanian
few kids have solved a problem OARECARE from textbook
'Few kids solved no matter what problem from the textbook.'
b. Maria nu poate să rezolve **o** problemă **OARECARE**.
Maria NEG can SUBJ solve a problem OARECARE
'Maria cannot solve just any problem.'

Recall that these EIs do not have NPI-uses, and hence are typically ruled out under downward-entailing operators. Here however, we see that emphatic stress, which I assume to signal focus, enables their occurrence in these environments, and (28b) for instance conveys that the speaker doubts that Gianni saw any old student, and thinks Gianni saw some special student. A similar reading arises if a modal is present in the structure, as in (29b), where the free choice effect is denied. The main issue to be dealt with in this connection concerns the way the presence of focus affects the meaning of the EI.

Given the parallel treatment of EIs and disjunction, it seems reasonable to look for an answer by considering what happens with focus on scalar items outside the polarity system. Implicatures typically disappear under downward-entailing operators, but it is well-known that focus on the implicature trigger signals that the implicature is retained (e.g., Horn 1989, Chierchia, Fox, and Spector 2012 among others), as illustrated in the following example repeated from above:

(30) Verdi didn't compose *La Traviata* OR *Aida*, he composed both.

How is this effect of focus derived on the alternative-based approach we are pursuing? Recall that disjunction optionally activates scalar and possibly domain alternatives. When active, scalar alternatives lead to the scalar implicature, i.e., the exclusive interpretation, whereas (recursive) exhaustification over domain alternatives is responsible for the free choice effects arising in modal contexts (cf. (8)–(9) above). Let us assume that in the sentence in (30) only scalar alternatives are active and see how the exclusive construal of disjunction comes about. If exhaustification applies above negation, the assertion entails all its alternatives and hence the enriched meaning would be identical to the assertion (cf. (23) above). To derive the correct interpretation of (30), we must assume that the exhaustification operator applies below negation, as in the following LF:

(31) $\neg$ O (Verdi composed La Traviata or Aida)

Focus thus simply signals that the (scalar) alternatives are active and exhaustification takes place within the scope of negation. Could we envisage a similar solution for EIs? The answer is negative: EIs *obligatorily* activate both scalar and domain alternatives, and consequently, if exhaustification were to take place in the scope of negation, the associated LF of (28a) would be as follows:

(32) a. Nessuno$_i$ O [t$_i$ ha letto un libro qualunque]
b. O [t$_i$ ha letto un libro qualunque]

This however does not seem a viable option: exhaustification in (32b) yields ungrammaticality (something which can be easily checked) – in the absence of a modal, the scalar and the free choice implicature contradict each other. On the basis of this, we must conclude that exhaustification applies above negation, at least in the absence of modal operators. In other words, the assumption that exhaustification takes place below negation can only be exploited in modal contexts, leaving us with no (or a different) explanation for the "not just any" reading arising in non-modal contexts. But the examples in (29) above show that the "not just any" reading arises regardless of whether a modal "intervenes" between the downward-entailing operator and the EI, if the EI is focused. So we are back to our original question: how does focus lead to the "not just any" interpretation of a total variation EI like *un NP qualunque/oarecare*?

In principle, there are two options we could pursue. Focus can either affect the way in which alternatives get factored into meaning (i.e., mode of exhaustification) or can have an effect on the alternatives considered for exhaustification. The first line of analysis is pursued in Crnič (2011a), who convincingly argues (building mainly on Krifka 1995; Chierchia to appear a) that stressed *any* behaves on a par with emphatic NPIs and selects for exhaustification via silent *even* (as defined in (5b)). The assumption that the presence of focus involves *even*-like exhaustification is exploited to derive the licensing of stressed *any* in non-downward-entailing contexts (e.g., non-monotone quantifiers or desire predicates). It remains to be seen to what extent this solution is applicable to EIs, a matter I will leave for future research. In the remainder of this chapter, I would like to explore the latter option, namely the hypothesis that focus affects the alternatives to which the exhaustification operator O applies. More precisely, I will defend the claim in (33):

(33) Focus adds domain alternatives.

This hypothesis is directly inspired by the treatment of Chinese *wh*-indefinites in Liao (2011).[9] Let me briefly review the relevant aspects of her proposal, and then show how it extends to EIs.

In a detailed study of Chinese *wh*-indefinites, within the alternative-based framework adopted here, Liao discusses focused *wh*-phrases in negative sentences, illustrated in the following example:[10]

(34) Zhangsan mei mai **shenme** shu. (Mandarin Chinese, Liao 2011: 88)
Zhangsan NEG buy what book
a. 'Zhangsan didn't buy any book.'
b. 'Zhangsan didn't buy any special book.'

The *wh*-indefinite *shenme* can acquire either an NPI-reading (34a), or the interpretation in (34b), whereby Zhangsan did buy some (ordinary) book. *Wh*-indefinites are similar to EIs in that they activate both scalar and domain alternatives (of any size). The NPI-reading is obtained along the lines of (23) above. More relevant for our present purposes is the second construal of the *wh*-indefinite in (34). According to Liao, this can be derived by conjecturing that (34) involves focus and the presence of focus leads to the consideration of a domain wider than the one initially associated with the assertion. The desired interpretation then comes about in the following way. Assuming Rooth's (1992) focus theory, and putting the entire proposition in (34) in focus, its LF representation is as in (35a):

(35) a. $O_C\ [\sim_C [\neg \exists x \in D \cap \text{book}\ [\text{bought}(ZS,x)]]_{[+F]}]$
b. $C = \{\neg \exists x \in D \cap \text{book}\ [\text{bought}(ZS,x)], \neg \exists x \in D' \cap \text{book}\ [\text{bought}(ZS,x)],$
$\text{where } D \subset D'\}$

Focus adds alternatives that range over the wider domain D′, i.e., the second alternative in the set in (35b). Since this proposition is stronger than the assertion, it will get excluded through exhaustification. Once we put together the assertion and the derived implicatures, the resulting interpretation is that Zhangsan didn't buy any book in D, but he did buy some book in D′.[11]

Liao's proposal provides a straightforward account for the "not just any" reading of the focused EIs in (28) and (29). To see this in more detail, consider once again the following sentence:

(36) Gianni non ha letto **un** libro **QUALUNQUE**. Italian
Gianni NEG has read a book QUALUNQUE
'Gianni didn't read just any book.'

Recall that a total variation EI like *un qualunque* lexically activates scalar and subdomain alternatives, given in (37)–(38). As we have already seen in (23), exhaustification applied above negation is vacuous (all alternatives are entailed by the assertion), i.e., it returns the assertion: Gianni didn't read any book in D, where D is {a,b,c}:

(37) a. ASSERTION: $\neg \exists x \in D[\text{one}(x) \wedge \text{book}(x) \wedge \text{read}(G,x)]$
b. SC-ALT = $\{\neg \exists x \in D[n(x) \wedge \text{book}(x) \wedge \text{read}(G, x)]: \text{one} < n\}$
c. D-ALT = $\{\neg \exists x \in D'[\text{one}(x) \wedge \text{book}(x) \wedge \text{read}(G, x)]: D' \subseteq D\}$

(38) a. $\neg(a \vee b \vee c)$ — ASSERTION
b. $\neg(a \wedge b)$ $\neg(b \wedge c)$ $\neg(a \wedge c)$ — SC-ALT
$\neg(a \wedge b \wedge c)$
c. $\neg(a \vee b)$ $\neg(b \vee c)$ $\neg(a \vee c)$ — D-ALT
$\neg a$ $\neg b$ $\neg c$
d. $O\neg(a \vee b)$ $O\neg(b \vee c)$ $O\neg(a \vee c)$ — EXH D-ALT
$O\neg a$ $O\neg b$ $O\neg c$

Since the NPI reading is disallowed by "proper strengthening" (see (26) above), this configuration is normally ruled out for *un qualunque*. In the absence of focus, this sentence is ungrammatical. But here the EI is focused and consequently, the LF for (36) is as in (39a). Following Liao's proposal reviewed above (formulated as in (33)), we assume that the presence of focus adds domain alternatives, i.e., leads to the consideration of a superset of D, namely D′= {a,b,c,d}:

(39) a. $O_C$ [$\sim_C$ [ un libro qualunque$_{[+F]}$ [ Gianni didn't read $t_i$]]]
b. $\{\neg \exists x \in D'[\text{one}(x) \wedge \text{book}(x) \wedge \text{read}(G, x)]: D' \subseteq D \text{ or } D \subseteq D'\}$

Exhaustification applies to this enlarged set and seeks to eliminate stronger alternatives. The alternatives in (38) are all entailed by the assertion (i.e., $\neg(a \vee b \vee c)$), but the alternative based on D′ ($\neg(a \vee b \vee c \vee d)$) is not. So through exhaustification, it will be excluded. The resulting meaning can be represented as in (40):

(40) $O_C$ [Gianni didn't read un libro qualunque] =
$= \neg \exists x \in D[\text{one}(x) \wedge \text{book}(x) \wedge \text{read}(G,x)] \wedge \neg([\neg \exists x \in D'[\text{one}(x) \wedge \text{book}(x) \wedge \text{read}(G,x)])$, where $D \subseteq D'$
$= \neg \exists x \in D[\text{one}(x) \wedge \text{book}(x) \wedge \text{read}(G,x)] \wedge \exists x \in D'[\text{one}(x) \wedge \text{book}(x) \wedge \text{read}(G,x)]$

According to (40), the sentence in (36), with *un libro qualunque* focused, is interpreted as saying that Gianni did not read a book in the initially considered domain of quantification, but he did read a book in some other, special domain. This does not explain how the book in the "special" domain is singled out. However, there is little doubt that it is a contextual matter, and a pragmatic effect of having changed the initial domain. Importantly, it is not something that comes from how exhaustification proceeds. For this proposal to work and derive the intended reading, it is crucial that the set considered at the final level of exhaustification (i.e., exhaustification applying to the lexically activated alternatives *plus* those brought in by focus) includes alternatives that are not entailed by the assertion. This ensures that we get a coherent meaning after applying O. But the choice of D and D′ is regulated by pragmatic factors. As we have seen in the previous example, a reasonable way to get the right result (and thus explain why focus rescues sentences like (40)) is by adding alternatives to D. But there are cases involving a different strategy. For example, imagine the initial D is set to the books on a given reading list. Clearly one can use (40) in this situation and add a continuation like *I read the most difficult one* (on the list).[12] What this means is that the difference between the books that have not been read (D) and the one(s) that have been read (D′) is established by bringing in additional factors (e.g., difficulty). I do not have a full story on how the various contextual factors may affect the observed readings. But I hope the general line of reasoning is clear even in the absence of more precise assumptions on the choice of domains. What matters for our present purposes is that focus on total variation EIs adds domain alternatives, thus offering a way to avoid the ungrammaticality of configurations like (40).[13] In DE-contexts, the addition of non-entailed alternatives amounts to the consideration of super-domains (something we represented by adding alternative *d* to the initial domain of books).

In the following, I will extend this proposal and exploit the hypothesis in (33) to account for the restrictions governing focus on partial variation EIs like *vreun* or *un qualche*.[14]

## 3.2 *Partial variation and focus*

In the previous section, we have seen that EIs like *un NP qualunque* or *oarecare* can be focused, acquiring a "not just any" reading in DE-contexts. In order to make sense of this behavior, I have adopted the proposal in Liao (2011) whereby focus adds domain alternatives to the set of lexically activated alternatives.

I now turn to what I think is a previously unnoticed restriction, namely the impossibility of Romanian *vreun* to associate with focus, illustrated below: as soon as *vreun* is focused in the sentences in (41), they become deviant:[15]

(41) a. *Nimeni nu are **VREUN** bilet la concert. Romanian
Nobody NEG have.3SG VREUN ticket to concert
'Nobody had any ticket to the concert.'
b. Se poate ca Maria să meargă la **VREUN** concert diseară.
REFL may that Maria SUBJ go to VREUN concert tonight
'Maria might go to some concert tonight.'

The fact that *vreun* cannot be stressed is surprising, on at least two grounds. First, we have just seen that EIs like *un qualunque/oarecare* can be focused. Second, *vreun* also has an NPI use, and NPIs are well-known to be able to carry emphasis (cf. (27)). So no matter how we look at the data in (41), we are faced with a puzzle. Moreover, as illustrated in (42), this restriction seems to be shared by other partial variation EIs – focus on *algún* or *un qualche* is systematically rejected:

(42) a. *Dudo que María tenga **ALGUNA** entrada para el concierto. Spanish
doubt.1SG that Maria has ALGUN ticket for the concert
'I doubt that Maria has any ticket to the concert.'
b. *Es possible que María vaya a **ALGÚN** concierto esta noche.
is possible that Maria goes to ALGUN concert this night
'It's possible that Maria goes to some concert tonight.'
c. *Voglio imparare a suonare **UN QUALCHE** strumento musicale. Italian
want.1SG learn to play A QUALCHE instrument musical
'I want to learn to play some musical instrument.'

The conclusion that can be drawn from these facts is that partial variation EIs cannot be focused, unlike total variation EIs, NPIs, or simple indefinites, to which they are closely related. How can an alternatives-and-exhaustification approach accommodate this behavior? Ideally, from the interaction between lexically activated alternatives and focus activated alternatives. Recall that the sole difference between *un oarecare* and *vreun* (and more generally between total and partial variation EIs) lies in the set of subdomain alternatives they activate, which must consist of all subdomains of the relevant quantificational domain for the former, and singleton subdomains only for the latter. Accordingly, if we pursue the same line of reasoning as before, we expect the (im)possibility to associate with focus to be somehow related to this difference. In other words, the fact that *vreun* activates singleton domain alternatives has to be incompatible with the posited effect of focus on domain alternatives. In the following, I will argue that this route can be fruitfully pursued to capture the restriction in (41b), and suggest that this explanation can be extended to the partial variation EIs exemplified in (42). I briefly return to the negative polarity uses of *vreun* in Section 4.

In the previous section, we accounted for the interpretation of the focused occurrences of EIs like *un oarecare* by assuming that focus adds domain alternatives to the set of lexically activated alternatives. Recall that on the present approach, the choice of the relevant quantificational domain D is a matter of pragmatics, but the subdomains are semantically determined and must consist of all subdomains of D (a property that is responsible for the total variation inference). Consequently, the only way to add domain alternatives (in the presence of focus) is by extending the initial domain, thus making exhaustification apply over both sub- and super-domain alternatives. This delivers the right interpretation.

Things are different for partial variation EIs. In particular, their lexically determined alternatives are different, in that they are restricted to singleton domain alternatives. As shown in Section 2.2, this assumption derives the fact that EIs like *vreun* or *un qualche* always prompt partial variation. I will now argue that it is this very same restriction to singleton alternatives that can explain the ban on focus illustrated in (41b). To see this, consider the set of domain alternatives lexically activated by *vreun* (in a context with three elements in D):

(43) $\Diamond a \quad \Diamond b \quad \Diamond c$

In the absence of focus, the sentence is grammatical and triggers a partial variation inference. Once we bring in focus, domain alternatives must be added to the set in (43). Here however, we can include domain alternatives that look as in (44a), i.e., non-minimal subdomains, and as a result, exhaustification will apply to the set in (44b). Once we allow for pre-exhaustification of these alternatives, and put together the assertion with the derived (scalar and free choice) implicatures, through steps familiar from Section 2.2 above, we wind up with the total variation meaning in (44c).

(44) a. $\Diamond (a \vee b) \quad \Diamond (b \vee c) \quad \Diamond (a \vee c)$
b. $\Diamond (a \vee b) \quad \Diamond (b \vee c) \quad \Diamond (a \vee c)$
$\Diamond a \quad \Diamond b \quad \Diamond c$
c. $O \Diamond (a \vee b \vee c) = \Diamond (a \vee b \vee c) \wedge$ (= Assertion)
$\neg\Diamond (a \wedge b) \wedge \neg\Diamond (a \wedge c) \wedge \neg\Diamond (b \wedge c) \wedge$ (= Scalar Implicature)
$\Diamond a \wedge \Diamond b \wedge \Diamond c$ (= Total Variation)

This state of affairs is not tolerated by *vreun*, which lexically encodes a ban on total variation, as extensively argued in Fălăuş 2012. The gist of the proposal I am referring to can be summarized as follows. Romanian *vreun* is only felicitous in contexts where one of the alternatives in the quantificational domain can be excluded (although the speaker does not necessarily know which one). In other words, instead of triggering the partial variation inference (i.e., *some but not necessarily all*), it imposes a stronger – anti-total variation – restriction (i.e., *it is necessary that not all* alternatives constitute viable options). This requirement is built in the semantics of *vreun*, an idea that is formally implemented by assuming that *vreun* includes among its alternatives the total variation element *un oarecare* (and its alternatives). Essentially, the total variation inference normally associated with *un oarecare* (i.e. $\Diamond a \wedge \Diamond b \wedge \Diamond c$) gets added to the set of alternatives in (43) and excluded via exhaustification, as sketched in (45):

(45) a. $O \Diamond (a \vee b \vee c)) = \Diamond (a \vee b \vee c) \wedge \neg\Diamond (a \wedge b) \wedge \neg\Diamond (a \wedge c) \wedge \neg\Diamond (b \wedge c)$
$\wedge \Diamond a \rightarrow (\Diamond b \vee \Diamond c)$
$\wedge \Diamond b \rightarrow (\Diamond a \vee \Diamond c)$
$\wedge \Diamond c \rightarrow (\Diamond a \vee \Diamond b)$
$\wedge \neg (\Diamond a \wedge \Diamond b \wedge \Diamond c)$
b. $= (\Diamond a \wedge \Diamond b) \vee (\Diamond a \wedge \Diamond c) \vee (\Diamond b \wedge \Diamond c)$ (= Partial Variation)
$\wedge \neg(\Diamond a \wedge \Diamond b \wedge \Diamond c)$ (= Ban on Total Variation)

This derives the correct "partial variation only" associated with *vreun* and accounts for its restricted distribution (most prominently its exclusion from deontic contexts), a property that is not directly relevant here. The crucial aspect of the analysis is that the lexical semantics of *vreun* encodes a ban on total variation. Focus on the other hand derives total variation, as illustrated in (44). This correctly accounts for the clash observed in (41b): the alternatives brought in by focus conflict with the standard meaning of *vreun*. On the theory outlined here, the non-association of *vreun* with focus in modal contexts receives a fairly principled explanation, based on two independently motivated assumptions, namely the constraint on singleton subdomains and the role of focus.

Crucial to the analysis proposed above is the hypothesis that focus affects the set of domain alternatives considered for exhaustification. Importantly, the shape of the domain alternatives that get added through focus depends on the shape of the lexically activated subdomains. In case the initial domain alternatives are singletons, focus brings in larger (i.e., non-singleton) subdomains. If focus were allowed to add further singleton domain alternatives (like for example in the case of total variation EIs), we would expect to get a partial variation inference that holds for a wider quantificational domain. The fact that this never happens indicates that the effect of focus on the domain alternatives is constrained by the lexical alternatives.[16]

This brings us to *un qualche* and *algún*, which are similar to *vreun* in that they never trigger total variation inferences. However, they are not so strictly incompatible with total variation set-ups: the sentence in (42c) for example, without focus on *un qualche*, is perfectly acceptable in a context where the speaker would be happy to play any musical instrument, without excluding any relevant alternative. In other words, unlike in the case of *vreun*, nothing in the meaning of *un qualche* (or *algún*) enforces partial variation. Focus is nevertheless infelicitous, as indicated in (42). On the present line of analysis, this means that these EIs disallow total variation (although this requirement is not as strong as in the case of Romanian *vreun*). A plausible way of thinking about this is in terms of a blocking effect: the fact that both Spanish and Italian have total variation elements (*un NP qualsiasi/cualquiera*) arguably blocks the possibility of the partial variation item to sustain the total variation inference triggered by focus. This leaves open the possibility that if for some reason (or for some speakers) this blocking effect can be overridden, focus becomes acceptable. Further empirical investigations are needed to see if this expectation is borne out in Spanish and Italian.

A related prediction made by the account outlined here is that an EI that can convey both partial and total variation inferences should be able to associate with focus, and the presence of focus should correlate with total variation. As shown in the next section, there is interesting preliminary evidence that German *irgendein* verifies this prediction.

### *3.3* Irgendein *and focus*

The previous section proposed an explanation for the fact that *vreun* does not associate with focus in modal contexts. Building on the conjecture that focus adds domain alternatives, we have tied the behavior of *vreun* to the activation of singleton domain alternatives and the ban on total variation which is part of its core meaning. Furthermore, we have seen evidence indicating that this restriction is shared by other partial variation EIs. What all these EIs have in common is the fact that they can never trigger total variation. This option however is available for the German EI *irgendein*, as illustrated in the following examples repeated from Section 2.2:

(46) a. Maria muss **irgendeinen** Arzt heiraten. German
Maria must *irgendein* doctor marry.
'Maria must marry a doctor, any doctor.'
b. Juan muss in **irgendeinem** Zimmer im Haus sein.
Juan must in *irgendein* room in_the house be
'Juan must be in some room of the house.'

As discussed in detail in Aloni and Port (2010), the sentence in (46a) receives a total variation interpretation, whereby any doctor could satisfy the modal requirement. The epistemic statement in (46b) on the other hand is most readily used in partial variation scenarios (e.g., the hide-and-seek context in (15)). The precise distribution of the partial vs. total variation inferences is not directly relevant for our present purposes. What is crucial to the current discussion is that the configurations where *irgendein* associates with total variation seem to require focus. According to Haspelmath (1997: 249), "in the free choice function, the *irgend*-series may occur, but it *must* be stressed":

(47) Dieses Problem kann **IRGENDJEMAND** lösen German
This problem can IRGENDJEMAND solve
'This problem can be solved by ANYONE.'

Similar observations can be found in Aloni and Port (2011), who furthermore note that *irgend-* cannot be stressed in contexts where it triggers partial variation (i.e., episodic and epistemic modal contexts):

(48) a. # **IRGENDJEMAND** hat angerufen. German
IRGENDJEMAND has called
'SOMEONE called, I don't know who.'
b. # Maria muss **IRGENDEINEN** Dokter geheiratet haben.
Maria must IRGENDEIN doctor married have
'Maria must have married SOME doctor, I don't know who.'

I think the data require closer scrutiny, but if these facts turn out to be solid, we have a further argument in favor of the hypothesis that focus leads to the addition of domain alternatives. As mentioned in Section 2.2 above, Chierchia (to appear a) suggests that *irgendein* can activate both singleton and non-singleton subdomains, but the larger alternatives are optional. By default, exhaustification applies to the active singleton alternatives (together with the scalar alternatives), yielding partial variation. If on the other hand *irgendein* occurs in a context where total variation is enforced (by the operator in the context of occurrence, in particular by deontic modals, cf. Fălăuş to appear b and Aloni and Franke, this volume), *irgendein* is focused.[17] As soon as focus is present (i.e., non-minimal domains are considered for exhaustification), *irgendein* winds up sustaining the total variation inference. Put another way, focus is required to avoid drawing the weaker, partial variation inference.[18] A more careful empirical investigation is clearly needed before drawing any conclusions on the interaction between the "licensing" operators, the interpretation of *irgendein* and focus. But the evidence available at this point provides interesting support in favor of the correlation between focus and total variation observed for the Romance EIs discussed in the previous sections.

## 4. Further issues and concluding remarks

This chapter examined the interaction between epistemic indefinites and focus, and proposed an alternative-based account for the observed patterns, within the framework developed in Chierchia (to appear a). The facts that I have considered here provide preliminary evidence in favor of a correlation between the strength of the free choice inference and the possibility to bear focal stress. More specifically, we have seen that whereas total variation EIs can be focused (and give rise to a "not just any" reading in DE-contexts), partial variation EIs disallow focus. This difference among EIs was argued to follow from the interaction between lexically activated alternatives and focus triggered alternatives, which get factored into meaning in essentially identical ways (through the application of a covert operator akin to *only*). Drawing on a hypothesis put forth in Liao (2011), we assumed that the role of focus is to add domain alternatives to the set of alternatives activated by the EI, and showed that the way this gets realized depends on the shape of the domain alternatives lexically activated by the EI. These assumptions enabled us (i) to capture the non-association with focus of partial EIs as a conflict between lexically induced and focus driven alternatives, and (ii) to derive the readings attested for the focused occurrences of total variation EIs. If this proposal is on the right track, the different interaction between EIs and focus is derivable from independently motivated properties of (domain) alternatives.

There are several issues that our discussion left open and which call for further research. One important set of issues concerns the behavior of partial variation EIs in contexts that license NPIs. In particular, as illustrated in (41a) above, the use of *vreun* as an NPI is also incompatible with focus. This restriction sets *vreun* apart from other NPIs, which are well-known to be able to bear focal stress.[19] At this point, I do not have an explanation for this fact and further empirical investigation will need to determine whether this restriction is shared by any other NPIs across languages. Let me simply mention two ways of accounting for stressed NPIs that are compatible with the present alternative-based framework and which could in principle serve as a starting point for any analysis of the unexpected behavior of *vreun*. The first one is due to Krifka (1995) and Lahiri (1998), and has been recently taken up in Crnič (2011a). It consists in assuming that the licensing of stressed NPIs (on a par with minimizers like *lift a finger*) involves an *even*-like exhaustification operator (EmphAssert in Krifka's proposal). For the NPIs to be licit, the presuppositions triggered by the covert *even* need to be satisfied in the context of utterance.

A related account of stressed NPIs is pursued in Chierchia (to appear a), which embeds the ideas developed in Krifka (1995) in the general theory of alternatives and exhaustification adopted here. The assumption that NPIs obligatorily activate alternatives is argued not only to be responsible for their distribution (as sketched in Section 2.1), but also to determine their behavior under contrastive focus, illustrated in (49):

(49)

| | |
|---|---|
| a. Dialogue I | b. Dialogue II |
| A: Do you have an egg? | A: Do you have any egg? |
| B: No. | B: No. |
| A: Maybe a pickled one? | A: Maybe a pickled one? |
| B: I don't have ANY egg. | B: *I don't have AN egg. |

The contrast between (49a) and (49b) is captured by assuming (i) that *any* activates subdomain (and scalar) alternatives which call for the insertion of the covert exhaustification operator O, and (ii) Rooth's anaphoric principle of focus interpretation. Roughly speaking, the contrastively focused expression must find an "antecedent" in the context, which must be a member of the focus value of the contrastively stressed counterpart. Since the focus value of a sentence involving *any* includes its lexically determined alternatives, the anaphoric condition can be satisfied only if the domain associated with the simple indefinite is a subset of the domain associated with *any*. This derives the observation that *any* seems to indicate reference to a wider domain of quantification, when contrasted with other existentials.

It remains to be seen to what extent the behavior of *vreun* in NPI-contexts, namely the fact that it disallows focus, can be captured along the lines of the theories mentioned above. I will leave this as a point for future investigation.

A related question arises in connection with the behavior of partial variation EIs that do not have NPI-uses, e.g., *un qualche*. Within the present framework, this is derived from a constraint on the mode of exhaustification (i.e., selection of $O_{PS}$, discussed in Section 2.3). In this respect, it is similar to the total variation *un qualunque*, which doesn't have an NPI-interpretation either. But whereas focus provides a way to rescue the use of the total variation EI *un qualunque* in DE-contexts (and acquire a "not just any" reading), this option is not available for partial variation EIs. More research is necessary to understand the constraints on the alternatives induced by focus and its rescuing effects.[20]

Finally, the chapter dealt with a small number of EIs and further empirical study is required before assessing the cross-linguistic validity of the observed correlation between focus and free choice inference. The interaction between EIs and overt focus markers (such as focus-sensitive particles, *only*, *even*, *at least*) can shed further light on the restrictions governing the interaction between EIs and focus. Whatever properties will be uncovered through future research, the facts considered here indicate that this is an interesting area of investigation, and the alternative-based approach is well equipped to accommodate the observed patterns. Not only can the interaction with focus contribute to a better understanding of the properties of EIs (and more generally of polarity sensitive elements), but it also provides an interesting empirical domain for exploring the relation between lexically induced and focus alternatives. The results can turn out to be relevant to the current debates concerning the possible unified treatment of different phenomena that make reference to sets of alternatives.[21]

**Acknowledgments**

I am extremely glad and honored to contribute to this volume and have the opportunity to thank Gennaro Chierchia and honor his inspiring work. Gennaro is the first to have made semantics meaningful to me and working with him is a constant and very pleasant reminder of how serious and beautiful is the project on which I embarked. His confidence broadened my views beyond what I thought possible, thus making everything more challenging; his incredibly generous and continuous support help me stay focused and optimistic all throughout. I wish to thank two anonymous reviewers and the audience at *ZAS* for thoughtful feedback and valuable suggestions on previous versions of this material. All errors are of course my own. This research was financially supported by the Spanish Ministry of Science and Innovation (FFI2011–29218), the Basque Government (GIC07/IT-769–13) and the University of the Basque Country – UPV/EHU (UFI11/14).

NOTES

1. On the use of the *namely* test in connection with free relatives, which also have an ignorance or an indifference reading, see e.g., Dayal (1997), Fintel (2000c), Rawlins (2008). An interesting comparison between *wh-ever* relatives and EIs like *some or other* can be found in Dayal (2009).
2. See Gajewski (2002) and Chierchia (to appear a) for details on when and why contradictions can give rise to ungrammaticality.
3. In the following, I omit the subscript indicating the set of propositions with respect to which exhaustification takes place (cf. C in (5a)). Unless mentioned otherwise, this set includes both scalar and (possibly pre-exhaustified) domain alternatives.
4. Where "guitar" is an abbreviation for "you study guitar," "$\Diamond$ guitar" for "you may study guitar," and similarly for all other alternatives.
5. "Pre-exhaustification" of domain alternatives corresponds to "recursive exhaustification" in Fox (2007a) (and is closely related to the anti-exhaustivity implicature in Kratzer and Shimoyama 2002). As correctly observed by a reviewer, for more complex sets of alternatives, it is important that pre-exhaustification takes place with respect to sets of alternatives that are Innocently Excludable, in the sense of Fox (which roughly speaking ensures that the elimination of one element will not lead to the arbitrary inclusion of another element). See Chierchia (to appear a) for a detailed discussion of these issues.
6. This is due to the following equivalences:
   $\neg(\Diamond \text{ guitar} \wedge \neg \Diamond \text{ violin}) = (\Diamond \text{ guitar} \rightarrow \Diamond \text{ violin})$
   $\neg(\Diamond \text{ violin} \wedge \neg \Diamond \text{ guitar}) = (\Diamond \text{ violin} \rightarrow \Diamond \text{ guitar})$.
7. Excluding an exhaustified alternative like $\neg O \neg (a \vee b) = \neg(\neg(a \vee b) \wedge c)$ amounts to $c \rightarrow (a \vee b)$, and similarly for all other alternatives.
8. Insofar as I can tell, French *un quelconque* behaves similarly (see Jayez and Tovena 2006). Alonso-Ovalle and Menéndez-Benito (2011) claim that the Spanish EI *un cualquiera* receives the "not just any" interpretation in downward-entailing contexts without any focus operator or emphatic stress. My informants disagree. More research is required to identify the source of this difference in judgments.
9. Chierchia (to appear a) mentions Liao's treatment of Chinese *wh*-indefinites as a promising way to derive the "not just any" reading of EIs like *un qualsiasi*, without however getting into the details of this proposal (at least in the draft version available to me upon completion of this chapter). The present discussion can be viewed as an attempt to pursue this route and extend it to partial variation EIs.
10. The present chapter deals only with structures that do not involve any overt focus particle, but it should be mentioned that Liao provides a detailed account of a further focus-related configuration, namely the interaction between *wh*-indefinites and *dou*. She argues that *dou* is a focus marker, which introduces an additive presupposition and a universality requirement, and furthermore signals the application of the *even*-exhaustification operator. This derives the fact that the presence of *dou* leads to a free choice/universal use of Chinese *wh*-indefinites. For extensive discussion of the role of focus in the two configurations, the reader is referred to Liao (2011).
11. Liao further discusses the pragmatic assumptions needed to derive the fact that Zhangsan bought some ordinary book. Since this is slightly different from the reading we want to derive for EIs, I will not get into the details of her proposal, and simply note that the relevant pragmatic constraints may differ.

12. I'm grateful to an anonymous reviewer for drawing my attention to this issue.
13. Chierchia (to appear a) discusses universal free choice items like *any* or *qualsiasi* in sentences like *It is not true that Gianni read ANY book he found* (in denial contexts). He suggests that focal stress indicates uniformly that exhaustification (which derives a universal reading of the free choice item) takes place within the scope of negation, resulting in a "not every" interpretation. The "not just any" reading, which is also possible, stems from an additional scalar alternative ("We may assume that after D-exhaustification, *any* may get an existential scalar alternative, a change prompted by the fact that exhaustification yields a universal reading" – Chierchia to appear a: Ch. 6, p. 28). It is not entirely clear to me how this works for *any*, and so it is difficult to compare this proposal with the one advocated here. Note however two differences with EIs, which indicate that perhaps different routes need to be pursued for different elements. First, I have discarded the hypothesis that EIs allow for exhaustification below negation (see the discussion of (32) above). Second, EIs do not yield universal readings, and consequently, the motivation for the additional scalar alternative seems to be absent. The two proposals however converge in assuming that the reading whereby John read a *special* book (or set of books) should be attributed to pragmatic factors. For now, I remain neutral on the derivation of the "not just any" reading of universal free choice items.
14. This analysis raises the question of the interaction between focus and *un oarecare* in modal contexts. The facts are not entirely clear at this point. Many speakers resort to the universal free choice *orice* "any" or a construction equivalent to *a book, any book* instead of focusing *un oarecare*. For the speakers who accept it, focus on *un oarecare* results in stronger free choice effects, i.e., the freedom of choice holds of a larger number of alternatives. Similar considerations hold for Spanish *un cualquiera*. This is consistent with the present proposal: if to the initial assertion $\Diamond$ (a $\vee$ b $\vee$ c), we add an alternative, high exhaustification applies to $\Diamond$ (a $\vee$ b $\vee$ c $\vee$ d). This yields the free choice effects discussed in Section 3, the only difference being that these effects are perceived as stronger as a result of having extended D.
15. This claim obviously does not apply to corrective focus, which can affect any linguistic expression, e.g., *In my dialect, I pronounce [vrun], not [vréun].*
16. This brings into focus a crucial difference between the present proposal and the domain widening approach due to Kadmon and Landman (1993), to which it may look similar. On their proposal, polarity sensitive items like *any* must widen domains and are subject to a constraint that domain widening is acceptable only if it leads to strengthening. On the alternative-based approach advocated here, domain widening effects may arise only in the presence of focus, which triggers the addition of alternatives to the set of active subdomain alternatives. Whether or not the initial quantificational domain gets eventually widened depends on the shape of the lexically constrained subdomains. See Chierchia (to appear a) for more extensive discussion of the issues raised by the original domain widening hypothesis.
17. To my knowledge, the only other context where *irgendein* requires focus are comparatives. For an interesting account of this fact, which I think is amenable to the alternative-based account pursued here, see Aloni and Roelofsen (2011).
18. As pointed out by an anonymous reviewer, this raises the question of why focus on *irgendein* is disallowed in epistemic contexts. Given our current assumptions, we would expect focus to be possible and trigger total variation effects, contrary to what

seems to be the case. This suggests that total variation is blocked in epistemic contexts, for reasons yet to be explained. A proper answer to this question must be postponed until the empirical facts become better understood.

19. There are interesting, conflicting reports concerning stressed *irgendein* in DE-contexts. According to Kratzer and Shimoyama (2002: 14), the "not just any" reading emerges in the presence of negation (and other DE-operators). On the analysis proposed here, this interpretation is derived from the consideration of super-domain alternatives (added by focus), as discussed in Section 3.2. On the other hand, Aloni and Port (2011) report an NPI reading for examples like (i):

    (i) Niemand hat **IRGENDEINE** Frage beantwortet.
    nobody has IRGENDEIN question answered
    'Nobody answered ANY question.'

    At this point, it is not entirely clear to me what is the difference in interpretation between (i) and its equivalent without focus. If the effect is akin to the domain widening attested for stressed *any* and other NPIs, it will have to be derived through whatever mechanism turns out to be responsible for the behavior in (49).

20. See Liao (2011) for an explanation of the fact that focus cannot rescue polarity sensitive items in episodic sentences.

21. See e.g., Fox and Katzir (2011) for a unitary theory of alternatives for both scalar implicatures and association with focus.

22. The EI itself never conveys total variation. The "no(/yes)" choice reflects the fact that *un qualche* (just like Spanish *algún*) is compatible with total variation contexts, e.g. *Voglio imparare a suonare un qualche strumento musicale* 'I want to learn to play some musical instrument' can be used by a speaker who would be happy to play any musical instrument. This is a logical consequence of the fact that total variation entails partial variation. In contrast to this, *vreun* is only compatible with partial variation contexts, and thus qualifies as a "strict" partial variation EI. I come back to this issue in Section 3.2.

# 5 On the free choice potential of epistemic and deontic modals

*Maria Aloni and Michael Franke*

## 1. Introduction

A number of constructions in various languages display a different behavior in the scope of epistemic and deontic modals. For example, the German indefinite determiner *irgendein* gives rise to different inferences under the two kinds of modals (Aloni and Port 2010; Kratzer and Shimoyama 2002). Furthermore, while the Romanian determiner *vreun* is licensed under epistemic modals, but not under deontic modals (Fălăuş 2009), concessive scalar particles like Slovenian *magari* are licensed under deontic modals but not under epistemic ones (e.g. Crnič, 2011b). Although seemingly a diverse set of observations, there is a curious commonality in the proposed explanations for the relevant data: all of the three case studies independently assume that deontic and epistemic modals have different *free choice (FC) potential*, in the sense that these modals differ in the way that they license so-called FC-inferences. We consider FC-inferences to be inferences of the form in (1a)/(1b) and (2a)/(2b) associated with either existentials or disjunctions under modals, as in (1c) and (2c) respectively:

(1) a. $\Box\exists x: \phi(x)$
b. $\Diamond\exists x: \phi(x)$
c. $\forall x: \Diamond\phi(x)$

(2) a. $\Box(p_1 \vee p_2 \vee \ldots p_n)$
b. $\Diamond(p_1 \vee p_2 \vee \ldots p_n)$
c. $\forall i \in \{1, 2, \ldots, n\}: \Diamond p_i$

While epistemic FC-inferences, i.e., FC-inferences associated with epistemic modals, mostly seem to be well-behaved pragmatic inferences outside of compositional semantics, deontic FC-inferences seem able to penetrate into the computation of semantic values much more freely. It is this *Modal Variability Hypothesis*, as we will call it, that is the main object of scrutiny in this chapter.

We argue that the hypothesized differences in FC-potential are not due to a sharp semantic contrast between modalities, but propose a pragmatic explanation for the Modal Variability Hypothesis. We acknowledge the possibility, explored in great depth by Chierchia (2006, to appear a) and others, of (quasi-)

pragmatic inferences taking effect "locally" during the composition of semantic meaning, but we still argue for a genuine pragmatic perspective on the distribution of such local pragmatic effects. We suggest that whether a pragmatic inference reliably enters semantics proper is a matter of *pragmatic fossilization*: since deontic FC-inferences are of a different type of information than epistemic FC-inferences, the former are more readily adaptable to the computation of semantic values.

Our main argument for the pragmatic difference between deontic and epistemic information hinges on the contextual variability of *universal FC-inferences*, i.e., FC-inferences that apparently occur in the scope of universal quantifiers, as is the case when an utterance of (3a) conveys the strengthened meaning expressed in (3b).

(3) a. All of the boys may go to the beach or to the cinema.
b. ⇒ All of the boys may go to the beach and all of the boys may go to the cinema.

We argue that the availability of universal FC-inferences depends, among other things, on the contextual relevance of the inference in question. Contrasting situations in which deontic and epistemic universal FC-inferences do or do not arise, we argue that deontic FC-inferences are more clearly relevant for practical purposes than their epistemic counterparts. This suggests that deontic information is more readily perceived as "base-level" information about what the actual state of affairs is than epistemic information. In turn, this makes plausible why, from a diachronic perspective, deontic FC would fossilize sooner and/or more readily than epistemic FC.

The proposed intuitive difference in relevance for "base-level" information can be made tangible in dynamic semantics. In standard dynamic accounts of epistemic modality (Veltman 1996; Gillies 2004; Yalcin 2007), epistemic modals are not eliminative updates, but tests on whether the currently accumulated information supports or is compatible with some piece of further information. In contrast, deontic modal statements that provide directly useful information about practically relevant permissions and obligations are most plausibly treated as base level informative, on a par with propositional information. We show that the difference between deontic and epistemic FC-inferences clearly shows in a dynamic semantics in the way that the former are *persistent*, while the latter are not only not persistent but even *anti-persistent*. Persistent information survives information growth; anti-persistent information survives information loss.

The chapter is structured as follows. After reviewing the relevant data and theories on Romanian *vreun*, Slovenian *magari* (and related constructions), and German *irgendein* in Section 2, we formulate the Modal Variability Hypothesis in Section 2.4. Section 3 discusses but dismisses an obvious semantic explanation of modal variability implemented in an alternative-based framework (Aloni 2007b; Chierchia to appear a). Building on data concerning universal

FC-inferences in Section 4, Section 5 states our pragmatic explanation of modal variability. Section 6, finally, tries to corroborate the informal picture by tracing the underlying intuitions in dynamic semantics. Section 7 concludes with some reflections on the conceptual consequences of our proposal.

## 2. Data in support of modal variability

In this section, we briefly review the main properties of Romanian *vreun* (Fălăuş 2009, 2011, 2012), Slovenian *magari* (and related constructions) (Crnič 2011b), and German *irgendein* (Aloni and Port 2010; Kratzer and Shimoyama 2002), focusing on their behavior in modal contexts. We also sketch three of the most recent accounts of these data sets. Interestingly, all of these analyses assume a different FC-potential for deontic and epistemic modals. We therefore formulate the Modal Variability Hypothesis in Section 2.4.

### *2.1 Romanian* vreun

Epistemic indefinites are existential constructions that signal ignorance or indifference on the part of the speaker. Romanian *vreun* is an example of an epistemic indefinite with a very limited distribution (Fălăuş 2009, 2011, 2012): its occurrences are restricted to negative polarity and a subset of modal contexts. We will focus here on the behavior of *vreun* in epistemic and deontic contexts. As Fălăuş reports, *vreun* is licensed under epistemic modals, as illustrated in (4), while it is ungrammatical under deontic modals, as illustrated in (5).

(4) Trebuie/Poate să fie vreun angajat care lucrează până târziu.
must/may SUBJ be.3SG *vreun* employee who work.3SG until late
'It must/might be some employee working late.'

(5) # Trebuie/Pot să citesc vreo carte până mâine.
must/can SUBJ read.1SG *vreun* book by tomorrow
'I must/can read some book by tomorrow.'

An interesting question concerns the type of modal inference *vreun* sustains in examples like (4). Following Alonso-Ovalle and Menéndez-Benito (2010), Fălăuş distinguishes between standard FC-inference, which, adopting terminology from Chierchia (to appear a), she labels as total variation, and a weaker partial variation inference:

(6) a. Total variation: $\forall x \Diamond \phi$
all alternatives in the relevant domain qualify as a possible option
b. Partial variation: $\exists x \exists y (\Diamond \phi(x) \wedge \Diamond \phi(y) \wedge \neg x{=}y)$
more than one (but not necessarily all) alternatives in the relevant domain qualify as a possible option

Using examples like (7), Fălăuş shows that *vreun* in epistemic contexts merely conveys partial variation effects (Fălăuş 2011: 418):

(7) E posibil ca Irina să se fi întâlnit cu vreun prieten, dar nu poate
be.3SG possible that Irina SUBJ REFL be met with *vreun* friend, but NEG can
fi Luca, tocmai l-am văzut.
be Luca, just CL.3SG.MASC-have.1SG seen
'It is possible that Irina met some friend, but it cannot be Luca, I have just seen him.'

But in addition to this, *vreun* seems actually to be incompatible with situations in which total variation would hold, as illustrated by the following example (Fălăuş 2012: 38):

(8) SHELL GAME SCENARIO: The shell game requires three shells or boxes and a small ball. The ball is placed under one of the shells and then the operator quickly shuffles the shells around. In order to win, the player has to correctly identify the shell containing the ball.

(9) Mingea trebuie să fie în vreo cutie.
ball_the must SUBJ be.3SG in *vreun* box
'The ball must be in a box.'

According to Fălăuş (2012), example (9) cannot be used in the scenario described in (8) because the context makes it clear that the ball could be in *any* of the three shells under consideration. *Vreun* then seems to express, beside partial variation, also an anti-total variation inference:

(10) Anti-Total variation: $\neg\forall x\Diamond\phi$
not all alternatives in the relevant domain qualify as a possible option

To explain these facts Fălăuş proposes an analysis couched in the alternative-based approach developed in Chierchia (2006, to appear a). Chierchia's proposal has two main ingredients: (i) all polarity items (including negative polarity items, FC-items, and epistemic indefinites) activate alternatives; (ii) active alternatives require the application of an independently established mechanism of exhaustification (e.g. Fox 2007a), which otherwise would be optional. Differences between different items are accounted for in terms of variation in (i) the type of alternatives they may activate (e.g. scalar, domain, singleton domain alternatives), and (ii) the mode of exhaustification they employ (see Chierchia to appear a; Fălăuş 2009, this volume for details). In this approach, different types of alternatives give rise to different modal inferences: recursive exhaustification with respect to domain alternatives derives total variation effects; recursive exhaustification with respect to *singleton* domain alternatives derives partial variation effects (Fălăuş 2009, 2011, 2012; Alonso-Ovalle and Menéndez-Benito 2010).

On Fălăuş' account, *vreun* activates singleton domain alternatives. Through recursive application of an exhaustivity operator in the style of Chierchia (2006) and Fox (2007a), this derives partial variation effects under epistemic modals; see (11a). But in addition to this, as we saw, *vreun* should also encode a ban on total variation, represented in (11b). In Fălăuş (2012), inference (11b) is derived by exhaustification with respect to 'complex' alternatives brought about by the competition of *vreun* with the Romanian epistemic 'total variation' indefinite *un oarecare* (see Fălăuş 2012, for details). This ban on total variation explains example (9), but it would also explain why *vreun* is excluded from deontic sentences under the assumption that existentials under deontic modals give rise to total variation (FC) inferences for independent reasons, as illustrated in (12):[1]

(11) Epistemic: Trebuie/Poate să fie vreun angajat care lucrează până târziu.
a. Partial variation: $\exists x \exists y\ (\Diamond_e\ \phi(x) \wedge \Diamond_e\ \phi(y) \wedge \neg x=y)$
b. Anti-total variation: $\neg \forall x\ \Diamond_e\ \phi$

(12) Deontic: #Trebuie/Pot să citesc vreo carte până mâine.
a. Partial variation: $\exists x \exists y\ (\Diamond_d\ \phi(x) \wedge \Diamond_d\ \phi(y) \wedge \neg x=y)$
b. Anti-total variation: $\neg \forall x \Diamond_d\ \phi$
c. Total variation: $\forall x \Diamond_d\ \phi$ ($\Rightarrow$ contradiction)

Crucial to this explanation is that total variation (FC) inferences are independently generated under deontic modals, but not under epistemic modals. It is important to stress that a different method from Chierchia/Fox's recursive exhaustification should be employed here to derive (12c). Indeed, Chierchia/Fox's exhaustivity operator is blind towards the difference between epistemic and deontic modals. If total variation is derivable via this operator under deontic modals, it will also be derivable under epistemic modals, unless we assume that *vreun* activates domain alternatives under deontic modals, and singleton domain alternatives under epistemic ones. But why would different sets of alternatives be selected by *vreun* under different types of modals?

To summarize, under the assumption that *vreun* activates singleton domain alternatives and 'complex' alternatives, Fălăuş derives partial variation and anti-total variation inferences via (recursive) application of Chierchia/Fox's exhaustification. To derive the systematic exclusion of *vreun* from deontic sentences one needs the additional assumption that total variation (FC) inferences are independently generated for *vreun* under deontic modals by a method which is different from Chierchia's or Fox's exhaustification. In Section 3 we will propose an explicit implementation of the strategy illustrated in (12) which derives (12c) as an entailment, employing the analysis of deontic modals developed in Aloni (2007b).

## 2.2 Concessive scalar particles

Crnič (2011b) uses **magari* as a blanket term for concessive scalar particles including Greek *esto ke* (Giannakidou 2007), Spanish *aunque sea* and *siquiera* (Alonso-Ovalle 2009; Lahiri 2010), and Slovenian *magari/makr*. There are two main kinds of environments in which **magari* can occur: in downward entailing contexts, where it is glossed with *even*, and under priority modals. Priority modals include imperatives, as (13), deontic, bouletic and teleological modals. Crucially, **magari* is reported not to be licensed under epistemic modals (Crnič 2011b: 4).

(13) Preberi magari Sintaktične Structure!
read.IMP *magari* Syntactic Structures
'Read at least Syntactic Structures!'

According to Crnič, **magari* spells out two operators that he calls EVEN and AT LEAST,[2] defined as follows ($\leq_c$ stands for *at most as likely as*, and Heim and Kratzer's (1998) notation for presupposition is assumed):

(14) $[[\text{EVEN}]]^{g,c} = \lambda C . \lambda p : \forall q \in C\, [\neg( p = q) \rightarrow p <_c q].\ \lambda w . p(w)$

(15) $[[\text{AT LEAST}]]^{g,c} = \lambda C . \lambda p . \lambda w . \exists q \in C\, [q \leq_c p \wedge ( p(w) \vee q(w))]$

For example, assuming that C consists of the propositions that Peter won bronze, that he won silver and that he won gold, i.e., the focus-semantic value of the prejacent:

(16) $[[[\text{EVEN C}]\ \text{Peter won gold}_F\ ]]^{g,c}$ (w) is defined only if it is least likely that Peter won gold. If defined, it is true iff Peter won gold in w.

(17) $[[[\text{AT LEAST C}]\ \text{Peter won bronze}_F\ ]]^{g,c}$ (w) is true iff Peter won bronze or silver or gold in w.

The distribution of **magari* is regulated by the inferences that these two operators generate. As illustrated in (18), in positive episodic environments, **magari* is predicted to be out because it produces contradictory presuppositions: in (18f), (bronze $\vee$ silver $\vee$ gold) cannot be less likely than the other alternatives in $C^0$, because the latter asymmetrically entail the former.

(18) a. # Peter won **magari* a bronze$_F$ medal.
b. # $[_{ZP}$ [EVEN $C^o$ $[_{XP}$ [AT LEAST C] Peter won a bronze$_F$ medal]]]
c. $[[C]]^{g,c}$ = {bronze, silver, gold}
d. $[[XP]]^{g,c}$ = (bronze $\vee$ silver $\vee$ gold)
e. $[[C^o]]^{g,c}$ = {bronze $\vee$ silver $\vee$ gold, silver $\vee$ gold, gold}
f. $[[ZP]]^{g,c}$ (w) is defined only if
(bronze $\vee$ silver $\vee$ gold) $<_c$ (silver $\vee$ gold), gold.
If defined, it is true iff Peter won bronze or silver or gold in w.

In deontic modal sentences like (19), the modal can crucially intervene between EVEN and AT LEAST. Assuming that deontic modals when applying to an existential sentence return a strengthened FC-meaning, see (19d), the presupposition of EVEN, fleshed out in (19f) can now be satisfied: since no entailment relation obtains between the relata, the presupposition is consistent and, as Crnič observes, it is also plausible: that you are allowed to win an unremarkable bronze medal (and silver and gold) can be less likely than that you are required to win some shinier medal (silver or gold, just gold).

(19) a. You must win **magari* a bronze$_F$ medal.
b. $[_{ZP}$ [EVEN $C^o$]$[_{XP}$ $\Box_d$ [[AT LEAST C] you win bronze$_F$]]]
c. $[[\,C]]^{g,c}$ = {bronze, silver, gold}
d. $[[XP]]^{g,c} = \Box_d (\text{bronze} \vee \text{silver} \vee \text{gold}) \wedge (\Diamond_d \text{bronze} \wedge \Diamond_d \text{silver} \wedge \Diamond_d \text{gold})$
e. $[[\,C^o]]^{g,c} = \{\Box_d (\text{bronze} \vee \text{silver} \vee \text{gold}) \wedge (\Diamond_d \text{bronze} \wedge \Diamond_d \text{silver} \wedge \Diamond_d \text{gold})\}$,
$\Box_d (\text{silver} \vee \text{gold}) \wedge (\Diamond_d \text{silver} \wedge \Diamond_d \text{gold}), (\Box_d \text{gold} \wedge \Diamond_d \text{gold})]$
f. $[[ZP]]^{g,c}$ (w) is defined only if
$\Box_d (\text{bronze} \vee \text{silver} \vee \text{gold}) \wedge (\Diamond_d \text{bronze} \wedge \Diamond_d \text{silver} \wedge \Diamond_d \text{gold}) <_c$
$\Box_d (\text{silver} \vee \text{gold}) \wedge (\Diamond_d \text{silver} \wedge \Diamond_d \text{gold}), \Box_d \text{gold} \wedge \Diamond_d \text{gold}$
If defined, it is true iff you must win bronze or silver or gold in w.

To derive FC-effects with priority modals, Crnič (2011b) adopts the mechanism developed in Aloni (2007b), but he observes that any mechanism which generates FC-effects in the grammar could be employed as well.[3] Crucial to this explanation of the distribution of **magari* is again the assumption that deontic modals and epistemic modals have a different FC-potential.[4] We have to derive the tendency that **magari* occurs solely under priority modals. If FC-effects were generated in the grammar also with epistemic modals, we would miss this generalization.

To summarize, on Crnič's (2011a) account **magari* is correctly predicted to be excluded from positive episodic sentences because it produces a contradictory presupposition. In a deontic sentence like (19), if embeddable FC-inferences are generated, no contradictory presupposition is produced and **magari* is predicted to be grammatical. To explain the systematic exclusion of **magari* from epistemic contexts, we have to assume that potentially rescuing FC-inferences are not generated by the grammar under epistemic modals (unless we want to rely on at least dubious alternative explanations in terms of implausible presupposition).

### 2.3 *German* irgendein

The German epistemic determiner *irgendein* is felicitous in positive episodic contexts where it gives rise to an ignorance effect (epistemic partial variation), but it can also be used in downward-entailing contexts where it expresses a plain narrow scope existential meaning (Aloni and Port 2010; Kratzer and Shimoyama 2002).

(20) Irgendein Student hat angerufen, (#nämlich Peter).
*irgend*_one student has called, (#namely Peter)
'Some student called. The speaker doesn't know who it was.'

(21) Niemand hat irgendeine Frage beantwortet.
nobody has *irgend*_one question answered
'Nobody answered any question.'

Quite puzzling is the different behavior *irgendein* displays under epistemic and deontic modals:

(22) a. Epistemic: $\Box_e$ (. . . irgend . . . ) $\Rightarrow$ partial variation
b. Deontic: $\Box_d$ (. . . irgend . . . ) $\Rightarrow$ total variation

Under epistemic modals, *irgendein* gives rise to a partial variation inference: Aloni and Port (2010) observed that example (24) can be used in the HIDE AND SEEK SCENARIO described in (23), where a statement like (25), employing a genuine FC-item which induces total variation, would be inappropriate (see also Lauer 2010 for similar observations).

(23) HIDE AND SEEK SCENARIO: María, Juan, and Pedro are playing hide-and-seek in their country house. Juan is hiding. María and Pedro haven't started looking for Juan yet. Pedro believes that Juan is not hiding in the garden or in the barn: he is sure that Juan is inside the house. Furthermore, Pedro is sure that Juan is not in the bathroom or in the kitchen. As far as he knows, Juan could be in any of the other rooms in the house. (Alonso-Ovalle and Menéndez-Benito 2010: 6)

(24) Juan muss in irgendeinem Zimmer im Haus sein.
Juan must in *irgend*_one room in_the house be
'Juan must be in some room of the house.'

(25) Juan might be in any room of the house.

Under deontic modals, instead, *irgendein* can give rise to a total variation inference, as illustrated by example (26) from Kratzer and Shimoyama (2002). The example is ambiguous between a wide scope epistemic interpretation for the indefinite represented in (26a) and a lower scope FC-interpretation represented in (26b).[5]

(26) Mary musste irgendeinen Mann heiraten.
Mary had_to *irgend*_one man marry
a. 'There was some man Mary had to marry. The speaker doesn't know who it was.'
b. 'Mary had to marry a man; any man was a permitted marriage option for her.'

Aloni and Port (2010) analyze epistemic indefinites as existentials with two additional characteristics: (i) they induce an obligatory domain shift; and (ii) they are licensed only if such a shift is for a reason. Differences between different epistemic indefinites can be captured in terms of the different kinds of domain shift they can induce. German *irgendein* is assumed to be able to shift the domain of quantification in two different ways: it can either shift method of identification (conceptual-cover shift, henceforth, CC-shift), or it can widen the domain (domain widening, henceforth DW). CC-shifts are justified only if otherwise, i.e., with respect to the old (default) method of identification, the speaker would not have been able to identify the witness of the existential claim. DW is justified only if it does not create a weaker statement.

The operation of DW is well-known since Kadmon and Landman (1993). The intuition behind the notion of a CC-shift is best illustrated by an example. Assume you know that Macky Sall is the new president of Senegal, but you have never seen the man and therefore you would not be able to point him out. Consider now the sentence "You know who the president of Senegal is" used in the following two contexts: (a) during an exam on African politics; (b) at a party with many African leaders where you need to find Macky Sall for an interview. Intuitively, in context (a) the sentence would be judged true: you know that Macky Sall is the president of Senegal, so you know who the president of Senegal is. In context (b), instead, the sentence would be judged false: as far as you know, this person could be the president of Senegal or that person over there, so you don't know who the president of Senegal is. Individuals, like Macky Sall, can be identified in various ways: by name, by ostension, or by description. Our evaluation of knowledge attributions seems then to depend on what identification method is at play in the context of use. In context (a) where identification by name is sufficient, the sentence is true; in context (b), where identification by ostension is required, the sentence is false. Aloni (2001) accounted for these facts by formalizing identification methods in terms of conceptual covers (sets of individual concepts satisfying certain constraints) and assuming that (i) quantificational expressions quantify over conceptual covers, rather than over sets of individuals *simpliciter*, and (ii) different covers can be selected as domain in different contexts.

The main intuition behind Aloni and Port (2010) is that referents of epistemic indefinites like *irgend*-indefinites are typically identified via a method different from the one required for knowledge. The notion of a CC-shift is the technical counterpart of this intuition. Suppose $m$ is the cover representing the identification method contextually required for knowledge. Then *irgend*-indefinites, at least in their specific uses, signal an obligatory shift to a cover $n$ different from $m$, i.e., they existentially quantify over a cover which represents a method of identification which is not the one at play in the relevant context. For example, in context (b) above, a specific use of an *irgend*-indefinite would signal a shift to a method of identification, say *n*, different from ostension, and a sentence of the form $\phi$(irgend-indefinite) such as (27) in its specific reading, analyzed as an existential sentence in a dynamic semantics, would say that there is an individual d, identified by method *n*, which satisfies $\phi$.

(27) Ich muss irgendeinen (bestimmten) Mann interviewen.
I have_to *irgend*_one (certain) man interview
'I have to interview a (certain) man, I don't know who.'

If the witness of the existential claim were also identifiable by ostension, such a CC-shift would be vacuous in this context. By assuming that only non-vacuous CC-shifts are justified, Aloni and Port (2010) derive cover-dependent partial variation effects for specific uses of *irgendein*, namely that the witness of the existential claim cannot be identified by the identification method at play, e.g., in context (b), ostension. This accounts for examples (20) and (26a). Partial variation effects of *irgendein* under epistemic modals, as in (24), are explained by CC-shift in a similar fashion (see Aloni and Port 2010, for details). Occurrences in downward-entailing environments, like (21), are explained by DW.

Deontic FC-uses of *irgendein*, as in (26b), constitute a potential problem for the approach. Under a standard analysis of deontic modals, neither CC-shift nor DW is justified; the latter fact is shown in (28a). So Aloni and Port's analysis wrongly predicts that *irgendein* is infelicitous under deontic modals. Assume now a grammar that generates (total variation) FC-effects for existentials under deontic modals. Then, extending the domain of an existential under a modal no longer leads to a weaker statement if we incorporate its universal FC-inference as in (28b):

(28) a. $\Box\exists x\varphi \models \Box\exists x_{DW}\,\varphi$ without FC-inference
b. $\Box\exists x\varphi \wedge \forall x\,\Diamond\varphi \not\models \Box\exists x_{DW}\,\varphi \wedge \forall x_{DW}\,\Diamond\varphi$ with FC-inference

DW would then be justified in this case, *irgendein* would be correctly predicted to have deontic FC-uses. Again for this analysis to work, (total variation) FC-inferences should be automatically generated with deontic modals, but not with epistemic modals, otherwise the felicity of (24) in the HIDE AND SEEK SCENARIO would remain unexplained.

To summarize, in Aloni and Port (2010) German *irgendein* is an existential which triggers an obligatory domain shift (either CC-shift or DW), which has to come for a reason. Ignorance uses of *irgendein* (specific or under epistemic modals) are explained by CC-shift, occurrences in downward-entailing environments by DW. Deontic FC-uses can be also explained by DW, but only if FC-inferences are incorporated. Again, FC-effects should be independently generated to rescue *irgendein* under deontic modals, but not under epistemic modals.

### 2.4 Modal variability

In summary, this section presented three case studies that independently of each other provided indirect evidence for the hypothesis in (29) below:

(29) **Modal Variability Hypothesis**
Deontic and epistemic modals have a different FC-potential. In particular, deontic FC seems to enter into the recursive computation of compositional semantic values, whereas epistemic FC does not.

Of course, the evidence in favor of (29) is only indirect: it is the *assumption* of (29) that helps explain the intricate modal data from three different languages. But in that case, it is worthwhile to inquire why exactly (29) should hold.

We suggest here that deontic and epistemic modality differ in the kind of information they provide. The former is able to penetrate into the compositional computation of semantic values because it conveys information of the *right type* more reliably than epistemic modality does. This is not as aberrant and arbitrary a proposal as it might sound. Evidence comes from the availability of FC-inferences in embedded contexts, in particular from FC-inferences scoping under universal quantifiers, so called *universal FC-inferences*, which we present in Section 4. Interestingly, the difference we argue for can be formalized rather nicely in dynamic semantics, where indeed epistemic and deontic modals are often treated differently. To flesh out our proposal in a formal way, we therefore present a toy fragment of a dynamic semantics for both modalities in Section 6 where we trace the intuitive pragmatic differences that we propose are relevant for (29) to a notion of *persistence* of the FC-inference. But before doing so, Section 3 attempts to formulate a straightforward explanation for (29) in terms of a *formal/sortal* difference between deontic and epistemic modals, and identifies the problems faced by this approach.

## 3. Semantic explanations for modal variability

A natural way to implement the Modal Variability Hypothesis assumes a formal/sortal difference between deontic and epistemic modals: FC-inferences are derived as semantic entailments for disjunctions and existentials under the former, but not under the latter. We are not aware of any such account in the literature, so we attempt to develop one that is as viable as possible. This hypothetical analysis adopts Chierchia's (to appear a) framework of polarity and free choice and attempts to accommodate the phenomena we discussed in Sections 2.1 and 2.3, namely the different behavior of *vreun* and *irgendein* under deontic and epistemic modals, by employing, within Chierchia's framework, an explicit semantic analysis of deontic FC-inferences along the lines of Aloni (2007b).

The main motivation for adopting Aloni's (2007b) analysis comes from the following considerations. A first potential difficulty for an entailment account of deontic FC-inferences is that it would predict total variation effects for all indefinites under deontic modals, even unmarked ones as in "John may/must marry someone," which clearly does not entail that any person is a permissible marriage option for John. Aloni's (2007b) analysis provides a potential way out of this difficulty by allowing two different representations for indefinites – an alternative-inducing and a flat representation – and by letting modals be sensitive to the alternatives generated in their scope. Only alternative-inducing indefinites give rise to free choice entailments on this account. Unmarked indefinites can then be required to adopt flat representations.

According to Aloni (2007b), alternative-inducing representations of indefinites generate a genuine set of propositional alternatives, but not flat representations:

(30) Alternative inducing representation:
a. Logical Form: $\exists p(p \wedge \exists x(p = \varphi(x)))$ b. Alternatives: $\{\varphi(d_1), \varphi(d_2), \ldots\}$

(31) Flat representation:
a. Logical Form: $\exists x\ \varphi(x)$ b. Alternatives: $\{\exists x\ \varphi(x)\}$

Possibility modals and imperatives (but nothing prevents us from extending this analysis to necessity modals as well)[6] are assumed to entail that all alternatives generated in their scope should be compatible with the relevant modal base:

(32) Building on Aloni (2007b):
a. $\Diamond\phi$ is true in w iff *every* alternative induced by $\phi$ is *compatible* with the set of accessible worlds $\lambda v.\, wRv$;
b. $\Box\phi$ is true in w iff *every* alternative induced by $\phi$ is *compatible* with the set of accessible worlds $\lambda v.\, wRv$ and *at least one* alternative induced by $\phi$ is *entailed* by $\lambda v.\, wRv$.

On this analysis of modality, only alternative-inducing indefinites give rise to FC-inferences in modal environments. Unmarked indefinites like *someone* can be then required to employ flat representations. Marked indefinites like *irgendein* and *vreun* instead should use alternative-inducing representations. FC-effects would be generated solely for the latter.

Let's adopt the analysis of modality in (32), but solely for priority modals. Since FC-inferences would be generated under priority modals but not under epistemic modals, the distribution of concessive scalar particles would be explained along the lines of Crnič (2011b). As for epistemic indefinites, adopting Chierchia's (to appear a) alternative-based account, we could assume that both *irgendein* and *vreun* generate singleton domain alternatives as in (30b). Under epistemic modals, via recursive exhaustification in the vein of Chierchia or Fox we can derive partial variation effects, as in example (11) from Fălăuş. Under deontic modals, total variation effects are independently derived because of (32). *Vreun* would then be predicted to be out under deontic modals, because of a clash between the deontic FC-entailment and the lexically encoded ban on total variation, as in example (12). The different behavior of *irgendein* under deontic and epistemic modals would also be accounted for: semantic total variation would be derived under the former (via (32)), and obligatory pragmatic partial variation effects would be generated under the latter (via recursive exhaustification). There are however a number of problems for this strategy.

First of all there are other examples of marked indefinites for which we want to derive partial variation under epistemic modals, but, as it seems, no total variation under deontic or other priority modals, like Spanish *algún* or Italian *un qualche*. Let us illustrate these facts for the Italian case. The compatibility of (33) with the HIDE AND SEEK SCENARIO in (23) shows that in epistemic contexts *un qualche* only generates partial variation effects (Aloni and Port 2010):

(33) Juan deve essere in una qualche stanza della casa.
Juan must be in *un qualche* room of_the house
'Juan must be in some room of the house.'

That *un qualche* does not give rise to total variation effects under priority modals is demonstrated by the following example from the web, where the continuation explicitly specifies that not any kind of basic skill is enough:

(34) Per diventare traduttore devi avere un qualche tipo di base. Di sicuro
to become translator must.2SG have *un qualche* kind of basic_skill. Of sure
devi saper leggere e in alcuni casi devi anche sapere scrivere.
must.2SG know read and in some cases must.2SG also know write.
'To become a translator you must have some basic skills. For sure you must be able to read and in some cases you must also know how to write.'

Why do these examples constitute a problem for the strategy we are investigating in this section? To generate epistemic partial variation in Chierchia's approach we need to assume that *un qualche* activates singleton alternatives, but then, given (32), total variation under priority modals would be automatically generated as well (unless we assume that in Italian priority modals behave differently than in Romanian and German, which seems quite implausible).

A second more conceptual problem of this implementation is that there is no reason why the generation of deontic FC-inferences formalized in (32) should not automatically extend to epistemic modals. The difference in FC-potential between epistemic and deontic modals would be stipulated. Why would only the latter be sensitive to the alternatives generated in their scope?[7]

A final and quite general problem with a semantic explanation of (29) is that the to-be-explained difference in FC-potential does not seem to be a black-and-white matter, but rather calls for a more nuanced picture of why only some FC-inferences penetrate into compositional semantics. This is the topic of the following section.

## 4. Contextual-variability of universal free choice

In order to come to grips with the variable FC-potential of deontic and epistemic modals, this section looks more closely at the behavior of disjunction in the scope of these modals. FC-inference can arise for both deontic and epistemic modals if they embed a disjunction, as witnessed by the following examples:

(35) a. You may go to the beach or to the cinema. (Kamp, 1973)
b. ⇒ You may go to the beach and you may go to the cinema.

(36) a. Mr. X might be in Victoria or in Brixton. (Zimmermann, 2000)
b. ⇒ Mr. X might be in Victoria and Mr. X might be in Brixton.

But also other modalities, e.g., ability modals, *can* give rise to FC-inferences:

(37) a. Hans can play the violin or the trombone.
b. ⇒ Hans can play the violin and Hans can play the trombone.

Moreover, as observed by Klinedinst (2006), Eckardt (2007), and Fox (2007), FC-like inferences may even arise for disjunctions when embedded under non-modal existential constructions (38).

(38) a. Some of the guests had burgers or fruit salads.
b. ⇒ Some of the guests had burgers and some of the guests had fruit salads.

Under a standard semantic analysis of the components involved, all of these putative FC-inferences would not be considered semantic entailments. This could mean that these inferences are pragmatic inferences, but it could also mean that the standard semantics is wrong. The main argument why these inferences are probably *not* semantic entailments comes from the observation that FC-inferences do not seem to arise in all downward-entailing environments, such as in the scope of quantifier *none*:

(39) a. None of the boys may go to the beach or to the cinema.
b. ⇒ All of the boys are not permitted to go to either.
c. ⇏All of the boys are permitted one option, but none is free to choose.

(40) a. None of the agents might be in Victoria or in Brixton.
b. ⇒ All of the agents must be somewhere other than Victoria or Brixton.
c. ⇏For all agents x, either (i) it is conceivable that x is in Victoria and it is certain that x is not in Brixton, or (ii) it is conceivable that x is in Brixton and it is certain that x is not in Victoria.

So far the picture seems quite homogeneous, with different kinds of modals (and even non-modal constructions) giving rise to FC-inferences, with some evidence that these are pragmatic entailments. But the impression of peaceful homogeneity is spoiled, when we look at how readily FC-inferences associated with disjunctions and different modals embed. Indeed, in spite of the data in (39) and (40), there is not a total ban on FC-inferences possibly occurring in the scope of other logical operators. It has been observed, for instance, that FC-inferences associated with disjunction under deontic modals apparently can take scope under universal quantifiers, so-called *universal free choice* (henceforth: UFC) (cf. Chemla 2009b, for empirical evidence):

(41) a. All of the boys may go to the beach or to the cinema.
b. ⇒ All of the boys may go to the beach and all of the boys may go to the cinema.

For our purposes here it is important to notice that UFC does *not* arise as readily for other sorts of modals. More concretely, the apparent strength of UFC seems to depend on the kind of modality. This was suggested first by Geurts and Pouscoulous (2009) based on introspective judgments, but is also backed-up by empirical data (van Tiel 2011). The study of van Tiel provides clear evidence that deontic UFC, as in (41) is much more readily endorsed by the participants than epistemic UFC, as in (42).

(42) a. According to the professor, every research question might be answered by a survey or an experiment.
b. ⇒ According to the professor, every research question might be answered by a survey, and, according to the professor, every research question might be answered by an experiment.

On a coarse-grained picture, the different UFC-potential of deontic and epistemic modals seems to support the Modal Variability Hypothesis in (29): deontic FC-inferences infiltrate compositional semantics, epistemic FC-inferences do not, or at least not to the same degree. The problem is that this coarsed-grained picture is too coarse-grained. As soon as we zoom in, we realize that there is a devil in the quantitative details. The problem is that the Modal Variability Hypothesis in (29) would rather lead us to expect that while deontic UFC is readily attested, epistemic UFC should be impossible, or at least very inaccessible. But that is not supported by van Tiel's data: epistemic UFC *is* attested, but much less prominent than deontic UFC. In other words, although (29) does square well with the qualitative difference in UFC-potential of deontic and epistemic modals, it does not square well with the more nuanced quantitative picture.

Of course, there can be many factors figuring into the explanation why epistemic UFC is less readily attested. We could think that epistemic FC is more computationally costly than deontic FC (irrespective of which system computes these inferences), or less available for other reasons – reasons that lie outside of formal semantics proper. In essence, this is exactly the line of explanation that we would like to explore here. We would like to suggest for consideration the idea that the strength of an FC-inference is relative to the *relevance* of the inferred information.[8,9] To demonstrate this, we consider sentences that could give rise to UFC-inferences in two contexts each: one which makes the UFC-inference relevant for practical purposes and one which does not (cf. Malamud forthcoming, for a similar approach to the interpretation of plural definites). Our main argument is that contexts of the former type are not equally natural for different kinds of modals, suggesting that the availability of embedded FC-inferences depends on pragmatic factors of relevance of information in context.

Let's consider a "neutral" case first, namely the UFC-potential of ability modals. The study of van Tiel attests only very little UFC-potential to ability modals. And, indeed, it is also intuitive that the sentence in (43a) does not readily invite the UFC-inference in (43b).

(43) a. Everybody at the ILLC can play the violin or the trombone.
b. $\Rightarrow_?$ Everybody at the ILLC can play the violin, and everybody at the ILLC can play the trombone.

However, the availability of (43b) as an inference from (43a) seems to depend crucially on the context of utterance and, in particular, on the relevance of the information in (43b). To see this consider two scenarios:

(44) SCENARIO 1: After many of the established musicians had to cancel on short notice due to a flu epidemic, your task is to re-assemble an improvised university orchestra. The dean has given you permission to recruit and assign to instruments whoever you like. However, it is essential for the quality of the performance that you do not recruit people for instruments that they cannot play. You know that we know our fellow colleagues (and we know that you know . . .). Time is short and the only piece of information that you get from us is (43a). After that you go pick arbitrary members of the ILLC (possibly none) and assign them to instruments.

(45) SCENARIO 2: You claim that researchers at the ILLC, though certainly capable logicians, are lacking in musical talent, as nobody is able to play an instrument. We rebut your statement using (43a).

When uttered in a context like (45), the sentence (43a) clearly does *not* convey the strengthened meaning in (43b). In contrast, when uttered in a context like (44), it seems to us that (43a) *does* convey (43b). It seems to us that, when you get the information in (43a) in context (44), it would be justified for you to assign to either the violin or the trombone any member of the ILLC you choose. If we had not meant you to do that, we should have given you more specific information. In other words, the UFC-inference in (43b) is available in (44) but not (45) because the question whether the "ability predicate"

(46) $\lambda x \lambda y$. x is able to play instrument y

holds true of any arbitrary member of the ILLC and any arbitrary relevant instrument is of acute practical relevance in context (44), but not in context (45).

We suggest that the availability of UFC-inferences under deontic and epistemic modals similarly depends on matters of contextual relevance. Take the more critical case of epistemic UFC. We claim that whether an utterance of (47a) triggers the UFC-inference in (47b) depends on context, similarly to the previous case of ability modals.

(47) a. According to Inspector Clouseau, everybody at the ILLC might have strangled Prof. X or shot Prof. Y.
b. $\Rightarrow_?$ According to Inspector Clouseau, everybody at the ILLC might have strangled Prof. X, and, according to Inspector Clouseau, everybody at the ILLC might have shot Prof. Y.

To test this intuition, consider again two scenarios:

(48) SCENARIO 1: There has been a triple murder at the university. Professors X, Y, and Z have been strangled, shot, and poisoned respectively. Each murder occurred at a different time. (Chief!) Inspector Clouseau is present to investigate. Going somewhat out of his way, Clouseau sticks to antiquated method, the Art of Deduction, and considers any university employee a suspect for a particular murder who has no alibi for the time of that murder. Clouseau has assigned three helpers to lead interviews, one for each case. Your job is to send each employee of the university home or to one of the three interviewers concerned with the case for which the person is a suspect. This is the first round of interrogation, so the only thing that really matters is that nobody is assigned to an interview if she is not a suspect for that case. Again time is short and the only information you get from Clouseau's assistant, Cato Fong, is (47a). After that your task is to schedule everybody from the ILLC for interviewing or to send us home.

(49) SCENARIO 2: We demand that everybody at the ILLC is obviously innocent, but Cato Fong dismisses our demand by uttering (47a).

In context (49), the UFC-inference in (47b) clearly does not heavily invite itself, because it is not relevant in this context. But in the context (48), where it is relevant for your practical choice of action whether the "epistemic relation"

(50) $\lambda x \lambda y$. Clouseau considers it possible that x is the murderer of y

is true of each member of the ILLC and each victim in question, the UFC-inference does seem to arise. Of course, the example is quite contrived and set up deliberately so that Clouseau's epistemic state about whether x is a suspect for case y matters for practical purposes. But the artificiality of this context is exactly what we are interested in. We hypothesize that, in general, it takes rather exceptional and involved situations in which an epistemic UFC-inference would arise because "epistemic relations" like (50) are seldom practically relevant.

This is different for deontic UFC in context. Let's consider the question whether (51a) gives rise to the UFC-inference in (51b).

(51) a. Everybody at the ILLC is entitled to a pay raise or a research assistant.
b. $\Rightarrow_?$ Everybody at the ILLC is free to choose between pay raise and assistant.

Parallel to the previous cases, here are two scenarios, one which makes the UFC inference practically relevant, and the other one which does not.

(52) SCENARIO 1: It is your task to make sure that none of the employees of the university lays claims on bonuses that she is not entitled to. When it comes to the ILLC, the dean tells you (51a).

(53) SCENARIO 2: A research institute receives the predicate "distinguished" if all of its members are entitled to at least one bonus from the university's special bonus programme. You claim that the ILLC is not distinguished, we correct you stating (51a).

According to our intuitions, the UFC-inference in (51b) clearly arises in context (52), and not, or at least clearly less strongly, in context (53). The context (52) is one where it is a relevant issue whether the "deontic predicate"

(54) $\lambda x \lambda y$. x is entitled to bonus y

is true of all relevant x and y. What is interesting for our argument is that the context (52) does not at all seem very contrived or artificially set up. If at all, then it's rather (53) that appears less natural or common.

Of course, having provided only one pair of contexts for each case, we extrapolate from a weak inductive basis here, but we still feel that there is a general difference in the naturalness of contexts in which UFC-inferences for different types of modals would be (practically) relevant. We suggest that this is due to a *pragmatic circumstance*: whether information expressed by modalized predicates like (46), (50), or (54) are frequently relevant for concrete practical purposes.

## 5. Modal variability from pragmatic relevance

If the picture we just sketched is correct, then a pragmatic explanation for the Modal Variability Hypothesis pops into view, especially when we consider a diachronic perspective: if putative FC-inferences of different modal flavors differ in the frequency or strength of their contextual relevance, and so are available more or less frequently/strongly, then, over time, this will lead to differences in the extent to which these inferences could infiltrate compositional semantics. Essentially, this is a direct application of the well-established notion of *pragmatic fossilization* that yesterday's pragmatics will gradually become tomorrow's semantics.[10]

More concretely, suppose a community of language users has available two kinds of constructions, type-1 and type-2. Type-1 constructions are able to give rise to deontic FC-inferences; type-2 to epistemic FC-inferences. Suppose further that these FC-inferences are originally entirely pragmatic and do not enter the recursive computation of semantic values at all. But now let's also assume, as we tried to make plausible above, that deontic FC-inferences are more readily available than epistemic FC-inferences if we look at a random sample of conversational contexts in which either type of construction is used. In that case, if pragmatics fossilizes, then it must be that deontic FC-inferences, simply due to a slight advance in contextual prominence, would be more prone to enter the compositional computation of semantic values. As the differences in informational relevance are presumably universal, the hypothesized asymmetry in the pattern of fossilization would likewise presumably be universal.[11] Consequently, the Modal Variability Hypothesis might be a true empirical generalization at the current stage of language evolution, not because of a strong sortal difference between modalities, but because of a tendentious pragmatic difference that is operative on a long time scale.

Essentially, this diachronic view endorses the general possibility of "local implicatures" in the spirit of Chierchia (2006, to appear a, to appear b) and Chierchia *et al.* (2012), but also adds its own particular flavor to the overall picture. Chierchia's approach to "grammaticalized implicatures" has obvious empirical advantages over purely pragmatic approaches when it comes to *positive fit* to the empirical data: allowing pragmatic inferences to systematically intrude into compositional semantics yields more fine-grained, but also seemingly better empirical predictions in many domains of application than standard "globalist" accounts of pragmatic inferences (cf. Chierchia *et al.* 2012; Sauerland 2012, for recent arguments). But allowing implicatures into compositional semantics runs the risk of generating problems with *negative fit*: the generating power of potential "local implicatures" is overwhelming and not borne out empirically. For instance, lacking special intonation that might trigger alternative pragmatic processes, FC-inferences do not arise in the scope of *none* as in (39). To cope with issues of "negative fit," usually some variant of the *strongest meaning hypothesis* of Dalrymple *et al.* (1998) is employed (cf. Chierchia to appear b; Chierchia *et al.* 2012; Sauerland 2012). Roughly speaking, the strongest meaning hypothesis states that if two alternative semantic interpretations are available, then *ceteris paribus* the semantically stronger one is to be preferred. Unfortunately, the case of modal variability cannot be explained by appeal to a strongest meaning hypothesis. Adding FC-inference to an existential modal sentence always creates a stronger meaning irrespective of the nature of the modal. Hence, the strongest meaning hypothesis cannot explain any differences in FC-potential. Consequently, the pattern of available local pragmatic effects must be explained in a different way. This is exactly where our present proposal adds to the picture. The proposed diachronic perspective vindicates the general possibility of local pragmatic effects, but both adds a general explanation for patterns of distribution of local pragmatic effects, and also yields, not a black-or-white picture, but the more nuanced quantitative perspective that, arguably, the empirical data demand.

To make these ideas at least somewhat more precise, we would like to conclude by sketching the outlines of a framework, couched in dynamic semantics, that shows how deontic, but not epistemic FC-inferences could be treated as embeddable pragmatic effects, because of a difference in the usual base-level relevance of the information conveyed by these modals in discourse (cf. Aloni 2012).

## 6. Deontic and epistemic FC in discourse

To account for the different discourse behavior of deontic and epistemic FC, we will adopt a dynamic account of epistemic modality (Gillies 2004; Veltman 1996; Yalcin 2007) combined with a more classical approach to deontic modality and propose a genuinely dynamic mechanism to generate and incorporate pragmatic inferences which is sensitive to the differences between the two modalities. We will assume that FC-inferences of a given form $\phi$ are *implicatures* that can be captured by specifying a set of states in which $\phi$ would optimally or rationally be uttered by a speaker (given the usual assumptions of cooperativity, mutual recognition of relevance of information etc.). Aloni (2007a) and Franke (2011), among others, both spell out systems that give us exactly that, and we will stay close to these accounts, but nothing hinges on specifics here. Also, our exposition here focuses on FC-inferences derived from disjunction, but this too is for convenience only. The crucial bit is the integration of the information provided by deontic and epistemic FC-inferences into the discourse: only deontic FC-inferences are *persistent* and therefore can be fully integrated (via Aloni's (2012) +I-operator) into the dynamic process of interpretation in a non-trivial way. The reason why deontic and epistemic information is treated differently in dynamic semantics is, we suggest, exactly the difference in practical relevance of information of that kind, as argued above in Section 4.

### *6.1 Modals in dynamic semantics*

In dynamic semantics (Chierchia 1995; Heim 1983a; Kamp and Reyle 1993), meanings are identified with *context change potentials.*[12] In the simplest case, an *information state* is a set of possible worlds that captures different ways the world could be, according to the mutually accepted information of the discourse so far. The meaning of a sentence (represented by a logical formula) is captured by defining its context change potential as a function that specifies how that sentence would transform any given information state into another information state. In the simplest case of propositional information uptake, a sentence like "it is raining" would simply rule out all worlds in the input state where it is not raining.

Crucial for our purposes is the analysis of epistemic and deontic modals. Following standard treatments (Gillies 2004; Veltman 1996; Yalcin 2007), epistemic modals are evaluated as *tests* on the input state. Essentially, an epistemic modal statement, be it universal $\Box_e\phi$ or existential $\Diamond_e\phi$, tests whether the current information state $\sigma$ contains the information in $\phi$ already (for $\Box_e\phi$) or whether $\sigma$ is compatible with the information in $\phi$ (for $\Diamond_e\phi$). This is because an information state as such is already an epistemic notion: it contains the possibilities currently not ruled out by accepted factual information. In contrast to epistemic modals, the most straightforward evaluation of deontic modals is not as tests but as informative updates that can also rule out some but not all possibilities from an input information state.[13] In that case, deontic statements, $\Box_d\phi$ and $\Diamond_d\phi$, receive a classical interpretation: $\Box_d\phi$ discards a possible world w from an input state if $\phi$ is false in some world deontically accessible from w; $\Diamond_d\phi$ discards a possible world w from an input state if $\phi$ is false in all worlds deontically accessible from w. This implementation is reasonable because deontic information is not on a par with epistemic information states, but rather what the latter are about. In rough but accessible terms, the difference between modals in dynamic semantics comes down to this: deontic information is what information states are *about*, epistemic information is what information states *are*.

Of course, information states could be defined to be *about* epistemic information as well. In this case we would essentially lift the notion of an information state to a higher-order object. The point of interest here is *not* that this cannot or should not be done. The point is that the most straightforward way of treating modals in dynamic semantics neatly formalizes exactly the hypothesis that we worked out previously, namely that normally in discourse deontic information and epistemic information are not relevant *in the same way.*

### *6.2 Implicatures in dynamic semantics*

The difference in dynamic impact of deontic and epistemic modals will naturally also show in the impact of deontic and epistemic FC-implicatures. In order to see this, it is necessary, firstly, to spell out the FC-implicatures in question in a format suitable for integration into a simple dynamic framework and, secondly, to define a mechanism for the dynamic uptake of implicatures.

In order to be able to merge implicated information with information states in dynamic semantics, we consider the implicatures of an utterance of $\phi$ as what is *supported*, in the dynamic sense (see Appendix 5A), by any *optimal* information state for $\phi$. Recently a number of algorithms have been proposed to compute optimal states suitable for our present purposes (e.g., Aloni 2007a; Franke 2009, 2011; Schulz 2005).[14] Although there are minor differences in the way optimal states are derived in these systems, these do not affect our argument, so that, for illustration, we will only consider the most recent approach of Franke (2009, 2011). Franke calculates optimal states as the outcome of reasoning rationally about language use and interpretation in a formal game-theoretic model of the context of utterance. Essentially, this kind of reasoning gives rise to a mapping between forms $\phi$ as possible speaker utterances and information states $t$ of the speaker as the receiver's interpretation of $\phi$. These mappings constitute an equilibrium between the speaker's use of language and the receiver's interpretation in an abstract language game that captures basic Gricean assumptions about conversational behavior. Let opt($\phi$) be the set of states $t$ such that ($\phi$, $t$) is optimal in this equilibrium sense. Within a dynamic setting, the implicatures of an utterance of $\phi$ are then defined as what is *supported* in any state in opt($\phi$) but not entailed by $\phi$ itself.

**Definition 1 (Implicature)** $\psi$ is an implicature of $\phi$ iff $\sigma \models \psi$ for all $\sigma \in \text{opt}(\phi)$, while not $\phi \models \psi$.

To give an example, assume that our dynamic model contains a simple set W = $\{w_a, w_b, w_{ab}, w_\varnothing\}$ as our logical space, where a, b $\in$ P are proposition letters and the index in $w_x$ gives the proposition letters true in world $w_x$. For example, in $w_a$, a is true and b is false, whereas in $w_\varnothing$ both a and b are false. For the case of a plain disjunction like (55a), Franke (2009, 2011) predicts as unique optimal state the state in (55b) (assuming a and b are both relevant and that a, b, and $a \wedge b$ are alternatives to $a \vee b$).

(55) a. $a \vee b$ [plain disjunction]
b. $\text{opt}(a \vee b) = \{\{w_a, w_b\}\}$
c. predicted implicatures: $\Diamond_e a \wedge \Diamond_e b, \Box_e \neg(a \wedge b), \neg(a \wedge b), \ldots$

The information state $\{ w_a, w_b \}$ describes a belief state of an agent who believes that exactly one out of a and b is true and is uncertain which one. That $\{ w_a, w_b \}$ is optimal means that $a \vee b$ is predicted to be the most rational/pragmatically efficient sentence to use for a speaker in such a state. If the speaker had known which of a and b is true, she would have played the language game better saying so, and similarly had she thought that a and b are both true. Some of the implicatures of an utterance of (55a) are given in (55c). Implicatures are thus inferences from the abducted rational explanation of the speaker's observed behavior.

Examples (56) and (57) similarly give the predictions of Franke (2009, 2011) for disjunction under epistemic modals. Epistemic FC-implicatures are derived for both the possibility and the necessity case.[15]

(56) a. $\Diamond_e (a \vee b)$ [epistemic possibility]
b. $opt(\Diamond_e (a \vee b)) = \{\{w_a, w_b\}, \{w_a, w_b, w_\varnothing\}\}$
c. predicted implicatures: $\Diamond_e a \wedge \Diamond_e b, \neg \Diamond_e (a \wedge b), \ldots$

(57) a. $\Box_e (a \vee b)$ [epistemic necessity]
b. $opt(\Box_e (a \vee b)) = \{\{w_a, w_b\}, \{w_a, w_b, w_{ab}\}\}$
c. predicted implicatures: $\Diamond_e a \wedge \Diamond_e b, \neg \Box_e (a \wedge b), \ldots$

To be able to state the predictions for deontic modality, let's fix that with $R_d \subseteq W \times W$ being the deontic accessibility relation of the underlying model; $R_d(w) = \{v \in W \mid \langle w, v\rangle \in R_d\}$ is the deontic possibility correspondence. Franke's system then computes the following optimal states (and thereby implicatures) for disjunctions under deontic modals:

(58) a. $\Diamond_d (a \vee b)$ [deontic possibility]
b. $opt(\Diamond_d(a \vee b)) = \{\{w \in W \mid R_d(w) = \{w_a, w_b\}\},$
$\{w \in W \mid R_d(w) = \{w_a, w_b, w_\varnothing\}\}\}$
c. predicted implicatures: $\Diamond_d a \wedge \Diamond_d b, \neg\Diamond_d(a \wedge b), \ldots$

(59) a. $\Box_d(a \vee b)$ [deontic necessity]
b. $opt(\Box_d (a \vee b)) = \{\{w \in W \mid R_d(w) = \{w_a, w_b\}\}\}$
c. predicted implicatures: $\Diamond_d a \wedge \Diamond_d b, \neg \Box_d(a \wedge b), \ldots$

Given a notion of implicature in terms of optimal states, the next question to address is how optimal states should be merged with information states in dynamic semantics. The most natural way of doing so is simply to add the information that is contained in *all* the optimal states in $opt(\phi)$ after updating with $\phi$ (cf. Aloni 2012):

**Definition 2 (Implicature uptake)** $\sigma[\phi+I] = \sigma[\phi] \cap \bigcup(opt(\phi))$.

As a first illustration consider the uptaking of the implicatures of plain disjunction, starting from a state of minimal information:

(60) $\{w_a, w_b, w_{ab}, w_\varnothing\}[(a \vee b) + I] = \{w_a, w_b, w_{ab}\} \cap \{w_a, w_b\} = \{w_a, w_b\}$

We first update with $a \vee b$, which eliminates $w_\varnothing$, and then intersect the output state with the optimal state for $a \vee b$. The resulting state supports both the scalar implicature $\neg (a \wedge b)$, and the clausal implicature $\Diamond_e a \wedge \Diamond_e b$. However, there is a crucial difference between these two inferences, the first is persistent, the second is anti-persistent:

(61) $\phi$ is persistent iff if $\sigma \models \phi$ and $\tau \subseteq \sigma$, then $\tau \models \phi$.

(62) $\phi$ is anti-persistent iff if $\sigma \models \phi$ and $\sigma \subseteq \tau$, then $\tau \models \phi$.

In a propositional system, $\sigma$ is at least as strong as $\tau$ iff $\sigma \subseteq \tau$. Negative sentences like $\neg(a \wedge b)$ are persistent because they assert the unavailability of a possibility, namely the possibility that a and b are both true. Eliminating possibilities (going to a smaller state) will never make that possibility available. Epistemic possibility sentences like $\Diamond_e a \wedge \Diamond_e b$ instead are not persistent because they express the availability of two epistemic possibilities that might fail to be available as soon as more information is achieved (if the state gets smaller). Actually $\Diamond_e a \wedge \Diamond_e b$ is anti-persistent because if an epistemic possibility is available, it will stay available if we enlarge our state.

Since $\sigma[\phi + I] \subseteq \sigma[\phi]$ (by definition of +I in terms of intersection), uptaking anti persistent implicatures is vacuous in the following sense: if $\psi$ is anti-persistent and $\sigma[\phi + I] \models \psi$, then $\sigma[\phi] \models \psi$. As we saw, epistemic FC-implicatures are anti-persistent. Deontic FC-implicatures instead are persistent: $\Diamond_d a \wedge \Diamond_d b$ expresses a property of all available possibilities, namely that they can deontically access both a-worlds and b-worlds. Adding possibilities might affect the validity of this universal property, but eliminating possibilities will not. But then uptaking epistemic FC-implicatures is vacuous, while uptaking deontic FC-implicatures is not:

(63) $\sigma[\phi + I] \models \Diamond_e a \wedge \Diamond_e b$ implies $\sigma[\phi] \models \Diamond_e a \wedge \Diamond_e b$
$\sigma[\phi + I] \models \Diamond_d a \wedge \Diamond_d b$ doesn't imply $\sigma[\phi] \models \Diamond_d a \wedge \Diamond_d b$

Examples (64) and (65) illustrate these facts.

(64) $\{w_a\}[\Box_e (a \vee b) + I] = \{w_a\} \cap \{w_a, w_b, w_{ab}\} = \{w_a\}$

(65) $\sigma[\Box_d (a \vee b) + I] = \sigma \cap \{w \in W \mid R_d (w) = \{w_a , w_b\}\}$
$= \{w \in W \mid R_d (w) = \{w_a, w_b\}\}$
where $\sigma = \{w \in W \mid R_d (w) = \{w_a\}\} \cup \{w \in W \mid R_d (w) = \{w_a, w_b \}\}$.

These considerations of persistence tell us that epistemic FC-inferences (due to anti-persistence and vacuity) are not relevant in the usual information-accumulating sense of dynamic semantics. Deontic FC-implicatures, on the other hand, are. Again, we need to stress for clarity that we do not claim that the dynamic formalization as such *proves* that this contrast is real across the board, but merely pins down in a formally traceable manner our intuition that epistemic and modal information are not on equal footing in normal information-seeking discourse.

We conclude this section by briefly discussing how the dynamic account we have just sketched can be employed to explain the three case-studies which constituted our point of departure. Let us assume that such a dynamic account would extend to existential statements in much the way one would expect with only deontic FC-inference derivable via application of +I (see Aloni 2012):

(66) Deontic: $\Box_d \exists x \phi + I \models \forall x \Diamond_d \phi$

(67) Epistemic: $\Box_e \exists x \phi + I \models \forall x \Diamond_e \phi$

*Concessive scalar particles*. Given the fact that only deontic FC-implicatures can be uptaken in a non-vacuous way, the possibility of adding +I can rescue *magari under deontic, but not under epistemic modals. Assuming a dynamic version of Crnič (2011b), the scalar presupposition triggered by EVEN in the deontic case is plausible (68c), while in the epistemic case it is contradictory (69c).

(68) a. You must win **magari* a bronze$_F$ medal.
b. EVEN$_C$$^{o}$' [$\Box_d$ [AT LEAST$_C$ [you win bronze$_F$ ]] + I]
c. Scalar presupposition triggered by EVEN:
$\Box_d$ (bronze $\vee$ silver $\vee$ gold) $\wedge$ ($\Diamond_d$ bronze $\wedge$ $\Diamond_d$ silver $\wedge$ $\Diamond_d$ gold) $<_c$ $\Box_d$ (silver $\vee$ gold) $\wedge$ ($\Diamond_d$ silver $\wedge \Diamond_d$ gold), $\Box_d$ gold $\wedge$ $\Diamond_d$ gold

(69) a. #You must have won **magari* a bronze$_F$ medal.
b. EVEN$_C$$^{o}$ [$\Box_e$ [AT LEAST$_C$ [you have won bronze$_F$ ]] + I]
c. Scalar presupposition triggered by EVEN:
$\Box_e$ (bronze $\vee$ silver $\vee$ gold) $<_c$ $\Box_e$ (silver $\vee$ gold), $\Box_e$ gold

*Epistemic indefinites*. Building on Aloni and Port (2010), we propose that both *irgendein* and *vreun* are existentials which trigger an obligatory domain shift (either CC-shift or DW), which has to come for a reason. Recall that DW is justified only if it does not create a weaker statement, and that under a modal, as shown in (28) here rewritten as (70), DW ceases to create a weaker statement only if FC-inferences are incorporated:

(70) a. $\Box \exists x \varphi \models \Box \exists x_{DW} \varphi$ without FC-inference
b. $\Box \exists x \varphi \wedge \forall x \Diamond \varphi \not\models \Box \exists x_{DW} \varphi \wedge \forall x_{DW} \Diamond \varphi$ with FC-inference

But then since only deontic FC-inferences can be uptaken in a non-vacuous way (66), when incorporating FC-implicatures via +I, DW can be justified in the *deontic* case, but not in the *epistemic* case:

(71) Deontic: $\Box_d \exists x\ \phi + I \not\models \Box_d \exists x_{DW}\ \phi + I$ DW justified
Epistemic: $\Box_e \exists x\ \phi + I \mid\not\models \Box_e \exists x_{DW}\ \phi + I$ DW unjustified

Normally optional, +I becomes then obligatory in uses of *irgendein* under deontic modals: CC-shifts are vacuous in these contexts and without implicature uptake DW would also have been unjustified. Total variation (FC) effects are then predicted to arise systematically for the German indefinite in deontic contexts:

(72) Mary musste irgendeinen Mann heiraten.
Mary had_to *irgend*_one man marry
'Mary had to marry a man; any man was a permitted marriage option for her.'
a. # $\Box_d \exists x\, \phi$ — neither CC-shift, nor DW can apply
b. $\Box_d \exists x \phi$ +I — with FC-inference DW can apply

To account for the exclusion of Romanian *vreun* from deontic contexts, we follow Fălăuş (2009, 2011, 2012) in assuming that *vreun* expresses a ban on total variation.[16] But then rescuing the indefinite under deontic modals via +I is no longer possible:

(73) # Trebuie să citesc vreo carte până mâine.
must SUBJ read.1SG *vreun* book by tomorrow
'I must read some book by tomorrow.'
a. # $\Box_d \exists x \phi$ — neither CC-shift, nor DW can apply
b. # $\Box_d \exists x \varphi$ +I — clashes with anti-total variation

The epistemic case works similarly for Romanian and German. As shown in (71), DW cannot apply under epistemic modals, but then CC-shift must apply and only a cover-dependent partial variation effect is generated:

(74) a. Juan must be in *irgendeinem/vreun* room of the house.
b. $\Box_e \exists x \phi$ — only CC-shift can apply, partial variation generated

The infelicity of *vreun* in the SHELL GAME SCENARIO described in (8) can be accounted for again in terms of a clash with an independently generated anti-total variation inference.

## 7. Conclusion

Summing up, we have here reviewed evidence from three independent case-studies that the FC-inferences associated with deontic modals appear more "semanticized" than their epistemic counterparts. Taking the possibility of local pragmatic effects seriously, but noting that the usual explanation for the distribution of local pragmatic effects in terms of the *strongest meaning hypothesis* (cf. Chierchia to appear b; Chierchia *et al.* 2012; Sauerland 2012) does not apply in the case at hand, we tried to give a diachronic pragmatic explanation for the different degree to which deontic and epistemic FC-inferences penetrate into compositional semantics. Our proposal revolves around the notion of pragmatic fossilization, and we argued that deontic FC-inferences are practically relevant more often than epistemic FC-inferences.

We discussed data on universal FC-inferences in favor of this claim and showed how this difference cashes out in dynamic semantics as a difference in persistence of the FC-information. In sum, according to our proposal, it is essentially basic features of contextual relevance that affect why some inferences penetrate compositional semantics more readily than others, even to the extent that these asymmetries in fossilization patterns inform grammaticality judgments (as in the case of *vreun* or **magari*).

An important conceptual question is how this explanation of the Modal Variability Hypothesis relates to the "grammatical view" of scalar implicatures, as championed by Chierchia (2006, to appear a) and others. As mentioned before, our account acknowledges the possibility of local pragmatic effects, but, migrating beyond applications of the strongest meaning hypothesis, we have tried to give a diachronic pragmatic explanation for the distribution of these. This essentially commits us to a particular interpretation of the "grammatical view." In a recent paper, Chierchia (to appear b) argues that the "grammatical view" of scalar implicature calculation *can* (but need not) be seen as a stepwise expansion of the more confined classical Gricean reasoning that has long been taken for gospel (Grice 1975). But it can also be considered a purely grammatical thing. What we suggested in this chapter commits us to consider the "grammatical view" in the first manner, as *intrinsically pragmatic*, even if integrated into formal semantic theory – that is, subject to general functionalist considerations about language use. This is opposed to a *strictly* grammatical view which would consider language an object of inquiry on its own, detached from issues of language use, that would then not admit functional considerations to play a role in explanations of local pragmatic effects.

Even if equivalent in terms of actual predictions, there is a conceptual difference between these two perspectives on the "grammatical view" that shows if we look at which *auxiliary assumptions* would be deemed feasible to adapt the formalism to new sets of empirical data. The data we discussed in Section 2 is such a set of novel empirical data that challenges the current formulation of the "grammatical view," in particular, its sole reliance on the strongest meaning hypothesis to account for the distribution of embedded implicatures. To account for (something like) the Modal Variability Hypothesis, an intrinsically pragmatic grammatical view can appeal to differences in frequencies of contextual relevance. But a strict grammatical view cannot. Viable explanations for the strict grammatical view could involve stipulating (and motivating) formal differences in the way different modals interact with domain alternatives and the like. No knock-down argument has been given here that the Modal Variability Hypothesis cannot be explained in terms of a strict grammatical view. But the burden of proof that modal variability is amenable to a strictly non-pragmatic explanation lies with those who favor this view.

## Acknowledgments

This research has been largely inspired by the work of Gennaro Chierchia: mostly by his recent research on free choice and local implicatures but also by his less recent contributions on dynamic semantics. Maria Aloni would further like to thank Gennaro Chierchia for supervising her 1996 Master thesis on "Dynamic semantics and epistemic modalities," and for his contagious passion for linguistic research: as this article tries to demonstrate, in even the most intricate empirical data some logical pattern can be found. We also thank Stephanie Solt and four anonymous reviewers for helpful comments, as well as the financial support of the Netherlands Organization for Scientific Research (NWO).


## Appendix 5A Formal definitions supporting Section 6

Let P be a set of *proposition letters* and, with $p \in P$, let $L^*$ be the *propositional base language*, i.e., the smallest set that contains P such that if $\phi, \psi \in L^*$, then also $\neg\phi \in L^*$ and $\phi \wedge \psi \in L^*$. Let L be the *modal language* we are interested in that, for simplicity, does not allow nesting of modal operators, defined in the usual way as the smallest set that contains $L^*$ such that if $\phi, \psi \in L$, then also $\neg\phi \in L$ and $\phi \wedge \psi \in L$ and if $\phi \in L^*$, then also $\Box_e\phi \in L$ and $\Box_d\phi \in L$. Additionally, the usual notational variants apply:

$$\phi \vee \psi \equiv \neg(\neg\phi \wedge \neg\psi) \qquad \Diamond_e\phi \equiv \neg\Box_e\neg\phi \qquad \Diamond_d\phi \equiv \neg\Box_d\neg\phi.$$

A *model* for language L is a triple $M = \langle W, V, (R_d) \rangle$ such that: W is a set of worlds, $V: W \times P \rightarrow \{0, 1\}$ is a *valuation function*, and $R_d \subseteq W \times W$ is a *deontic accessibility relation*. We require that $R_d$ is *serial*, i.e., for each $w \in W$ there is some $v \in W$ such that $\langle w, v \rangle \in R_d$. We define static truth conditions for a formula $\phi \in L^*$ with respect to a model and a world in that model in the standard way:

$$\begin{array}{lll} M, w \vDash p & \text{iff} & V(w,p) = 1 \\ M, w \vDash \neg\phi & \text{iff} & \text{not } M, w \vDash \phi \\ M, w \vDash \phi \wedge \psi & \text{iff} & M, w \vDash \phi \text{ and } M, w \vDash \psi \\ M, w \vDash \Box_d\phi & \text{iff} & \text{for all } v \in W: <w, v> \in R_d \rightarrow M, v \vDash \phi \end{array}$$

Entailment is defined as usual: $\phi \models \psi$ iff for all M, w if $M, w \models \phi$, then $M, w \models \psi$.

An information state $\sigma$ based on a given model M with possible worlds W is just a subset of W. Let $\Sigma_M$ be the set of all information states for model M. The semantics for expressions in L is given for a fixed model M in terms of *context change potentials*, i.e., a function $\Sigma_M \times L \rightarrow \Sigma_M$. Using standard notation this function is defined as follows:

$$\begin{array}{llll} \sigma\,[p] & = & [w \in \sigma | M, w \vDash p] & \\ \sigma\,[\neg\phi] & = & \sigma - \sigma[\phi] & \\ \sigma\,[\phi \wedge \psi] & = & \sigma[\phi][\psi] & \\ \sigma\,[\Box_e\phi] & = & \{w \in \sigma | \sigma[\varphi] = \sigma\} & \text{(test)} \\ \sigma\,[\Box_d\phi] & = & \{w \in \sigma | M, w \vDash \Box_d\phi\} & \text{(eliminative update)} \end{array}$$

The dynamic interpretation of epistemic modals is a *test*: update with $\Box_e\phi$ either yields the input state or the empty set. This is because epistemic information is of a higher-order type than base-level information. Deontic modality, however, is defined as an eliminative update that adds information *in the same way* as propositional information. Finally, we say that an information state σ that is non-empty *supports* a formula ϕ, $\sigma \models \phi$, iff $\sigma[\phi] = \sigma$.

## NOTES

1. Fălăuş does not explicitly work out this line of explanation, but this seems to be her strategy as is clear from passages like the following: "... I take these facts to indicate that deontic modals with existentials activating alternatives in their scope have a strong free choice flavor, i.e., they give rise to a total variation inference. As we have seen, epistemic operators do not impose such a requirement. This distinct behavior should follow from the semantics of these modals, something which cannot be properly explored here" (Fălăuş 2012: 43).
2. These analyses are not necessarily faithful to the meaning of English *even* and *at least*.
3. Indeed, Crnič (2011a) adopts Fox's (2007a) approach to generate FC-effects, but as we have already observed, Fox's machinery is blind towards the differences between deontic and epistemic modals and therefore overgenerates: potentially rescuing FC-inferences are derived also in the scope of epistemic modals. Crnič (2011a) notes this problem and expresses a hope that it might disappear on the account of the differences in felicity of the scalar presuppositions triggered by EVEN. For example, for a doxastic sentence like "John thinks that Peter wins **magari* a bronze medal," Crnič (2011a) predicts the quite implausible presupposition "that there is an alternative that is more likely than that John thinks that Peter won a medal and that he might have won any medal" (Crnič 2011a: 126). We agree that this presupposition is implausible (see also our discussion in Section 4), but it is not contradictory (in contrast to the presupposition triggered by EVEN in (18)). But then such an explanation might be too weak for a proper account of the systematic exclusion of **magari* from epistemic contexts.
4. See Crnič (2011a: 11, footnote 12). In the same footnote, Crnič also mentions a different possible strategy to account for the data building on Heim's (1992) non-monotonic, preference-based semantics for bouletic modals. If deontic modals were non-monotonic, we would not need to rely on an FC-effect to account for the data. Crnič (2011a) discusses this strategy in more detail, but, as far as we understand, dismisses it because of lack of independent evidence for the non-monotonic behavior of deontic operators.
5. In FC-uses, *irgendein* is typically stressed. Notice that stressing *irgendein* under epistemic modals as in (24) results in oddity.
6. Actually Aloni's (2007b) assumption that under necessity modals no FC-inferences are generated was crucial for her explanation of the distribution of *any* in terms of Kadmon and Landman's (1993) analysis. In this section we will adopt Chierchia's account of polarity and free choice, therefore that assumption is no longer needed.
7. Most semantic theories of FC-inferences do share this problem with Aloni (2007b) (also Barker 2011) with the exception of performative accounts like van Rooij (2000). Performative accounts however fail to explain FC-inferences of non-performative uses of deontic modals (e.g., in the past tense).

8. An alternative explanation of the variability in UFC-potential revolves around the notion of *homogeneity*. The idea is that the availability of an UFC-inference like in (41) is proportional to the plausibility of the assumption that everybody in the group has the same rights, i.e., that the group is homogeneous (Franke 2011; van Tiel 2011). Our proposal here is orthogonal to this issue. According to the picture sketched here, homogeneity assumptions may very well affect the availability of UFC-inferences for de-contextualized sentences. All we claim here is independent of that: we argue merely that, if a proper context is supplied, then the contextual relevance of certain information will affect the availability of an UFC-inference. It is not crucial for our purposes here whether homogeneity assumptions mingle in some fashion or other with considerations of relevance.
9. It is important to note that we propose that it is the inferred *information* that is at stake, not the relevance of contextually given *alternatives*. This is important, because, as a helpful reviewer correctly pointed out to us, the subsequent discussion about differences in contextual availability of UFC could possibly be accounted for as well by a theory that treats UFC inferences purely as a grammatical phenomenon in the vein of Chierchia (2006, to appear a, to appear b) or Chierchia *et al.* (2012) with a pragmatic constraint on contextually relevant alternatives. However, we are not sure, at the present moment, how suitable and justified restrictions on relevant alternatives could do the trick. This is not to say that this is necessarily impossible, but until proven, we stick to the distinction between relevant information and relevant alternatives and therefore prefer accounts where both relevant interpretations *and* relevant alternatives are explicitly handled, such as done in optimality theory (e.g., Aloni 2007a), game-theoretic approaches (e.g., Franke 2011) or Geurts's (2011) intention-driven account. Be that as it may, this issue does not really matter for our overall argument.
10. Grice already stated: "It may not be impossible for what starts life, so to speak, as a conversational implicature to become conventionalized" (Grice 1975: 58). This idea has been later explored by many researchers, notably Hopper and Traugott (1993).
11. A reviewer raised an important point here, namely whether we would predict different stages of fossilization in different languages and/or for different types of modals. To answer this question, more detailed and more quantitative data would be necessary. In principle, we would expect some differences, but the main tendency that deontic FC-inferences fossilize stronger and more readily should be universally attested.
12. A fragment of a minimal system that covers the formal details necessary for our present concerns is given in Appendix 5A.
13. Another natural idea is to treat deontic modals as performative elements that change obligations and permissions (e.g., Kamp 1973; van Rooij 2000), which is straightforwardly modeled in dynamic semantics. However, we believe that performative analyses are problematic, for instance, because they cannot straightforwardly explain FC-inferences in the past tense, etc. (see also note 7). It is therefore often attempted to derive performative effects from informative uses of deontic modals, e.g., under the assumption that the speaker is an authority (e.g., Kaufmann 2012).
14. Other approaches to the calculation of FC-implicatures (e.g., Fox 2007a) would equally qualify, but would require more conceptual shifting to yield a description of optimal states.

15. To be able to distinguish between partial variation and total variation we would need at least three alternatives. For $\Diamond/\Box$ (a $\vee$ b $\vee$ c) Aloni (2007a), for example, does indeed predict the total variation FC-implicature $\Diamond a \wedge \Diamond b \wedge \Diamond c$ without further ado; Franke's system needs extra assumptions, but can achieve the same thing.
16. This ban on total variation should be derived as a blocking effect. The availability of a specialized total variation indefinite in Romanian (but not in German) blocks the FC-interpretation of *vreun* expressed in (73b). No other interpretation is compatible with the felicity conditions. The indefinite is predicted to be out under deontic modals.

# 6 Implicatures of modified numerals

*Clemens Mayr*

## 1. Introduction

While bare numerals such as in the sentence in (1) usually receive an exact-interpretation, numerals modified by comparative *more than* or superlative *at least* such as in (2) do not give rise to such an interpretation.

(1) Three boys attended the party.

(2) a. More than three boys attended the party.
b. At least three boys attended the party.

Krifka (1999) and Fox and Hackl (2006) show that this state of affairs is surprising. If a scalar implicature were factored into the basic meaning of the sentences in (2), an exact-interpretation should result. For instance, for (2b) a scalar implicature negating the stronger alternative proposition *at least 4 boys attended the party* would have the effect that exactly three boys attended the party, where the implicature is combined with the basic interpretation of (2b).

The present chapter has three main objectives: first, I will discuss novel data that strongly suggest that the examples in (2) should be treated on a par. On the one hand, numerals modified by *more than* are shown to not have scalar implicatures in exactly those environments where numerals modified by *at least* lack them as well. On the other hand, it is furthermore shown that if one of the two types of modified numerals occurs embedded in an environment where a scalar implicature is nevertheless triggered, the same holds for the other. Second, by investigating these details, I suggest a new descriptive generalization which any account of (2) should incorporate. Third, I argue that currently existing accounts for the facts in (2) are not completely satisfying empirically. The fully predictive theory by Fox and Hackl (2006), in particular, unfortunately only covers cases with comparative *more than* going against the picture argued for in this paper. Because of this defect, I turn to the discussion of two closely related approaches. Both stipulate certain alternatives that are put to use by the implicature generating mechanism, and in both accounts the alternatives are of such a form that negating one of them contradicts the negation of another one. Thus neither is negated, and no scalar implicature is derived. On both accounts it moreover follows that when embedded under certain operators the modified numeral can introduce an implicature. But I also show that the accounts of the facts in (2) both have certain problems. First, I discuss accounts making use of *exactly n* alternatives for modified numerals (for instance, Spector 2005). Both the neo-Gricean version and the grammatical view of scalar implicatures are shown to run into problems: they predict truth conditions that are too strong. Another theory making use of non-monotonic alternatives is suggested. It will, however, be seen that unless a way is found to contextually restrict the set of available alternatives, truth conditions are predicted that are again not in accordance with our intuitions.

The paper is structured as follows: in Section 2 I review the neo-Gricean theory of scalar implicatures and the problem presented by the data in (2). Section 3 discusses some novel data and presents evidence that the facts in (2) should be handled by one theory by investigating in detail under which circumstances scalar implicatures appear for modified numerals. Section 4 proposes a novel generalization. Section 5 argues that existing accounts run into problems with the data discussed in the preceding sections. In Section 6, I present the two related approaches relying on the structure of the alternatives to account for the problem. Section 7 concludes the paper.

## 2. The problem

### *2.1 Gricean reasoning and bare numerals*

It has long been noted that numerals should not receive an exact-interpretation but rather an at-least-interpretation as their basic non-strengthened denotation.[1] The exact-interpretation intuitively associated with sentences embedding a numeral should be treated as resulting from an inference, in particular a scalar implicature based on the hearer's reasoning employing Grice's 1975 maxim of quantity (cf. Gazdar 1979; Horn 1972; Levinson 1983, a.m.o.). The maxim of quantity essentially states that if two sentences $\varphi$ and $\psi$ are both relevant in the conversation, and $\varphi$ is more informative than $\psi$ – i.e., the denotation of $\varphi$ asymmetrically entails the one of $\psi$ – and the speaker believes both $\varphi$ and $\psi$ to be true, the speaker should choose $\varphi$ over $\psi$.

Consider a current version of this theory, often called neo-Gricean. (3) has an exact-inference. In particular it has the inference associated with it that Jack did not read (at least) four books (non-entailment inferences are represented by $\rightsquigarrow$ throughout the chapter) or any larger number of books. This taken together with the basic inference obtained from the assertion that Jack read at least three books derives the strengthened inference that Jack read exactly three books.

(3) Jack read three books.
⤳ Jack did not read four books or more.

According to Horn (1972) scalar items are lexically collected in sets ordered by informativeness. The following are relevant Horn-sets {or, and}, {some, all}, {1, 2, 3, 4, …}. From these sets of scalar alternatives one derives a set of alternative sentences *Alt*(S) for a given sentence S by replacing the members of a given Horn-set with each other (Sauerland 2004). The neo-Gricean version of the maxim of quantity can then be stated as follows:

(4) Maxim of quantity
In world w of evaluation if $\varphi$ and $\psi$ are both relevant in the conversation, $\varphi \subset \psi$, $\varphi \in \mathrm{Alt}(\psi)$, and the speaker believes both $\varphi(w) = 1$ and $\psi(w) = 1$, the speaker should choose $\varphi$ over $\psi$.

For (3) this means that the hearer reasons as follows: the speaker believes that Jack read at least three books, which corresponds to the literal interpretation of (3). This is the basic inference in (5a), and it follows from Grice's maxim of quality, which says that a speaker should not present something as true that she believes to be false. Moreover, *Alt* (3) includes the stronger propositions that Jack read four books, that Jack read five books and so on. Since these would also have been relevant to the topic of conversation, the speaker should have chosen one of these stronger propositions if she believed them to be true. But the speaker did not choose any of them. The hearer therefore concludes that the speaker does not believe any of these to be true (in particular, (5b) follows). Sauerland (2004: 383) argues that if nothing in the context precludes it, the hearer will further strengthen (5b) to (5c), that is, the speaker does not believe that Jack read four books. In particular, this process of strengthening is allowed to apply when no contradiction results.[2] In the present example strengthening (5b) to (5c) does not lead to a contradiction. The stronger inference (5c), together with the speaker's belief that the basic meaning of (3) is true, leads the hearer to conclude (5d), which is equivalent to the strengthened inference that the speaker believes that John read exactly three books (in the following $B_S p$ denotes *'the speaker believes p'*).

(5) a. *Basic inference of* (3): $B_S$(that Jack read at least 3 books)
b. *Scalar inference of* (3): $\neg B_S$(that Jack read at least 4 books)
c. *Strengthened scalar inference of* (3): $B_S \neg$(that Jack read at least 4 books)
d. *Strengthened inference of* (3):
$B_S$(that Jack read at least 3 books) $\wedge$ $B_S \neg$(that Jack read at least 4 books)

It can now be seen why Horn-alternatives are necessary. Without such stipulated alternatives one would derive for (3) also an alternative proposition stating that Jack read three books but not four. This alternative is also strictly stronger than the basic interpretation of (3), and therefore by the same reasoning process as discussed above, the inference that the speaker does not believe that Jack read three books but not four would be drawn, i.e., the speaker does not believe that Jack read exactly three books. But if that inference were derived, the strengthened scalar inference in (5c) could not be drawn. Together with the basic inference it would contradict the inference that the speaker does not believe that Jack read exactly three books. In fact, this latter inference could also not be strengthened to the inference that the speaker believes that Jack did not read exactly three books. Together with the basic inference it would entail that Jack read more than three books. But this contradicts the basic scalar inference in (5b). In other words, no strengthened inference could be drawn at all. For this reason the problem that would arise without Horn-alternatives is termed the symmetry problem. No strengthened scalar inference as in (5c) could ever be drawn.[3]

Evidence for the claim that numerals have the at-least-interpretation as their denotation and moreover form a Horn-set can be attained when embedding them in downward-entailing (DE) contexts. It is known that implicatures tend to disappear in such environments (cf. Chierchia 2004; Gazdar 1979). This makes the prediction that the exact-interpretation of *three* in (3) should disappear or be weakened when the sentence is embedded in a DE context if the exact-interpretation is derived via an implicature. If *three*, however, had the exact-interpretation as its denotation, DE contexts should not affect the availability of the exact-interpretation. Embedding (3) in DE contexts such as clausal negation (6a), the antecedent of a conditional (6b), or the restrictor of a universal quantifier (6c) suggests that the former option is correct because in these contexts the exact-interpretation of the numeral *three* is systematically suspended.[4]

(6) a. Jack didn't read three books.
$\rightsquigarrow$ Jack didn't read four books.
b. If Jack read three books, he can participate in the course.
$\rightsquigarrow$ If Jack read four books, he can participate.
c. Everyone who read three books can participate.
$\rightsquigarrow$ Everyone who read four books can participate.

## 2.2 *The absence of implicatures with modified numerals*

Krifka (1999: 258) notes that sentences embedding *at least n* – that is, numerals *n* modified by the superlative *at least* – do not lead to an implicature that *not at least n + 1*. If (7) licensed such an inference, it would be taken to imply that Jack read exactly three books.

(7) Jack read at least three books.
$\not\rightsquigarrow$ Jack did not read at least four books.

Fox and Hackl (2006: 540) note that numerals *n* modified by the comparative *more than* similarly do not give rise to an implicature that *not more than n + 1*. Otherwise (8) would imply that Jack read exactly four books.

(8) Jack read more than three books.
⇝̸ Jack did not read more than four books.

This behavior is unexpected. If scalar implicatures are derived as argued, then (7) and (8) should have the unobserved interpretations, and if bare numerals form a Horn-set even more so. Two types of approaches have been suggested to deal with these data to my knowledge. On the one hand, *at least* has been claimed by Krifka (1999) and Nouwen (2008) to behave similar to *only* in that it consumes the scalar alternatives in its scope (Rooth 1992) and leaves no alternatives to be evaluated for higher operators, i.e., the implicature generating mechanism has no alternatives to operate on because *at least* uses up the alternatives of the numeral. On the other hand, Fox and Hackl (2006) propose a detailed theory of why implicatures are missing for *more than n*, making use of the assumption that all measurement scales in natural language are dense. Their argument does not carry over to *at least n*. Therefore another theory, for instance one like the first one mentioned, is needed on top of Fox and Hackl's (2006) one.[5] In the following section I will discuss data that suggest that this position is untenable: implicatures appear under certain conditions for both *more than n* and *at least n*. And crucially these conditions are the same for both types of modified numerals.[6] This does not follow from Fox and Hackl's (2006) account, and is also unexpected if *at least* consumes the alternatives of the numeral. I will return to their account in Section 5, where in addition I point out a false empirical prediction.

## 3. Characterization of the problem

### *3.1 Fox and Hackl's 2006 observation and a novel observation*

Modified numerals do sometimes have scalar implicatures: Fox and Hackl (2006: 544) make the crucial observation that universal modals reintroduce the implicature of *more than n* (9), whereas existential modals do not do so (10). In other words, in case *more than n* is embedded under a universal modal, an exact interpretation becomes available, but not if it is embedded under an existential modal.

(9) Jack is required to read more than three books.
⇝ Jack is not required to read more than four books.

(10) Jack is allowed to read more than three books.
⇝̸ Jack is not allowed to read more than four books.

From this observation Fox and Hackl proceed to develop an interesting analysis, which will be discussed in detail in Section 5 below. As will be seen there, their analysis correctly captures the fact that *more than n* only triggers a scalar implicature when embedded under a universal modal. They do not intend their analysis to be applied to numerals modified by the superlative *at least*. That is, the non-availability of a scalar implicature in (7) should have different roots than the one in (8).

Fox and Hackl do not note that *at least n* shows a behavior parallel to the one of *more than n* when it comes to the appearance of scalar implicatures under embedding. Only in a sentence where *at least n* is embedded under a universal modal does the exact interpretation become possible:

(11) Jack is required to read at least three books.
⇝ Jack is not required to read at least four books.

(12) Jack is allowed to read at least three books.
⇝̸ Jack is not allowed to read at least four books.

The parallelism observed between *more than n* and *at least n* is interesting insofar as it might suggest that a unified approach to the lack of scalar implicatures in (7) and (8) could after all be called for, contrary to Fox and Hackl's (2006) suggestions. In the following, I investigate when scalar implicatures appear with modified numerals and when they do not do so strengthening this initial suspicion.

### 3.2 *When are scalar implicatures generated?*

Universal modals allow for the appearance of scalar implicatures with both *more than n* and *at least n*. This leads us to expect that conditionals should also license scalar implicatures with modified numerals under Stalnaker's (1975) analysis and the approach advocated by Kratzer (1979, 1986) where conditionals are analyzed with implicit universal quantification. This is indeed the case. (13a) implies that there is a world where John is well prepared and he read exactly four books, whereas (13b) implies that there is a world where John is well prepared and he read exactly three books.[7]

(13) a. If John is well prepared, he read more than three books.
⇝ Not in all worlds where John is well prepared he read more than four books.
b. If John is well prepared, he read at least three books.
⇝ Not in all worlds where John is well prepared he read at least four books.

Embedding the modified numeral in the restrictor of the universal quantifier does not affect the availability of the implicature, which has not been pointed out to my knowledge. Only the entailment pattern is reversed, as the restrictor of a conditional is DE and DE contexts change entailment patterns. Therefore the stronger alternatives to, say, *three* are now all the numerals smaller than *three*. (14a) suggests that there is a world where John read exactly three books and he is not well prepared. Similarly, in (14b) there is a world where John read exactly two books and he is not well prepared.

(14) a. If John read more than three books, he is well prepared.
↝ Not in all worlds where John read more than two books, he is well prepared.
b. If John read at least three books, he is well prepared.
↝ Not in all worlds where John read at least two books he is well prepared.

Fox and Hackl (2006: 576) note that not only do universal modals allow for the appearance of scalar implicatures with *more than n*, universal quantifiers over individuals do so as well (15a). That is, (15a) does have the inference that at least one person wrote exactly four books. I add that the same holds for *at least n*, (15b). It suggests that someone wrote exactly three books.[8]

(15) a. Everyone wrote more than three books.
↝ Not everyone wrote more than four books.
b. Everyone wrote at least three books.
↝ Not everyone wrote at least four books.

As with conditionals, we find that parallel behavior can be observed by embedding the modified numerals in the restrictor of the universal quantifier. (16a) and (16b) suggest that there is someone who read exactly three books and someone who read exactly two books, respectively, who did not participate.

(16) a. Everyone who read more than three books participated.
↝ Not everyone who read more than two books participated.
b. Everyone who read at least three books participated.
↝ Not everyone who read at least two books participated.

Furthermore, a DE quantifier like *no one* has the same effect, with the caveat that *at least* is not perfect in the scope of negation, presumably due to the fact that *at least n* is a positive polarity item and can therefore not occur under negation.[9] It seems, however, that *at least* is more acceptable in the restrictor of the negative quantifier, which would suggest that it is a local positive polarity item. (17a) implies that someone wrote exactly three books, and (17b) that someone wrote exactly two books. (18a) implies that someone who read exactly three books participated, and (18b) suggests that someone who read exactly two books participated.

(17) a. No one wrote more than three books.
↝ Someone wrote more than two books.
b. ?No one wrote at least three books.
↝ Someone wrote at least two books.

(18) a. No one who read more than three books participated.
↝ Someone who read more than two books participated.
b. No one who read at least three books participated.
↝ Someone who read at least two books participated.

Comparative quantifiers like *more than half of the NPs* also allow for the scalar implicature associated with modified numerals to be generated. (19a) implies that some students wrote exactly four books, while (19b) implies that some of the students wrote exactly three books.

(19) a. More than half of the students wrote more than three books.
↝ At most half of the students wrote more than four books.
b. More than half of the students wrote at least three books.
↝ At most half of the students wrote at least four books.

Moreover, we observe that distributive conjunctions of individuals show a parallel behavior. The examples in (20) suggest that one of John and Mary wrote exactly four books or exactly three books.

(20) a. John and Mary both wrote more than three books.
↝ Not both of John and Mary wrote more than four books.
b. John and Mary both wrote at least three books.
↝ Not both of John and Mary wrote at least four books.

The facts about *no one*, the comparative *more than half*, and distributive conjunction have not been noticed to my knowledge. Let me now turn to discussion of environments where scalar implicatures are not generated.

### 3.3 *When are scalar implicatures not generated?*

We already know that an exact-interpretation is not generated when modified numerals occur non-embedded or under an existential modal. To this list we can add embedding under sentential negation. For discussion of the sentences to follow it is important to have in mind the surface scope interpretation of the relevant sentences. Since the negation is DE, the strength of the alternatives is, of course, reversed. Consider (21a) under this aspect first. It does not seem to imply that Jack read exactly three books, which would be expected if the implicature noted were available. Notice moreover that *not more than n* is equivalent to *at most n*, where *at most* is DE. In other words, (21a) is equivalent to (21b), and it is clear that (21b) does not have the exact-interpretation either.

(21) a. Jack didn't read more than three books.
↝̸ Jack read more than two books.
b. Jack read at most three books.
↝̸ Jack didn't read at most two books.

Similarly, (22a) does not have the exact-interpretation, i.e., it does not have the interpretation that Jack read exactly two books. But (22a) is slightly degraded due to the positive polarity status of *at least n*.[10] The situation is, however, clearer with (22b). Note that *not at least n* is equivalent to *fewer than n*, where *fewer than* is of course DE. (22b) clearly does not have the exact-interpretation.

(22) a. ?Jack didn't read at least three books.
$\not\rightsquigarrow$ Jack read at least two books.
b. Jack read fewer than three books.
$\not\rightsquigarrow$ Jack didn't read fewer than two books.

In other words, the situation observed is parallel to the one discussed for positive environments in that for both types of modified numerals no scalar implicature is generated. And importantly, sentential negation does not pattern with negative quantifiers like *no one* discussed in (17) and (18), which *do* allow scalar implicatures to be generated for modified numerals embedded under them. This difference has not been discussed in the literature so far.

Because of the fact that modified numerals embedded under existential modals do not generate scalar implicatures, we expect that no implicature is generated either when it is embedded in the antecedent of a conditional with an existential modal. This is the case, as (23) shows:

(23) a. If Jack read more than three books, he is allowed to participate.
$\not\rightsquigarrow$ There is no world where Jack read more than four books and he participates.
b. If Jack read at least three books, he is allowed to participate.
$\not\rightsquigarrow$ There is no world where Jack read at least four books and he participates.

Fox and Hackl (2006: 576) also note that existential quantifiers ranging over individuals do not license a scalar implicature for *more than n* (24a). Let me add that we can make the same observation for *at least n* (24b). From what we have seen so far we also expect that modified numerals embedded in the restrictor of an existential quantifier should behave in exactly the same way. This is borne out as shown in (25).

(24) a. Someone wrote more than three books.
$\not\rightsquigarrow$ No one wrote more than four books.
b. Someone wrote at least three books.
$\not\rightsquigarrow$ No one wrote at least four books.

(25) a. Someone who read more than three books participated.
$\not\rightsquigarrow$ No one who read more than four books participated.
b. Someone who read at least three books participated.
$\not\rightsquigarrow$ No one who read (at least) four books participated.

Finally, given that conjunction and disjunction can be seen as a form of universal and existential quantification, respectively, and that embedding of

Table 6.1. *Abbreviations: +: scalar inference possible; −: scalar inference impossible; root: non-embedded context; ¬: sentential negation; ∀: universal quantifier; □: universal modal; ∃: existential quantifier; ◇: existential modal; ¬∃: negative quantifier; >1/2: comparative quantifier; ∧: conjunction; ∨: disjunction. The number below each abbreviation in the top row indicates the section where the relevant data are discussed.*

| Context / Modified Numeral | root (3.2) | ¬ (3.3) | ∀ (3.2) | □ (3.2) | ∃ (3.3) | ◇ (3.3) | ¬∃ (3.2) | >1/2 (3.2) | ∧ (3.2) | ∨ (3.3) |
|---|---|---|---|---|---|---|---|---|---|---|
| more than *n* | − | − | + | + | − | − | + | + | + | − |
| at least *n* | − | − | + | + | − | − | + | + | + | − |

modified numerals under conjunction does allow for scalar inferences, we expect that such inferences are not generated by embedding under a disjunction of individuals. Again, this expectation is confirmed by the novel data in (26).

(26) a. John or Mary wrote more than three books.
⇝̸ Neither John nor Mary wrote more than four books.
b. John or Mary wrote at least three books.
⇝̸ Neither John nor Mary wrote at least four books.

### 3.4 The distribution of scalar implicatures for modified numerals

Given the discussion in this section an empirical picture summarized by Table 6.1 presents itself. Here all the embeddings for modified numerals discussed above are collected. I do not discriminate between restrictor and scope of quantifiers, as we did not find any difference in the behavior of these two environments. Moreover, conditionals are not listed as separate environments. Their behavior is completely dependent on the type of modal chosen.

Fox and Hackl (2006) already observed that universal quantifiers and existential quantifiers allow for the generation of scalar implicatures associated with *more than n*. The novel observations, which will be seen to be crucial later on, are the following: first, sentential negation and negative quantifiers behave differently. Only the latter allow for scalar implicatures of embedded modified numerals, and therefore we cannot conclude that negation in general blocks such inferences. Second, conjunction and disjunction of individuals also differs along the universal–existential divide in that only the former constitute environments for scalar implicatures of modified numerals. But crucially third, comparative quantifiers like *more than half* behave differently from ordinary existential quantifiers in that they do allow for scalar implicatures. In other words, it is not the case that existential quantification per se blocks scalar inferences of modified numerals. And finally, superlative *at least n* is not inherently different from comparative *more than n* when it comes to scalar implicatures. The two types of modified numerals behave in a completely parallel fashion, at least with regards to the environments summarized above. This is, of course, not to say that they might not differ in other respects.

## 4. Towards a generalization

On the basis of the empirical discussion in the preceding section, I now point out an almost obvious difference between examples with modified numerals showing a scalar implicature and examples not doing so. I submit that this fact cannot be a coincidence and propose that it should be the backbone of the descriptive generalization that we wish to account for.

There is a feature that all the examples in Subsection 3.2 share, and that is absent from all the examples surveyed in Subsection 3.3: notice that in the cases where no scalar implicature is generated in a sentence $Op\varphi$ – with $Op$ being a possibly null operator – the interpretation that would have resulted if an implicature had been generated would be entailed by the *basic* interpretation of $Op\psi$, which is just like $Op\varphi$ except that the modified numeral has been replaced by an *exactly n* expression. This is obvious for the cases not involving any quantification. But for the examples involving existential quantifiers this is also the case. Consider (27a) and (27b) again, repeated from (24) above. Factoring in the implicature would have the consequence that (27a) would have as its interpretation the proposition that someone wrote more than three books and no one wrote more than four books. (27b) would have the interpretation that someone wrote three books and no one wrote four books. In other words, in each case the strengthened interpretation of the sentence is entailed by the basic interpretation of a minimally differing sentence with an *exactly n* expression.

(27) a. Someone wrote more than three books.
$\not\leadsto$ No one wrote more than four books.
b. Someone wrote at least three books.
$\not\leadsto$ No one wrote (at least) four books.

The cases in (27) differ from the ones in (28), repeated from (15) above. The strengthened interpretation in (28a) is not entailed by the proposition that everyone wrote exactly four books. And the strengthened interpretation of (28b) is not entailed by the proposition that everyone wrote exactly three books. Both of these propositions would be the basic interpretations of sentences differing from the ones in (28) only in the fact that the modified numeral has been replaced by an *exactly n* expression.

(28) a. Everyone wrote more than three books.
⇝ Not everyone wrote more than four books.
b. Everyone wrote at least three books.
⇝ Not everyone wrote four books.

Parallel facts can be shown to hold for the other operators embedding modified numerals. It is thus natural to conclude that a scalar implicature for a modified numeral like *more than n* or *at least n* is generated whenever this does not partially undo the truth-conditional contribution of *more than* or *at least* and reduces it to essentially the contribution that *exactly* would make for all worlds or individuals quantified over by the embedding operator if such an operator exists. In other words, the scalar implicature is generated as long as a world or individual can remain after strengthening the basic meaning of the sentence such that *more than* or *at least* makes a truth-conditional difference for that world or individual when compared to *exactly*. Simply put, the potential strengthened interpretation of a sentence with a modified numeral in it and all its implicatures factored in ($[[\ ]]^S$) should not be entailed by the basic interpretation of an alternative sentence with an *exactly n* expression in it:

(29) **Generalization**
For any $\varphi$ with a modified numeral $\alpha$ *n* in it, a scalar implicature for $\alpha$ *n* is generated iff $[[\psi]]$ does not entail $[[\varphi]]^S$, where $\psi$ is just like $\varphi$ except that $\alpha$ *n* is replaced by *exactly n+1*, *exactly n−1*, or *exactly n*.

Given this generalization it is furthermore natural to expect that the exact-interpretation of numerals should play a role in the account of the absence of scalar implicatures for modified numerals. Two such possible approaches will be discussed in Section 6. But before doing so, I will discuss in some more depth previous analyses and point out some problems for them.

## 5. "Density" plus something else

In this section I discuss an approach to numerals modified by comparative *more than* which crucially relies on the property of density. It will be seen that another ingredient is needed in order to also account for numerals modified by superlative *at least*. Two things will be argued: first, suggestions found in the literature as to what this additional ingredient might be are not on the right track. Second and more importantly, an approach relying on density makes wrong predictions when it comes to embedding under negation.

Fox and Hackl (2006) argue for the following principle (also cf. Fox 2007b; Nouwen 2008):

(30) **The Universal Density of Measurements (UDM)**
Measurement scales needed for natural language semantics are *always* dense.
(Fox and Hackl 2006: 542)

That is, scales in natural language are set up in such a way that for any two degrees there are infinitely many degrees between the former two. In other words, for any $n$ and $n + \varepsilon$ there is a degree $n + \delta$ such that $n < n + \delta < n + \varepsilon$. This assumption has the consequence that the Horn-set for numerals is not the scale of cardinal numbers $\{1, 2, 3, \ldots\}$ but rather a dense scale. What does this mean for the data at hand? Assume with Hackl (2000) that comparative quantifiers contain a silent *many*. (31) on its basic interpretation then states that the comparative quantifier *more than two girls* applies to a set of degrees $d$ such that there is an individual $x$ that John kissed and the cardinality of $x$ is larger than $d$. This is equivalent to (32a). It is therefore required that John kissed more than two girls, i.e., he kissed $2 + \varepsilon$ girls. But since the number scale is dense, it follows that he also kissed $2 + \varepsilon/2$ girls. The implicature generating mechanism now negates all stronger alternatives to (32a).[11] The potential implicature states that for any degree $d$ larger than $2$ it is not the case John kissed more than $d$-many girls. So he did not kiss more than $n + \varepsilon/2$ girls. But this is contradictory because by the basic interpretation of the assertion in (32a) it is required that John kissed $2 + \varepsilon$ girls. Contradictory implicatures are not generated. Thus (31) is predicted to not have an exact-interpretation.

(31) John kissed more than two girls.

(32) a. $[[(31)]] = \exists x[|x| > 2$ and John kissed $x$ and $x$ is a girl$]$
b. $\forall d[d > 2 \rightarrow \neg$(John kissed more than $d$-many girls)$]$

This type of explanation does not carry over to examples with modification by *at least*. The basic interpretation of (33) states that there is an individual of at least three girls such that John kissed that individual. This is equivalent to saying that John kissed $3$ girls or $3 + \varepsilon$ girls. The potential implicature for (33) states that for all degrees $d$ larger than 3 it is not the case that John kissed at least $d$-many girls. In other words, it cannot be the case that John kissed (at least) $3 + \varepsilon$ girls. But this implicature is consistent with the assertion in (34a), and we get the strengthened interpretation $[[\ ]]^S$ in (34c), where the negated stronger alternatives have been factored into the basic meaning, saying that John kissed exactly three girls.

(33) John kissed at least three girls.

(34) a. $[[(33)]] = \exists x[|x| \geq 3$ and John kissed $x$ and $x$ is a girl$]$
b. $\forall d[d > 3 \rightarrow \neg$(John kissed at least $d$-many girls)$]$
c. $[[(33)]]^S = \exists x[|x| = 3$ and John kissed $x$ and $x$ is a girl$]$

Thus clearly density only predicts the absence of any scalar implicature for sentences with *more than n* in them. Fox and Hackl (2006: fn. 4) suggest that *at least n* is different from *more than n* and the unavailability of the implicature with the former should be accounted for independently.[12] Nouwen (2008) for related reasons suggests to follow Krifka (1999) in the assumption that *at least* consumes the alternatives of the numeral, similar to the effects of the ~ operator argued for by Rooth (1992) (also cf. Beck 2006), so that the implicature generating mechanism has no alternatives to work on anymore. Is such an assumption realistic?

### 5.1 *Similarities between* at least n *and* more than n

As discussed in Subsection 3.1, Fox and Hackl (2006: 544) observe that universal modals reintroduce the implicature of *more than n*, as in (35) repeated from (9) above. Existential modals, however, do not do so, as in (36) repeated from (10) above.

(35) Jack is required to read more than three books.
$\rightsquigarrow$ Jack is not required to read more than four books.

(36) Jack is allowed to read more than three books.
$\not\rightsquigarrow$ Jack is not allowed to read more than four books.

The difference between embedding *more than n* under a universal modal and under an existential one follows naturally under Fox and Hackl's (2006) proposal. Consider first (35). The basic meaning in (37a) states that in all worlds Jack reads more than three books. This means that in all worlds *w* there is a degree $\varepsilon$ such that Jack reads $3 + \varepsilon$ books in *w* and that therefore Jack reads $3 + \varepsilon/2$ books in *w*. The potential implicature in (37b) states that for each degree *d* greater than *3* there is a world *w* such that Jack does not read more than *d*-many books in *w*. If we assume that the modal base over which the modals quantify are the set of worlds corresponding to the dense degrees *d* greater than *3*, then it follows that for each *d* there is a world where Jack reads at most *d*-many books. But the basic meaning in (37a) and the implicature in (37b) are consistent. It is possible that Jack reads more than three books in each world and moreover that for each degree *d* larger than *3* there is a world where Jack reads at most *d*-many books. The strengthened interpretation in (37c) is derived: there is a world where Jack does not read more than four books.[13]

(37) a. $[[(35)]] = \forall w \exists x[|x| > 3$ and Jack reads $x$ and $x$ is a book in $w]$
b. $\forall d[d > 3 \rightarrow \neg\forall w$[Jack reads more than $d$-many books in $w$]
$= \forall d[d > 3 \rightarrow \exists w[\neg$(Jack reads more than $d$-many books in $w$)]
c. $[[(35)]]^S = \forall w \exists x[|x| > 3$ and Jack reads $x$ and $x$ is a book in $w]$ and $\exists w \neg \exists x[|x| >$ 4 and Jack reads $x$ and x is a book in $w]$

The exact interpretation for (36), however, is not allowed. The basic interpretation in (38a) states that in some world Jack read more than three books, i.e., there is a world $w$ where Jack reads $3 + \varepsilon$ books, and thus Jack reads $3 + \varepsilon/2$ books in $w$. The potential implicature requires that for all degrees $d$ greater than $3$ there is no world where Jack read more than $d$-many books, (38b). In particular, it requires that there is no world where Jack read more than $3 + \varepsilon/2$ books. But this contradicts the basic meaning stating that in $w$ Jack read $3 + \varepsilon$ books, and therefore strengthening does not apply.

(38) a. $[[(36)]] = \exists w \exists x[|x| > 3$ and Jack read $x$ in w and $x$ is a book in $w]$
b. $\forall d[d > 3 \rightarrow \neg\exists w[$Jack reads more than $d$-many books in $w]$

But recall that we saw in Section 3 that *at least n* shows a completely parallel behavior to the one of *more than n* when it comes to the appearance of scalar implicatures in embedded contexts. In particular, if *at least n* is embedded under a universal modal, the exact interpretation becomes possible, as in (39) repeated from (11). But this is not the case if *at least n* is embedded under an existential modal, as in (40) repeated from (12).

(39) Jack is required to read at least three books.
$\rightsquigarrow$ Jack is not required to read (at least) four books.

(40) Jack is allowed to read at least three books.
$\not\rightsquigarrow$ Jack is not allowed to read (at least) four books.

I said that Fox and Hackl (2006) do not intend their proposal to capture numerals modified by *at least n*. Nevertheless it is interesting to note for further discussion what their account would predict for the data in (39) and (40). Consider first (39). The basic meaning says that in all worlds $w$ there is a degree $\varepsilon$ such that Jack reads $3$ books or $3 + \varepsilon$ books in $w$, (41a). The potential implicature states that for each degree $d$ greater than $3$ there is a world $w$ such that Jack reads fewer than $d$-many books in $w$. If the modal base is again the set of worlds corresponding to the dense degrees greater than or equal to $3$, the basic meaning and the implicature are consistent: it is possible that in each world Jack reads three books or more while there still being for each degree $d$ greater than $3$ a world where he reads fewer than $d$-many books, as long as he reads at least three books in each of these worlds. But then it follows that there is no degree $d$ greater than $3$ such that Jack must read at least $d$-many books. Strengthening can apply, (41c).

(41) a. $[[(39)]] = \forall w \exists x[|x| \geq 3$ and Jack reads $x$ in $w$ and $x$ is a book in $w]$
b. $\forall d[d > 3 \rightarrow \neg\forall w[$Jack reads at least $d$-many books in $w]$
$= \forall d[d > 3 \rightarrow \exists w[\neg($Jack reads at least $d$-many books in $w)]$
c. $[[(39)]]^{S} = \forall w \exists x[|x| \geq 3$ and Jack reads $x$ and $x$ is a book in $w]$ and $\exists w \neg\exists x[|x| > 3$ and Jack reads $x$ and $x$ is a book in $w]$

What about (40)? Its basic meaning states that there is a world *w* such that Jack reads *3* books or $3 + \varepsilon$ books in *w*. But the implicature would state that for all degrees *d* greater than *3* there is no world such that Jack reads at least *d*-many books in *w*. It follows that Jack cannot read $3 + \varepsilon$ books in *w*. Nevertheless the implicature is consistent with the basic interpretation, as the strengthened meaning in (42c) would imply that Jack is only allowed to read exactly three books, contrary to fact.

(42) a. $[[(40)]] = \exists w \exists x[|x| \geq 3$ and Jack reads $x$ in $w$ and $x$ is a book in $w]$
b. $\forall d[d > 3 \rightarrow \neg\exists w[$Jack reads at least $d$-many books in $w]$
c. $[[(40)]]^S = \exists w \exists x[|x| = 3$ and Jack reads $x$ and $x$ is a book in $w]$

The fact that the density-based approach predicts an implicature for (40) is not in itself problematic. We already know that the account is not meant to be applied to data with numerals modified by *at least*. But it must be noted that the parallel behavior of *at least n* and *more than n* makes us suspect that the density-based account misses a generalization. In other words, we have cast some initial doubts on the density-based approach to missing implicatures for *more than n*. Moreover, the observation that *at least n* does sometimes have a scalar implicature as in (39) is at odds with Krifka's (1999) and Nouwen's (2008) assumptions that *at least* consumes the alternatives of the numeral. If the latter were the case, implicatures should also be unavailable for (39). But then it follows that this analysis cannot be the independent theory needed by Fox and Hackl (2006) in order to make the correct predictions with respect to *at least n*.[14]

I will now show that the density approach runs into more severe problems once embedding under negation is considered.

## 5.2 Embedding under negation

Remember from Subsection 3.3 that both types of modified numerals do not generate scalar implicatures when embedded under sentential negation. Furthermore recall that due to the equivalence between *not more than* with *at most n*, on the one hand, and between *not at least n* and *fewer than n*, on the other hand, we also do not observe scalar inferences in these latter cases. (43) and (44) are repeated from (21) and (22), respectively.

(43) a. Jack didn't read more than three books.
↛ Jack read more than two books.
b. Jack read at most three books.
↛ Jack didn't read at most two books.

(44) a. ? Jack didn't read at least three books.
↛ Jack read at least two books.
b. Jack read fewer than three books.
↛ Jack didn't read fewer than two books.

What does the density-based approach predict for the data above? Let us start by considering (43a). The basic meaning states that Jack read 3 or fewer books, (45a), i.e., Jack read *3* books or Jack read $3 - \varepsilon$ books. The implicature says that for all degrees *d* smaller than *3* it is not the case that Jack didn't read more than *d*-many books, i.e., Jack read more than *d*-many books. Therefore Jack read more than $3 - \varepsilon$ books. But the implicature is consistent: it follows that Jack read exactly three books, (45c), contrary to fact.

(45) a. $[[(43a)]] = \neg\exists x[|x| > 3$ and Jack read $x$ and $x$ is a book]
b. $\forall d[\mathrm{d} < 3 \rightarrow$ Jack read more than $d$-many books]
c. $[[(43a)]] = \exists x[|x| = 3$ and Jack read $x$ and $x$ is a book]

The reasoning for (43b) is, of course, almost parallel. The basic meaning states that Jack read *3* books or Jack read $3 - \varepsilon$ books, (46a), while the implicature says that for all degrees *d* smaller than *3* it is the case that Jack read more than *d*-many books, (46b). Therefore Jack read more than $3 - \varepsilon$ books. So Jack read exactly three books, (46c).

(46) a. $[[(43b)]] = \exists x[|x| \leq 3$ and Jack read $x$ and $x$ is a book]
b. $\forall d[d < 3 \rightarrow \neg$(Jack read at most $d$-many books)]
c. $[[(43b)]]^S = \exists x[|x| = 3$ and Jack read $x$ and $x$ is a book]

Consider now (44a). Its basic interpretation is that Jack read fewer than 3 books, (47a). That is, Jack read $3 - \varepsilon$ books and therefore it is not the case that he read $3 - \varepsilon/2$ books. But the potential implicature states that for all degrees *d* smaller than 3 Jack read at least *d*-many books (47b), from which it follows that Jack read at least $3 - \varepsilon/2$ books. This is a contradiction and the implicature is not generated.

(47) a. $[[(44a)]] = \neg\exists x[|x| \geq 3$ and Jack read $x$ and $x$ is a book]
b. $\forall d[d < 3 \rightarrow$ Jack read at least $d$-many books]

Again, the reasoning for (44b) is parallel to the one just given. The basic meaning says that Jack read $3 - \varepsilon$ books and therefore he did not read $3 - \varepsilon/2$ books, (48a). The implicature would require that he read at least $3 - \varepsilon/2$ books (48b), which would be contradictory.[15]

(48) a. $[[(44b)]] = \exists x[|x| < 3$ and Jack read $x$ and $x$ is a book]
b. $\forall d[d < 3 \rightarrow \neg$(Jack read fewer than $d$-many books)]

The situation observed is problematic for Fox and Hackl's (2006) account. Recall that according to this approach, the exact-interpretation for numerals modified by comparative *more than* is absent due to the hypothesized density of measurement scales. The absence of such an interpretation for numerals modified by superlative *at least* is in need of an independent explanation, as density alone would predict precisely that interpretation. As shown in the present subsection, however, the pattern switches when the modified numerals are embedded under negation: on the one hand, the absence of an exact-interpretation for *more than n* now does not follow from density anymore but would rather be predicted by it. The absence of such an interpretation for *at least n*, on the other hand, does now follow from density. This is unexpected and problematic because the account for *more than n* in positive environments is lost in negative ones. Moreover, it seems that a generalization is missed: as I already argued in Section 3 above, in the same environments where numerals with comparative modifiers do not have an exact-interpretation, numerals modified with superlative modifiers do not do so either. And the same holds for the environments where an exact-interpretation is available. In a way this is to be expected given that comparative *not more than n* can be replaced by superlative *at most n* and superlative *not at least n* can be replaced by *fewer than n* (but cf. Geurts and Nouwen 2007). This immediately predicts that we should observe a parallel behavior for *fewer than n* and *at most n* when embedded under negation. The former is equivalent to *at least n*, whereas the latter can be expressed by *more than n*. Neither of them appears to have the exact-interpretation: (49) does not imply that Jack read exactly four books. Again, (49) is not perfect given the positive polarity status of superlative *at most*. And (50) does not imply that Jack read exactly three books. Crucially, Fox and Hackl (2006) would predict the latter.

(49) ?Jack didn't read at most three books.
$\not\rightsquigarrow$ Jack read at most four books.

(50) Jack didn't read fewer than three books.
$\not\rightsquigarrow$ Jack read fewer than four books.

Finally, to complete the empirical picture, observe that scalar implicatures reappear under necessity modals for both *at most n* and *fewer than n*, whereas such inferences are absent under existential modals:

(51) a. Jack is required to read at most three books.
$\rightsquigarrow$ Jack is not required to read at most two books.
b. Jack is allowed to read at most three books.
$\not\rightsquigarrow$ Jack is not allowed to read at most two books.

(52) a. Jack is required to read fewer than three books.
$\rightsquigarrow$ Jack is not required to read fewer than two books.
b. Jack is allowed to read fewer than three books.
$\rightsquigarrow$ Jack is not allowed to read fewer than two books.

Embedding under negation has been shown to be problematic for Fox and Hackl (2006), as density does not make the correct predictions for *more than n* in such environments. It predicts no implicature. It must, however, be noted that Nouwen (2008: Section 6.2) adduces evidence in favor of a density-based approach by looking at the complex numeral *no more than n*. He notes that there is a difference between the examples in (53): *no more than n* lends itself much more easily to an exact-interpretation than *not more than n* does. The former thus behaves as predicted by Fox and Hackl (2006).

(53) a. Jack didn't read more than three books.
↝̸ Jack read more than two books.
b. Jack read no more than three books.
↝ Jack read exactly three books.

Nouwen derives the difference in (53) by assuming that sentential negation *not* always has widest scope – in particular, wider scope than the exhaustivity operator leading to strengthened readings (cf. Subsection 6.1.3 below) – whereas *no* in *no more than n* does not. If this much is guaranteed, the strengthened reading of (53a) will be derived without taking negation into account. The result is, of course, contradictory given density. In the case of (53b), however, negation is part of the material strengthened, and thus density predicts a scalar implicature. The problem for such an approach is to account for the most salient reading of (54), where *only* has widest scope saying that Mary is the only person who did not read *Anna Karenina*. This reading should not be possible given Nouwen's assumptions, as sentential negation has obligatorily widest scope.

(54) Only Mary didn't read *Anna Karenina*.

Thus, while the facts seen with *no more than n* are interesting in their own right, they do not lend strong support to Fox and Hackl's (2006) approach given that the stipulation regarding obligatory widest scope for sentential negation does not seem to be warranted given (54) and many similar data. Therefore the problem discussed in this section does not disappear (as acknowledged to some extent by Nouwen 2008 himself). I must also add that it is not clear what should be responsible for the different status of (53a) and (53b). I can only speculate that it must be somehow connected to the fact that *no more than n* is a lexically complex item, whereas *more than n* obviously does not form a lexical item together with sentential negation. Here it should also be noted that we should expect the more compositional nature of (53a) to be a more reliable window into what is really going on with modified numerals under negation than the lexically somewhat idiosyncratic *no more than n*.

I thus conclude that Fox and Hackl's (2006) approach is problematic nonetheless.

## 6. The limits of two related accounts

Consider the sentences in (55a) and (55b). When are such sentences typically uttered by a speaker?

(55) a. At least three boys left.
b. More than three boys left.

One particularly salient type of context where such sentences can be uttered felicitously is the one where the speaker does not know how many boys exactly left. Assume otherwise. In particular, assume that the speaker knows that exactly four boys left. In such a situation the basic interpretation of both (55a) and (55b) would be felicitous. Nevertheless one would probably judge the speaker to be not very cooperative because the utterances in (55) would be slightly misleading. In other words, upon hearing one utter (55a), the hearer draws the ignorance inference that the speaker fails to believe that exactly three boys left. In fact, it seems that (55a) has the ignorance inference that for any number *n* larger than three the speaker fails to believe that *n*-many boys left. There are two ways to account for this I can think of. Unfortunately, both run into problems of their own. Let me discuss each of the approaches in turn now.

For concreteness let us make the rather uncontroversial assumption for the following discussion that the interpretations of sentences (55a) and (55b) involve existential quantification as in (56a) and (56b), respectively.[16]

(56) a. $[[(55a)]]^w = \exists x[|x| \geq 3 \wedge \text{boy}_w(x) \wedge \text{left}_w(x)]$
b. $[[(55b)]]^w = \exists x[|x| > 3 \wedge \text{boy}_w(x) \wedge \text{left}_w(x)]$

### *6.1* exactly n *alternatives*

Given the descriptive generalization argued for, one might suspect that the following is a plausible account of the data discussed. One might want to argue that it is literally *exactly-n*-alternatives that create a problem for the generation of scalar implicatures. In this subsection I show that such an account faces at least one big problem under a Gricean theory of scalar implicatures. For reasons of space, I will only show how such an account would work for numerals modified by superlative *at least*. The problem shows up for comparative modifiers as well, though.

Assume that *at least n* has two types of alternatives. It has alternatives of the form {exactly *n*, *exactly n+1*, *exactly n+2*, . . .}. Moreover it has scalar alternatives where only the numeral is replaced by another, stronger numeral. The alternatives for the sentence in (57) are then as in (58).

(57) At least three boys left.

(58) *Alt*([[At least three boys left]]) = {exactly 3 boys left, exactly 4 boys left, . . . , at least 3 boys left, at least 4 boys left, . . .}

Note that the alternatives in (58) are partially ordered by entailment. All the alternatives entail the basic meaning of (57) – that is, all entail that at least three boys left. Let us see how the neo-Gricean reasoning described in Subsection 2.1 for the strengthening of bare numerals would handle the case of (57).

A hearer of (57) draws the basic inference in (59a). That is, given the maxim of quality the hearer concludes that the speaker believes the plain meaning of (57), which says that at least three boys left. Employing the maxim of quantity, the hearer reasons about the strictly stronger alternatives, which would have been relevant for the discussion: if the speaker believed that exactly three boys left or that exactly four boys left (and similarly for any higher numeral), the speaker would have said so. Since she did not say so, she does not believe these alternative propositions to be true. This derives the ignorance inference in (59b). In a completely parallel fashion, the hearer reasons about the derived scalar alternatives in (58). If the speaker had evidence that at least four boys left, she would have said so. She did not do so. Therefore she does not believe that the stronger scalar alternatives are true, (59c).

(59) a. *Basic inference of* (57): $B_S$(that at least 3 boys left)
b. *Ignorance inference of* (57):
$\neg B_S$(that exactly 3 boys left) $\wedge$ $\neg B_S$ (that exactly 4 boys left) $\wedge \ldots$
c. *Scalar inference of* (57):
$\neg B_S$(that at least 4 boys left) $\wedge$ $\neg B_S$ (that at least 5 boys left) $\wedge \ldots$

The next question is whether any of the inferences in (59) can be strengthened. This is only possible if no contradiction arises. First, the hearer will not derive the stronger inference that the speaker believes it to be false that exactly three boys left. Otherwise it would entail together with the basic inference that the speaker believes it to be true that at least four boys left. But this contradicts the scalar inference in (59c), which says that the speaker does not believe that at least four boys left.

How about the scalar inference in (59c) – can it be strengthened? If the speaker believed that it is false that at least four boys left, she would have to believe that exactly three boys left, given the basic inference. But this contradicts the ignorance inference in (59b). It can be seen that we are essentially facing the symmetry problem discussed in Subsection 2.1: the hearer can neither conclude that the speaker believes it to be false that exactly three boys left nor that she believes it to be false that at least four boys left. But this also means that we have (almost) solved our initial problem. Sentences with non-embedded *at least n* do not appear to give rise to scalar implicatures. The strengthened interpretation derived so far is then as in (60).

(60) *Strengthened interpretation of* (57):
$B_S$(that at least 3 boys left) ∧
¬$B_S$(that exactly 3 boys left) ∧ ¬$B_S$(that at least 4 boys left)

*6.1.1 Reappearance of scalar implicatures* Recall that scalar implicatures of modified numerals appear when embedded under universal quantifiers, but not when embedded under existential ones, as first noted by Fox and Hackl (2006). In terms of our descriptive generalization this means that a scalar implicature appears whenever the embedding operator has the effect that the strengthened interpretation is not entailed by the basic interpretation of a minimally differing sentence with an *exactly n* expression. Consider the examples with *at least n* from above:

(61) Jack is required to read at least three books.
⇝ Jack is not required to read at least four books.

(62) Jack is allowed to read at least three books.
⇝̸ Jack is not allowed to read at least four books.

The relevant alternatives for (61) are as in (63).

(63) *Alt*([[Jack is required to read at least three books]]) = {Jack is required to read exactly 3 books, Jack is required to read exactly 4 books, . . ., Jack is required to read at least 3 books, Jack is required to read at least 4 books, . . .}

A strengthened interpretation of (61) where the ignorance and scalar inferences have been further strengthened as in (64) is possible. It is non-contradictory for the speaker to believe that Jack must read three books while at the same time believing that he neither must read exactly three nor at least four books.

(64) *Strengthened interpretation of* (61):
$B_S$(that Jack is required to read at least 3 books) ∧
$B_S$¬(that Jack is required to read exactly 3 books) ∧
$B_S$¬(that Jack is required to read at least 4 books)

The alternatives for (62) are as in (65).

(65) *Alt*([[Jack is allowed to read at least three books]]) =
{Jack is allowed to read exactly 3 books, Jack is allowed to read exactly 4 books, . . ., Jack is allowed to read at least 3 books, Jack is allowed to read at least 4 books, . . .}

This time a strengthened interpretation saying that the speaker believes that Jack is allowed to read at least three books but also believes that he is neither allowed to read exactly three books nor to read at least four books is contradictory – that is, the ignorance and scalar inferences cannot be further strengthened. The strongest interpretation possible is thus the one in (66).

(66) *Strengthened interpretation of* (62):
$B_S$(that Jack is allowed to read at least 3 books) ∧
¬$B_S$(that Jack is allowed to read exactly 3 books) ∧
¬$B_S$(that Jack is allowed to read at least 4 books)

A parallel account can be given for *more than n*. Therefore an approach making use of *exactly n* alternatives correctly accounts for the reappearance of scalar implicatures under certain operators. Spector (2005) offers an account of the present problem along the lines just discussed. He proposes that *more than n* actually has the same formal alternatives as the disjunction *n + 1 or more*. As is well known the symmetry problem arises in disjunction independently. I will now turn to a problem. It is both a problem for Spector's more limited account and for the more general version discussed above.[17]

*6.1.2 A problem* What about the alternative propositions with numerals larger than 4? So far we have ignored the ignorance and scalar inferences for higher numerals. Notice that both the non-strengthened ignorance inference and the scalar inference for the sentence *At least three boys left* in (67), repeated from (59) above, contain further conjuncts that are said to not be believed by the speaker.

(67) a. *Basic inference of* (57): $B_S$(that at least 3 boys left)
b. *Ignorance inference of* (57):
¬$B_S$(that exactly 3 boys left) ∧ ¬$B_S$(that exactly 4 boys left) ∧ . . .
c. *Scalar inference of* (57):
¬$B_S$(that at least 4 boys left) ∧ ¬$B_S$(that at least 5 boys left) ∧ . . .

The question arises whether the hearer can conclude for any numeral *n* larger than 4 that the speaker has the belief that it is false that exactly *n*-many boys left.

The hearer cannot conclude that for all numerals *n* larger than 3 that the speaker believes that not exactly *n*-many boys left. Together with the basic inference that the speaker believes that at least three boys left, this would entail that she also believes it to be the case that exactly three boys left. But this contradicts the ignorance inference in (67b). But the hearer could conclude that for any numeral *m* larger than 4 the speaker believes it to be false that exactly *m*-many boys left. Note that this does not clash with the ignorance inference: the speaker is still allowed to not believe the propositions that exactly three boys left and that exactly four boys left to be true. Moreover, the hearer could then also conclude that the speaker believes the scalar alternatives with numerals larger than 4 to be false. In other words, it would follow that the speaker believes that fewer than five boys left. Together with the basic inference a strengthened interpretation would follow that says that the speaker believes that either exactly three or exactly four boys, but not more left, given in (68) with the problematic part in boldface. Clearly, this interpretation is not attested for (57).[18]

(68) *Strengthened interpretation of* (57):
$B_S$(that at least 3 boys left]) ∧
¬$B_S$(that exactly 3 boys left) ∧
¬$B_S$(that at least 4 boys left) ∧
**$B_S$(that at least 5 boys left) ∧ $B_S$(that at least 6 boys left), ∧ . . .**

A fully parallel problem would arise for a sentence with a numeral modified by comparative *more than*. This means that a scalar implicature is after all derived for modified numerals *at least n* and *more than n*, namely one stating that *not at least n + 2* and one stating *not more than n + 2* is the case, respectively. That is, it appears that the initial problem has just been shifted one level up on the number scale, and we have only partially accounted for the problem. It is important to see the nature of the problem a little clearer. The result that no scalar implicature for the numeral *n + 1* is generated was obtained because the basic inference of the sentence (57) sets a lower bound on how many boys left, namely three. Because of this and the respective ignorance inference the scalar inference where *three* is replaced by the next larger numeral cannot be strengthened. But for scalar alternatives where *three* is replaced with a numeral at least as large as five this strategy does not work: the basic inference does not set a sufficiently high lower bound on how many boys left. Thus we see that a neo-Gricean framework following Sauerland (2004) makes wrong predictions for modified numerals when employing *exactly n* alternatives. I will now briefly show that a grammatical account of scalar implicatures faces a similar problem when using *exactly n* alternatives.

*6.1.3 A grammaticality-based version* The grammatical view of scalar implicatures (cf. Chierchia 2006, Chierchia *et al.* 2012; Fox 2007a) derives the strengthened interpretation of a sentence with a Horn-alternative in it by employing an exhaustivity operator O. That is, they assume that the strengthened interpretation of a sentence like *Jack read three books*, i.e., its exact-interpretation, is derived by applying an operator O such as (69) similar to *only* to the proposition denoted by the sentence, the prejacent (cf. Krifka 1995). This operator states that the prejacent is true and that all alternatives to the prejacent in the set C are either entailed by it or false. In other words, all alternatives to the proposition that Jack read three books not entailed by it must be false. As a consequence it must be false that Jack read four books or any larger number of books.

(69) $[[O]](C_{<<s,t>,t>})(p_{<s,t>})(w_s) = p(w) = 1 \wedge \forall q \in C[q(w) = 1 \rightarrow p \subseteq q]$

Following Fox (2007a), who in turn follows Groenendijk and Stokhof (1984) and Sauerland (2004), let us moreover adopt a version of the exhaustivity operator O that only negates those alternatives in C whose negation does not automatically require the truth of some other alternative in C. These alternatives are called the *innocently excludable* ones. What this does is to spare those alternatives from negation that would otherwise contradict each other. That is, the negation of these alternatives is not factored into the strengthened interpretation. The definition of O is as in (70) (cf. Fox 2007a: (61)).[19]

(70) $[[O]](C_{<<s,t>,t>})(p_{<s,t>})(w_s) = p(w) = 1 \wedge$
$\forall q \in C$ [q is innocently excludable given $C \wedge p \not\subseteq q \rightarrow q(w) = 0$]
(where q is innocently excludable given C if $\neg\exists q' \in C[p(w) \wedge \neg q(w) \rightarrow q'(w)]$)

If *At least 3 boys left* has the alternatives in (71), repeated from (58), a parallel problem to the one raised for the neo-Gricean account follows: negating, on the one hand, *exactly 3 boys left* would automatically include *at least 4 boys left* given the basic meaning of the sentence under discussion. Due to the basic meaning of the sentence, it would similarly follow that negating *at least 4 boys left* would automatically include *exactly 3 boys left*, because it would require that fewer than four boys left. Therefore the scalar implicature that exactly three boys left is not generated. Negating *at least 5 boys left*, on the other hand, does neither automatically include *at least 4 boys left* nor *exactly 3 boys left* (nor *exactly 4 boys left*): if fewer than five boys left, this is compatible with exactly three or exactly four boys leaving. Similarly, the negation of *exactly 4 boys left* would neither automatically include *at least 3 boys left* nor *at least 5 boys left* (nor *at least 4 boys left*): the negation of the non-monotonic *exactly 4 boys left* is compatible with at least three boys leaving – that is, exactly three boys leaving given the basic meaning of the sentence – and with at least five boys leaving. Therefore alternatives with a higher numeral than 4 can be negated deriving again the problematic reading in (72).

(71) *Alt*([[At least three boys left]]) = {exactly 3 boys left, exactly 4 boys left, . . ., at least 3 boys left, at least 4 boys left, . . .}

(72) that at least 3 boys left ∧ ¬ that at least 5 boys ∧ ¬ that at least 6 boys left ∧ . . .

The problem discussed is thus rather theory-independent.

## 6.2 *Non-monotonic alternatives*

Consider now an account where *at least* and *more than* themselves come with lexical alternatives.[20] In particular, the following Horn-sets are proposed: {*at least, at most*} and {*more than, fewer than*}. It is important to see that the alternatives in these sets are not ordered by monotonicity.[21] This means that for the sentences in (73), the alternatives in (74a) and (74b) are derived, respectively.

(73) a. At least three boys left.
b. More than three boys left.

(74) a. *Alt*([[At least three boys left]]) = {at least 3 boys left, at least 4 boys left, . . ., at most 3 boys left, at most 4 boys left, . . .}
b. *Alt*([[More than three boys left]]) = {more than 4 boys left, more than 5 boys left, . . ., fewer than 4 boys left, fewer than 5 boys left, . . .}

The goal is to create a symmetry problem by employing the alternatives given so that no scalar implicature is derived. For concreteness let us assume the grammatical view of scalar implicatures.[22] The LFs assumed for (73a) and (73b) are as in (75a) and (75b), respectively.

(75) a. O [C [at least three boys left ] ]
b. O [C [more than three boys left ] ]

Consider what the assumptions just laid out do for the example in (73a). O asserts that the prejacent is true – that is, it is true that at least three boys left. Which of the alternatives in (74a) are innocently excludable? Consider first the alternative *at most 3 boys left*. Negation of that alternative would require that at least four boys left. That is, the alternative *at least 4 boys left* would be automatically true, i.e., included in the strengthened meaning. Therefore *at most 3 boys* is not innocently excludable. Negation of the alternative *at most 4 boys left* would require the truth of the alternative *at least 5 boys left*. Again, *at most 4 boys left* is not innocently excludable. For completely parallel reasons *at-most*-alternatives with numerals larger than 4 are not innocently excludable either.

Consider next the *at-least*-alternatives. Of course *at least 3 boys left* cannot be negated. This would contradict the prejacent, which is required to be true. The negation of *at least 4 boys left* would entail together with the truth of the prejacent that exactly three boys left. But this would require the truth of the alternative *at most 3 boys left*. And therefore *at least 4 boys left* is not innocently excludable. Similarly, the negation of *at least 5 boys left* would require the truth of the alternative *at most 4 boys left*. Therefore it is not innocently excludable. And the same holds for *at-least*-alternatives with numerals larger than 5. None of them is innocently excludable.[23]

None of the alternatives in (74a) is innocently excludable. To see clearer what O defined as in (70) achieves, notice that the negations of these alternatives would contradict each other. For instance, the negation of *at least 4 boys left* – that is, the proposition that fewer than four boys left – contradicts the negation of the alternative *at most 3 boys left* – that is, the proposition that more than three boys left. The negation of both alternatives cannot be true at the same time. O therefore does not negate them. In other words, they are not innocently excludable. But from this it follows that the strengthened interpretation of (73a) is equivalent to its basic interpretation. It does not have a scalar implicature.

For parallel reasons no implicature is generated for (73b) with comparative *more than n*, where the alternatives are as in (74b). The alternative *fewer than 4 boys left* can be negated given the basic interpretation of (73b). The negation says that at least four boys left, which is just the basic interpretation of (73b). That is, the negation forces the inclusion of *more than 3 boys left*, which is innocent. But *fewer than 5 boys left* cannot be negated. It would automatically make the alternative *more than 4 boys left* true. It is not innocently excludable. And the same holds for *fewer-than*-alternatives with larger numerals. They are all not innocently excludable.

The alternative *more than 4 boys left* cannot be negated. Doing so would automatically include the alternative *fewer than 5 boys left*. Similarly the alternative *more than 5 boys left* cannot be negated either. It would force the inclusion of the alternative *fewer than 6 boys left*. Again, the same holds for *more-than*-alternatives with numerals larger than 6. None of them is innocently excludable. Thus no scalar implicature is generated for (73b), and its strengthened interpretation is just its basic interpretation.

It should be noted that the negated versions of *more than n* and *at least n*, as well as the modified numerals *fewer than n* and *at most n* discussed in Subsection 5.2 work in a fully parallel way to the cases discussed here. They will not exhibit any scalar implicatures either.

*6.2.1 Reappearance of scalar implicatures* Let us now look at embedded modified numerals with the examples in (76) and (77) repeated once more from above.

(76) Jack is required to read at least three books.
$\leadsto$ Jack is not required to read at least four books.

(77) Jack is allowed to read at least three books.
$\not\leadsto$ Jack is not allowed to read at least four books.

The symmetry problem does not arise for (76). The relevant alternatives are as in (78).

(78) *Alt*([[Jack is required to read at least three books]]) =
{Jack is required to read at least 3 books, Jack is required to read at least 4 books, . . ., Jack is required to read at most 3 books, Jack is required to read at most 4 books, . . .}

Can the *at-most*-alternatives be innocently excluded? The negation of the alternative *Jack is required to read at most 3 books* says that there is a world where Jack reads more than three books. In the example (73a) discussed above negation of the *at most 3* alternative automatically led to the inclusion of the *at least 4* alternative. Not so in this case: if there is a world where Jack reads more than three books, it does not follow that in all worlds Jack reads more than three books, as would be required by inclusion of the alternative *Jack is required to read at least 4 books*. Similarly, negation of *Jack is required to read at most 4 books* does not lead to the inclusion of the alternative *Jack read at least 5 books*. Parallel considerations apply for the remaining *at-most*-alternatives.

Consider next the *at-least*-alternatives. Negation of *Jack is required to read at least 3 books* is prohibited by the basic meaning of (76). *Jack is required to read at least 4 books*, however, can be innocently excluded. In particular its negation does not lead to the automatic inclusion of *Jack is required to read at most 3 books*. If there is a world where Jack reads fewer than 4 books – as the former requires –, it does not follow that in all worlds Jack reads fewer than 4 books – as the latter requires. The same holds for alternatives with larger numerals. We thus get the strengthened interpretation for (76) in (79), which is the desired outcome.

(79) [[Jack is required to read at least three books]]$^S$ =
Jack is required to read at least 3 books $\wedge$ for any $n > 3$ he is not required to read at least $n$-many books $\wedge$ for any $m \geq 3$ he is not required to read at most $m$-many books

Consider now (77), which has the alternatives in (80).

(80) *Alt*([[Jack is allowed to read at least three books]]) = {Jack is allowed to read at least 3 books, Jack is allowed to read at least 4 books, . . ., Jack is allowed to read at most 3 books, Jack is allowed to read at most 4 books, . . .}

Negating the alternative *Jack is allowed to read at most 3 books* automatically includes the alternative *Jack is allowed to read at least 4 books*. The negation of the former states that there is no world where Jack reads at most three books, i.e., in all worlds he reads at least four books. Thus the latter must be true. Similar considerations hold for the other *at-most*-alternatives.

Negating the alternative *Jack is allowed to read at least 4 books* would mean that in all worlds Jack reads fewer than four books. Therefore the alternative *Jack is allowed to read at most 3 books* would have to be true. In sum, none of the alternatives is innocently excludable, and the strengthened interpretation of (77) is equivalent to its basic meaning. In other words, the present theory correctly distinguishes between (76) and (77).

It is fairly easy to see that a parallel account for numerals modified by comparative *more than* embedded under universal or existential quantifiers can be given. Moreover, the remaining operators discussed in Subsection 3.2 that do lead to scalar implicatures are treated on a par by the present account, which might not always be desirable, unless something is said in addition. Let me turn to this problem.

*6.2.2 Another problem* Consider again the example with distributive conjunction of individuals, (81) repeated from (20a).[24]

(81) John and Mary both wrote more than three books.
⇝ Not both of John and Mary wrote more than four books.

It has the relevant alternatives in (82).

(82) *Alt*([[John and Mary both wrote more than three books]]) =
{John and Mary both wrote more than 4 books, John and Mary both wrote more than 5 books, . . . , John and Mary both wrote fewer than 4 books, John and Mary both wrote fewer than 5 books, . . .}

The alternative *John and Mary wrote fewer than 4 books* is innocently excludable. Its negation says that either John or Mary wrote at least four books. This does not contradict the basic meaning of (81). But it also does not require any other alternative to be true, which is to be expected given what was shown in the preceding subsection. The same holds for any alternative of the form *John and Mary wrote fewer than n books* with $n \geq 4$. But then the strengthened interpretation of (81) amounts to (83), which requires that one of John and Mary wrote at most five books and for any numeral $n$ at least as high as 4 one wrote at least $n$ books. In other words, one of John and Mary must have written an infinite amount of books.

(83) $[[\text{John and Mary both wrote more than three books}]]^S$ =
John and Mary both wrote more than 3 books, for any $n \geq 5$ either John or Mary wrote at most $n$-many books, for any $m \geq 4$ either John or Mary wrote at least $m$-many books

This is a serious problem, and it generalizes to modified numerals embedded under other universal operators. The problem might not appear to be as severe for (84) repeated from (76). But even here the strengthened interpretation given in (79) above will have the consequence that for any $n$ larger than three Jack is allowed to read at least $n$ books, an interpretation we would normally not associate with (84).

(84) Jack is required to read at least three books.
⇝ Jack is not required to read four books.

I do not see any particularly insightful way how to deal with this problem at the moment. It might be possible to restrict the set of alternatives. That is, if we restrict the set of available alternatives for (84) to alternatives with numerals between three and, say, nine, it would only follow that for any $n$ larger than three and not larger than nine that Jack is allowed to read $n$ books. In other words, Jack is allowed to read between three and ten books. Nothing is said about alternatives with larger numerals. Clearly, the requirement previously derived for (81) that one of John and Mary wrote an infinite number of books goes away, at least to some extent. Restricting the set of alternatives contextually might even make sense intuitively. When (84) is uttered, it does not appear that the alternative *Jack is required to read at least 100 books* is particularly relevant. But it is unclear to me at the moment how we can restrict the alternatives precisely in the way we want it so that no problems arise. I must leave this for future research. If this part can be further spelled out, then we might have reason to adopt an account of modified numerals with non-monotonic alternatives over one with *exactly n* alternatives, it seems.

## 7. Conclusion

In the present chapter I did the following things: first, I provided novel evidence suggesting that the varying absence and presence of scalar implicatures with numerals modified by comparative *more than* and superlative *at least* has very similar roots, if not the same root. I therefore argued against certain views on this topic found in the literature. Second, I suggested a new empirical generalization covering the data discussed. Third, I showed that existing analyses dealing with implicatures of modified numerals do not account for the full empirical generalization, as they only deal with one type of modified numerals. In particular, I argued that both a density-based account[25] and a focus-operator-based one make certain unwelcome predictions. Finally, I discussed and compared two related alternative approaches that could be taken to analyze the novel data collected. Both have their problems regardless of whether a neo-Gricean or a grammatical view of implicatures is taken. While the ultimate account of the puzzle discussed thus remains to be determined, it should, however, be noted that one of the two alternative accounts – that is, an account relying on non-monotonic alternatives for modified numerals – might be successful if an insightful way is found how the contextually relevant alternatives are to be restricted. I sketched what the necessary ingredient should look like. I therefore hope that this positive outlook provides opportunity for future research on this issue.

## Acknowledgments

I dedicate the chapter to Gennaro Chierchia, whose insightful work inspired the research reported. I wish to thank him for his support over all these years. For helpful discussion and criticism I thank Anton Benz, Angelika Kratzer, Uli Sauerland, Stephanie Solt, and two anonymous reviewers. Moreover I thank the editors, in particular Ivano Caponigro who has provided very useful feedback. Part of the research for this paper was funded by grant A925/1–4 awarded to Uli Sauerland by the DFG.

NOTES

1. When talking about the neo-Gricean theory, I will refer to the meaning obtained before the scalar implicatures are factored in as the basic or the non-strengthened inference. The meaning where the implicatures are factored in is called the strengthened inference. When talking about the grammatical theory of scalar implicatures I will mostly replace "inference" by "meaning."
2. This step does not follow from Gricean reasoning as such. In order for it to go through, it is necessary to assume that a speaker is opinionated with respect to the truth of the alternatives of a given sentence (cf. the discussion by Sauerland 2004, Fox 2007a, but also Gazdar 1979).
3. For discussion of the symmetry problem see Fox (2007a) (also cf. Kroch 1972). The symmetry problem arises whenever one inference prohibits the strengthening of another inference, and vice versa.
4. Breheny (2008) casts doubt on the significance of data similar to (6). In particular, he shows that the inference can go in both directions depending on the context – that is, both upper- and lower-bounded implicatures are available with bare numerals in DE environments. This, of course, speaks against an implicature-based analysis of the exact-interpretation of bare numerals and in favor of a lexical analysis. Also cf. Kennedy's arguments in this volume in favor of a semantically driven approach to the exact-interpretation of numerals. I do not want to take a stance in this debate as it is orthogonal to the main argument of this chapter. In other words, even if the exact-interpretation of bare numerals should be accounted for by a lexical analysis, the puzzle to be discussed shortly remains.
5. There is one more type of account exemplified by Spector (2005) to be discussed in Section 6.
6. There are in fact more cases of modified numerals (for instance, *no more than n*, *between $n_i$ and $n_j$*), classified by Nouwen (2010) into two subtypes. For discussion of *no more than n* see Subsection 5.2.
7. The inverse scope reading does not seem to be particularly salient in examples with conditionals where the modified numeral is in the consequent and should thus not interfere with the judgments. This is possibly due to a prohibition against inverse scope readings that would be stronger than the respective surface scope reading (Mayr and Spector 2011).
8. The inverse scope interpretation is nonsensical for (15a) and (15b) in normal contexts, because usually not everyone writes the same books. Similar considerations apply to examples below.
9. Geurts and Nouwen (2007), however, suggest that numerals modified by superlatives are not positive polarity items but rather modal expressions. Modal expressions, they argue, are more restricted in distribution than non-modal ones.
10. (22a) is acceptable under the inverse scope interpretation saying that at least three books are such that Jack did not read them. This is as expected from positive polarity items (cf. Szabolcsi 2004 a.o.) but tangential to the present discussion.
11. Together with Chierchia (2006); Chierchia *et al.* (2012); Fox (2007a) a.o., Fox and Hackl (2006) assume the so-called grammatical theory of scalar implicatures. See Subsection 6.1.3 below for discussion of how the negation of stronger alternatives works technically.

12. For arguments that *at least n* and *more than n* are inherently different see Geurts and Nouwen (2007); Nouwen (2008, 2010). For reasons of space I cannot discuss their proposal in more detail.
13. In order to account for scalar implicatures of *more than n* embedded under *every*, Fox and Hackl (2006) have to resort to an infinite domain of individuals over which the universal quantifier ranges, so that no contradiction arises under the density-based approach for the example (15a) (*Everyone wrote more than three books*) when the scalar implicature is factored in. The infinite set of dense degrees is distributed over the infinite set of individuals. How would they deal with scalar implicatures generated by *more than n* under conjunction as in (20a) (*John and Mary both wrote more than three books*) above, which can be seen to involve universal quantification of some sort? It appears that one has to assume that at the level where strengthening happens the universal conjunction ranges over an infinite set of individuals as well. That is, the restricted set provided by *John and Mary* must somehow be ignored at this level. Otherwise the implicature associated with (20a) would be blocked by density. Specific assumptions about granularity can guarantee this.
14. An anonymous reviewer points out that Fox and Hackl (2006) make the predictions with respect to *at least n* discussed here only insofar as the meaning for *at least n* given in the text is assumed. This is correct. Another semantics for *at least n* can always be developed. The challenge, however, is to have it behave in parallel to *more than n* given the discussion in the previous sections. But this latter fact is not straightforwardly derivable if the two types of modified numerals have completely independent meanings.
15. Two things should be noted for (43b) and (44b). The basic meanings given for them in (46a) and (48a), respectively, entail that Jack read at least one book. However, this does not seem to be required by either of them, as shown by the non-contradictory sentences in (i). Barwise and Cooper's (1981) Generalized Quantifier theory does not make this prediction (cf. the discussion by Krifka 1999).

    (i) a. Jack read at most three books, in fact he read none.
        b. Jack read fewer than three books, in fact he read none.

    This fact is, however, not problematic for the argument given in the text. For (46) observe that even if *at most 3* includes the possibility of zero books, it would still follow that Jack read $3 - \varepsilon$ books, which is compatible with the implicature that he read more than $3 - \varepsilon$ books. That is, an exact-interpretation is predicted. Similarly, for (48): even if it were possible that Jack read zero books, it is true that he read $3 - \varepsilon$ books and therefore that he did not read $3 - \varepsilon/2$ books. The latter is at odds with the implicature, and it would thus not be generated. Second, the interpretations given do not guarantee that Jack did not read more than three books because of cumulativity, as Krifka (1999) shows.
16. What is more controversial is how these interpretations are compositionally derived. The generalized quantifier tradition, on the one hand, would argue that the modifier and the numeral form a constituent taking the NP as a restrictor (cf. Barwise and Cooper 1981, Keenan and Stavi 1986). Krifka (1999) and Geurts and Nouwen (2007), on the other hand, claim that the NP and the numeral form a constituent. The modifier only supplies the modification of the numeral. The existential import is derived from existential closure. This latter option needs some additional

assumptions. I do not want to take a side in this debate. Christopher Kennedy in this volume has some related discussion.

17. Also see Fox (2007b) for another problem in relation with Spector's account.
18. For readability, the strengthened ignorance inferences for numerals larger than 4 have been left out. That is, the inference that the speaker believes it to be false that exactly five boys left has been left out, and the same for larger numerals.
19. Actually Fox (2007a) shows that the definition of *innocent exclusion* should make reference to that subset of C that only contains propositions that are non-weaker than p. For present purposes it seems to me that (70) suffices.
20. I especially thank Uli Sauerland (p.c.) for helpful discussion on this subsection.
21. This contradicts Matsumoto's (1995) assumptions that the fundamental condition on Horn-sets is that the alternatives are ordered by monotonicity.
22. Nothing said below really hinges on this. The neo-Gricean view could also be adopted. Given that the alternatives employed are not ordered by strength some complications might arise that could, for instance, be overcome by employing the maxim of quality instead of the maxim of quantity (cf. Sauerland 2012).
23. Note that there are in fact also alternatives with numerals smaller than 3. Consider the alternative *at least 2 boys left*. It is entailed by the basic interpretation of (73a). By the semantics of O in (70) it therefore cannot be negated. The same holds of course for *at least 1 boy left*. Consider next the negation of the alternative *at most 2 boys left*. It forces the inclusion of the alternative *at least 3 boys left,* which is just the basic meaning of the sentence. Thus it is innocently excludable. The same holds for *at most 1 boy left*. Thus these alternatives do not affect the overall result obtained for (73a).
24. I thank an anonymous reviewer for pointing out this problem, which I had noticed independently after having submitted the paper. I was unable to find a fully satisfying solution to this issue.
25. This raises the question of whether the universal density of measurement is needed at all for natural language semantics. Fox and Hackl (2006) argue that it is, for instance, also needed to account for weak island phenomena. If Abrusán and Spector (2011), however, are on the right track, then there might be a density-independent way to analyze weak islands.

# 7 A scalar semantics for scalar readings of number words

*Christopher Kennedy*

## 1. Introduction

Number words have played a central role in debates about the relation between context and meaning for decades. While current analyses of these terms and the sentences in which they appear differ in their details, they typically agree that interpretations of sentences containing number words crucially involve pragmatic enrichment of a more basic meaning. In the first part of this chapter, I present a set of challenges for existing semantic and pragmatic accounts of number word meaning. In the second part, I develop and motivate a fully semantic and compositional analysis of scalar readings of sentences containing numerals, in which number words denote generalized quantifiers over degrees, and scalar readings arise through scopal interactions between number words and other constituents, rather than through pragmatic enrichment.

### *1.1 The Classic Analysis*

The dominant view of number word meaning – or more accurately, the contribution of number words to sentence and utterance meaning – comes from Horn 1972:

> Numbers, then, or rather sentences containing them, assert lower-boundedness – *at least n* – and given tokens of utterances containing cardinal numbers may, depending on the context, implicate upper-boundedness – *at most n* – so that the number may be interpreted as denoting an exact quantity. (Horn 1972: 33)

Horn's analysis is based on the observation that number words appear to pattern with other scalar terms in leaving open whether propositions involving higher quantities are true, while generating entailments that propositions involving lower quantities are false, as illustrated by the examples in (1).

(1) a. Kim read three of the articles on the syllabus, if not more/#fewer.
b. Kim read most of the articles on the syllabus, if not all of them/#many of them.

Although an assertion of the first part of (1a) (*Kim read three of the articles on the syllabus*) would usually be taken to communicate the information that

Kim didn't read more than three books, just as the first part of (1b) would be taken to mean that Kim didn't read more than merely most of the books (i.e., that Kim didn't read all of them), the fact that (1a–b) can be followed by *if not more/ all* is taken as evidence by Horn that the UPPER BOUND inference associated with utterances of these sentences (*not four, five, six...*; *not all*) is a conversational implicature. In contrast, the infelicity of the *if not fewer/many* continuations is taken as evidence that the LOWER BOUND inference (*at least three*; *more than half*) is an entailment.

The details of Horn's account of the "exact quantity" interpretation of sentences with number words – what Horn (1992) calls the TWO-SIDED meaning – runs as follows. Assume that sentences containing number words entail a lower bound, so that the first part of (1a) is true just in case the number of articles read by Kim is equal to or greater than three. If this is correct, then any sentence just like (1a) in which *three* is replaced by a number word that introduces a lower bound greater than 3 (*four, five, six*, etc.) entails (1a). On the assumption that a speaker intends to be as informative as possible without saying something that she knows to be false, in accord with Grice's Maxims of Quality and Quantity, an utterance of (1a) instead of a stronger alternative generates the implicature that the speaker believes that none of the alternatives are true. The resulting combination of sentence meaning (*the number of books Kim read is equal to or greater than three*) and implicature (*for all n greater than three, the speaker doesn't believe that the number of books Kim read is equal to or greater than n*) corresponds to the two-sided meaning.

Additional evidence for the Classic Analysis comes from the interpretation of sentences in which number words occur in a downward-entailing context. Unlike (1a), an utterance of (2a) is most naturally understood as conveying the information that everyone who missed three *or more* of the questions failed the exam, not as a claim that everyone who missed exactly three of the questions failed; (2b–c) are understood in a similar way.

(2) a. Everyone who missed three of the questions failed the exam.
b. Everyone who missed some of the questions failed the exam.
c. Everyone who missed most of the questions failed the exam.

The difference between these examples and the ones in (1) is that the kind of entailment pattern that motivates an analysis of the upper-bounding interpretations of (1a–b) in terms of scalar implicature does not obtain, because the numeral and scalar quantifiers appear in a downward-entailing context. Replacing *three* in (2a) with a numeral higher in the counting list does not generate an entailment to (2a) (given lower-bounded truth conditions); instead the entailment relations are flipped: if it is true that everyone who missed at least three of the questions failed the exam, then it is true that everyone who missed at least four, five, six, etc. failed. The Classic Analysis therefore predicts that examples like (2) should not have two-sided interpretations, which indeed appears to be the case.

Horn's version of the Classic Analysis is a neo-Gricean one, but its general features are shared by "grammatical" theories of scalar implicature as well (e.g. Chierchia 2004, 2006; Chierchia *et al.* 2012; Fox 2007a; Magri 2011; Mayr this volume, etc.). In these approaches, the upper-bounding inference is introduced compositionally by an exhaustivity operator EXH which composes with a sentence, computes a set of alternative meanings for the sentence in a way that is fully parallel to the reasoning outlined above, and returns a meaning that consists of the original sentence meaning plus a denial of its stronger alternatives. The central difference between the neo-Gricean version of the Classic Analysis and the grammatical one is that on the former view, the two-sided understanding of the utterances in (1) is part sentence meaning, part speaker meaning; while on the latter view, it is entirely a matter of sentence meaning, and so can interact compositionally with other expressions. However, both versions of the Classic Analysis share two core features. First, upper-bounding inferences arise through consideration and subsequent exclusion of stronger scalar alternatives. Second, upper-bounding inferences of numerals and other scalar terms (both quantifiers like *some, many, most* as well as modals, aspectual verbs, and so forth) are derived in exactly the same way. As we will see below, these two features lead to problems for both versions of the Classic Analysis.

### *1.2 Number word meaning*

Before moving to a discussion of these problems, I want to point out that although the Classic Analysis is often thought of as an analysis of the meanings of number words themselves, this is incorrect. As the quote from Horn (1972) makes clear, it is instead an analysis of the information conveyed by an utterance of a sentence containing a cardinal numeral. As such, it is compatible with several distinct hypotheses about the meanings of number words themselves and the way in which the "basic" lower-bounded semantic content is introduced. There are three main approaches that have been taken in the literature.

The first is to analyze number words as quantificational determiners, as in Barwise and Cooper (1981). On this view, the hypothesis that numerals introduce lower-bounded content reflects one of two potential analyses of the denotation of the determiner, specifically the one in (3a) (using the numeral "three" as an example), in which it introduces a lower bound on the cardinality of the intersection of the determiner's restriction and scope.

(3) a. $[[\text{three}]] = \lambda P \lambda Q.|P \cap Q| \geq 3$
b. $[[\text{three}]] = \lambda P \lambda Q.|P \cap Q| = 3$

This denotation contrasts with the one in (3b), advocated by Breheny (2008), which introduces a two-sided meaning as a matter of semantic content, and so represents a significantly different hypothesis about how two-sided inferences are generated.

The second option is to treat number words as cardinality predicates, or properties of pluralities, as in Chierchia (2010); Krifka (1999); Landman (2003, 2004); Rothstein (2011) (or, in a more elaborate way, Ionin and Matushansky 2006). This approach typically assumes a denotation along the lines of (4), where # returns the number of atoms that comprise a plural individual.

(4) $[[\text{three}]] = \lambda x.\#(x) = 3$

Even though the number word introduces a relation to an exact quantity (which accounts for obligatory two-sided interpretations of predicate numerals; see Geurts 2006), the resulting truth conditions for a sentence in which a numeral modifies a noun are lower-bounded, thanks to existential closure over the individual argument. The truth-conditional content of the first part of (1a), for example, is as shown in (5) (ignoring partitivity).

(5) $\exists x[\mathbf{read}(x)(\text{kim}) \wedge \mathbf{articles}(x) \wedge \#(x) = 3]$

(5) entails the existence of a plurality of books read by Kim of size three, but does not rule out the existence of pluralities of greater size, and so has lower-bounded truth conditions. However, this analysis can be turned into one that introduces two-sided truth conditions either by adding an extra condition to the effect that the plurality which satisfies the cardinality predicate uniquely satisfies it (Nouwen 2010), or by type-shifting the predicate denotation into a determiner meaning (Geurts 2006).[1]

A third option is to treat numerals as singular terms, as advocated by Frege (1884), i.e., as names of numbers. Recasting Frege's view in the context of contemporary semantic theory, we may assume a model-theoretic interpretation in which numbers are of the same semantic type as the objects introduced by measure phrases like *two meters* and quantified over by comparatives and other kinds of quantity morphology, i.e., type d (for DEGREES; see e.g., Cresswell 1976; Kennedy 1999; Klein 1991; Stechow 1984, and many others). Like these other expressions, number words must compose with an expression of type $\langle d, \alpha \rangle$; such an expression can be derived from the quantificational determiner or adjectival meanings of number words by abstracting over the position of the numeral in the metalanguage representation of the meaning, deriving either the "parameterized" quantificational determiner in (6a) (Hackl 2000) or the gradable adjective in (6b) (Cresswell 1976; Krifka 1989).[2]

(6) a. $[[\text{MANY}_{\text{Det}}]] = \lambda n \lambda P \lambda Q.\ |P \cap Q| \geq n$
b. $[[\text{MANY}_{\text{Adj}}]] = \lambda n \lambda x.\#(x) = n$

Composing (6a) or (6b) with the singular term denotation for e.g. *three*, namely the number 3, then gives back the determiner meaning in (3a) or the cardinality predicate meaning (4), respectively.[3] This approach is similar to the previous two in making the number word part of a determiner or adjective meaning (and in this way, it can accommodate whatever syntactic evidence there might be for one analysis or the other), but differs crucially in allowing for more independence between the numeral and the rest of the nominal projection: since the numeral itself is a syntactic and semantic argument, rather than a determiner or a modifier, it may have an interpretive independence from the rest of the nominal. Specifically, it can in principle take scope independently from the rest of the nominal projection. This will turn out to be crucial in the alternative to the Classic Analysis that I will propose in Section 3.

## 2. Challenges to the Classic Analysis

In this section, I will discuss a number of problems for the Classic Analysis, which challenge both the view that number words introduce lower-bounded sentence meaning, and the view that the upper-bounding inference and two-sided speaker meaning is derived in the same way for number words as it is for other scalar expressions.

### *2.1 Two-sided meaning and semantic composition*

In a neo-Gricean model of speaker meaning, conversational implicatures are based partly on contextual information, partly on reasoning based on the Cooperative Principle, and partly on sentence meaning. Because sentence meaning is part of the input to implicature calculation, a prediction of the neo-Gricean model is that implicatures are invisible to semantic composition. This is a central tenet of the neo-Gricean program, and is the basis for its resulting "simplification" of semantics. In the case of number words, if they introduce only lower-bounded semantic content, with two-sided meanings arising as implicatures, the prediction is that only lower-bounded content should interact compositionally with other expressions in a sentence. As it turns out, there is reason to believe that this prediction is wrong, and that instead number words interact with other expressions in a way that indicates that two-sided inferences are a matter of semantic content. I will examine three such cases here: interactions with negation, quantifiers, and modals.[4]

*2.1.1 Interactions with negation* Consider first the question–answer dialogue in (7). If the semantic content of B's response to A involves a lower-bounded meaning for the number word, then her denial amounts to the claim that it is false that she has at least three children. This is consistent with her follow-up in (7B-i), but it should be contradicted by her follow-up in (7B-ii).

(7) A: Do you have three children?
B: No, I don't have three children.
(i) I have two.
(ii) I have four.

In fact, either (7B-i) or (7B-ii) is a perfectly acceptable way for B to elaborate on her initial denial that she has three children. Horn (1972) was well aware of this, and argued that only B's response in (7B-i) involves a negation of the semantic content of the number word. (7B-ii), on the other hand, is an instance of METALINGUISTIC NEGATION, in which B's use of negative morphology is designed to signal that the upper-bounding implicature should be suppressed.

However, this analysis has been challenged in recent years, including by Horn himself. Horn (1992) observes that in question–answer contexts, putative denials of an upper bound inference in answers with number words have a different status from those involving clear scalar quantifiers. He points to pairs like the following, observing that B's response in (8) is perfectly acceptable even with a neutral intonation, but B's response in (9) is acceptable only with the strong intonational prominence on *all* that is indicative of a metalinguistic interpretation.

(8) A: Did you read three of the articles on the syllabus?
B: No, I read four of them.

(9) A: Did you read many of the articles on the syllabus?
B: ?No, I read all of them.

Horn (1996b) elaborates on this difference with a discussion of examples like those in (10).

(10) a. ? Neither of them read many of the articles on the syllabus. Kim read one and Lee read them all.
b. ? Neither of them started the assignment. Kim didn't even look at it, and Lee finished it.
c. ? Neither of them liked the movie. Kim hated it, and Lee absolutely loved it.

The negative quantifier in the first sentence of these examples can in principle be understood either semantically or metalinguistically. If it is understood semantically, it interacts with the lower-bounded semantic content of the scalar quantifier *many*, the aspectual verb *start*, and the scalar verb *like*, generating the meaning that it is false of the two individuals picked out by *them* (Kim and Lee) that an appropriate lower bound was reached. (The number of articles read was below the threshold for counting as "many"; the assignment was not started; the evaluative attitude towards the movie is insufficient to count as liking it.) If it is used metalinguistically, with appropriate intonational prominence on the scalar term, it can deny the corresponding scalar inference: "*Neither of us LIKED the movie. We both LOVED it!*" The examples in (10) are strange because they require us to simultaneously understand the negative quantifier semantically and metalinguistically, something that is evidently impossible, or at the very least triggers a zeugma effect. If number words are semantically lower-bounded and only pragmatically upper-bounded, then we should see exactly the same infelicity in (11), but this is not the case:

(11) Neither of them read three of the articles on the syllabus. Kim read two and Lee read four.

This example is perfect, even without special intonational prominence on the number word. This is expected only if the number word introduces two-sided semantic content, which can then be targeted by the negative quantifier, deriving the intuitively correct truth conditions for (11): it is false of both Kim and Lee that they each read exactly three articles on the syllabus.

The interaction of negation and number words is a problem for both the neo-Gricean and grammatical variants of the Classic Analysis, though in different ways. As noted above, the neo-Gricean analysis must explain apparent denials of the upper bound as instances of metalinguistic negation, a move that does not appear to square very well with the facts. The grammatical approach can in fact account for the facts by hypothesizing that EXH, the exhaustivity operator involved in generating upper-bounding inferences, can be inserted below negation. In the case of (11), for example, the relevant reading can be derived by assuming the representation in (12a), which derives the truth conditions paraphrased in (12b) (keeping things informal for now).

(12) a. Neither of them EXH [read three of the articles on the syllabus]
b. For each $x \in$ {Kim, Lee}, it is not the case that:
(i) x read at least three articles and
(ii) it is not the case that x read more than three articles

To satisfy the negation, it is necessary for each of Kim and Lee to make one of (12b-i) or (12b-ii) false; this will be the case if they read fewer than three articles ((12b-i) false) or more than three articles ((12b-ii) false), i.e., if the two-sided truth conditions fail to hold.

However, note that in the examples under consideration here, the upper-bounding inference appears in a downward-entailing context. As I mentioned in Section 1.1, it is generally the case that scalar implicatures disappear in such contexts. This is expected in a neo-Gricean framework, because such contexts invert entailments, and explains why (9) and (10) are odd. At the same time, this is precisely why examples like (8) and (11) are such problems for the neo-Gricean version of the Classic Analysis: if the two-sided interpretation of number words derives from a scalar implicature, then it should disappear in downward-entailing contexts, contrary to fact.

In contrast, the fact that scalar implicatures generally disappear in downward-entailing contexts does not follow automatically in the grammatical theory of scalar implicatures, and this difference is precisely what gives the grammatical version of the Classic Analysis the tools it needs to derive two-sided meanings for number words in the examples above. But instead of solving the problem, this just creates a new one: if examples like (8) and (11) show that EXH can be inserted in a downward-entailing context, generating two-sided inferences for number words, then why can it evidently not be inserted in the corresponding examples in (9) and (10)?

In fact, according to Chierchia *et al.* (2012), insertion of EXH in such examples is possible, but dispreferred. Chierchia *et al.* point out that whenever a weak scalar term is part of a propositional constituent S that occurs in a downward-entailing context, then adjunction of EXH to S derives a meaning that is asymmetrically entailed by the corresponding structure without EXH. This allows them to appeal to a "strongest meaning" principle as a way of limiting upper-bounding inferences in downward-entailing contexts: insertion of EXH is dispreferred if it results in a weaker meaning. This is a default constraint, but it is not a hard one, as it can be violated in the right context. On this view the unacceptability of (9) and the examples in (10) is indicative of the constraint in action, while the fact that strong phonological emphasis on the scalar terms can improve the examples indicates that the constraint can be bypassed.

Regardless of whether this line of thought is a correct or fruitful way of understanding the distribution of upper-bounding inferences with scalar terms in general (a debate that I do not wish to engage here), it does not provide a way of salvaging the Classic Analysis of number words. The problem, quite simply, is that there is no evidence that two-sided interpretations of sentences with number words are dispreferred in downward-entailing contexts, or that it is necessary to add a special prominence or emphasis on the number word to derive this meaning. Quite the opposite: in the examples considered above, the two-sided interpretations appear to be the default, and need not be signaled by special intonational prominence. In short, the central challenge for the grammatical version of the Classic Analysis is the same as the one faced by the neo-Gricean version: sentences with number words systematically have two-sided meanings in contexts in which other scalar terms do not.

*2.1.2 Interactions with quantifiers* Interactions with universal and negative quantifiers make the same point. Earlier I presented (2), repeated below, as evidence that upper-bounding inferences disappear in the scope of a universal quantifier.

(2) a. Everyone who missed three of the questions failed the exam.
b. Everyone who missed some of the questions failed the exam.
c. Everyone who missed most of the questions failed the exam.

While it is true that (2a) is most naturally understood as conveying the information that everyone who missed three or more of the questions failed, we actually cannot be sure that this is because *three* introduces lower-bounded content. Even if *three* introduced two-sided content, (2a) would still be true in a situation in which everyone who missed three or more of the questions failed the exam, because such a situation is also one in which everyone who missed exactly three questions failed.[5] We could then explain our understanding of the message conveyed by an utterance of (2a) in terms of a particularized scalar implicature: generally, missing more questions on an exam is worse than missing fewer, so if it's true that everyone who missed exactly three questions failed, we can reason that everyone who missed more than three failed too (cf. Breheny 2008).

But more importantly, it is easy to construct examples in which sentences containing numerals in downward-entailing quantifier restrictions clearly have two-sided truth conditions. Consider, for example, a test-taking situation in which there are five answers, and students are rewarded with different color stars depending on how well they do: students who get exactly three correct answers receive a red star; students who get exactly four correct answers get a silver star, and students who get five correct answers get a gold star. In this scenario, the sentences in (13) can be understood in two different ways. They both can be understood in a way parallel to (2a), with the number word introducing a lower bound, in which case they falsely describe the situation under consideration. This reading might indicate the existence of lower-bounded truth conditions, but it could also be the result of pragmatic reasoning, as described above.

(13) a. Everyone who correctly answered three of the questions got a red star.
b. No one who correctly answered three of the questions got a gold star.

However, both of the sentences in (13) also can be understood as saying something true about the situation in (12), a result that is possible only if the number words are understood as providing both a lower and upper bound on the number of missed examples, i.e., only if the sentences have two-sided interpretations.

The same cannot be said of the examples in (14), in which the number words are replaced by scalar determiners. These sentences are unambiguously false as descriptions of the situation described above, which means that they have only their "basic," lower-bounded truth conditions.

(14) a. Everyone who correctly answered most of the questions got a red star.
b. No one who correctly answered most of the questions got a gold star.

The absence of two-sided readings in (14a–b) is expected on the neo-Gricean version of the Classic Analysis, but the presence of two-sided readings in (13a–b) is not. In the absence of strong intonational prominence on the scalar words (something not required for the numerals), these readings can be derived in the grammatical version of the Classic Analysis by inserting EXH in the relative clause (despite the fact that this is a downward-entailing context), but then we incorrectly predict two-sided readings to be equally accessible in (14a–b).

*2.1.3 Interactions with modals* Let us finally consider sentences in which number words appear in the scope of a modal verb.[6] At first glance, the interaction of modals and number words appears to provide strong evidence that the lower bound inference is a constituent of the semantic content of sentences containing number words. In the examples in (15), the number word is part of the semantic scope of the modal, and is understood as though it introduces lower-bounded semantic content (Carston 1998; Scharten 1997).

(15) a. In Britain, you have to be 18 to drive a car.
b. Mary needs to get three As if she wants to graduate.
c. Recipients of the education benefit must have two children enrolled in primary school.

An utterance of (15a), for example, is most naturally understood as an assertion that in all worlds consistent with the relevant regulations, one must be at least 18 to drive, i.e., that 18 is the minimum legal driving age. Likewise, (15b) places a lower bound on the number of As Mary needs to graduate, and (15c) implies that anyone with two or more students in primary school will get the benefit. These readings are exactly what we expect if number words have lower-bounded semantic content, and if only the semantic content of the expression that provides the scope of the modal (the infinitival clause) plays a role in determining the truth conditions of the sentence.[7]

(15a–c) can also have two-sided understandings, in which an upper bound is placed on the obligation: (15b), understood in this way, says that Mary needs to get three As to graduate, but she does not need to get more than three As. This reading can be derived in the usual way, either as a quantity implicature or by inserting EXH at the root.

The problem is that examples like (15a–c) can, in addition, have a two-sided understanding which is not derivable as a scalar implicature, at least not in the normal way. Such interpretations are stronger than the ones I just described:

instead of merely placing an upper bound on what is required, they involve requirements which are themselves upper-bounded. World knowledge makes such readings implausible for (15a–b), but they emerge quite clearly in (16a–b), for example.

(16) a. In "Go Fish," each player must start with seven cards.
b. Assignments have to be five pages long.

The point of (16a) is to say that the rules of "Go Fish" stipulate that players begin with exactly seven cards. Likewise, (16b) can be used to convey the information that acceptable assignments are no more and no less than five pages long. Here again, the upper-bounding inference appears to be part of the semantic content of an expression that composes with another element of the sentence, something that is problematic for the neo-Gricean version of the Classic Analysis.

The facts can be accommodated by the grammatical version of the Classic Analysis by inserting EXH below the modal (cf. Chierchia *et al.* 2012). As with the other phenomena we looked at, however, this would again predict a parallelism between number words and other scalars that is not actually observed. Consider the following scenario. A major midwestern research university seeks to build up enrollments in its for-profit MA program by requiring Ph.D.-granting departments to identify applicants to their graduate programs who are promising and likely to accept an offer of admission, but not fully competitive for the Ph.D. program, and then to pass them on for consideration by the MA program admissions staff. The administration wants to maximize the applicant pool, but not overwhelm the limited MA program staff. In such a context, (17a) is most naturally understood as imposing a two-sided obligation: the Linguistics Department must send over ten applicants, and may not send over more than ten applicants.

(17) a. The Linguistics Department is required to select ten of its Ph.D. program applicants for consideration by the MA program.
b. The Linguistics Department is required to select some of its Ph.D. program applicants for consideration by the MA program.

(17b), on the other hand, does not have an understanding in which the requirements prohibit selection of Q of the Department's Ph.D. applicants, where Q is a scalar alternative to *some*. That is, although norms of behavior and expectation typically ensure that a department given the instructions in (17b) will not send all – or even most or many – of its Ph.D. applicants to the MA program (don't make the MA people do too much work; save some applicants for the Ph.D. program), (17b) cannot be understood as an actual rule prohibiting such a move.

The preceding examples all involve interactions between number words and universal modals. But number words also interact in an interesting and very important way with existential modals. In particular, existential modals naturally give rise to readings in which number words are associated only with an upper-bound (Carston 1998; Scharten 1997). (18a) is understood to say that as long as Lee has 2000 or fewer calories, there will be no problem of weight gain; (18b) gives prisoners permission to make up to three phone calls, and (18c) licenses attendance in six courses or fewer.

(18) a. Lee can have 2000 calories without putting on weight.
b. Prisoners are allowed to make three phone calls.
c. You may take six courses next year.

Carston (1998) claims that the salient, upper-bounded interpretation of such examples cannot be accounted for on the Classic Analysis, but this is not correct: as I will show below, it can be derived in the usual way, as a scalar implicature. More significantly, given the traditional approaches to the semantic analysis of number words discussed in Section 1.2, the upper-bounded reading can *only* be derived as an implicature, regardless of whether we assume that number words introduce lower-bounded or two sided content. To see why, let us take a close look at the analysis of (18c).

First, observe that the upper-bounded reading is consistent with a *de dicto* interpretation of the nominal, so we need to be able to derive it when the nominal takes scope under the modal. Then assume that the numeral either introduces lower-bounded content, or two-sided content, in one of the ways discussed in Section 1.2. If the numeral introduces lower-bounded content, we get the truth conditions informally stated in (19a); if it introduces two-sided content, we get the truth conditions in (19b).

(19) a. $\exists w \in Acc_{w0}$[the *number of courses you take in* $w \geq 6$]
b. $\exists w \in Acc_{w0}$[the *number of courses you take in* $w = 6$]

On either of these options, the truth-conditional content of (18c) is exceedingly weak: there is a deontically accessible world in which you take at least/exactly six courses. Neither of these meanings forbids enrollment in more than six courses, and neither expressly allows enrollment in fewer than six. And indeed, (18c) can be understood in this weak way. However, it is far more natural to understand it in a stronger way, which forbids enrollment in more than six courses, but allows enrollment in six or fewer. This is the upper-bounded reading which Carston claims to be unavailable to the Classic Analysis.

In fact, this meaning is straightforwardly derivable as an implicature, given either the one-sided semantics in (19a) or the two-sided semantics in (19b). In particular, we can derive the inference that registration in more than six classes is prohibited as a scalar implicature from (19a), since it is asymmetrically entailed by alternatives in which the number word is replaced by a higher value. The resulting implicature – *for all n greater than 6, there is no deontically accessible world in which the number of courses you take is at least n* – gives the upper-bound and the strong meaning typically associated with an utterance of this sentence. Somewhat surprisingly, if the basic meaning of the number word involves two-sided content, as in (19b), the strong reading *cannot* be derived as a scalar implicature, because (19b) is not entailed by alternatives in which 6 is replaced by higher values. But both the upper-bound inference and the inference that lower quantities are allowed can be derived as a particularized conversational implicature from general reasoning about permission (Breheny 2008).[8]

The significance of the upper-bounded reading of sentences like (18a–c), then, is not that it presents a particular problem for the Classic Analysis, as Carston claims, but is rather that this is a reading which is only derivable via the implicature system, no matter which of the traditional hypotheses about the semantic content of number words we adopt. This means that if we can find evidence that these readings are derived semantically, rather than pragmatically, we have a strong reason to reconsider the traditional semantic assumptions about number word meaning. And indeed, there is evidence that the one-sided, upper-bounded readings we are interested in here are not (or at least do not have to be) derived via implicature, but are instead a matter of semantic content. One piece of evidence will be discussed in the next section, where we will see that there are populations of speakers who systematically fail to calculate scalar implicatures, yet not only assign two-sided meanings to sentences with number words, but also appear to understand sentences like those in (18) in the usual, strong way. Both facts are problematic for accounts of scalar readings of number words that crucially invoke the scalar implicature system.

The second piece of evidence comes from examples similar to the ones we have already been considering, in which the upper-bounding inference is retained in a context in which implicatures normally disappear. To set up the example, imagine a situation in which there are three different groups of people who can be distinguished according to how many of four possible exemptions they are allowed to claim on their tax returns: zero for individuals in Group A, two for individuals in Group B, and four for individuals in Group C. These individuals are members of an exemption-maximizing but law-abiding society, so everyone in Group A claims zero exemptions, everyone in Group B claims exactly two, and everyone in group C claims exactly four. Now consider the following utterances as descriptions of this situation:

(20) a. No individual who was allowed to claim two exemptions claimed four.
b. No individual who was allowed to claim some exemptions claimed four.

(20a) has a reading in which it is true in this scenario, because the quantifier restriction is understood to pick out individuals who were allowed to claim two exemptions, and not allowed to claim more than two exemptions, i.e., the ones in Group B. This is an upper-bounded reading, but it occurs in a downward-entailing context (and in the argument of a logical operator), which we have already seen is a context that is resistant to implicature calculation. And indeed, (20b), in which the number word is replaced by the scalar quantifier *some*, is clearly false in this situation, because the quantifier is understood to range over all individuals who were allowed to claim exemptions, which includes the ones in Group C. The sentence does not have a reading in which the restriction ranges over individuals who were allowed to claim some exemptions but not allowed to claim all exemptions. This would exclude the individuals in Group C, and would make the sentence true.

These facts provide further evidence, in addition to what we have seen so far, that upper-bounding inferences in sentences with number words are a matter of semantic content, and as such, they provide yet another argument for rejecting the Classic Analysis. But the real significance of these facts is that they give us new insight on what an alternative analysis of number word meaning must look like: it should be one that generates an upper-bounding inference for sentences with existential modals as a matter of semantic content. We have just seen that none of the semantic analyses discussed in Section 1.2 has this feature, including ones which posit two-sided semantic content for number words. The right analysis, then, is going to look different from what we have seen so far. In Section 3, I will say what I think it should look like; before doing that, though, I want to take a look at some experimental data which provides additional support for the conclusions that we have reached here.

### 2.2 *Experimental studies of number word meaning*

In addition to the kinds of semantic facts we have been discussing, there is a large set of experimental evidence based on different methodologies and studies of both child and adult behavior which indicates that two-sided interpretations of sentences with number words are retained in contexts in which upper-bounded interpretations of other scalar terms disappear. For example, in separate studies involving the Truth Value Judgment Task, Noveck (2001) and Papafragou and Musolino (2003) found that children (unlike adults) fail to assign upper-bounded readings to sentences with weak modals, scalar quantifiers, and aspectual verbs (e.g., *might*, *some*, *start*), but consistently assign two-sided interpretations to corresponding sentences with number words. Hurewitz *et al.* (2007) and Huang *et al.* (2009) achieved similar results in picture-matching and act-out tasks, and Huang and Snedeker (2009) found an asymmetry between number words and scalar terms in a set of eye-tracking experiments that suggested the same conclusion. Huang and Snedeker (2009) moreover showed that in a task in which adults' calculation of upper-bounding implicatures were suppressed for the scalar quantifier *some*, they were retained for numerals.

Taken as a whole, these studies provide evidence that two-sided interpretations of sentences with number words are available to speakers and in contexts in which two-sided interpretations of other scalar terms are not. The developmental work is particularly important, because it shows that during a stage in which children generally tend not to compute scalar implicatures (though they can do so when other cognitive demands are decreased, and the communicative task is highlighted; see Papafragou and Tantalou 2004), they nevertheless consistently assign two-sided interpretations to sentences with number words. The behavioral data thus supports the same conclusion that we drew in the previous section from observations about the linguistic data: two-sided interpretations of number words are not derived in the same way as two-sided interpretations of other scalar terms. The most straightforward explanation for the full pattern of data is that two-sided readings are not derived via the implicature system, whatever that may be (neo-Gricean or grammatical; generalized or particularized), but instead arise in a fully compositional way, in virtue of the meanings of the number words themselves – meanings which are evidently different from the options we considered in Section 1.2, given what we saw with existential modals in the previous section.[9]

The experimental literature also includes (at least) one apparent challenge to this conclusion, however. Musolino (2004) reports a set of experiments which show that in contexts in which adults most naturally understand sentences containing number words in a one-sided way – either as introducing only a lower bound on a particular quantity, or as introducing only an upper-bound – children do the same.[10] For example, children heard sentences like the following in a scenario in which an "owner" character has more objects than another character needs. (21) was presented in a context in which Troll needs just two cookies for a party, and Goofy presents him with a tray containing four cookies.

(21) Let's see if Goofy can help the Troll. The Troll needs two cookies. Does Goofy have two cookies?

Children systematically respond "yes" to the question, which means that they understand it in a one-sided, lower-bounded way. Similarly, when (22) is used to describe a situation in which Troll has missed only one hoop, children report that he does in fact win the coin, which indicates that the number word imposes at most an upper-bound on number of misses, but not a lower one.

(22) Goofy said the Troll could miss two hoops and still win the coin. Does the Troll win the coin?

Unfortunately, we do not know from Musolino's experiments whether children understand this sentence to actually impose an upper bound, because he did not consider scenarios in which more than two hoops were missed. My own experience with five-year olds tells me that the typical child knows exactly what would make the Troll lose here – missing more than two hoops – and I'm sure that other parents, aunts, uncles, and older siblings will agree with me on this. This hunch should be confirmed experimentally, but if it turns out to be correct, we have a significant puzzle not only for the Classic Analysis of number word meaning, but also for alternatives which posit two-sided semantic content. The problem, as we saw in the previous section, is that given the current options for number word meaning, an upper-bounding inference for examples with existential modals, like (22), can only be generated by implicature: because the truth-conditional content alone does not preclude the existence of deontically accessible worlds in which more than two hoops are missed. This result is in conflict with all the other evidence suggesting that children do not calculate upper-bounding implicatures for scalar terms, including for modals.

### 2.3 *Summary*

Summarizing, we have now seen compelling evidence that the upper-bounding inference which gives rise to two sided interpretations of sentences with number words is a matter of semantic content. The first kind of evidence comes from interactions between sentences containing number words and other logical operators that show that two-sided inferences are a matter of semantic content. This is a serious problem for Horn's original neo-Gricean version of the Classic Analysis, a fact that has already been pointed out in the literature by many researchers, including by Horn himself (Horn 1992; see also Breheny 2008; Carston 1988, 1998; Geurts 2006; Koenig 1991; Sadock 1984; Scharten 1997). The grammatical version of the Classic Analysis can accommodate the compositional facts by inserting an exhaustivity operator in the minimal clause containing the number word, but then predicts that other scalar terms should just as easily give rise to two-sided interpretations in the same contexts, contrary to fact. In short, on either version of the Classic Analysis, it remains a mystery why number words easily introduce two-sided content into the truth conditions, while other scalar terms do not.

A second type of evidence for the same conclusion comes from experimental results which show that sentences with number words strongly prefer two-sided interpretations, even in contexts and developmental stages in which sentences with other scalar terms are assigned one-sided interpretations. These results complement the linguistic data and indicate that two-sided interpretations of sentences with number words are a matter of semantic content, and not derived by whatever reasoning or mechanisms are involved in assigning upper-bounding inferences to sentences containing other kinds of scalar terms. At the same time, children in the relevant developmental stage are also able to correctly assign one-sided interpretations to sentences containing number words in contexts in which adults do the same. The crucial question, then, is:

what is the crucial difference between the contexts in which only two-sided meanings appear to be available and those which also allow one-sided readings? Let us now answer that question, and see how it leads to a new, fully semantic analysis of scalar readings of number words.

## 3. Numerals denote generalized quantifiers over degrees

### *3.1 Scalar readings of comparative numerals*

The generalization that emerges from both the linguistic and experimental literature is that two-sided readings are the norm, but that the two classes of one-sided readings (lower and upper-bounded) appear most naturally in sentences that contain other logical operators, in particular modals. Moreover, as originally observed by Scharten (1997), there is a pattern of interaction: lower-bounded readings are associated with sentences in which number words occur in the scope of a universal (typically deontic) modal, and upper-bounded readings are associated with sentences in which number words occur in the scope of an existential (deontic) modal. The following examples illustrate the pattern:

(23) *Lower-bounded interpretations*
   a. In Britain, you have to be 17 to drive a motorbike and 18 to drive a car.
   b. Mary needs three As to get into Oxford.
   c. Goofy said that the Troll needs to put two hoops on the pole in order to win the coin.
   d. You must provide three letters of recommendation.
   e. You are required to enroll in two classes per quarter.

(24) Upper-bounded interpretations
   a. She can have 2000 calories a day without putting on weight.
   b. You may have half the cake.
   c. Pink panther said the horse could knock down two obstacles and still win the blue ribbon.
   d. You are permitted to take three cards.
   e. You are allowed to enroll in four classes per quarter.

All of these sentences also allow for two-sided interpretations, though in most of the examples in (23), real-world knowledge renders such a reading unlikely, and for the examples in (24), such a reading results in exceedingly weak truth conditions, as we saw in Section 2.1.

The ambiguity of number words in modal contexts is strikingly similar to a pattern of ambiguity that has been previously discussed in the literature, involving the interaction between modals and comparatives (see e.g., Bhatt and Pancheva 2004; Hackl 2000; Heim 2000; Nouwen 2010). Consider, for example, (25a–b).

(25) a. Kim is required to take fewer than three classes.
b. Kim is allowed to take fewer than three classes.

(25a) has a reading in which the maximum number of courses that Kim is allowed to take is fewer than three; i.e., enrollment in three or more is prohibited. This is similar to the two-sided interpretation of the corresponding sentence with a bare numeral, where *fewer than three* is replaced by *three*. (25a) has a second reading, however, in which the minimum number of courses that Kim is required to take is fewer than three, e.g., Kim must take two, but is allowed to enroll in more. This reading is parallel to the one-sided, lower-bounded reading of the corresponding sentence with the bare numeral. (25b) is similar. One reading allows enrollment in two or fewer courses, but says nothing about enrollment in three or more courses; this is parallel to the weak, two-sided reading of the sentence with the bare number word. The other reading forbids enrollment in more than two courses; this is parallel to the upper-bounded, one-sided reading of the sentence with the bare number word.

Hackl (2000) shows that the ambiguity of sentences like (25) can be explained as a scope ambiguity arising from the interaction of the modal verbs and the comparative. Crucial to the analysis is the hypothesis that a comparative numeral like *fewer than three* is not an unanalyzed, complex quantificational determiner with the denotation in (26a) (as in e.g., Barwise and Cooper 1981; Keenan and Stavi 1986), but is rather a full-fledged generalized quantifier on its own, with the denotation in (26b).

(26) [[fewer than 3]]
a. $\neq \lambda P_{\langle e,t\rangle}\lambda Q_{\langle e,t\rangle}.|P \cap Q| < 3$
b. $= \lambda D_{\langle d,t\rangle}.\max\{n|D(n)\} < 3$

On this view, comparative numerals denote generalized quantifiers over degrees (type $\langle\langle d, t\rangle, t\rangle$). They combine with a degree property that is created by abstracting over a degree argument position inside the nominal projection, which we may assume to be introduced by the null cardinality predicate MANY discussed in Section 1.2, and return true just in case the maximal degree (number) that satisfies the property is greater or less than (depending on the type of comparative) the degree (number) corresponding to the modified numeral.[11] Like other quantificational expressions, comparative numerals must take scope. This means that in sentences containing modal verbs, such as (25a–b), we predict an ambiguity depending on whether the comparative numeral scopes below or above the modal.

In the case of (25a), if the comparative has narrow scope relative to the modal, we derive the proposition in (27a); if it has wide scope relative to the modal, we derive the proposition (27b).

(27) a. $\lambda w.\forall w' \in Acc_w[\max\{n|\exists x[\mathbf{classes}(w')(x) \wedge \#(w')(x) = n \wedge \mathbf{take}(w')(x)(\mathbf{kim})]\} < 3]$
b. $\lambda w.\max\{n|\forall w' \in Acc_w[\exists x[\mathbf{classes}(w')(x) \wedge \#(w')(x) = n \wedge \mathbf{take}(w')(x)(\mathbf{kim})]\} < 3$

(27a) is fairly straightforward: it is true of a world iff in every world deontically accessible from it, the maximum number of classes taken by Kim is less than three. (27a) is therefore false of a world if there are worlds deontically accessible from it in which Kim takes three or more classes; this is the "two-sided" interpretation. (27b) is a bit more complex. It is true of a world *w* iff the maximum *n*, such that in every world deontically accessible from *w* there is a plurality of classes taken by Kim of size *n*, is less than three. In this case, the argument of the modal is a proposition with lower-bounded truth conditions: the proposition that there is a plurality of classes of size *n* taken by Kim, for some value of *n*. This means that the set of values that the comparative is maximizing over represents the numbers of enrolled-in classes that all of the deontically accessible worlds agree on; maximizing over this therefore derives the *minimum* enrollment requirements, making (27b) false of a world if there are no worlds deontically accessible from it in which enrollment in at least two classes is required. This is the one-sided, lower-bounded interpretation of (25a).

Turning to (25b), the two scope relations in (26) derive the truth conditions in (28a–b), which are a bit easier to understand.

(28) a. $\lambda w.\exists w' \in Acc_w[\max\{n|\exists x[\mathbf{classes}(w')(x) \wedge \#(w')(x) = n \wedge \mathbf{take}(w')(x)(\mathbf{kim})]\} < 3]$
b. $\lambda w.\max\{n|\exists w' \in Acc_w[\exists x[\mathbf{classes}(w')(x) \wedge \#(w')(x) = n \wedge \mathbf{take}(w')(x)(\mathbf{kim})]\} < 3$

(28a) is true of a world just in case there is a world deontically accessible from it in which the maximal number of classes that Kim takes is less than three; this is the "two-sided," weak reading of (25b), which merely allows enrollment in two or fewer classes, and doesn't forbid anything. (28b), on the other hand, is true of a world just in case the maximal *n*, such that there is a world deontically accessible from it in which Kim takes *n* courses, is less than three. This is the one-sided, upper-bounded reading of (25b), which forbids enrollment in greater than two classes.

Stepping back a bit, let us observe that there are two components to this analysis of the ambiguity of sentences containing comparative numerals and modals. The first is the hypothesis that comparative numerals are generalized quantifiers over degrees, which can take scope independently of the nouns that they are in construction with in the surface form, and so can interact scopally with the modals. The second is the hypothesis that part of the truth-conditional content that a comparative numeral contributes involves maximization over the degree property denoted by its semantic scope, an operation (or its equivalent) which is necessary to get the comparative truth conditions right.[12] I would now like to propose that both of these features are also present in the semantics of bare numerals, in a way that derives the facts discussed in the previous section.

### *3.2 Unmodified numerals as degree quantifiers: deriving scalar readings as scope ambiguities*

Let us begin with scopability. That bare numerals must be able to take scope independently of the rest of the nominal has recently been argued by Kennedy and Stanley (2009). Kennedy and Stanley base their argument on the interpretation of "average" sentences such as (29a–b).

(29) a. The average American family has 2.3 children.
b. American families on average have 2.3 children.

What is important to observe about these examples is that they do not entail the existence of families with 2.3 children. This is in contrast to (30a–b), which are odd precisely because they do introduce such an entailment.

(30) a. ?A normal American family has 2.3 children.
b. ?American families in general have 2.3 children.

The oddity of (30a–b) is expected if the denotation of the verb phrases in these examples is as in (31), which is what we would expect if 2.3 denotes a degree and directly saturates a degree position introduced by $\text{MANY}_{\text{Adj}}$.[13]

(31) $\lambda x.\exists y[\mathbf{have}(y)(x) \wedge \mathbf{children}(y) \wedge \#(y) = 2.3]$

(31) is a property that is true of an object if it has a quantity of children of size 2.3; assuming the truth conditions of (30a–b) entail that there are families which have such a property, we have an explanation for why the examples sound strange.

Conversely, the fact that the examples in (29) do not entail of any families that they have such an odd property suggests that (31) is not the denotation of a constituent in the logical forms of these examples. And according to Kennedy and Stanley, the reason that (31) is not the denotation of a constituent of the logical form of these examples is because the numeral can (and must, in these cases) take scope independently of the rest of the nominal and outside of the verb phrase, just as we saw above with comparative numerals. This derives the relation between individuals and the (whole) number of children they have shown in (32), which then feeds into the semantics of *average* to derive correct truth conditions for the sentence as a whole.

(32) $\lambda n\lambda x.\exists y[\mathbf{have}(y)(x) \wedge \mathbf{children}(y) \wedge \#(y) = n]$

Let us now turn to maximization. Kennedy and Stanley assume that when a bare numeral like *three* takes scope, it either retains its status as a singular term and denotes the number 3, or it can be lifted in the standard way to a type ⟨⟨d, t⟩, t⟩ generalized quantifier denotation $\lambda P_{\langle d,t \rangle}.P(3)$. If scope-taking is optional, then a simple example like (33) has the three possible logical analyses shown in (33a–c).

(33) Kim has three children.

a. $\exists x[\mathbf{have}(x)(\mathbf{kim}) \wedge \mathbf{children}(x) \wedge \#(x) = 3]$

b. $\lambda n.\exists x[\mathbf{have}(x)(\mathbf{kim}) \wedge \mathbf{children}(x) \wedge \#(x) = n](3)$

c. $[\lambda P.P\,(3)](\lambda n.\exists x[\mathbf{have}(x)(\mathbf{kim}) \wedge \mathbf{children}(x) \wedge \#(x) = n])$

It is easy to see that these three parses are logically equivalent, and moreover have lower-bounded truth conditions. The two scope-taking parses in (33b) and (33c) provide a way of explaining why a numeral need not be interpreted in its base position, explaining the *average* data, but we need to add something else in order to explain the pattern of data we have seen in this chapter.

In particular, what we need to add is maximization over the degree property that constitutes the numeral's scope, as shown in (34) for the bare numeral *three*.

(34) $[[\text{three}]] = \lambda D_{\langle d,t \rangle}.\max\{n \mid D(n)\} = 3$

According to (34), *three* is a property of properties of degrees – a generalized quantifier over degrees – which is true of a degree property just in case the maximal number that satisfies it equals 3. The denotation of *three* in (34) is just like the denotation of *fewer than three* in (26b), except that the maximal number that satisfies the scope predicate is required to be equal to 3, rather than to be less than 3. If *three* takes sentential scope in (34), composition with the degree property that provides its scope gives the truth conditions in (35).

(35) $\max\{n \mid \exists x[\mathbf{have}(x)(\mathbf{kim}) \wedge \mathbf{children}(x) \wedge \#(x) = n]\} = 3$

These are two-sided truth conditions: (35) is true just in case the maximal *n* such that Kim has (at least) *n* children is equal to 3, i.e., just in case Kim has exactly three children. This analysis therefore straightforwardly accounts for the linguistic and experimental data discussed in Sections 2.1 and 2.2 which indicate that sentences with numerals can have two-sided semantic content.

More significantly, this analysis correctly derives lower-bounded and upper-bounded readings of sentences with bare numerals in modal contexts in exactly the same way that we saw for comparative numerals: as a scopal interaction between number words and modals. Consider first the case of universal modals. The sentence in (36) can be interpreted either with the number word inside the scope of the modal, deriving the proposition in (36a), or with the modal inside the scope of the number word, deriving the proposition in (36b).

(36) Kim is required to take three classes.

a. $\lambda w.\forall w' \in Acc_w[\max\{n \mid \exists x[\mathbf{classes}(w')(x) \land \#(w')(x) = n \land \mathbf{take}(w')(x)(\mathbf{kim})]\} = 3]$

b. $\lambda w.\max\{n \mid \forall w' \in Acc_w[\exists x[\mathbf{classes}(w')(x) \land \#(w')(x) = n \land \mathbf{take}(w')(x)(\mathbf{kim})]]\} = 3$

(36a) is true of a world if in every world deontically accessible from it, the maximum number of classes taken by Kim is three. This is the two-sided reading. (36b) is true of a world if the maximum number, such that in every world deontically accessible from it there is a plurality of classes of at least that size taken by Kim, is three. This means that the minimum number of deontically acceptable classes is three, which is the lower-bounded meaning.

In the case of a sentence with an existential modal like (37), we get exactly the same scopal relations, but the resulting truth conditions are quite different:

(37) Kim is allowed to take three classes.

a. $\lambda w.\exists w' \in Acc_w[\max\{n \mid \exists x[\mathbf{classes}(w')(x) \land \#(w')(x) = n \land \mathbf{take}(w')(x)(\mathbf{kim})]\} = 3]$

b. $\lambda w.\max\{n \mid \exists w' \in Acc_w[\exists x[\mathbf{classes}(w')(x) \land \#(w')(x) = n \land \mathbf{take}(w')(x)(\mathbf{kim})]]\} = 3$

(37a) is the "weak" reading, which merely says that there is a deontically accessible world in which the maximum number of classes taken by Kim is three. (37b) is true of a world if the maximum number, such that *there is a deontically acceptable world in which Kim takes at least that many classes*, is three. On this reading, the proposition is false of a world if there is another world deontically accessible from it in which Kim takes more than three classes. This is the strong reading of (37), and unlike all of the traditional analyses of number word meaning, the proposal I am advocating here derives it as a matter of semantic content. This is an extremely positive result, given the evidence we saw in Sections 2.1 and 2.2 which indicated that this reading is in fact a matter of semantic content, and not derived via implicature.

### 3.3 *Revisiting the evidence for lower-bounded content*

The semantic analysis of numerals as generalized quantifiers over degrees that I presented in the previous section has a clear advantage over the alternatives that we examined in Section 1.2 in that it both derives the correct scalar readings of numerals in the correct modal contexts as a matter of semantic content, and also correctly predicts that numerals can introduce two-sided semantic content in non-modalized sentences. However, the latter result immediately raises an important question: what about the data that motivated the neo-Gricean account in the first place? For example, how do we explain the fact that the continuation *if not more* in (38a) does not give rise to a contradiction, and the fact that (38b) is most naturally understood as saying that everyone who missed three questions *or more* failed the exam?

(38) a. Kim read three of the articles on the syllabus, if not more.
b. Everyone who missed three of the questions failed the exam.

There are at least three ways to bring examples like these in line with my proposals. The first is to maintain the strong hypothesis that numerals always denote degree quantifiers with denotations like (34), so that (38a–b) both have semantic content, but then to attempt to explain the appearance of one-sided readings in non-modalized examples as particularized conversational implicatures (Breheny 2008), or as the result of an interaction with a covert modal (cf. Nouwen 2010). The former approach would work for (38b): if missing exactly three questions is sufficient to fail the exam, then surely missing more questions is too, while missing fewer questions may not be. For (38a), we could hypothesize the presence of an implicit relativization of the assertion to worlds compatible with my knowledge state, with the follow-up *if not more* provided as a way of indicating uncertainty about the completeness of my knowledge. Note that I am not proposing that the numeral takes scope over an implicit epistemic modal; rather, I am suggesting that the first part of (38a), two-sided content and all, is claimed to be true only in worlds compatible with my knowledge, and the second part is a way of saying that I am open to the possibility that my knowledge is partial, and so does not in fact rule out the possibility that a variant of this sentence containing a higher-valued numeral could be true of the actual world.[14]

A second option, which also maintains the strong hypothesis that numerals always have quantificational denotations like (34), is to hypothesize that the individual variable contributed by the nominal with which the numeral composes can be existentially bound either below the numeral (as I have been tacitly assuming so far) or above it. (I am grateful to Paul Marty for suggesting this approach.) On this view, the first half of (38a) is ambiguous. If the individual variable is existentially bound below the numeral, as shown in (39a), we derive two-sided truth conditions, as we have already seen.

(39) a. $\max\{n \mid \exists x[\mathbf{read}(x)(\mathbf{kim}) \wedge \mathbf{articles}(x) \wedge \#(x) = n]\} = 3$
b. $\exists x[\max\{n \mid \mathbf{read}(x)(\mathbf{kim}) \wedge \mathbf{articles}(x) \wedge \#(x) = n\} = 3]$

If, however, the individual variable is existentially bound above the numeral, we get lower-bounded truth conditions: (39b) is true just in case there is a plurality of books that Kim read whose maximal size is three, which rules out lower values but not higher ones. Whether this option is a viable alternative or not depends mainly on compositional considerations, in particular on where and how existential closure over the individual argument is introduced.

The final – and perhaps most likely – option is to hypothesize that the quantificational denotation of a number word is derived from a more basic singular term denotation. On this view, number words are in effect polysemous between the denotations in (39a) and (39b) (continuing to use *three* as our example).

(40) [three] =
a. 3
b. $\lambda D_{\langle d,t\rangle}.\max\{n \mid D(n)\} = 3$

As we have already seen, combination of the singular term denotation of a numeral with e.g. an adjectival analysis of MANY derives lower-bounded truth conditions, so the consequence of hypothesizing (40a) as a potential denotation for the numeral is that lower-bounded truth conditions become available across the board, and in particular for non-modalized sentences like (40a–b). This should not create any problems, since the data we considered in the first part of the chapter showed only that two-sided content must be an option, not that one-sided, lower-bounded content is *not* an option.[15]

I do not have space here to conduct a full exploration of these three options, but I will briefly mention two factors that may argue in favor of the third approach. First, if the basic denotation of a numeral is a number (if numerals are singular terms), we can construct a simple mapping to the denotations of modified numerals such as *more/fewer than three*, *at least/most three*, and so forth: they are mappings from denotations like (40a) to denotations like (40b), with the appropriate ordering relation substituted for "=" (>, <, ≥, ≤, etc.).[16] In Kennedy (2011) I show how this move allows us to explain a number of puzzles involving modified numerals and modals discussed by Nouwen (2010).

Second, it may be possible to say simply that the singular term meaning of the numeral is the lexical meaning, and to derive the maximal degree meaning in (40b) in a quite general way, without any assumptions specific to numerals. Specifically, we could assume that numerals in general are number-denoting singular terms, but like e.g. proper names, when they take scope they undergo a Montagovian type-shift to a generalized quantifier denotation: in the case of *three*, a move from 3 to $\lambda D_{\langle d,t\rangle}.D(3)$. As we saw in the previous section, this move alone does not derive interesting truth-conditional results. However, if we further assume that the generalized quantifier denotation composes with an exhaustivity operator of the sort originally proposed in Groenendijk and Stokhof (1984) to derive exhaustive readings of answers to questions (see also Rooij and Schulz 2004; Schulz and Rooij 2006; Zeevat 1994), then we should be able to derive an interpretation that is equivalent to (40b). Working out the details of this hypothesis is beyond the scope of the current chapter, but it seems like a promising approach. In particular, it may provide a nice account of some facts involving the interaction of questions and context in the promotion of two-sided readings discussed by Scharten (1997).

## 4. Conclusion

I hope to have done two things in this chapter. First, I have tried to show that sentences containing numerals can have two-sided meanings as a matter of semantic content, rather than as the result of implicature calculation. Previous work has come to similar conclusions (Breheny 2008; Carston 1988, 1998; Geurts 2006; Horn 1992; Koenig 1991; Sadock 1984; Scharten 1997); one of the contributions of the current chapter is to show that even the "grammatical" account of scalar implicature runs into many of the same problems as the neo-Gricean one. Second, I have argued for a new semantic analysis of number words as generalized quantifiers over degrees, true of a property of degrees D just in case the maximal degree that satisfies D is equal to a specific value (a number). I showed that this account generates two-sided interpretations in the basic case, and that scalar (upper/lower-bounded) readings of sentences containing numerals arise through scopal interactions with modals.

I would like to close by briefly comparing my proposal to one with a much longer history. The idea that number words denote second-order properties rather than determiners, cardinality predicates, or singular terms is not new: this idea goes back to Frege (1884), who considers an analysis of numbers as second-order properties of individuals before eventually rejecting it in favor of a treatment of numbers as singular terms, and it has been more recently proposed by Scharten (1997). The Fregean analysis of *three* as a second-order property of individuals, for example, can be stated as in (41a); the "neo-Fregean" analysis of *three* as a second-order property of degrees that I have proposed in this chapter is repeated in (41b) for comparison.

(41) a. $[[\text{three}]] = \lambda P_{\langle e,t\rangle}.\#(\{x \mid P(x)\}) = 3$
b. $[[\text{three}]] = \lambda D_{\langle d,t\rangle}.\max\{n \mid D(n)\} = 3$

The Fregean analysis also returns two-sided truth conditions for the basic cases we are interested in, and it has the advantage of not necessitating the introduction of degrees into the semantics. Space unfortunately prohibits a full examination of how the Fregean semantics interacts with modals; the various scope configurations do not derive exactly the same truth conditions as the degree quantifier analysis (because the Fregean semantics tracks individuals across worlds, rather than degrees), but it may be that the same range of readings eventually emerges.

One potential advantage of the degree-quantifier analysis of numerals is that it fits seamlessly into a quite general, well-motivated, and well-understood syntax and compositional semantics for quantity and degree constructions in the nominal projection. Number words stand alongside comparatives and other degree words (*too*, *how*, *so*, etc.) as expressions that provide information about the quantity of objects that satisfy the nominal description by saturating a degree argument position in an (overt or covert) occurrence of MANY. Because this position is distinct from the individual argument position that the nominal itself saturates, these words can take scope independently of the nominal, as we have seen. It may be that an equally general syntax and semantics can be developed for numerals and degree words under a Fregean analysis (see Scharten 1997 for some first steps in this direction), but this is an investigation that I will have to leave for another time.

## Acknowledgments

This chapter took a long time to write, and I am grateful to the people who provided helpful criticism and advice along the way: Ivano Caponigro, Gurpreet Rattan, Pete Arlenga, Paul Marty, Rick Nouwen, Yoad Winter, two anonymous reviewers (whose comments I have not been able to fully address in the space of this chapter, but which will be helpful as I continue with this project), and audiences at Queens University, the University of Kyoto, the University of Chicago, the University of Southern California, the University of Rochester, Harvard University, XPRAG 2011 and Semantics and Linguistic Theory 21. I am very pleased to have the opportunity to publish this chapter in a volume in honor of Gennaro Chierchia, whose work has inspired my thinking about quantity and scalar meaning in the nominal projection.

NOTES

1. Geurts shows that both the two-sided and lower-bounded determiner meanings can be derived from the cardinality predicate meaning in using standard type-shifting principles, and uses this to build a "polysemy" analysis of number word meaning which can accommodate most of the facts we will discuss in the next section, with the exception of those involving existential modals.
2. In fact, Cresswell (1976) and Krifka (1989) treat nouns themselves as type ⟨d, ⟨e, t⟩⟩, basically incorporating the meaning of $\text{MANY}_{\text{Adj}}$ into the meaning of the noun. I actually prefer this way of doing things for English, but since working it out requires dealing with issues of composition that are orthogonal to the purposes of this chapter (having to do with how the degree argument gets passed up, and how it gets saturated in the absence of an overt numeral), I will stick with the compositionally simpler $\text{MANY}_{\text{Adj}}$ version of the analysis.
3. An apparent disadvantage of this kind of analysis is that it must stipulate that MANY is deleted (or unpronounced) when it composes with a numeral, though it may turn out that there is a principled explanation for this. Note in particular that other putative degree-denoting expressions either allow deletion of their corresponding scalar predicates in prenominal position (i) or require it (ii):

   (i) 2 meter (long) board
   (ii) a 10 kilogram (*heavy) stone

Murphy (1997) proposes that reason that *heavy* must be omitted in (ii) is because the measure phrase unambiguously determines the dimension of measurement. (This is not the case in (i), where *2 meters* could be a measure of length, width, depth, etc.) It is tempting to apply the same reasoning to the case of numerals and MANY in English, since MANY is (by hypothesis) the only scalar predicate that numerals combine with. This would lead us to expect that if a language had more than one type of MANY-term, it would need to be expressed, a scenario that sounds very much like a classifier system.

4. Space considerations preclude a discussion of the full range of data that has been presented in recent years as evidence for two-sided content in number words; so I focus here on a few cases that I think make the point in a particularly clear and relevant way. For additional discussion, though, see Breheny (2008); Bultinck (2005); Carston (1998); Geurts (2006); Koenig (1991); Krifka (1999); Sadock (1984); Scharten (1997).
5. The crucial difference between lower-bounded content and two-sided content is that the former would be true and the latter false if e.g., some people missed four or more questions and all of them failed, but nobody missed exactly three questions. But this situation is not really a problem, given the existence presupposition of the relative clause. Indeed, the fact that (2a) appears to presuppose only that there are some people who missed exactly three questions on the exam, and not that there are some people who missed more than three questions, could potentially be interpreted as another argument that number words introduce two-sided semantic content.
6. I restrict my attention here to interactions between number words and deontic modals, mainly because focusing on one case is sufficient to make the main point that number words are able to introduce two-sided truth-conditional content, and because deontic modals support the construction of fairly clear examples. However, I will say a bit more about the relation between number words and other kinds of modals in Section 3.
7. As pointed out by Geurts (2006), these examples also appear to challenge a semantic analysis of number words as two-sided quantificational determiners (as in (3b)), a position that is advocated by Breheny (2008). Breheny acknowledges this challenge, and attempts to derive the appearance of one-sided content in examples like (15) pragmatically.
8. The reasoning goes roughly as follows. Knowing that it is permissible to take exactly six courses does not allow one to conclude that it is permissible to take more than six courses, because doing so would involve a greater use of existing resources. On the other hand, if it is permissible to take six courses, then surely it is not a problem to take five or fewer, because that would involve a smaller use of existing resources.
9. Though see Barner and Bachrach (2009) for an alternative explanation of the difference between numerals and other scalar terms, which is based on the idea that the alternatives involved in computing implicatures for numerals are easier for children to access, given their knowledge of the counting list. I do not have space here to adequately assess this interpretation of the data, other than to point out that in addition to its plausibility as an account of the developmental facts, it should be assessed in light of facts like those discussed in Section 2.1 (and additional facts discussed in the papers mentioned in note 4), which give us strong reasons to believe that two-sided inferences in sentences containing number words are a matter of semantic content, not implicature.
10. The following is a simplification and condensation of Musolino's study; please see the original article for the full details of design and statistical analysis of results, as

well as a discussion of controls and adult responses, which were exactly as one would expect.

11. As noted in Section 1.2, Hackl treats MANY as a determiner that introduces existential quantification over the individual argument of the noun. As such, MANY and its nominal argument constitute a DP which must themselves take scope, resulting in a "split-scope" analysis of DPs with comparative numerals. I adopt the "$\text{MANY}_{\text{Adj}}$" (cardinality predicate) analysis mainly to keep the logical forms simpler, but my proposals are entirely consistent with the "$\text{MANY}_{\text{Det}}$" analysis. Hackl also treats the numeral part of the comparative numeral complex as the remnant of a clausal structure, derived by ellipsis, an option that I will not discuss here.
12. As we saw in Section 1.2 and above, the combination of MANY plus existential quantification over the individual argument of the noun gives the scope expression a "Classic Analysis" semantics, so it picks out all the numbers/degrees such that there is a plurality of objects of at least that size which satisfy the restrictions imposed on the nominal argument.
13. Clearly, if the numeral is a degree-denoting singular term, then $\text{MANY}_{\text{Adj}}$ cannot actually be a relation between pluralities and cardinalities, which is how I have been describing it so far. It must instead take quantities of stuff as its input, which may be composed of atoms as well as parts, and return a value that represents the measure of that stuff relative to a stuff-appropriate counting metric (possibly provided by the noun denotation; cf. Krifka 1989; Salmon 1997), with the values not limited to ones corresponding to whole numbers (cf. Fox and Hackl 2006). Quantities of children are normally not measured in this way, but many other things are, for example:

    (i) It normally takes one bushel of apples to make 4 gallons of apple juice, each bushel is 42 pounds of apples, each pound is 3 apples, so it would take **3.7 apples** to make 15.2 fluid ounces of apple juice. (www.chacha.com/question/how-many-apples-does-it-take-to-make-15.2-fl-oz)

    Gennaro Chierchia (p.c.) wonders whether the use of the decimal in *3.7 apples* is natural language. Perhaps not; on the other hand, we would like to understand why such expressions so naturally slot into the same position as cardinals once they have been introduced into the language.
14. In fact, if my overall analysis is on the right track, then I predict that numerals can never take scope over epistemic modals. An empirical generalization that has emerged from research on degree quantification over the past fifteen years or so is that degree quantifiers may take scope higher than some kinds of quantificational expressions but not others (see e.g., Bhatt and Pancheva 2004; Hackl 2000; Heim 2000; Kennedy 1999; Lassiter to appear; Takahashi 2006). In particular, while degree quantifiers may scope above deontic modals of the sort we looked at in the previous sections, they may not take scope above epistemic modals (Büring 2007). So the fact that (i) lacks a "strong" reading, to the effect that it is epistemically impossible that Kim read more than three articles on the syllabus, is expected under the current proposal.

    (i) Kim might have read three of the articles on the syllabus.

15. Note also that for sentences like (40b) – and more generally for any structure in which the numeral appears in a downward-entailing context – a parse in which the numeral is hypothesized to have the denotation in (40a) will result in more informative truth conditions than one in which the numeral is hypothesized to have the denotation in (40b), and so might represent a preferred parse given general informativity principles. What is important, though, is that both readings are derived fully semantically; neither invokes the implicature system.
16. A modifier like *exactly*, on the other hand, which also introduces an equality relation, can be analyzed as a "slack regulator" in Lasersohn (1999): its function is not to introduce a truth-conditional mapping from a lower-bounded interpretation to a two-sided one, but just to signal increased pragmatic precision.

# 8 Presupposition projection from quantificational sentences: trivalence, local accommodation, and presupposition strengthening

*Danny Fox*

The main goal of this chapter is to make sense of conflicting data pertaining to the way quantifier phrases project the presuppositions of their arguments. More specifically, I will try to argue that the facts can be understood within trivalent approaches to presupposition projection,[1] when coupled with two independently needed mechanisms: (i) one which strengthens presuppositions (needed to deal with the so called "proviso problem"), and (ii) another which incorporates presuppositions into truth conditions at various scope positions ("local accommodation"). A secondary goal is to provide some sketchy remarks on how the trivalent predictions could be derived in a classical bivalent system with the aid of a modified bridge principle – a modification of the principle suggested in Stalnaker (1978) to connect formal presuppositions to pragmatic conditions of language use.[2]

The chapter is organized as follows. The first three sections will present empirical challenges for a theory of presupposition projection that come from quantificational sentences. We will see that the challenges come from three sources of variability in judgments. The first pertains to differences among individual speakers: some speakers report judgments that are consistent with extremely weak presuppositions whereas the judgments of other speakers require much stronger presuppositions – in some cases it looks like universal projection is required. The second source of variability pertains to the nature of the quantifier: it seems that the strong judgments require a distinction among different quantifiers (some quantifiers appear to project universal presuppositions whereas others do not). The third source of variability pertains to the nature of the presupposition trigger: all quantifiers and all speakers appear to provide evidence for universal projection in the case of so-called strong triggers.

Section 4 will introduce the predicted presupposition of Strong Kleene. Section 5 will explain the way that judgments (the strong judgments) can be derived from these predictions if presuppositions are collapsed with assertions. Section 6 will problematize this observation, noting that collapsing assertion and presupposition is not necessarily a sound move if presuppositions are viewed as providing admittance conditions.

Section 7 will characterize a very specific prediction that follows from the Strong Kleene system when presuppositions are taken to provide admittance conditions. The prediction is based on the fact that universal projection is never derived directly in Strong Kleene, but is, instead, the result of presupposition strengthening (global accommodation). We will see evidence that when presupposition strengthening is not required given contextual assumptions, universal projection is never supported by data (for any combination of speaker, trigger, and quantifier). Sections 8–11 will discuss two mechanisms in detail (local accommodation and presupposition strengthening) and will argue that the patterns of variability can follow from the claim that local accommodation is impossible for strong triggers and is dispreferred for certain speakers (in any position but the matrix). Section 12 will outline a way of deriving the results reported here in a bivalent system with a modified bridge principle.

## 1. Projection from the nuclear scope: a complicated empirical terrain

Consider the sentences in (1) under an interpretation in which the pronoun *his* is bound by the quantificational subject.

(1) a. Some boy drives *both* of his cars to school.
b. Every boy drives *both* of his cars to school.
c. No boy drives *both* of his cars to school.

In all of these sentences the word *both* (a presupposition trigger) introduces a presupposition of some sort, one that affects the presupposition of the sentence. If we want to understand the way the presupposition of the sentence is affected by the presupposition of *both*, i.e., the way in which the presupposition triggered by *both* projects, it is very useful to be able to state the presupposition triggered by *both*. But how should that be done?

In analogy with simple sentences that contain the word *both*, one would be tempted to state this as the presupposition that some particular person has exactly two cars. But who is that person? It should be the person that the pronoun *his* refers to. But we know that there is no such person: the pronoun has no reference (independently of an assignment function); rather it serves as a variable bound by the quantificational subject.[3] So the problem of presupposition projection exemplified here is one of determining ways in which an assignment dependent presupposition projects (and becomes assignment independent) once a variable is bound. Let us, then, adopt the notation of e.g. Sandt (1989) and write the presupposition of the nuclear scope as a subscript that contains a variable bound outside the subscript:

(2) a. Some boy λx. x drives *both* of x's cars to school$_{\text{x has two cars}}$.
b. Every boy λx. x drives *both* of x's cars to school$_{\text{x has two cars}}$.
c. No boy λx. x drives *both* of x's cars to school$_{\text{x has two cars}}$.

Our problem of presupposition projection is to determine and explain the presupposition for sentences of the form $Q(A)(\lambda x.A(x)_{p(x)})$, where p(x) is the (assignment dependent) presupposition of the nuclear scope.[4]

One important challenge in addressing this problem is that the facts are far from clear. In fact, different authors have made different empirical claims about the relevant presuppositions. Heim (1983b), who pointed out the significance of the problem to debates about presupposition projection, suggested that all quantificational sentences presuppose that every individual in the domain of quantification satisfies the presupposition of the nuclear scope – that $Q(A)(\lambda x.B(x)_{p(x)})$ presupposes $\forall x(A(x) \rightarrow p(x))$.[5] Beaver (2001), by contrast, argued that this universal presupposition is too strong, and suggested that all the sentences have, instead, an existential presupposition: $\exists x A(x) \wedge p(x)$.

Chierchia (1995) was, as far as I know, the first to suggest that the situation is more nuanced. Specifically, he suggested that both an existential and a universal presupposition are possible and that they follow from two available representations. Chemla (2009a) presented evidence that the presupposition depends on the choice of quantifier, that for some quantifiers a universal presupposition is too strong, but for others an existential presupposition is too weak. Finally, Charlow (2009) argues that, despite initial appearances, the true presuppositions are universal and that the appearance of weaker presuppositions should be attributed to the fact that certain presuppositions can sometimes be cancelled (to the process of local accommodation).

## 2. Some evidence that different quantifiers behave differently

Heim (1983b) pointed out that people do not tend to draw a universal inference for existential sentences such as those in (1a). This observation was consistent with her claims about universal projection for quantificational sentences, given her assumption that indefinites are not quantificational. However, if one treats indefinites as existential quantifiers, the observation seems to argue that a universal presupposition is not, in general, correct. Furthermore, it seems to argue against the recent proposal of Schlenker (2008a) that derives universal projection based on the meaning of the relevant sentences, independently of assumptions about the syntax and semantics of the indefinite phrase itself.

It has been noted in the literature that the empirical issue (even when limited to indefinites) is not straightforward, given the availability of "implicit domain restriction." It is well established that quantificational domains are determined not only by overt restrictors, i.e., that implicit contextual restriction is often available. So, in order to rule out universal projection, one needs to factor out domain restriction. However, it has also been pointed out (in particular in Beaver 2001) that this can be done and that the initial suspicion that a universal inference is too strong for existential sentences is corroborated. The following (based on the combination of manipulations suggested by Beaver 2001 and Schlenker 2008a) illustrates the point.

(3) a. Half of the ten boys wrote two papers. Furthermore, one of the ten boys is proud of both of his papers.
b. Half of the ten boys wrote papers. #Furthermore, every one of the ten boys wrote excellent papers.

Given the contradictoriness of the universal sentence in (3b), it is reasonable to assume that in the context of (3) implicit domain restriction is impossible (an impossibility that should follow from the form of the partitive). The fact that the existential sentence in (3a) is entirely coherent (at least for most speakers) demonstrates that universal projection should not be derived for existential sentences (at least not all the time).[6]

For other quantificational sentences, the facts about presupposition projection are less clear. Universal sentences, such as (1b), clearly support a universal inference, but (as pointed out by Beaver) this need not have any consequences for presupposition projection – given that a universal inference ought to follow from the assertive component on its own. Negative existentials, such as that in (1c), should be more revealing, since a universal inference, if it were present, would probably not follow from the assertive component. The problem is that speakers' judgments do not seem to be uniform. Nevertheless, there do seem to be some speakers who get a universal inference, as suggested by the experimental work reported in Chemla (2009a). Furthermore, informal surveys I've conducted indicate that at least some speakers reject sequences of sentences parallel to what was acceptable in (3):[7]

(4) Half of the ten boys wrote two papers. (#)And/but none of the 10 boys is proud of both of his papers.

So we might conclude that a universal presupposition is true for negative existentials, as in (1c), but not for plain existentials as in (1a). This state of affairs is rather odd. One might think that (1c), which in a classical system (bivalent with no presuppositions) is the negation of (1a) should have the same presuppositions. More directly, the sentence in (1a) appears to support a universal inference (again, for some speakers) when it is transparently embedded under negation as in (5a) or under other "holes" for projection, such as the environment that forms polar questions (see Schlenker 2008a: 294, 2009: 3.1.1.).

(5) a. Not one of these 10 boys is [$t_1$ proud of both $his_1$ papers].
b. Is one of these 10 boys [$t_1$ proud of both $his_1$ papers]?

(6) Half of the ten boys wrote two papers. (#)Is one/any of the 10 boys proud of both of his papers?

The empirical conclusions seem to be rather complex. There seems to be at least some evidence that different quantifiers project their presuppositions differently. But the picture is far from clear given informal evidence for inter-speaker variation. There, thus, seems to be a clear goal for empirical research, namely to ascertain the range of variation in presupposition projection (i) across speakers, and (ii) across different quantificational constructions.

But the facts at the moment seem to be the following. The judgments of some speakers appear to show no evidence for universal projection in any quantificational environment. However, the judgments of other speakers appear to distinguish among different quantificational environments: in some environments, universal inferences seem to be derived (universal quantifiers, negative existentials, and existentials embedded under polar questions), but not in other environments (simple existentials).

## 3. Evidence that all quantifiers project universal presuppositions: Charlow (2009)

We have seen evidence that in simple existential sentences, in possible contrast to other quantificational sentences, presuppositions of the nuclear scope do not project universally. Charlow (2009), however, presented data suggesting that this holds only for certain presupposition triggers. Specifically, he observes that the presupposition triggered by *also* appears to yield a universal inference even in the scope of an existential quantifier. This is illustrated by the contradictoriness of (7) when compared to (3), or the more minimal counterpart in (8).[8]

(7) Just half of these 100 boys have smoked in the past. They have all smoked Nelson.
#Unfortunately, some of these 100 boys have also smoked $\text{Marlboro}_F$.
*Representation:*
Some of these 100 boys $\lambda$x. x has smoked $\text{Marlboro}_{\text{x has smoked Nelson}}$

(8) Just half of these 100 boys smoke. Unfortunately, some of these 100 boys advertise the fact that they smoke.
*Representation:*
Some of these 100 boys $\lambda$x. x advertises the fact that x $\text{smokes}_{\text{x smokes}}$

To deal with this complicated state of affairs, Charlow relies on the distinction between "soft" and "strong" triggers. It has been claimed that the presuppositions that are triggered by certain lexical items (so called soft triggers) are cancellable in certain environments more easily than the presuppositions triggered by other lexical items (strong triggers) (Abusch 2010; Chierchia and McConnell-Ginet 2000, and references therein). *Also*, and other so-called anaphoric triggers, appear to be strong triggers, as illustrated by the contrast in (9):[9]

(9) a. No, he is not interviewing the applicants; there are no applicants.
b. #No, he is not talking also to Bill; he didn't talk to anyone else.
c. After talking to Mary, did he also talk to Bill? #No, he didn't also talk to Bill; he (just) didn't talk to Mary.

Charlow's conclusion is that to study the true projection properties of quantifiers we ought to look at sentences containing strong triggers, such as (7). For other triggers, such as *both* and *the*, presupposition cancellation (a.k.a. local accommodation) is available (as illustrated in (9)), masking the true nature of things. From (7) we can conclude, Charlow argues, that all quantifier phrases, even those headed by existential quantifiers, project the presuppositions of their arguments universally.

This is an interesting proposal, but there are some puzzles that still ought to be addressed. Charlow has argued that all quantifiers project the presuppositions of strong triggers in the same way. But he did not address the differences between different quantificational environments that arise (at least for some speakers) with soft triggers. So, for example, under his proposal, the contrast between (1a) and (1c) is still mysterious, as is the effect of embedding in polar questions. Furthermore it seems that presupposition cancellation, or local accommodation, is easier when soft triggers occur in quantificational sentences, such as (8) and (1a), than in other environments, such as (9), and the reasons for this still need to be understood.

## 4. The presuppositions derived by Strong Kleene

In this section I present the predicted presuppositions of a theory that is based on a trivalent logic. The predictions will, at first, seem rather odd and my goals for the remainder of the chapter will be to argue that they might nevertheless be correct once investigated in conjunction with certain auxiliary hypotheses. The relevant trivalent logic (Strong Kleene) is based on a general recipe for transforming bivalent semantic values (functions from various domains to the two truth-values 0 and 1) into trivalent ones (functions from various domains to the three truth-values 0, 1, and #). The trivalent values, in turn, lead to predictions about presuppositions, once one adopts something like Stalnaker's Bridge Principle in (10) (see Beaver and Krahmer 2001).

(10) **Stalnaker's Bridge Principle**[10]
A truth denoting sentence S is assertable given a context set C only if $\forall w \in C$ [the denotation of S in w is either 0 or 1].

In other words, the semantics will make predictions about the conditions under which a sentence, S, receives a given truth-value, and these conditions, together with the bridge principle, will derive the presupposition of S – the presupposition that the semantic value of S is not the third value, #.

So our first step is to derive the trivalent truth conditions. For minimal sentences that contain a presupposition trigger, the truth conditions are derived based on stipulations (as in all systems), or on some independent theory (see, e.g., Abrusán 2011). For example *John drives both his cars to school* receives the third value if the number of cars John has $n_J$ is any number other than 2 and otherwise the sentence is true if John drives all of his cars to school, and false if not.

(11) [[John drives both of his cars to school]]
$= 1$ if $n_J = 2$ and $\forall x$ (Car-of-John(x) $\rightarrow$ Drive (J,x))
$= 0$ if $n_J = 2$ and $\exists x$ (Car-of-John(x) & $\neg$Drive (J,x))
$= \#$ otherwise

If we abstract over the position of *John* we derive the denotation of the nuclear scope in (1):

(12) Trivalent denotation of the nuclear scope in (Trivalent denotation of the nuclear scope 1a–c):
λx.
1 if x has exactly two cars and x drives both of x's cars to school
0 if x has exactly two cars and x doesn't drive at least one of x's cars to school
# if the number of cars x has is different from 2

What is needed, next, is a general recipe for transforming classical lexical entries to trivalent ones. To understand the Strong Kleene recipe it is useful to assume that the system is underlyingly bivalent and that the third value stands for either 0 or 1 – we just don't know which.[11] The way the third value projects is the way that uncertainty projects.

Assume that a certain constituent receives the third value. This means that we don't know whether its value is 0 or 1. If we can determine the bivalent value of the entire sentence without knowing the value of the relevant constituent, the sentence would have that bivalent value. Otherwise – since we do not know the bivalent value of the entire sentence – it will receive the third value.[12] In order for this idea to apply more broadly, we will have to discuss cases in which trivalent functions serve as arguments of higher-order predicates.[13] We will focus here on the bit needed to deal with quantificational sentences, with the hope that the extension (to the general case) will be transparent.

Imagine that f is a function of type <e,t>, one which assigns the third value to certain elements in its domain ($D_e$). If we apply f to an element of type e, we will receive a truth-value by simple function application. But what if f is an argument of a quantifier, Q, (type <et,t>)? In order to understand what happens, we need to continue to imagine that the system is underlyingly bivalent, and that cases in which f returns # indicate lack of knowledge pertaining to the bivalent value. What we want to know is under what conditions knowledge (or lack of knowledge) projects, i.e., under what circumstances the elements of type e for which f assigns the third value could be bypassed in determining the truth-value of Q(f). The answer is simple: elements can be bypassed when we would get the same value for Q(f), irrespective of the value that f assigns to them. And when does that happen? Whenever we get the same value under every replacement of f with what George (2010) calls a bivalent correction of f – a bivalent function, g, that agrees with f on all individuals to which f assigns a bivalent value.

(13) A function $g:X \rightarrow \{0,1\}$ is a *bivalent correction* of a function $f:X \rightarrow \{0,1,\#\}$ iff $\forall x[(f(x) = 0 \vee f(x) = 1) \rightarrow g(x) = f(x)]$

(14) **Strong Kleene:**
The denotation of S in w is
a. 1 if its denotation (in a bivalent system) would be 1 under every bivalent correction of sub-constituents.
b. 0 if its denotation would be 0 under every bivalent correction of sub-constituents.
c. # if neither (a) nor (b) hold.

Consider now the existential sentence in (1a), and assume that there is one boy $s_1$ who has (exactly) two cars and drives both of them to school. Since the denotation of the nuclear scope, (12), would map $s_1$ to true, every bivalent correction of (12) would map $s_1$ to true and the existential sentence in (1) would, thus, be true under any such correction. If there is no boy who has two cars and drives each of them to school, there will, of course, be at least one bivalent correction of the trivalent function that would make the sentence false. So having one boy who has two cars and drives each to school is the minimal condition that must be met for the sentence to be true under all bivalent corrections. For the sentence to be false under all bivalent corrections, it must be the case that all boys have two cars and no boy drives each of them to school. The sentence in (1a) is, thus, predicted to have a disjunctive presupposition: that some boy has two cars and drives them to school or that all boys have two cars and no boy drives each to school (equivalently: that some boy has two cars and drives each to school or that all boys have two cars).

For the sentence in (1b) to be true under all bivalent corrections of (12), it must be the case that every boy has two cars and drives each to school. For it to be false under all bivalent corrections there must be at least one counterexample: a boy who has two cars and doesn't drive each to school. The sentence will thus presuppose a disjunction as well: that some boy has two cars and doesn't drive one to school or that all boys have two cars. The sentence in (1c) is the negation of the sentence in (1a). It will thus be false whenever the latter is true and vice versa. Hence whenever one sentence has the same truth-value under all bivalent corrections of the partial function, the other will as well. They are thus predicted to have the same presuppositions.

(15) TRIVALENT PREDICTIONS:[14]

a. Some $boy_1$ [$t_1$ drives both $his_1$ cars to school]
*Presupposes*:
Either [Some boy has exactly two cars and drives each to school] or [Every boy has two cars]

b. Every $boy_1$ [$t_1$ drives both $his_1$ cars to school]
*Presupposes*:
Either [Some boy has exactly two cars and doesn't drive each to school] or [Every boy has two cars]

c. No $boy_1$ [$t_1$ drives both $his_1$ cars to school]
*Presupposes:*
Either [Some boy has exactly two cars and drives each to school] or [Every boy has two cars]

OK, so these are the presuppositions predicted by the system. On the face of it, they seem rather unintuitive: we clearly do not intuit these disjunctive statements as the presupposition of the sentence. But, as argued by many authors (see in particular Fintel 2000b), there is no reason to expect that the presuppositions of a sentence would be accessible to direct introspection. So we should ask whether these unintuitive presuppositions might be empirically adequate, and in particular, whether they might be adequate in addressing the empirical challenges presented at the end of Section 3.

My strategy in addressing this question will be based, at first, on the pretense that presuppositions can be collapsed with truth conditions. When this is done, we will derive differences between quantifiers that correspond, more or less, to what we've seen in Section 2. But we will still not understand the odd property of polar questions, (6), inter-speaker variation, or the difference between soft and strong triggers discussed in Section 3. My goal in the subsequent sections will be to show that the facts could be understood once we take seriously the Stalnakerian view of presuppositions as "admittance" conditions on the common ground, conditions that demand that certain things be presupposed *prior* to assertion.

## 5. Collapsing assertion and presupposition

So let's begin by pretending that we're allowed to think about the inferences of a sentence as simply following from the conjunction of assertion and presupposition, ignoring important issues pertaining to the special status of presuppositions as admittance conditions. Under this pretense, we straightforwardly predict the difference between existential and negative existential sentences discussed in Section 2. The two types of sentences have the same disjunctive presupposition. But, once we add the assertion, the negative existential sentence leads to a universal inference but the existential sentence does not:

(2) a. Some boy [x drives both of x's cars to school]$_{\text{x has (exactly) two cars}}$
*Presupposes*:
Either [Some boy has two cars and drives each to school] or [Every boy has two cars]
*Asserts:*
Some boy has two cars and drives each to school.
*Hence: no universal inference*

c. No boy [x drives both of x's cars to school]$_{\text{x has (exactly) two cars}}$
*Presupposes:*
Either [Some boy has two cars and drives each to school] or [Every boy has two cars]
*Asserts:*
It's not the case that some boy has two cars and drives each to school.
*Hence: a universal inference follows.*

Of course, also the universal inference of a universal sentence is predicted, though this is not particularly surprising (for reasons discussed in Section 2):

(2) b. Every boy [x drives both of x's cars to school]$_{\text{x has (exactly) two cars}}$
*Presupposes*:
Either [Some boy has two cars and drives each to school] or [Every boy has two cars]
*Asserts:*
Every boy has two cars and drives each to school.

Perhaps more surprising is the prediction that the negation of the universal statement will not be associated with a universal inference – a prediction that contradicts the assumption that universal quantifiers projected universal presuppositions, as most theorists assume. It is not obvious that this prediction holds in general, but some evidence that it might be correct comes from the following discourse (modeled on an example due to Beaver 1994: ex. 13).

(16) *Relevant context*: May and Jane are students trying to organize an event of some sort for which they need many cars.
*Mary*: There are many students around, hence many cars.
*Jane*: No, half of the students don't have a car.
a. Furthermore, some don't drive their car to school.
b. Furthermore, not every student drives his car to school.
c. #Furthermore, every student leaves his car at home.

The oddness of the variant of Jane's response in (16c) follows straightforwardly from the universal inference associated with this response. It also teaches us that in this kind of context, contextual restriction to individuals that satisfy the presupposition (the students that have a car) is not available. This sets the stage for our observation that the negative universal in (16b), just like the plain existential in (16a), is not associated with a universal inference.[15]

The observations we've made shed some positive light on the trivalent system, but there are a few questions, both empirical and conceptual, that need to be addressed.[16] The first question is based on the assumption that presuppositions should be viewed as admittance conditions. If so, it is not right to simply collapse assertion and presupposition. The combined effects of assertion and presupposition are indeed predicted to be inferences of a sentence, but there might be other predictions that follow from the special status of presuppositions, and the question is whether such predictions come out right under the trivalent theory. Other obvious questions pertain to the variability in judgments mentioned in Section 2 and to the strengthened presuppositions that arise when soft triggers are replaced with strong triggers, discussed in Section 3. Finally, there is also the observation that presuppositions of existential sentences such as (1a) appear stronger (at least for some speakers) when these sentences are further embedded to form polar questions, as seen in (5b) and (6), which has also not been addressed.

## 6. The oddness of the presupposition: qua presupposition

Consider again (2a), along with its presupposition and assertion:

(2) a. Some boy [x drives both of x's cars to school]$_{\text{x has (exactly) two cars}}$
*Presupposes:*
Either [Some boy has two cars and drives each to school] or [Every boy has two cars]
*Asserts:*
[Some boy has two cars and drives each to school]

The presupposition is the disjunction of two propositions, one of which is the universal statement that the presupposition holds of every individual in the domain of quantification, and the other of which is the assertion itself. Conjoining this disjunction with the assertion is, of course, equivalent to the assertion. Once the conjunction is completed we, thus, lose any trace of the presupposition, and, in particular, of the universal disjunct. That was our explanation for the lack of a universal inference for existential sentences.

But we did not consider the demands that the presupposition itself makes regarding what is presupposed *prior* to assertion. Under the Stalnakerian view that we've been assuming, sentences that have presuppositions can only be asserted and evaluated against an information state in which the presupposition is met (a common ground that entails the presupposition). So we must ask whether it is true that sentences such as (1a) can only be asserted when the disjunctive presupposition is entailed by the common ground. Addressing this question is no trivial matter given the ubiquity of presupposition accommodation (Karttunen 1974; Lewis 1979b). In other words, the Stalnakerian claim that presuppositions must be presupposed prior to assertion is based on a non-trivial idealization (abstracting away from accommodation) and deriving predictions is not going to be straightforward. Still the question is real and needs to be addressed (see Fintel 2000b, 2008).

One way to begin thinking about it is to investigate the various types of information-state that would entail the disjunctive presupposition, and for each type to ask how reasonable it is to assume that the sentence would be uttered with this type of information state as common ground.[17] The information states that entail the presupposition can be usefully divided into three types: one that entails the first disjunct (*some boy has two cars and drives each to school*), $T_1$, one that entails the second disjunct (*every boy has two cars*), $T_2$, and one that entails neither, yet entails the disjunction, $T_3$.[18] $T_1$ is inappropriate since it not only entails the presupposition but also the assertion itself: under $T_1$ the utterance is pointless (violating one of Stalnaker's basic principles).[19] $T_2$, which entails the universal statement, is appropriate. What about $T_3$? The problem with such an information state is that it would typically involve presupposition of a non-trivial, and implausible, connection between the two disjuncts. None of the disjuncts is itself believed to be true when this information state is taken to be common ground, yet there is a belief that if one of the disjuncts is false, the other is true. This does not seem like a very plausible information state to be in.[20]

So where does this leave us? It seems that the only plausible information state that (i) entails the disjunctive presupposition of (1a), and (ii) can serve as common ground for the utterance of (1a) is one where the universal statement that every boy has two cars is presupposed. So, once we insist on viewing presuppositions as admittance conditions, it is not at all clear that we can explain the fact that (1a) is not associated with a universal inference.

More generally, all the quantificational sentences we looked at involve disjunctive presuppositions for which a $T_3$ information state (one that entails the disjunction without entailing any of the disjuncts) is implausible – unless a lot of work is done introducing highly specific contextual assumptions. This means that $T_3$ would not be the type of information state in which the sentence would be uttered (at least not typically). Furthermore, it is easy to see that a $T_1$ information state – one which does not entail the universal statement (that all individuals in the domain of quantification satisfy the presupposition of the nuclear scope) – always makes the assertion either a contextual tautology or a contextual contradiction (in the cases we've looked at) leaving us with a $T_2$

information state (one in which the universal presupposition holds) as the only available option.[21]

This discussion is, of course, incomplete in that it is not accompanied with a perspective on the nature of accommodation – the process by which participants in the conversation (are expected to) accommodate their view of the common ground in light of the presuppositions of utterances. We could consider approaches to accommodation that would allow us to circumvent this problem, but I would like to suggest that the problem noticed above is real and is at the heart of the explanation for Charlow's observation that certain triggers appear to show evidence for universal projection. I will agree with Charlow that these triggers resist the process of local accommodation. However, I will disagree with Charlow's conclusion that quantifiers project a universal presupposition. I will argue, instead, that a universal inference follows from considerations of plausibility of the sorts sketched above. The considerations will be a bit more complicated once the process of accommodation is discussed along with theories of presupposition strengthening (proposed to resolve the so-called "proviso problem").

Some of the argument for viewing things from the trivalent perspective is that it will allow us to address the questions that were left open for Charlow. But before we get there, I would like to present a more direct argument for the trivalent predictions by drawing what I think is the clearest prediction, namely that every quantificational sentence with a presupposition in the nuclear scope will be admissible when a $T_3$ information state is plausible and taken to be common ground. Constructing sentences and contexts that make a $T_3$ information state plausible is going to be difficult, but this can be done systematically, once the general recipe is clear. The results will corroborate the predictions of the trivalent system for every combination of quantifier and presupposition trigger.

## 7. Getting rid of oddness

In this section, I will construct contexts in which a $T_3$ information state is the common ground (and the universal presupposition is not met). Against these contexts, I will investigate those sentences that out of context appear to support a universal inference. We will see that the sentences are admissible as predicted by the trivalent system.

### *7.1 Existential sentences embedded under polar questions*

In Section 2 we have seen evidence that existential sentences when used to form polar questions lead to the inference that the presupposition of the nuclear scope holds of every individual in the domain of quantification (examples (5b) and (6)). Our goal later on will be to interpret this fact as following from the implausibility of $T_3$, something that will require a way of distinguishing the polar question from unembedded existential sentences. But before we get there, I would like to motivate this line of attack by showing that when $T_3$ is plausible, the universal inference disappears (even for those speakers who, out of context, insist on a universal inference for polar questions).

Consider the polar question in (17). When uttered out of the blue, the sentence strongly suggests (for some speakers) that each of the two players has chips. This could be explained by the claim that existential sentences in polar questions project the presupposition of the nuclear scope universally. I would like to argue that the facts should be explained based on the implausibility of a $T_3$ context, one in which the only thing that is presupposed is the relevant disjunction (either both of the players have chips or one them has chips and is ready to cash them). This, as mentioned, is implausible because it suggests a connection between the two disjuncts (if one is false the other is true).

(17) Is one of the two card players ready to cash his chips?

This line of explanation would predict that if we establish the appropriate connection between the two disjuncts, the polar question will be appropriate and would not lead to a universal inference. The following argues that the prediction is correct:

(18) CONTEXT: John and Bill meet for a game of poker. The rules they set for their engagement are the following. They each give Jane 100 dollars and get chips in return. The game will continue until one of them has no more chips left. The moment this happens, the winner (the player that has 200 chips) can go to Jane and cash his chips. Fred (who knows the rules of engagement) is responsible for cleaning the room the moment the game is over. He calls Jane and asks the following question:
FRED TO JANE:Is one of the two players ready to cash his chips?

Another example that illustrates the same point is (19). Here it seems reasonable to believe that either all of the bankers have a fortune or one of them has a fortune that he acquired by wiping out some other banker (without believing one of the disjuncts). In other words $T_3$ is, once again, reasonable.

(19) Did any one of these bankers acquire his fortune by wiping out one of the others?
*Presupposition:* if none of these bankers acquired his fortune by wiping out one of the others, they all have a fortune.

So it might seem that we have provided important evidence for the disjunctive presuppositions, but as pointed out to me by Ben George, there is a serious confound here that needs to be addressed. Specifically, it is reasonable to propose that in both (18) and (19) the putative universal inference needs to be restated in light of consideration pertaining to the temporal interpretation of noun phrases. Moreover, once restated, it is no longer obvious that it is not met. Our discussion of (18), for example, took the universal inference to be the statement that both players have chips *at the time of utterance*. But if instead, we take the presupposition to be that both players have chips at *some time or other* (see Enç 1981, 1987), we notice that it is met and the initial suggestion (from Section 2) that existential sentences embedded under polar questions are associated with universal inferences is not affected. It is easy to see that the same issue arises for (19).

However, this confound can be overcome. In fact, there are two ways to overcome it, and both lead to the results predicted by the trivalent system. One way involves explicit reference to time within the relevant noun phrase ((20) and (21)) and the other involves contexts where the universal presupposition does not hold even after it is construed in the weak sense (with existential quantification over time) ((22), with the crucial sentence in italics).

(20) Did any one of these bankers acquire the fortune he deposited in the bank last week by wiping out one of the others?
*Presupposition*:if no banker acquired the fortune he deposited in the bank last week by wiping out one of the others, they each deposited a fortune last week.

(21) CONTEXT: same as in (18)
Is any one of the two players allowed to cash the chips that he now has in his possession?

(22) CONTEXT: Two partners (Bill and Fred) started a new company based on a new algorithm that they developed. If neither partner reveals the algorithm, they will both earn millions once the company goes public. If, however, one of them shares the algorithm with Tom – a well-known English businessman – before the company goes public, this partner will be getting millions from Tom but then the other partner will remain very poor.
*Will one of the two partners get his millions from Tom?*

## 7.2. *Strong triggers*

In Section 2 we looked at Charlow's evidence that strong triggers project universal presuppositions in quantificational sentences. Here, I would like to show that, also in the case of strong triggers, things appear to be different once $T_3$ is made plausible.[22] To see this, consider the following context:

(23) CONTEXT: The TV game show "diamonds are not enough" has the following format:
Every week, there are ten contestants and one million dollars to be spent on prizes for the contestants. As in many shows of this sort, there are all sorts of ways of scoring points – irrelevant for our purposes. What is important is that there are two possible outcomes:

*First Outcome:*If everyone scores less than 1000 points, the million dollars will be used to purchase 10 diamonds (each for 100K) and each contestant will receive a diamond. *Second Outcome:* Otherwise, the top-scoring contestant (the winner) will receive 500K and the 5 highest-scoring contestants (including the winner) will each receive a (100K) diamond.

a. Every week at least five of the ten contestants gets a diamond. I bet that this week one of the ten contestants will also get 500 K.
b. Every week at least five of the ten contestants gets a diamond. I wonder if this week one of the ten contestants will also get 500 K.

### *7.3 Universal sentences embedded under polar questions*

A universal sentence, such as (1b), leads to the universal inference that the presupposition of the nuclear scope holds of every individual in the domain of quantification. As mentioned in Section 5, this ought to follow from the assertive component on its own, and, therefore, need not argue for universal projection. Furthermore, the example in (16) where the universal sentence is negated seems to argue against a universal presupposition. However, a polar question formed from a universal sentence again leads to a universal inference (for example in (24) that each of the 3 boys has/had money).

(24) a. Did each of the 3 boys invest his money wisely?
b. It matters to me whether each of the 3 boys will invest his money wisely.

Later on, I will attempt to explain this special property of polar questions (observed already with existential sentences). But here I want to argue that things change once $T_3$ is made plausible. The argument is based on (25) with the crucial sentence in italics.

(25) John got money gambling in the racetrack. If he invests his money wisely, he will be able to pay Bill (who will have no money otherwise). If Bill gets money from John and invests it wisely, he will be able to pay Fred (who will have no money otherwise). If Fred has money and invests it wisely, he will be able to pay me, and otherwise I will have no money at all.
*So it matters to me quite a bit whether or not each of the three fellows will invest his money wisely.*

### *7.4 Negative existentials*

In Section 5 we derived the universal inference for negative existentials by considering the combined effect of assertion and presupposition. However, when a negative existential is embedded in various environments where the assertive component is modified, things might be different. In particular, if (1c) is embedded in a polar question, the assertive component is eliminated and we no longer predict a universal inference. So in principle, we could consider exactly the same manipulations we considered in Section 7.1, replacing an existential with a negative existential. Unfortunately, the results are not as natural as we would like, probably due to the special biases that are associated with negative polar questions (Romero and Han 2004).

For this reason, I will consider the same contextual manipulations but will look at constructions in which the negative existential is embedded in the antecedent of a conditional. First note that out of the blue, such embedding leads to a universal inference (for reasons that still need to be clarified) – in the case of (26) that both partners will get millions:

(26) If neither partner gets his millions from Tom, I will be quite content.

However, once $T_3$ is made plausible, this inference disappears, as in (27), where the context is the same as in (22) and the crucial sentence is in italics.

(27) CONTEXT: Two partners (Bill and Fred) started a new company based on a new algorithm that they developed. If neither partner reveals the algorithm, they will both earn millions once the company goes public. If, however, one of them shares the algorithm with Tom – a well-known English businessman – before the company goes public, this partner will be getting millions from Tom, but then the other partner will remain very poor.
*If neither partner gets his millions from Tom, I will be quite content.*

### 7.5 *Interim summary*

In this section, we focused on a peculiar property of the disjunctive presuppositions predicted by Strong Kleene (in conjunction with the bridge principle). This presupposition would be satisfied in three types of context, and the context which is crucial for zeroing in on the disjunctive nature of the presupposition, $T_3$, is implausible without some contextual background. The goal of this section was to provide the background and to show that when this is done a universal inference that is otherwise often attested is eliminated. This provides some support for the trivalent predictions, but as mentioned in Section 6, we still need to understand how the perspective on presuppositions as admittance conditions does not lead to universal inferences in all cases in which a $T_3$ information state is not plausible. In the next sections, we will try to address this question along with the question of variability in judgments.

## 8. Additional mechanisms

Our discussion to this point is incomplete for three reasons. First, as just mentioned, we seem to predict universal inferences in all but $T_3$ contexts, a prediction that appears to be wrong for certain quantifiers in combination with weak triggers. Second, we did not deal with inter-speaker variation, and third, we did not deal with cases in which the presupposition is not satisfied in the actual conversational context but needs to be accommodated (global accommodation).

In this section, I will deal with the first of these open issues by adopting Charlow's hypothesis that soft triggers (and only soft triggers) allow for local accommodation. I will view local accommodation as a process that collapses assertion and presupposition at various scope positions. The predictions described in Section 5 will be derived from applying local accommodation at the matrix level. Speaker variation, the second open issue, will be dealt with by the assumption that speakers vary in how easily they allow for local accommodation, and possibly in the scope position in which they prefer the process to apply. Finally, I will deal with the third issue, discussing the process of global accommodation, in light of the proviso problem, and the need for a mechanism of "presupposition strengthening."

## *8.1 Local accommodation*

Our first observation is that there are some individual differences in the distribution of universal inferences. To account for this observation, and for the contrast between strong and soft triggers, I would like to suggest that there is a process that collapses assertion and presupposition, which I will call (following Heim 1983b) local accommodation. I will assume that the relevant mechanism is a covert operator B (for Bochvar) which maps the third value to 0 (see Beaver and Krahmer 2001).

(28) $[[B]] = \lambda p_t.1$ if $p=1$, 0 if $p \neq 1$.

If a constituent receives the third value, applying B to it yields 0; in all other cases, B does not affect the value of the constituent to which it applies. If B applies to the nuclear scope of a quantificational expression, presuppositions get cancelled, and a universal inference will not surface unless it follows from the assertive component (as in simple universal quantification). If we apply B to the entire sentence, we collapse the assertion and presupposition of the entire sentence.

Our account in Section 5 of the difference between different quantificational expressions that embed weak triggers would thus follow if we assume that B applies at the matrix level. For the sake of illustration, consider (1c) with the two parses in (29).

(29) Two Parses of (1c):
a. No boy λx. B(x drives *both* of x's cars to school$_{x \text{ has two cars}}$)
b. B(No boy λx. (x drives *both* of x's cars to school$_{x \text{ has two cars}}$)

(29a) expresses a bivalent proposition which is true if and only if there is no boy for which the assertion and presupposition of the nuclear scope holds, i.e. iff the nuclear scope is false of every boy for which the presupposition holds. It is easy to see that no universal inference follows. (29b), by contrast, is true iff the disjunctive presupposition is true (every boy has two cars or some boy has two cars and drives both to school) and the second disjunct is false, which of course entail the first disjunct. It thus follows that every boy has two cars. For existential quantifiers, by contrast, both parses lack a universal inference. It is easy to see that applying B at the matrix level yields the results for universal and negative quantifiers discussed in Section 5.

To account for inter-speaker variation, I would like to propose that speakers vary in their ability (or tendency) to apply B in an embedded position. Some speakers can apply B within the nuclear scope while other speakers either avoid B or apply it at the matrix level. Speakers of the first sort will not report a universal inference, and speakers of the second sort will (for some quantifiers, when they apply B at the matrix level; for all quantifiers in a non $T_3$ context, when they avoid B altogether – as we will see shortly).[23] We might also predict a third type of speaker, one who does not apply B at all, for which a universal inference will be predicted for all quantifiers in all but the special scenarios discussed in Section 7.

To account for the behavior of strong triggers, I would like to agree with Charlow that such triggers resist local accommodation.[24] Under the implementation proposed here, this will be stated as a constraint banning application of B to a constituent that contains a strong trigger. However, given the discussion in Section 7 (and in particular 7.2.), I conclude (as already mentioned) that the universal inference associated with strong triggers does not follow directly from universal projection, but rather from the oddness of the disjunctive presupposition discussed in Section 6. But the discussion in Section 6 did not take into account situations in which the disjunctive presupposition is not part of the common ground at the time of assertion, i.e., the process of global accommodation (as opposed to local accommodation).[25] In the next subsection, I will argue that the empirical expectations do not change once global accommodation is taken into account.

## 8.2 *Global accommodation*

In Section 6 we discussed how a universal inference might follow for simple existential sentences that embed a presupposition trigger if we are serious in viewing presuppositions as admittance conditions (despite the fact that the universal inference does not follow directly from the trivalent truth conditions). Consider again (2a), under the assumption that B is not part of the syntactic representation.

(2) a. Some boy [x drive both of x's cars to school]$_{x \text{ has (exactly) two cars}}$
*Presupposes:*
Either [Some boy has two cars and drives each to school] or [Every boy has two cars]

We discussed three types of context where the disjunctive presupposition is met: $T_1$, where the first disjunct is presupposed and the sentence is a contextual tautology, $T_2$, where the universal disjunct is presupposed, and $T_3$, where neither disjunct is presupposed yet the disjunction is presupposed. Since the sentence is unassertable in $T_1$ and $T_3$ is implausible, we concluded that speakers are likely to draw a universal inference. This, one might suggest, is the account of the universal inference drawn with strong triggers under our assumption that B is not part of the syntactic parse.

But this account ignores situations where the disjunction is not presupposed but accommodated upon assertion. If we assume that accommodation is minimal and then followed by the assertion, we would not derive the universal inference. Hence we will not be able to account for Charlow's observation (or for better studied cases of presupposition strengthening discussed in Section 10).[26] I would therefore like to adopt the view that accommodation involves the postulation of a plausible common ground (Beaver 1999). In other words, accommodation cannot result in a $T_3$ context (unless a connection between the disjuncts is made plausible) and some form of "presupposition strengthening" is required (as assumed in various accounts of the proviso problem, to which we will return).[27] There are two types of strengthening that could be considered: $T_1$ and $T_2$. Since the sentence is unassertable in $T_1$, the only available option (among the two) is $T_2$. Hence, we predict a universal inference whenever B is not part of the parse.[28]

So where are we? We have seen that if B is not part of the parse, we predict a universal inference for all quantifiers and in all contexts other than the specialized contexts discussed in Section 7. We accounted for Charlow's observation (and the counterexamples discussed in 7.2.) under Charlow's assumption that strong triggers resist local accommodation, which for us is derived by B. When B is part of the parse, we cancel the presuppositions entirely when it applies to the nuclear scope. When it applies at the matrix level, we derive the differences among quantifiers discussed in Section 5. Differences among speakers are predicted if speakers vary in whether they allow B to apply locally.

In the next section, I would like to discuss what is predicted for polar questions (and other embeddings that modify the assertive component) given the perspective mentioned above. But first a small point about the ease of local accommodation. One issue that was mentioned for Charlow in Section 3 pertains to the argument for a distinction between soft and strong based on contrasts such as (9) repeated below:

(9) a. No, he is not interviewing the applicants; there are no applicants.
b. #No, he is not talking also to Bill; he didn't talk to anyone else.
c. After talking to Mary, did he also talk to Bill? #No, he didn't also talk BILL; he (just) didn't talk to Mary.

Under the current implementation, we would like to say that the contrast shows that inserting B below negation is possible when soft triggers are involved (9a), but not when strong triggers are involved ((9b) and (9c)). Our question for Charlow was why insertion of B below negation seems to be more marked than in the context of existential sentences. In particular, the first sentence in (9a), if uttered in isolation, would clearly lead to the inference that there are applicants. It is only upon hearing the second sentence that we consider a parse with local accommodation – one that avoids a contradiction. With existential sentences, we don't seem to need a continuation.

This question arises for the current proposal as well. But under the current proposal, we have two ways of addressing it that were not available for Charlow. One way is to assume that the markedness of embedding B below negation should not be attributed to a general dispreference for local accommodation. Rather, it is the result of a general dispreference for *embedded* B. In existential sentences, we can avoid a universal inference by applying B to the entire sentence, and this option is not dispreferred by the parser.

A second possibility, under the current proposal, is to claim that local accommodation (insertion of B) must be motivated. In (9a) it is motivated by the need to avoid a contradiction. In the absence of the continuation, it would not be motivated. In quantificational sentences, by contrast, local accommodation (either at a matrix or embedded position) is motivated by the desire to avoid an odd presupposition. The second possibility (which is not incompatible with the former) needs to be further articulated by specifying the set of considerations that could motivate local insertion of B. But we can already see that it ought to have predictions for other cases that involve odd presuppositions (and in particular for their embedding), predictions that I hope to return to at some point.[29]

## 9. Embedding under polar questions

Despite our evidence that certain quantificational sentences are not associated with universal presuppositions, we have seen that for some speakers, at least out of the blue, these sentences do lead to universal inferences when used to form polar questions ((5b), (6), (17), and (24)). We now can make sense of this observation. The trivalent presuppositions, if they are not strengthened, are odd in out-of-the-blue contexts (since they suggest an implausible connection between two unrelated propositions, the two disjuncts). This oddness can be circumvented by two means: local accommodation and presupposition strengthening. We have postulated that universal inferences with soft triggers result from a preference to apply B globally. But in polar questions B cannot apply globally (for type considerations). This, in and of itself, could serve to explain the preference for a universal inference.[30,31]

But there is also another possible explanation. Specifically, we might propose that the relevant strategy (the one employed by speakers who get a universal inference) involves applying B as high as possible given type considerations. Even under this strategy, polar questions would require presupposition strengthening, under Karttunen's assumption about their syntax. To see this, consider the polar question in (5b) under the Karttunen/Hamblin assumption that questions denote sets of propositions. If B applies to what Karttunen assumes is the proto-question, we will get two propositions in the denotations, one resulting from applying B to the existential sentence and the other from applying B to the negative existential:[32]

(30) [[ Is B [one of these 10 boys [$t_1$ proud of both $his_1$ papers]]? ]] = {p: p is the denotation of *B [one of these 10 boys [$t_1$ proud of both $his_1$ papers]]* or p is the denotation of *B not [one of these 10 boys [$t_1$ proud of both $his_1$ papers]]*} =
{that one of these 10 boys has two papers and is proud of both of them, that all of these 10 boys have two papers and none of them is proud of both of them}

In contrast to ordinary yes/no questions, there are states of affairs where neither proposition in the Hamblin denotation is true. Specifically, a proposition in the set is true iff the disjunctive presupposition of the existential is met (or equivalently of the negative existential). If we assume that a question presupposes that a member of its denotation is true,[33] we would be left with the disjunctive presupposition. This presupposition would need to be strengthened in out-of-the-blue contexts, yielding a universal inference.[34]

## 10. A mechanism for presupposition strengthening

Our discussion of presupposition strengthening is, as mentioned, parallel to various discussions in the literature of the proviso problem, illustrated by the following contrast.

(31) a. If John is a scuba diver, he will bring his wetsuit.
*Appears to presuppose:*If John is a scuba diver, he has a wetsuit.
b. If John is a scuba diver, he will bring his car.
*Appears to presuppose:*John has a car.

(31b) leads to the inference that John has a car, whereas (31a) does not appear to lead to the parallel inference that John has a wetsuit. In other words, the presupposition triggered by the definite description appears to project differently in the two sentences.

According to one influential account of this contrast, this appearance is misleading. The presupposition triggered by the definite description projects in the same way in both cases, resulting in the presupposition that if John is a scuba diver, he has a car/wetsuit.[35] The appearance of a different presupposition in (31b) is the result of presupposition strengthening. The account is identical in form to the proposal about presupposition projection made here. To see this, note first that the conditional presupposition is understood as a material conditional which can be re-stated as a disjunction: either John is not a scuba diver or he has a car/wetsuit.

Let's now divide contexts in which the presupposition is satisfied to three different types (along the lines of our discussion in Section 6): contexts in which the first disjunct is presupposed, $T_1$, contexts in which the second disjunct is presupposed, $T_2$, and contexts in which neither disjunct is presupposed yet the disjunction is presupposed, $T_3$. Both sentences share an important property, namely that both are not assertable in $T_1$ (conditionals are inappropriate when the antecedent is presupposed to be false). So, as in Section 6, we only need to consider $T_2$ and $T_3$. The difference between (31a) and (31b) is that in (31a) $T_3$ is a plausible context but not in (31b). The reason for this is that the two disjuncts in (31b) are not plausibly related to each other: we do not expect there to be a dependency between having a car and being a scuba diver. But in (31a) the connection is very plausible: there is obviously a connection between having a wetsuit and being a scuba diver. The implausibility of $T_3$ in (31b) leads to the inference that the relevant context is $T_2$ and hence that John has a car. In the case of (31a), this inference is not called for and hence we do not infer that John has a wetsuit.

In other words, we saw that the disjunctive presupposition of a conditional sentence sometimes gets strengthened to one of the disjuncts (the one that it can be strengthened to). This is exactly what was assumed for the disjunctive presupposition of a quantificational sentence. The question in both cases, however, is whether we need a special mechanism for this type of strengthening. The literature on this matter is divided. Still there are reasons to believe that a special mechanism is required (Geurts 1996; Katzir and Singh 2010; Singh 2007, 2008, 2009, 2010), reasons that I think are strengthened significantly if the trivalent theory of presupposition projection is correct.

One conceptual reason (stressed by Singh) pertains to the very nature of the problem: one in which a sentence is uttered with a presupposition that is too weak for minimal accommodation. In such a scenario the accommodated common ground would have to entail some new information stronger than the presupposition itself. But the space of possible strengthenings is in principle larger than the one we considered. After all, a disjunction is entailed by many propositions besides those denoted by the disjuncts. So in order for the account of presupposition strengthening to stand on firm grounds, we should have some characterization of the space of possible strengthenings that we ought to consider (see note 18).

Geurts has made a more concrete argument based on cases for which presupposition strengthening is impossible: sentences that have presuppositions that are too weak for minimal accommodations and nevertheless cannot be strengthened (yielding pragmatic deviance). The response to this argument has been to point out special properties of Geurts's sentences that are in conflict with presupposition strengthening, in particular certain implicatures (Beaver 2006; Heim 2006; Pérez Carballo 2007, 2009). In light of this impasse, it would be good to ask whether there are pairs of sentences that have exactly the same semantic properties and the same presupposition and nevertheless yield different forms of presupposition strengthening.[36] If such sentences exist, that could strongly support an account in terms of a specialized mechanism.

With this in mind, consider the following pairs of questions under the assumption that the trivalent presuppositions are correct:

(32) a. Does one of your two sons drive his car to school?
b. #Does one of your two sons have a car and drive it to school or do both your sons have a car and neither drives it to school?

If trivalent presuppositions are correct (and if B is not inserted in (32a) at the most embedded position), the two sentences in (32) share the following presupposition: Either (p) one of your two children has a car and drives it to school or (q) both of your children have a car and neither drives it to school. Furthermore, they ask for exactly the same information: they have {p,q} as their Hamblin denotation.[37] But still they feel very different. For (32b), the disjunctive presupposition is perceived and the result is some form of pragmatic deviance. (32a), by contrast, is an entirely natural question where the disjunctive presupposition is not perceived: some speakers report a universal inference, whereas others do not. To explain this, we've hypothesized that either B is inserted at a low position, thus cancelling the presupposition altogether, or the resulting structure yields the implausible presupposition of (32b), which escapes pragmatic deviance through presupposition strengthening to a universal inference.

The obvious question to ask is why presupposition strengthening can't apply to (32b), thus eliminating deviance. My answer to this question is based on Singh's claim that we need a theory of presupposition strengthening which specifies the space of potential strengthenings from which participants in a conversation might select the most plausible one. More specifically, I would like to adopt Schlenker's (2011) theory of the set of alternatives. Schlenker proposes that this set is derived by computing the admittance conditions while ignoring the identity of certain sub-constituents of the relevant sentence, where ignoring a sub-constituent is interpreted in a very special way. Specifically, to ignore the identity of a sub-constituent, X, while computing admittance conditions is intended to mean that the admittance conditions must be satisfied *no matter what the identity of X is*. In other words:

(33) *Sloppy notation:* When S(X) refers to a sentence that contains a constituent X, S(X') will refer to the result of substituting X with X' in S.
Let S(X) be a sentence with presupposition p, $p^+$ is a possible strengthening of p if $p^+ = \cap\{p' : \exists X'\ X'$ has no presupposition trigger and p' is the presupposition of S(X')$\}$

I would like to add to (33) the assumption that representations such as those in (2) are real, in particular, that a subscript on a constituent has reality (independent of the identity of the constituent). From this it follows that the part of the nuclear scope that does not include the subscript can be substituted independent of the subscript. With this assumption at hand, we derive the desired results: the universal inference turns out to be a potential strengthening of all simple quantificational sentences. Specially, the universal inference results from ignoring the identity of the (unsubscripted) nuclear scope, i.e., for every quantifier we've considered, Q, (in fact for every conservative quantifier):[38]

(34) EVERY (A) $(\lambda x.p(x)) =$
$\cap\{p: \exists Z$ p is the trivalent presupposition of $Q(A)(\lambda x.Z_{p(x)})\}$

## 11. Conclusions

In this chapter I've attempted to deal with presupposition projection from the nuclear scope of quantificational sentences. My goal was to deal with a very complicated empirical picture, one that involved variance among quantificational determiners, presupposition triggers, and individual speakers. My starting point was the observation that despite this variability one fact seems to be constant, namely the acceptability of the relevant sentences in $T_3$ contexts.

I took this as important evidence for the trivalent system. In order to deal with variability, I capitalized on the oddness of the trivalent presupposition in out-of-the-blue contexts. I suggested that there are two different mechanisms that can deal with this oddness: local accommodation and presupposition strengthening. Furthermore, I assumed that the former is dispreferred for some individuals (in any position but the matrix) and unavailable for all individuals when strong triggers are involved.

## 12. Postscript: a bivalent perspective

Finally, I would like to point out that the results reported here can be obtained in a bivalent system in which Stalnaker's Bridge Principle in (10) is modified. Potential motivations for such a system are the following:

(35) i. It will straightforwardly extend to an account of the presuppositions of non-truth denoting expressions, e.g., questions (which Stalnaker's principle is silent about).
ii. Its conceptual grounding will not be based on the epistemic reasoning that was used to introduce the trivalent system – reasoning that is not obviously appropriate for presupposition projection.

In the system we sketched in this chapter, trivalent semantic values are computed (via the Strong Kleene recipe) and these truth conditions, in turn, yield admittance conditions via Stalnaker's Bridge Principle. In the alternative bivalent system, trivalent semantic values are not computed at all and instead admittance conditions are stated directly via a modification of Stalnaker's principle. The modified principle (like Schlenker's 2008a principle) makes direct reference to the minimal sentences dominating a presupposition trigger. Such sentences must have a two-dimensional representation, which can be annotated using subscripts. The subscript plays a role in the admittance condition but not in the semantics, which is, as mentioned, standard and bivalent.

Imagine that $S_p$ is a minimal sentence dominating a presupposition trigger and that p is the "atomic presupposition" (the one that results from the lexical stipulations). The problem of presupposition projection is to determine the contribution of $S_p$ to the admittance conditions of a sentence φ that dominates $S_p$, $\varphi(S_p)$. Instead of computing trivalent truth conditions, we can encode the contribution of $S_p$ directly to admittance conditions for φ (conditions that are independent on the semantic type of φ, (35i)).

Keeping to the format of (10), this will be implemented by a constraint on the set of worlds compatible with the common ground, which we've simply called the context C. Let's start with the simple case in which p contains no free variables that are bound outside of p. In such a case it is meaningful to ask whether p is true in a given world in C. The intuition behind our constraint is based on the idea that $S_p$ is inadmissible in a world w (unverifiable, or problematic for some other reasons, see (35ii)) if p is false in w. Now assume that w is a member of C. To see whether p needs to be true in w, we need to know whether the value of $S_p$ in w is important/relevant for determining the value of φ. If the answer is yes, then p must be true in w. Otherwise it need not be.

(36) $\varphi(S_p)$ is assertable in C only if
$\forall w \in C$: Relevant($S_p$, $\varphi(S_p)$, w) → p is true in w.[39]

(37) $\text{Rel}(S_p, \varphi(S_p), w) \Leftrightarrow_{\text{def}} ([[\varphi(T)]]^w \neq [[\varphi(\bot)]]^w)$
Where $[[T]]^w = 1$ for all w and $[[\bot]]^w = 0$ for all w

The next two goals are to extend the system to atomic sentences that contain variables that are bound from the outside and to incrementalize the condition along the lines of Schlenker (2008a) (see Fox 2008). Unfortunately, there is no space for introducing the relevant machinery, so (for now) I will refer the reader to a detailed handout (Fox 2011: 19–31).[40]


## Acknowledgments

It is a huge honor to contribute a paper for this volume in celebration of Gennaro's birthday. I met Gennaro for the first time when he visited MIT while I was a first year graduate student. We discussed a paper that I had written and I was amazed by the combination of seriousness and generosity with which I was treated. Every meeting since then has been a huge pleasure, as well as a real source of inspiration. Gennaro's arrival at the Boston area in 2005 has immensely improved my quality of life, so all in all there is a great sense of gratitude: thank you Gennaro and Happy Birthday. This work owes an obvious debt to Schlenker's work on presupposition projection (see Fox 2008). It has been modified as a result of ongoing work with Yasu Sudo, Jacopo Romoli, and Martin Hackl (Sudo *et al.* 2012). Many thanks to two anonymous reviewers as well as to Ivano Caponigro, Emmanuel Chemla, Gennaro Chierchia, Alexandre Cremers, Luka Crnič, Paul Egré, Kai von Fintel, Ben George, Irene Heim, Ofra Magidor, Alejandro Pérez Carballo, Jacopo Romoli, Raj Singh, Benjamin Spector, Yasu Sudo, Steve Yablo, and especially to Philippe Schlenker.


NOTES

1. Beaver and Krahmer (2001); Fox (2008); George (2008, 2011); Krahmer (1998); Peters (1979). For discussion see also Beaver and Geurts (2011); Fox (2008); Schlenker (2008b).
2. As is clear from Fox (2008), my perspective on the topic relies heavily on the proposal of Schlenker (2008a), and, in particular, on the idea that the theory of presupposition projection should be divided into two components: (i) a conceptually simple theory of projection which has no left–right asymmetry and (ii) a principle that "incrementalizes" this theory of projection thus introducing asymmetry. The significance of Schlenker's work is not clear from the presentation in this chapter, which entirely avoids component (ii) (incrementalization). But avoiding this component would have been impossible without Schlenker's paper. Schlenker teaches us how to abstract away from left–right asymmetries and how to re-introduce them (by quantifying over "good finals"). When we wish to avoid incrementalization, we need to limit our attention to the problem of predicting presupposition projection from sentence final constituents, a problem for which the conceptually simple theory and its incrementalization are equivalent.
3. Unless we adopt a variable free semantics. Under variable free semantics we would be presenting the problems in a different format, but, as far as I can see, the issues would not be affected.
4. There are many issues about presupposition projection that this paper will remain silent about. One, which feels particularly pertinent, is projection out of the restrictor

of a quantifier. As pointed out in Beaver (2001) and Chemla (2009a), the projected presupposition appears to be much weaker than what is predicted by existing theories (including the trivalent theory). All I can offer at the moment is the hope that something can be said about local accommodation that would explain the relevant observations.

5. As we will see, Heim's position on indefinites, as in (1a), was different, given her assumption that they are not quantificational.
6. The situation is complicated somewhat if one adopts Schwarzschild's theory of wide scope indefinites (Schwarzschild 2002). Under this theory indefinites can appear to have unrestricted wide scope because they can quantify over singleton domains. However, note that this theory must distinguish indefinites from definite description, in that in the former the identity of the singleton domain cannot be common ground (Fintel 2000a). This raises an obvious question for presupposition projection, one that can be seen most clearly under von Fintel's assumption that the singleton domain is quantified over by an island insensitive existential quantifier. The problem of presupposition projection for Schwarzschild is to figure out the way in which the existential quantifier over domain restrictions projects the presupposition of its nuclear scope. The advantage of predictive theories of projection (such as the one we will be pursuing) is that they leave no wiggle room for stipulations.
7. Beaver (2001) discussed cases where the universal inference is not attested. My hope is that these can be reduced either to implicit domain restriction or to local accommodation. See Sudo (in progress) for arguments to this effect.
8. As noted by Charlow, one has to make sure that the focus particle is interpreted within the nuclear scope of the quantifier. This can be done (at least for many speakers) by placing it after the auxiliary, as in (7).
9. It seems to me that for Charlow's proposal to work, all non-anaphoric triggers must be treated as soft triggers. See Chemla and Schlenker (in press) for relevant discussion and experimental data. This is in conflict with what is assumed in some of the literature. I will, unfortunately, have to leave this conflict for some other occasion. Thanks to an anonymous reviewer for bringing up the issue.
10. This principle will be modified in Section 12 (as discussed in the introduction), circumventing the need for a trivalent system. Note that the principle, as it stands, does not apply to non-truth denoting sentences. The modified principle will apply to sentences of any semantic type.
11. One might claim that this epistemic justification is inappropriate for a theory of presupposition. This could serve as another motivation for exploring the alternative alluded to in Section 12.
12. In this sense Strong Kleene is very similar to a trivalent logic based on supervaluation. The difference is that a logic based on supervaluation is, so to speak, smarter in deciding whether it can ignore a third value: specifically, under supervaluation you consider bivalent corrections of the entire sentence instead of bivalent correction of a particular constituent (on its own). This difference is irrelevant for our purposes the moment the system is incrementalized (see Schlenker 2008c: appendix).
13. In George (2008), this is generalized to expressions that do not denote truth-values. However, I think that this will not affect our point about the bridge principle (see note 10).
14. Note that these disjunctive presuppositions are weaker than the universal projections assumed by Heim and stronger than the existential projections assumed by Beaver.

15. The facts in (16) would also follow from Beaver's assumption that the projected presuppositions are existential. As mentioned, Beaver himself presents cases of this sort. His assumption, however, will make predictions that are too weak for polar question. See Section 7.
16. Chemla (2009a) presents evidence that the DP *exactly 3 NP* does not project the presupposition of its scope universally. This observation is problematic for the trivalent system (see George 2008 for attempted corrections). I don't have a solution for this problem, but would like to explore it in conjunction with the yet unpublished proposal of Benjamin Spector that *exactly* in this context has the same meaning that it has elsewhere, namely that it serves to indicate a more stringent level of granularity than we would have otherwise. The meaning of *exactly 3* is derived by an "at least" meaning accompanied with an obligatory Scalar Implicature (required by the shift in granularity). It is my hope that the projection properties would follow from an independent study of the effects of Scalar Implicatures on presuppositions. The situation is further complicated by extremely interesting observations made in Sudo (2012).
17. This discussion owes, of course, quite a bit to earlier discussions in the literature of the proviso problem, which arises in the context of the conditional or disjunctive presuppositions predicted by Karttunen and Heim (see Section 10).
18. There is of course a multitude of ways to divide information states that entail a given proposition into different types. For example, we might exchange $T_2$ with a proper subset of information states, $T_2$', those that entail the proposition that every boy has two cars and no boy drives both his cars to school. We could then let $T_3$' be the remainder (the set of information states that entail the presupposition and are not of one of the other two types: $T_1$ or $T_2$'). In other words, we might begin with the non-simplified version of the disjunctive presupposition: the proposition that either some boy has two cars and drives both to school or that every boy has two cars and no boy drives both his cars to school. I don't think our conclusions would change, though things might be harder to see.

    $T_1$ and $T_2$' would be inappropriate for Stalnakerian reasons: one entails the assertion and the other its negation. $T_3$' violates none of the Stalnakerian principles. The question is whether there is a plausible information state of this type. The answer is, of course, yes: an information state that entails that every boy has two cars but does not determine whether every boy drives his cars to school is of type $T_3$' and seems plausible enough. But this discussion illustrates that it could be somewhat difficult to tell whether an information state individuated by its entailments is plausible. On the face of it $T_3$' might seem non-plausible, but here we see that we can find a specific version of it which is entirely natural. This raises the question of accommodation: when pragmatic presuppositions do not entail the presupposition of a sentence, interpreters need to figure out what type of information to accommodate and this could be far from trivial. See Section 10. Many thanks to Benjamin Spector and two anonymous reviewers.
19. In $T_1$ the common ground entails the assertion (hence the assertion is a contextual tautology).
20. Note that the same is not true of $T_3$' from note 18. In the case of $T_3$' there is a plausible connection between the two disjuncts. If every boy has two cars, it follows that if one disjunct is false, the other is true.

21. Since (1c) is the negation of (1a), $T_1$ will make the assertion a contextual contradiction. The discussion can be applied to other cases only if we are able to identify $T_1$–$T_3$. For the sentences in (1), I hope my intention was clear: $T_1$ refers to contexts in which the first disjunct in (15) is satisfied, $T_2$ to contexts in which the second disjunct is satisfied (the universal statement), and $T_3$ to contexts that satisfy the disjunction without satisfying either of the disjuncts. So (1b) will be a contextual contradiction in $T_1$, and the negation of (1b), in (16), will be a contextual tautology.

    For the discussion to generalize beyond (1), we have to first state the trivalent presupposition as a disjunction with the second disjunct being the universal statement (the predicted presupposition in Heim's system). The problem is that there is no unique statement of this sort (note 18), a problem very much related to the claim that there is a need for a mechanism of presupposition strengthening (Section 10).
22. One might attempt to derive all of the results of this section from local accommodation. Specifically, one might suggest that local accommodation is motivated, in the cases discussed here, by the contextual assumptions that make it clear that a universal presupposition is not met. The contrast between the facts in (23) and Charlow's example argues against this possibility.
23. In Sudo *et. al.* (2012), we found evidence that some speakers get a universal inference even for existential quantifiers that embed weak triggers. To accommodate this observation, we made a slightly different assumption about speaker variation, namely that some speakers avoid B altogether, whereas others tend to apply it, and then might select a scope position randomly.
24. Romoli (2012) points out that things need to be stated somewhat differently to accommodate cases in which a constituent embeds both a strong and a weak trigger and only the presupposition of the latter is cancelled. What it seems we will need is a process that "associates" with a particular presupposition trigger and only cancels that one. As far as I can see, this will be easier to implement in the system outlined in Section 12.
25. Terminology can be confusing given that the mechanism for local accommodation can apply globally (i.e., at the matrix level). In the system proposed here the results for matrix application of local accommodation and for global accommodation are quite different, given the phenomena of presupposition strengthening.
26. In earlier presentations of this material, I assumed such a model of accommodation, one in which presupposition strengthening was considered only if the result of minimal accommodation and assertion lead to an implausible information state.
27. This perspective is more reasonable than minimal accommodation if we are serious in viewing presuppositions as admittance conditions. If presuppositions are admittance conditions, the presupposition of a sentence has to be part of the common ground when the sentence is evaluated – under the appropriate idealization. In cases that deviate from this idealization, hearers have to figure out what contexts speakers took to be the common ground, and the relevant contexts have to be reasonable.
28. As discussed in Section 10 (based on Singh's work), one might argue that there are other options (besides $T_1$ and $T_2$) we ought to consider, e.g., specific instantiations of $T_3$ that are nevertheless plausible.

29. For example it would predict that local accommodation (below negation) would be easier in (i) than in (9a).

 (i) I don't think that if he flies to Paris his sister will pick him up.

30. Note that the same reasoning applies here. $T_1$ is not an available strengthening because it would make the question inappropriate (in that the answer is part of the common ground).

 It has been argued that questions are not always inappropriate when the answer, given the presupposition, must be part of the common ground – specifically that they can be used rhetorically (Guerzoni 2008). I would claim that this rhetorical effect can be achieved only if the answer must be part of the common ground under any type of accommodation, i.e., that one would prefer to accommodate a common ground that would make the question have a non-rhetorical interpretation. Thanks to Luka Crnič for raising this issue.
31. I haven't discussed the way presuppositions project by the operator that forms polar questions and how this might be explained in the trivalent system. The problem is that, at the moment, no predictions are made. Appropriate predictions are made by the system outlined in Section 12 (see Fox 2011). Thanks to Alexandre Cremers.
32. The same result would be achieved if B could apply point-wise to each member of the question denotation as in Kratzer and Shimoyama (2002).
33. This would follow from the *Ans* operator proposed in Dayal (1996) and further argued for in Fox and Hackl (2006) and Abrusán and Spector (2011).
34. This logic extends to the conditional in (26), which I will not go over here. The important observation is that conditionals do not entail that the antecedent is true. Hence applying B globally will not eliminate the implausibility of the inference of a connection between the two disjuncts.
35. Note that the trivalent approach predicts this uniform presupposition hence is committed to this line of analysis.
36. Other pairs to consider (inspired by Singh and Schlenker) are the following:

 (i) If John lives in Michigan and works as a corporate lawyer in Detroit, he will find a way to take advantage of his rights as a holocaust survivor.
 **Likely inference**: If John lives in Michigan, he has rights as a holocaust survivor.
 (ii) If John lives in a Midwestern state and works as a corporate lawyer in Detroit, he will find a way to take advantage of his rights as a holocaust survivor.
 **Likely inference**: If John lives in a Midwestern state, he has rights as a holocaust survivor.

37. The disjunctive presupposition for (32b) comes from the general observation about the presuppositions of questions. See note 33.
38. Another way of getting this strengthened meaning might be to consider substitution for the determiner:

$$\text{EVERY}\ (A)\ (\lambda x.p(x)) = \cap\{p: \exists Q\ Q \text{ a natural language quantifier } \&\ p \text{ is the trivalent presupposition of } Q(A)(\lambda x.Z_{p(x)})\}$$

39. This should be read as the value of S is relevant for the value of $\varphi$ in w.
40. In Fox (2011) I did not define local accommodation – the operator B. What seems to be needed is something like the following:

(i) $[[BS]] = \lambda w$. S is assertable in $\{w\}$ and $[[S]](w) = 1$.
To derive selective cancellation of presuppositions (see note 24), we will index subscript with B:

(ii) $[[B_iS]] = \lambda w$. $S_i$ is assertable in $\{w\}$ and $[[S]](w) = 1$ where $S_i$ is like S except that every subscript with an index distinct from i is deleted.
We will also need to exempt subscripts from (36) if they are co-indexed with B.

(iii) $\varphi(S_p)$ is assertable in C only if p is co-indexed with a c-commanding B or $\forall w \in C$: Relevant$(S_p, \varphi(S_p), w) \rightarrow$ p is true in w.

*Part III*

# From grammar to meaning: experimental insights

# 9 Unification in child language

*Stephen Crain and Rosalind Thornton*

## 1. Introduction

This chapter is, in some sense, an update on the 'nature versus nurture' debate in the realm of developmental semantics. We report the findings from experimental studies designed to adjudicate between a usage-based approach to language acquisition, and a nativist approach. The studies we review were inspired in large part by the model of the language apparatus proposed by Gennaro Chierchia (see especially Chierchia 2004). Several features of the model have been the focus of experimental investigations of child language, including children's sensitivity to scalar implicatures and their knowledge of several linguistic phenomena that, on the surface, do not appear to be related, but which Chierchia's model has sought to unify. More specifically, the same linguistic contexts that cancel scalar implicatures (downward-entailing contexts) are also contexts that license negative polarity items and ones that generate a "conjunctive" interpretation of disjunction. We have been investigating these properties in children's emerging grammars in two typologically distinct languages, Mandarin Chinese and English. In this chapter, we summarize some of the main findings of these investigations.

## 2. Two interpretations of disjunction

This section reviews the basic tenets of the alternative approaches to language acquisition that will feature prominently in the remainder of the chapter: the usage-based (nurture) approach and the nativist approach. To frame the discussion, we will focus on the interpretation of disjunction as seen from these alternative perspectives. First, preliminary remarks about the semantics of disjunction are in order.

### *2.1 Inclusive*-or

Suppose that after lunch, your friend tells you *Ted did not order pasta or sushi for lunch today.* If you are a native English speaker, you infer two things from your friend's remark: (i) that Ted did not order pasta for lunch today, and (ii) that Ted did not order sushi for lunch today. In deriving these inferences, your knowledge of English conforms to one of the patterns of logical inference in classical logic (i.e., one of de Morgan's laws). Interestingly, the joint inferences that Ted didn't order pasta, and didn't order sushi, depend on a particular interpretation of the English disjunction word "or". Namely, "or" must be assigned the truth conditions associated with inclusive-*or*, the meaning of disjunction in classical logic (where the symbol for disjunction is written "$\vee$"). So the interpretation English speakers assign to sentences like *Ted did not order pasta or sushi for lunch today* reveals that English "or" has the same meaning as the symbol "$\vee$" in classical logic. It will be useful to review the steps that take us from the assumption that "$\vee$" is inclusive-*or* in classical logic, to the conclusion that English "or" is inclusive-*or* in sentences like *Ted did not order pasta or sushi*. For this, we briefly review some of the relevant bits of classical logic.

In classical logic a formula of the form $(A \vee B)$ is true in three circumstances: (i) when only A is true, (ii) when only B is true, and (iii) when both A and B are true. It is this last circumstance that distinguishes inclusive-*or* from exclusive-*or*. Exclusive-*or* is false when both A and B are true. Assuming that disjunction is inclusive-*or*, the formula $(A \vee B)$ is only false when A and B are both false. In symbols, this is written $(\sim A \ \& \sim B)$. Our concern is with negative statements in human languages, such as the English sentence *Ted did **not** order pasta **or** sushi*. This sentence corresponds to the formula $\sim(A \vee B)$ in classical logic. We saw that the formula $(A \vee B)$ is false in classical logic just in case A and B are both false. Negation reverses truth-values. Therefore, the formula $\sim(A \vee B)$ is <u>true</u> just in case both A and B are false. That is, the formula $\sim(A \vee B)$ is logically equivalent to the formula $(\sim A \ \& \sim B)$. This yields one of de Morgan's laws of propositional logic. According to this one of de Morgan's laws, negated disjunctions make a "conjunctive" entailment: from $\sim(A \vee B)$ it is valid to infer $(\sim A \ \& \sim B)$.

This is precisely how negated disjunctions are interpreted in English. From the English statement (1), it is valid to infer (2). If (1) is true, then (2) must also be true.

(1) Ted did not order pasta or sushi.

(2) Ted did not order pasta and Ted did not order sushi.

This is circumstantial evidence that English "or" is inclusive-*or*, just as in classical logic.

## 2.2 *Exclusive*-or

Despite the circumstantial evidence that English "or" is inclusive disjunction, the literature on human reasoning, and the usage-based account of language acquisition, have reached a different conclusion. Advocates of this perspective contend that disjunction in human languages is exclusive-*or*, for both children and adults, except in special circumstances. This would seem to be a reasonable conclusion, because it is prefaced on the assumption that children learn the meanings of logical expressions from witnessing how people use these expressions in real-life situations.

Exclusive-*or* has been documented to be the dominant meaning of disjunction in real-life situations. For example, in a review of 240 transcriptions of audiotaped exchanges between 2- to 5-year-old children and their parents taken from the CHILDES database, Morris (2008) reports 465 uses of *or* out of a total of 100,626 conversational turns. For children, utterances in which disjunction meant inclusive-*or* were produced less than 10% of the time, and uses of *or* with an inclusive-*or* interpretation were produced by adults only slightly more often than this. A representative sample of the parental input to Adam and Eve from the Brown corpus (Brown 1973) is given in Crain *et al.* (2005). This sample illustrates the predominance of the exclusive-*or* interpretation of disjunction in the input to children.

In the reasoning literature, too, evidence has been offered to suggest that exclusive-*or* is the meaning of disjunction. Others are convinced that *or* is ambiguous between inclusive disjunction and exclusive disjunction, but that exclusive disjunction is the dominant meaning (e.g., Kegley and Kegley 1978; Richards 1978). Braine and Rumain (1981: 291) acknowledge the view that "equates *or* with standard logic," yet they reject this view on the grounds that "coherent judgments of the truth of *or*-statements emerge relatively late and are not universal in adults." They conclude that disjunction is exclusive-*or* more often than not, even for adults. In experimental settings, for example, if English-speaking children are asked by an experimenter to respond to simple instructions such as *Give me the red balloon or the blue balloon*, they never give the experimenter both the red balloon and the blue one. If English "or" is inclusive-*or*, it would be correct, from a logical point of view, to give the experimenter both balloons. Based on the absence of such responses, and many other findings, reasoning experts have inferred that, more often than not, the meaning of "or" in English is exclusive-*or*.

## 3. The usage-based approach

According to many scholars, knowledge of the meanings of linguistic expressions is acquired by language learners based on observations of the linguistic behavior of others; this is especially true of the meanings of logical expressions. We call this the usage-based account. Meaning must be manifested in use, on this perspective, because all there is to the meaning of a logical expression is the use that speakers make of it. Modern philosophy of language yields many endorsements of this approach to the acquisition of language, and especially the acquisition of the meanings of logical expressions. For example, the philosopher W. V. O. Quine (1992: 37–38) asserts:

In psychology one may or may not be a behaviourist, but in linguistics one has no choice. Each of us learns his language by observing other people's verbal behaviour and having his own faltering verbal behaviour observed and reinforced or corrected by others. We depend strictly on overt behaviour in observable situations. ... There is nothing in linguistic meaning beyond what is to be gleaned from overt behaviour in observable circumstances.

Dummett (1978: 216–217) explicitly adopts the usage-based approach to the meaning of logical expressions:

The meaning of a mathematical statement determines and is exhaustively determined by its use. The meaning of a mathematical statement cannot be, or contain as an ingredient, anything which is not manifest in the use made of it, lying solely in the mind of the individual who apprehends that meaning: if two individuals agree completely about the use to be made of the statement, then they agree about its meaning. The reason is that the meaning of a statement consists solely in its role as an instrument of communication between individuals, just as the powers of a chess-piece consist solely in its role in the game according to the rules.

Advocates of the usage-based approach are also well represented in the literature on child language. In this domain, advocates of the approach contend that "children acquire word uses closely related to those used in natural language input, only later using a word to convey a broader range of meanings" (Morris, 2008: 68; cf. Lieven *et al.* 1997; MacWhinney 2002; Tomasello 2003). The acquisition of the meanings of logical connectives, such as disjunction, is no exception. Citing the finding mentioned earlier – that exclusive-*or* dominates in the input to children – Morris (2008: 70) identifies an advantage to children in initially assigning the exclusive-*or* interpretation to disjunction words:

Interference with other possible meanings could increase the difficulty of acquiring the term; thus initial meanings should occupy a unique area in conceptual space. ... For example, while inclusive OR (A, B, A & B) overlaps with AND (A & B) in that the presence of both options is allowable, exclusive OR (A, B, but not both) has no overlap with AND, and thus should create less interference during acquisition.

Lacking relevant input, children learn the "formal logic" uses of disjunction words much later, according to Morris (2008: 82–84):

Through experience, children acquire additional non-core uses (e.g., assigning explicit truth-values) the conditions under which uses are appropriate (i.e., pragmatics), and form a more abstract connective representation (Gentner and Namy 2006).

The data demonstrate that initial language use of a connective is not identical to the logical use. ... Because the data demonstrate that children's initial uses are restricted to nonlogical functions, logical functions must be acquired.

> If connectives are a part of a syntax of thought, then what must be learned are conditions for use. ... If, however, logical functions are learned, then learning likely occurs in reasoning situations in which the goal of connective use matches a logical use. ... Importantly, there were nearly no examples of these contexts in the present data.

As all of these quotations make clear, the idea that logic is innate does not go down easily with many scholars. It almost seems to be presupposed in much of the literature, both on child language and on reasoning, that children acquire logic by observing the outward behavior of adult language users. Yet, as we will see, there is a growing body of evidence that clearly demonstrates that children initially assign the inclusive-*or* meaning to disjunction words across languages, despite the absence of decisive evidence from the input. This evidence is problematic for the usage-based account (Crain *et al.* 2006; Crain *et al.* 2005; Crain and Khlentzos 2008, 2010; Crain and Thornton 2006). Before we turn to the child language laboratory, the next step is to explain the apparent paradox: how the majority of disjunctive statements (and hence the input to children) can have the exclusive-*or* meaning of disjunction and, at the same time, all human languages, including all child languages, assign the inclusive-*or* meaning to disjunction.

## 4. The Gricean model

Grice (1975) proposed that the basic meaning of disjunction across human languages is indeed inclusive-*or*. To explain how the exclusive-*or* meaning is derived in "real-life" circumstances, the standard Gricean account takes the following line. Disjunction words and conjunction words form a scale < *or, and* >. The scale is ordered by information strength, from weakest to strongest, where a term α is "weaker" than another term β if β asymmetrically entails α (Horn 1996a). Since the truth conditions assigned to statements with conjunction are a subset of those that verify the corresponding statements with disjunction, statements with "and" asymmetrically entail the corresponding statements with "or". So, "or" is weaker than "and." When a speaker uses the weaker term "or", a scalar implicature of "exclusivity" is engaged. The trigger to the implicature is usually attributed to the Gricean conversational Maxim of Quantity, which entreats speakers to make their contributions as informative as possible. In adherence with this maxim, hearers generally assume that a speaker who uses "or" in describing a situation is not in a position to use the corresponding statement with the stronger term "and" (Grice 1975). Upon hearing a statement with "or", hearers therefore remove the truth conditions associated with "and" from the meaning of "or", yielding the exclusive-*or* reading of disjunctive statements (*A or B, but not both*). To see that sentences with "and" are true in a subset of the circumstances associated with "or," consider sentences (3) and (4).

(3) Ted ordered pasta or sushi.
C1: Ted ordered pasta, but not sushi
C2: Ted ordered sushi, but not pasta
C3: Ted ordered both pasta and sushi

(4) Ted ordered pasta and sushi.
C3: Ted ordered both pasta and sushi

On the basic meaning of disjunction (inclusive-*or*), (3) is true in circumstances C1-C3. Notice that the corresponding statement with conjunction (4) is true in just one of these circumstances, C3. According to the Gricean view, the statement with the weaker term ("or") induces a derived meaning that includes the negation of the stronger term ("not both") eliminating circumstance C3.

The Gricean view appeals to scalar implicatures to explain the findings from the reasoning literature that have been used to impugn the conclusion that disjunction words are inclusive-*or* in human languages. It is expected, on the Gricean approach, that when scalar implicatures are cancelled, the basic inclusive-*or* truth conditions will be assigned to sentences with disjunction. As Grice observed, scalar implicatures are cancelled, or at least diminished, in situations of uncertainty. When one is making a prediction, or making a bet, it is possible to use disjunction without invoking a scalar implicature.

Consider example (5). In a study by Gualmini *et al.* (2000), this sentence was uttered by a puppet, Kermit the Frog, who was invited to make wagers about the outcomes of a series of stories.

(5) *Kermit the Frog*: I bet that Batman will take a cake or an apple.

Following Kermit's statement in (5), several alternative outcomes were presented to children. On one outcome associated with (5), Batman ended up taking both a cake and an apple. The use of disjunction in (5) does not guarantee that this will be the outcome, but neither is this possibility excluded, since the outcome was still in dispute when Kermit produced (5). The finding was that 3- to 5-year-old English-speaking children accepted statements like (5) 98% of the time in situations where both disjuncts turned out to be true, i.e., when Batman took both a cake and an apple. When sentences describing past events were produced (*Batman took a cake or an apple*), children continued to accept statements with "or," whereas adults rejected them. In statements about past events, there is less uncertainty, so adults at least compute the scalar implicature when disjunction is used to describe past events. Where children are less sensitive to scalar implicatures than adults, children appear to be more logical. We will review some of the literature on children's sensitivity to implicatures in Section 8.

The Gricean model explains why an implicature of exclusivity is engaged in ordinary assertions with disjunction like (3), repeated here as (6). The Gricean model was extended by Gazdar (1979) to explain why people assign the truth conditions associated with inclusive-*or* in negated disjunctions like (7). According to Gazdar, scalar implicatures are often suspended under negation because the relative strength of scalar terms is the reverse of what it would be without negation. The use of 'or' in (7) results in a stronger statement than the corresponding statement with 'and' (8).

(6) Ted ordered pasta or sushi.

(7) Ted did not order pasta or sushi.
C1: Ted did not order pasta and Ted did not order sushi

(8) Ted did not order pasta and sushi.
C1: Ted did not order pasta and Ted did not order sushi
C2: Ted did not order pasta, but Ted did order sushi
C3: Ted did not order sushi, but Ted did order pasta

As indicated by the contexts given below the examples, statement (7) *Ted did not order pasta or sushi* is true in one circumstance, when Ted ordered neither dish. Notice that the corresponding statement with conjunction (8) *Ted did not order pasta and sushi,* is true in that circumstance (Ted ordered neither dish), and is also true in other circumstances (Ted ordered just one of the dishes). Therefore, negated disjunctions are true in a narrower range of circumstances than negated conjunctions, hence negated disjunctions are more informative (stronger). In subsequent work, Horn (1989) proposed that scalar implicatures are not just suspended under negation but, more generally, they are suspended in downward entailing contexts.

## 5. The unification of linguistic phenomena

If linguists are struck by the diversity of human languages, they are also struck by the common themes, i.e., the patterns that occur in individual languages, and across languages. Here is where Chierchia enters the picture. First, Chierchia (2004, 2006) sought to verify the conjecture by Horn (1989) that scalar implicatures are suspended in downward-entailing contexts. The strategy he followed was to see if three apparently unrelated linguistic phenomena were tied together by the semantic property of downward entailment. Although this correlation is mentioned in passing in Chierchia *et al.* (2004) and in Guasti *et al.* (2005), a detailed exposition of the correlation is reported in Chierchia (2004, 2006).

As we saw, one phenomenon that was hypothesized to be governed by downward entailment was the suspension of scalar implicatures (SIs). This indeed proved to be the case. Chierchia showed that, time and again, SIs were suspended, or 'recalibrated,' in downward-entailing environments. But, just as importantly for the present discussion, Chierchia showed that the suspension of SIs was correlated with two other linguistic phenomena. One is the interpretation of disjunction. Because it is anticipated that SIs are suspended in downward-entailing linguistic contexts, it follows that if the exclusive interpretation of disjunction is derived by a SI, then the "basic" inclusive meaning of disjunction should arise in downward entailing linguistic contexts. The third linguistic phenomenon was already well known from the seminal work of Fauconnier (1975) and Ladusaw (1979). This phenomenon is the licensing of negative polarity items (NPIs), such as English *any*. As Ladusaw (1979) had established, downward-entailing linguistic contexts license NPIs. Chierchia sought to show, then, that downward-entailing contexts tie these different linguistic phenomena together. In downward-entailing contexts, NPIs are licensed, and disjunction is assigned the inclusive-*or* interpretation, yielding conjunctive entailments.

All these facts are expected, as Chierchia pointed out, for the simple reason that downward-entailing linguistic contexts reverse entailment relations, as compared to ordinary (non-downward-entailing) linguistic contexts. To appreciate this insight, we first need to state what it means for an operator, or a linguistic environment, to be downward entailing (DE). The defining property of DE linguistic contexts is that they guarantee the validity of inferences from general statements to more specific statements. More specifically, these contexts license inferences from sentences with expressions that refer to sets of things (e.g., *fruit, car*) to sentences with corresponding expressions that refer to the subsets of those things (e.g., *apples, Prius*). Formally, a function $f$ is DE iff $f(A)$ entails $f(B)$, whenever $B \subseteq A$.

The class of downward-entailing operators in human languages includes negation, negative adverbs, certain prepositional phrases (but not others), certain determiners (but not others), verbs expressing minimum conditions, comparatives, and many others. In addition, there are downward-entailing linguistic environments, such as the antecedent of conditionals (but not the consequent). These operators and environments form a natural class in human languages, despite appearing to be a fairly motley collection of expressions and linguistic contexts.

Now let us look at how the semantic property of downward entailment provides a unifying account of several linguistic phenomena which, on the surface, look unrelated. To illustrate, we will use the three linguistics structures in (9). Notice first, that each of these linguistic contexts satisfies the defining property of downward entailment – they validate inferences from sets (speaking a Romance language) to their subsets (e.g., speaking French, speaking Spanish, speaking Italian). Example (9a) shows that the phrase headed by the determiner *every* in subject position is DE. The antecedent of a conditional statement is shown to be downward entailing in (9b), and (9c) shows that the preposition *before* is DE.

(9) a. Every student who speaks a Romance language likes to travel.
⇒ *Every student who speaks French likes to travel.*
b. If a student speaks a Romance language, she likes to travel.
⇒ *If a student speaks French, she likes to travel.*
c. John went to Europe before learning a Romance language.
⇒ *John went to Europe before learning French.*

We chose these linguistic contexts because, in each case, downward entailment is restricted to one structural position, or to one of a pair of lexical items. To see this, consider the "invalid" inferences from sets to their subsets in (10). The examples in (10) reveal that the set-referring expression, *Romance language*, cannot be replaced by the subset-referring expression, *French*, in the consequent clause of conditional statement, in the predicate phrase (nuclear scope) of the universal quantifier *every*, or in the complement of the preposition *after*. These "asymmetries" in DE linguistic contexts, as illustrated in examples (9) versus (10), will loom large in our later discussion of language learnability.

(10) a. Every student who likes to travel speaks a Romance language.
# ⇒ *Every student who likes to travel speaks French.*
b. If a student likes to travel, she speaks a Romance language.
# ⇒ *If a student likes to travel, she speaks French.*
c. John went to Europe after learning a Romance language.
# ⇒ *John went to Europe after learning French.*

A second feature of downward entailment is the licensing of negative polarity items (NPIs), such as English *any* (also *ever* and *at all*). Examples in (11a)–(13a) illustrate that *any* is welcome in the phrase headed by the determiner *every* in subject position, and in the antecedent of conditional statements, and following the preposition *before*. Examples (11b)–(13a) show, by contrast, that *any* is not licensed in the predicate phrase (nuclear scope) of the universal quantifier *every*, or in the consequent clause of conditional statements, or following the preposition *after*. Such asymmetries are potentially problematic for language learners.

(11) a. Every linguist who agreed with **any** philosopher is in this room.
b. *Every linguist who is in this room agreed with **any** philosopher.

(12) a. If **any** linguist enters the gym, then Geoff leaves.
b. *If Geoff leaves, then **any** linguist enters the gym.

(13) a. Geoff went to the gym before **any** linguist.
b. *Geoff went to the gym after **any** linguist.

A third phenomenon associated with downward entailment pertains to the interpretation of disjunction. In the scope of a DE operator, or in DE linguistic environments, disjunction is assigned its basic inclusive-*or* meaning. We know this, because disjunction licenses a conjunctive entailment in these environments (Boster and Crain 1993; Chierchia 2004, 2006; Crain *et al.* 2005; Crain and Khlentzos 2008). Example (14) shows that *or* generates a conjunctive entailment in the phrase headed by the determiner *every* in subject position; (15) shows that disjunction generates a conjunctive entailment in the antecedent of a conditional; and (16) shows that disjunction generates a conjunctive entailment in the scope of the preposition *before*.

(14) a. Every student who speaks French **or** Spanish passed the exam.
b. ⇒ Every student who speaks French passed the exam **and** every student who speaks Spanish passed the exam.

(15) a. If Ted **or** Kyle enters the gym, then Geoff leaves.
b. ⇒ If Ted enters the gym, then Geoff leaves **and** if Kyle enters the gym, then Geoff leaves.

(16) a. Geoff went to the gym before Ted **or** Kyle.
b. ⇒ Geoff went to the gym before Ted **and** Geoff went to the gym before Kyle.

(17) a. Every student who passed the exam speaks French **or** Spanish.
b. ⇒ Every student who passed the exam speaks French **or** Spanish (or possibly both).

(18) a. If Geoff leaves, Ted **or** Kyle enters the gym.
b. ⇒ if Geoff leaves, Ted enters the gym **or** Kyle enters the gym (or possibly both).

(19) a. Geoff went to the gym after Ted **or** Kyle.
b. ⇒ Geoff went to the gym after Ted **or** after Kyle (or possibly both).

Downward-entailing (DE) linguistic contexts are a common feature of human languages, so the unification of the linguistic phenomena observed for English should extend to even historically unrelated languages, such as Mandarin Chinese. We will illustrate this, first, using *ruguo* conditionals in Mandarin. *Ruguo*-conditionals correspond most closely to English *if…, then…* statements. We saw that the antecedent of an English conditional statement is downward entailing, so the statement *If a linguist bought a car, he got a rebate* entails *If a linguist bought a Prius, he got a rebate*. We also saw that the consequent clause of an English conditional is not downward entailing, so the statement *If a linguist got a rebate, he bought a car* does not entail *If a linguist got a rebate, he bought a Prius*. If the English examples are translated into Mandarin Chinese, the same asymmetry appears. That is, the antecedent clause of a *ruguo*-conditional is downward entailing in Mandarin, as shown in (20), but the consequent clause is not, as indicated by the "*" in (21).

(20) Ruguo yi-ge yuyanxuejia mai-le **qiche**, ta jiu na-le huikou.
If one-CL linguist buy-ASP car he then get-ASP rebate
'If a linguist bought a car, he got a rebate.'
⇒ Ruguo yi-ge yuyanxuejia mai-le **Puruisi qiche**, ta jiu na-le huikou.
If one-CL linguist buy-ASP Prius car he then get-ASP rebate
'If a linguist bought a Prius, he got a rebate.'

(21) Ruguo yi-ge yuyanxuejia na-le huikou, ta jiu mai-le **qiche**.
If one-CL linguist get-ASP rebate he then buy-ASP car
'If a linguist got a rebate, he bought a car.'
* ⇒ Ruguo yi-ge yuyanxuejia na-le huikou, ta jiu mai-le **Puruisi qiche**.
If one-CL linguist get-ASP rebate he then buy-ASP Prius car
'If a linguist got a rebate, he bought a Prius.'

Another linguistic phenomenon governed by downward-entailing linguistic contexts is the licensing of negative polarity items, such as English *any*. In Mandarin, the expression that corresponds most closely to the English NPI *any* is *renhe*. Mandarin *renhe* has the same pattern of distribution in *ruguo*-conditionals, as the English NPI *any* does in *if . . ., then. . .* conditionals. This is shown in (22).

(22) a. [$_{\text{ANTECEDENT}}$ Ruguo Yuehan chi-le **renhe** binjiling] [$_{\text{CONSEQUENT}}$ ta jiu shengbing].
'If John ate any ice cream, he became ill.'
b. [$_{\text{ANTECEDENT}}$ Ruguo Yuehan shengbing-le] [$_{\text{CONSEQUENT}}$ ta jiu chi ***renhe** binjiling].
'If John became ill, he ate *any ice cream.'

A third linguistic phenomenon that is governed by downward entailment involves the interpretation of words for disjunction in human languages, including English *or* and Mandarin *huozhe*. In the antecedent clause of a conditional statement, disjunction generates a conjunctive entailment. By contrast, when disjunction appears in the consequent clause, it does not generate a conjunctive entailment; instead, disjunction is assigned "disjunctive" truth conditions in the consequent clause. Mandarin works in exactly the same way. In the antecedent clause of a conditional statement, disjunction *huozhe* generates a conjunctive entailment, as illustrated in (23). When disjunction appears in the consequent clause in Mandarin, the interpretation is "disjunctive," as shown in (24).

(23) Ruguo Taide dian-le yidalimianshi **huozhe** shousi, name Maikesi dian-le pisa.
If Ted order-ASP pasta or sushi, then Max order-ASP pizza
'If Ted ordered pasta or sushi, then Max ordered pizza.'

(24) Ruguo Maikesi dian-le pisa, name Taide dian-le yidalimianshi **huozhe** shousi.
if Max order-ASP pizza, then Ted order-ASP pasta or sushi
'If Max ordered pizza, then Ted ordered pasta or sushi.'

As Chierchia (2004) points out, it is instructive to ask whether children could have plausibly learned when disjunction words generate a conjunctive entailment, and when they do not. If these facts are learned, then both English-speaking children and Mandarin-speaking children must have access to evidence that words for disjunction (English *or*; Mandarin *huozhe*) have different meanings when they appear in the antecedent clause of a conditional, as compared to when these same words appear in the consequent clause. Because this is a fact about meaning, Chierchia remarks, it seems highly unlikely that children have abundant experience relevant to this distinction.

Consider the asymmetries in the Mandarin examples (23)–(24). In both sentences, the disjunction word (*huozhe*) is permitted. So the relevant distinction is not based on a distributional analysis of the occurrence or non-occurrence of a particular (kind of) word. The relevant distinction is in the interpretation of disjunction: in (23) disjunction makes a conjunctive entailment, whereas in (24) disjunction is assigned "disjunctive" truth conditions. The distinction that children must draw concerns the different interpretations that the same disjunction words receive when they appear in different linguistic environments. Nevertheless, 3- to 5-year-old children have been found to correctly distinguish the meaning of disjunction words in these two positions (cf. Gualmini *et al.* 2003; Meroni *et al.* 2006; see Su 2011, for results from studies with Mandarin-speaking children).

Based on these joint facts that (a) young children know when disjunction does and does not generate a conjunctive entailment, and (b) children lack sufficient evidence in the input for this distinction, Chierchia (2004) concludes that acquiring the meaning of disjunction "yields a particularly strong version of the poverty of the stimulus argument." The findings from cross-linguistic research on child language, therefore, reinforce the nativist account of language acquisition, according to which children are innately endowed with 'deep-seated' linguistic principles that tie together a variety of linguistic phenomena which appear to be unrelated on the surface. Advocates of the theory of Universal Grammar refer to deep-seated regularities as "core" linguistic properties, as compared to 'peripheral' properties of languages. We discuss the core/periphery distinction in the next section.

## 6. Core versus periphery

Advocates of the theory of Universal Grammar have argued that the core/periphery distinction is significant. In contrast, advocates of a usage-based model of language acquisition have argued that the core/periphery distinction has little merit. For example, Goldberg (2006) makes the following remark: "[t]he impossibility of making a clear distinction between the core and the periphery of linguistic structure is a genuine scientific discovery, and it has far-reaching theoretical implications." According to usage-based theorists like Goldberg (2006) and Tomasello (2003), if a learning mechanism suffices for learners to acquire linguistic phenomena that lie at the periphery of human languages, then the same mechanism will surely also suffice for learners to acquire core linguistic phenomena.

This argument reveals how the notion "core" is understood by advocates of the usage-based approach. This view of the core/periphery distinction is revealed in another statement by Goldberg (2003: 14):

> In fact, by definition, the core phenomena are more regular, and tend to occur more frequently within a given language as well. Therefore if anything, they are likely to be easier to learn. Since every linguist agrees that 'peripheral', difficult cases must be learned inductively on the basis of the input, constructionists point out that there is no reason to assume that the more general, regular, frequent cases cannot possibly be.

Tomasello (2003: 104–105) concurs:

> not only must there be a mechanism for learning the idiosyncratic, but this mechanism produces an output that has all of the properties of core grammar, except for maximal generality.

As these quotations indicate, according to the usage-based model of language acquisition, core properties are ones with "maximal generality". Their effects are expected to appear with greater regularity in a language, as compared to peripheral phenomena. This invites the inference that children should have an even easier time learning core properties, as compared to peripheral properties, of the local language.

Proponents of Universal Grammar also contend that there are core properties shared by human languages, and that these properties express regularities. But, the kinds of regularities are not the same as those discussed by usage-based theorists. Here is an instructive quote by Chomsky (1965):

> The grammar of a particular language . . . is to be supplemented by a universal grammar that . . . expresses the deep-seated regularities which, being universal, are omitted from the grammar itself. Therefore it is quite proper for a grammar to discuss only exceptions and irregularities in detail. It is only when supplemented by a universal grammar that the grammar of a language provides a full account of the speaker-hearer's competence.

There are two noteworthy characteristics of the kinds of "deep-seated" regularities that are stated in the theory of Universal Grammar. First, these regularities are expressed universally and, second, they tie together a number of linguistic phenomena which, on the surface, appear to be unrelated.

## 7. Putting scalar implicatures into the semantics

Up to this point, all the research findings are compatible with the standard Gricean view of scalar implicatures. We have seen that scalar implicatures (SIs) are responsible for the exclusive-*or* interpretation of disjunction and SIs tend not to arise in downward-entailing (DE) contexts. Chierchia followed up some of the implicit predictions of the (neo-)Gricean approach, by showing that DE contexts have broader empirical coverage than had previously been documented. Not only do DE contexts suspend SIs, they also govern another two apparently unrelated linguistic phenomena; disjunction generates a conjunctive entailment in DE contexts, and NPIs are licensed in DE contexts. Chierchia introduced an additional claim, however, which represented a challenge to the standard Gricean view.

According to the standard Gricean view, there is a division of labour between the semantics and the pragmatics. SIs are a pragmatic phenomenon, and are computed globally, after the logical (truth-conditional) meaning of the sentence is composed. On Chierchia's model, by contrast, there is no division of labour; SIs are computed within the semantic component, alongside the logical meaning, as part of the on-line incremental composition of sentence meaning. Although we will leave it to others to discuss this particular feature of Chierchia's proposal in detail, it will be useful to present the basic idea behind the "localist" computation of SIs. This is useful in order to appreciate one of the conclusions that followed from this perspective on sentence meaning. It will suffice, for our purposes, to present one simple argument in favor of the localist view, and against the globalist view of the computation of scalar implicatures. This will give you the flavor of the difference that holds between these alternative views of the architecture of the language apparatus.

Consider sentence (25), which contains the existential indefinite *some*. This quantificational expression forms a scale with other quantificational expressions *many*, *most*, and *every*. The expression *some* is the weakest term on the scale <*some*, *many*, *most*, *every*>. This follows from the fact that a statement with *some* is asymmetrically entailed by the corresponding statements in which *some* has been replaced by *many*, *most*, or *every*. According to the standard Gricean account, therefore, (25) implies (but does not entail) that (26) is false.

(25) Gennaro is seeing *some* students.

(26) Gennaro is seeing *every* student.

On the Gricean account, scalar implicatures are a root phenomenon. They are applied to the output of the computational system, wherein the compositional semantic meaning of sentences is constructed. So, we might say that the semantics is responsible for the "logical meaning," and the pragmatics is responsible for implicatures. In any event, example (27) represents the Gricean "globalist" view of the application of the scalar implicature that is operative in (25).

(27) Globalist SI
Gennaro is seeing *some* students, and it is **not** the case that Gennaro is seeing *every* student.

On the "localist" view, by contrast, the logical meaning and implicatures are both computed within the semantic component of the language apparatus. This is represented in (28).

(28) Localist SI
Gennaro is seeing *some* students, though **not** *every* student.

Now we can appreciate the disjunction problem. Consider the disjunctive statement (29), in which *some* resides in the second disjunct.

(29) Gennaro is either at the pub or seeing *some* students.

On any account of SIs, (29) implies that Gennaro is not seeing *every* student. The accounts differ, however, on how this implicature comes about. According to the Gricean account, SIs are a pragmatic phenomenon, and are applied only after the compositional meaning of a sentence is constructed. On this approach, the implied denial of the stronger statement (that Gennaro is seeing *every* student) is a root phenomenon, as represented in (30).

(30) Globalist SI
Gennaro is either at the pub or seeing *some* students, and it is **not** the case that Gennaro is either at the pub or seeing *every* student.

Because negation is applied to the output of the compositional semantics, this leads to the unwanted consequence that both disjuncts are subsumed under negation. In English, as we saw, negated disjunctions generate a "conjunctive" entailment, as in one of de Morgan's laws of propositional logic: $\sim(A \vee B) \Rightarrow (\sim A \ \& \sim B)$. Applying this law to the negated disjunction in (30) yields the invalid inference in (31), which is clearly not part of the intended meaning of the sentence *Gennaro is either at the pub or seeing some students.*

(31) Gennaro is not at the pub.

Now suppose, instead, that implicatures are factored into semantic representations locally. Then, the semantic representation in (32) provides a snapshot of the output of the SI, as it applies to the example under consideration.

(32) Localist SI
Gennaro is either at the pub or seeing *some* students, though **not** *every* student.

There are far-reaching consequences of the localist perspective for language learnability. According to this view, scalar implicatures are computed alongside the truth-conditional meaning of a sentence. That is, SIs apply within the computational system of Universal Grammar. All things being equal, then, children should be expected to compute both aspects of the compositional meaning of sentences as early as they can be tested. Here is how Guasti *et al.* (2005: 670) put it:

Under this view, the logical and scalar meanings of statements are not clearly distinct, since implicatures are integrated during the course of their interpretation. As a consequence of the architecture of the language apparatus, we are not led to expect children to be less competent than adults in deriving the scalar meaning than in deriving the logical meaning. Given the assumption that both logical meaning and implicatures are computed within the semantic module, observed differences between adults and children are more likely to arise because the derivation of the scalar meaning adds to the complexity of language processing by consuming additional processing resources.

In view of the expectations of the localist account of scalar implicatures, it is worth taking the time to consider what we have found out about children's abilities to compute scalar implicatures.

## 8. Children's knowledge of scalar implicatures

In a series of studies, children have been found to compute scalar implicatures relatively late in the course of language acquisition. Even children as old as 11 have been found to accept weak scalar terms (*some*, *or*) to a far greater extent than adults do, in contexts in which the corresponding statements with stronger terms (*all*, *and*) are (also) true. For example, Smith (1980) found that 4- to 7-year olds interpreted *some* as meaning *some, and possibly all* in responding to questions like *Do some giraffes have long necks*? and Braine and Rumain (1981) found that 7- to 9-year olds interpreted *or* inclusively, assigning the meaning *A or B*, *and possibly both* to sentences of the form "A or B." In an important study, Noveck (2001) established that even 11-year-old children did not derive scalar implicatures to the same extent as adults do, though adults, too, failed to consistently compute scalar implicatures in some experimental conditions. Studies by Papafragou and Musolino (2003) and by Guasti *et al.* (2005) replicated the findings by Noveck (2001). In addition, they included experiments in which children were explicitly instructed to make decisions about the "informativeness" of different descriptions of the same object, rather than a judgment about truth or falsity. For example, children were shown a picture of a grape, and were asked whether it was better to use "grape" or "fruit" as a description. In this task, children's performance improved following training. However, when the same children were tested one week later, without additional training, it was found that the effect of the previous training did not persist, for most of the children. A number of other experimental studies have also shown that children's performance is task dependent (cf., Foppolo *et al.* 2012; Katsos and Bishop 2011; Pouscoulous *et al.* 2007).

Children have been found to successfully compute scalar implicatures, without training, in three experimental contexts. One was a new task reported in Chierchia *et al.* (2001), called the Felicity Judgment task. In this task, two puppets each offer a different description of a story, and children reward the puppet that "said it better." On the test trials, one of the puppets used *or*, and the other one used *and*. For example, one trial was about a group of farmers who were cleaning their animals. At the completion of the story, all the farmers had decided to clean a horse and a rabbit, among their other animals. The puppets then produced the statements in (33).

(33) a. Every farmer cleaned a horse or a rabbit.
b. Every farmer cleaned a horse and a rabbit.

Fifteen children participated in the study, with a mean age of 4;8 (range 3;2–6;0). Children correctly rewarded the puppet that produced the statement in (33b), with *and*, on 93% of the trials. Children clearly favored the puppet that had made the more informative statement, demonstrating that children as young as 3 years old have one piece of pragmatic knowledge, Grice's Maxim of Quantity.

In addition to the Felicity Judgment task, Meroni and Gualmini (2012) found that children successfully computed the scalar implicature associated with the indefinite NP *some* (i.e., *some, but not all*) in another task, developed by Zondervan (2006). In the task, the puppet made an assertion in response to a specific question, called the Question Under Discussion (QUD). In the assertions corresponding to *some*, children computed a scalar implicature if the QUD contained *all*, as in the question/answer pair in (34).

(34) a. Were all the hot-dogs delivered?
b. I think some hot-dogs were delivered.

In the context corresponding to (34), all the hot-dogs had been delivered. A group of fifteen English-speaking children (average age = 4;8) rejected the puppet's statement in (34b) 87% of the time.

Taken together, the findings show that children have no trouble computing scalar implicatures when they are exposed to both terms on the relevant scale: <*or, and*>, <*some, . . . all*>. Clearly, the observation made in previous studies – that children over-accept sentences with scalar terms, including disjunction and the indefinite *some* – was not the result of a lack of pragmatic knowledge, since exposure to both scalar terms sufficed to enable children to compute the corresponding scalar implicatures. However, children are not consistently exposed to both the weaker and the stronger term in ordinary conversational contexts. In many circumstances, children are exposed only to the weaker term, e.g., *or* or *some*, and they must compute the "derived" meaning representation, with the stronger term, without the aid of a puppet who produces a statement with the stronger term (as in the Felicity Judgment task), or an experimenter who poses a question that contains the stronger term (as in the QUD task).

According to the localist approach advocated by Chierchia, the computation of SIs involves two components. One component is the recursive interpretation of a sentence, including both its truth conditions, and the set of alternatives. The second component involves building and maintaining different representations of the sentence in working memory. Based on the findings of the Felicity Judgment task, and the task involving a QUD, it appears that children experience difficulty when they are required to compute the recursive interpretation of a sentence and calculate a scalar implicature, at the same time. In such circumstances, children's responses appear to be driven by considerations of truth or falsity, whereas adults are able to focus directly on the felicity of what is said, in preference to truth or falsity. This suggests that children's failure to compute SIs is due to processing limitations, such as verbal working memory, and not a deficit in semantic/pragmatic knowledge.

If this line of reasoning is correct, then children should perform in a more adult-like way in tasks that dramatically reduce processing demands, and in tasks that focus on the felicity of a statement rather than on its truth or falsity. A direct attempt to verify this prediction was conducted by Guasti *et al.* (2005), who sought to make the conversational exchanges in which children are engaged as close as possible to those that we all experience in everyday life. In ordinary conversational exchanges, speakers and hearers share a common conversational background, which they modify on the basis of the events that transpire in the context. We evaluate the information strength of the statements made by others by comparing them to a given context, to see if they conform to standard conversational norms. Based on these observations, Guasti *et al.* tested a group of 7-year-olds (i.e., the age of the youngest children in the Noveck study) using a Truth Value Judgment task (Crain and Thornton 1998). This task permits the experimenter to control the situational context and, "thereby, to establish the conditions that are prerequisite for computing scalar implicatures" (p. 685). More specifically, the experimental context in a Truth Value Judgment task can be partitioned into a Possible Outcome and the Actual Outcome. In the study under consideration, the Possible Outcome was part of the story that corresponded to the test sentence itself, and the Actual Outcome was a subsequent event that transpired which made the test sentence infelicitous. In short, the Actual Outcome served as the basis for rejecting the test sentence on the grounds that it was a Possible Outcome, but one that did not eventuate.

An example story featured five soldiers. The soldiers were instructed to travel abroad to collect treasure. Each of the soldiers could either go by motorbike or ride a horse. There was some discussion among the soldiers. Some soldiers said that they would like to go by motorbike, since motorbikes are fast. But, some other soldiers disagreed. These soldiers argued that gasoline is expensive and that it would be more fun to ride a horse. After more discussion, one by one, the soldiers decided to ride a horse. So at the conclusion of the story, *all* the soldiers rode a horse. Following the conclusion of the story, the puppet produced the test sentence (35).

(35) Some soldiers are riding a horse.

Now we can partition the story into the Possible Outcome and the Actual Outcome. The Possible Outcome corresponds to the point in the story at which some of the soldiers said that they preferred to ride a horse, since motorbikes consumed too much fuel. That point in the story, the Possible Outcome, corresponds to the test sentence: *Some soldiers are riding a horse*. The Actual Outcome is "what really happened" in the story; in the end, all of the soldiers rode a horse. This represents the reason that the test sentence is infelicitous.

Unlike many previous experiments, the rejection rate for the child subjects (75%) in the Truth Value Judgment task was not significantly different than the rejection rate for an adult control group (83%). The conclusion reached by Guasti *et al.* (2005: 692) is that the "crucial factors for enhancing the computation of implicatures are the availability of the relevant evidence and naturalness of the situation." Both of these factors were absent in the tasks in which children failed to compute implicatures. Although the findings are encouraging, the fact that the child subjects were 7 years old tempers the conclusions that can be reached. Children younger than 7 typically fail to compute scalar implicatures in tasks that do not involve making the alternative scalar terms explicit but, to date, it has not been demonstrated that children younger than 7 can successfully compute scalar implicature in the absence of explicit instruction, or tasks in which the relevant alternative scalar terms are not made overtly available for comparison.

## 9. Cross-linguistic variation

In the remainder of the chapter our attention will be directed to studies that were designed to assess children's knowledge of the semantic property of downward entailment. We will concentrate on negation, because this proved to be the most interesting, and the most challenging. We saw that negative statements in English, such as *Ted did* ***not*** *order pasta* ***or*** *sushi* generated a conjunctive entailment: (i) Ted did not order pasta, and (ii) Ted did not order sushi. We argued that negated disjunctions yield a conjunctive entailment in English because English "or" is inclusive-*or*, just as in de Morgan's laws of propositional logic, where it is valid to infer the negation of two propositions ($\sim A \& \sim B$) from one negated disjunction $\sim(A \vee B)$. The model Chierchia proposed anticipates that disjunction words in all human languages should be interpreted as inclusive-*or*, and that appearances to the contrary will be due, largely, to the influence of pragmatic implicatures. We would not expect disjunction to be interpreted as inclusive-*or* in some languages, but as exclusive-*or* in others. This would just make languages harder for children to learn.

We soon began to test this prediction in Japanese and in Mandarin Chinese, and we made a quite unexpected discovery (but cf. Szabolcsi 2002). When English sentences with negation and disjunction are translated into Japanese or into Mandarin Chinese, adult speakers of these languages did not judge these sentences to generate a conjunctive entailment. Consider the Mandarin example in (36).

(36) (Wo cai) Taide meiyou dian yidalimianshi huozhe shousi.
(I guess) Ted not order pasta or sushi
'It's either pasta or sushi that Ted did not order.'

It turned out that Mandarin contrasts with English in the way that the disjunction word, *huozhe*, is interpreted in sentences with negation, *meiyou*, as in (36). Adult speakers of Mandarin judge (36) to be true in three circumstances: (i) when Ted didn't order pasta, (ii) when Ted didn't order sushi, and (iii) when Ted didn't order either pasta or sushi. This is clearly not the conjunctive entailment that is generated by English speakers. How can this cross-linguistic variation be reconciled within the theory of Universal Grammar? Our proposal is that the variation involves a parameter. There are other possibilities to consider, however.

Let us quickly put to rest the possibility that the Mandarin disjunction word, *huozhe*, is exclusive-*or*. If this were the case, adult speakers of Mandarin would not interpret sentences like (36) in the way that they do. To see this, consider the logical formula ($A \oplus B$), where the symbol '$\oplus$' represents exclusive-*or*. This formula is true if exactly one of {A, B} is true. It follows that the negated disjunction, $\sim(A \oplus B)$, is false if exactly one of {A, B} is true. But as we saw, adult speakers of Mandarin accepted the negated disjunction in (36) when exactly one of the disjuncts is true, i.e., when Ted ordered pasta, but not sushi, or when Ted ordered sushi, but not pasta. These are the very circumstances in which negated disjunctions would be false if *huozhe* were exclusive-*or*. If *huozhe* were exclusive-*or*, sentence (36) would be true in just two circumstances: (i) when Ted ordered neither pasta nor sushi, and (ii) when Ted ordered both pasta and sushi. It is highly implausible, in our view, that negated disjunctions could be judged to be true, in any human language, in situations in which both disjuncts are true (see Crain and Khlentzos 2008 for further arguments that disjunction is not exclusive-*or* in human languages).

The observed differences in the interpretation of negated disjunctions across languages could be reconciled with the theory of Universal Grammar in (at least) two ways. First, negated disjunctions could have a different syntactic structure in some languages as compared to others. On this scenario, languages like Mandarin and Japanese might analyze negated disjunctions (e.g., (36)) as having two negated verb phrases, where the second verb phrase has undergone "disjunction reduction." Example (37) shows the underlying syntactic structure of the sentence *Ted did not order sushi or pasta*, according to this analysis. If the semantic interpretation is computed before the second VP is elided, this could explain the judgments made by speakers of Mandarin and Japanese in response to negated disjunctions

(37) Ted did not order pasta or ~~did not order~~ sushi.

On this account, languages like English do not undergo disjunction reduction. Because the semantic interpretation of negated disjunctions does not involve a second instance of negation in languages like English, disjunction directly licenses a conjunctive entailment.

A second account of the observed cross-linguistic variation was initially suggested by Szabolcsi (2002), and proposed more formally in work by Goro (2004, 2007). (For subsequent research adopting this proposal, see Crain 2008, 2012; Crain *et al.* 2007; Crain *et al.* 2006; Crain and Khlentzos 2008.) On this account, the cross-linguistic variation is due to a parameter, called the Disjunction Parameter. The Disjunction Parameter partitions languages into two classes. In one class of languages, disjunction is a positive polarity item. By definition, a positive polarity item (PPI) takes scope over (local) negation. In the other class of languages, according to the Disjunction Parameter, disjunction is not a positive polarity item, so the logical form mirrors the surface syntax in negated disjunctions, with negation taking scope over disjunction. So, the two values of the disjunction parameter distinguish languages according to the possible scope relations between negation and disjunction. On one value of the parameter, disjunction and negation are related by "inverse scope," because disjunction is a PPI. On the other value of the parameter, disjunction is not a PPI, so the scope relations are dictated by the surface syntax.

Let us indicate the parameter value on which disjunction takes scope over negation as OR = +PPI, and let OR = −PPI indicate the scope relations in languages where negation takes scope over disjunction. English takes the OR = −PPI value of the parameter. This is why *Ted didn't order pasta or sushi* generates a conjunctive entailment, as in classical logic. Notice that the symbol for negation takes scope over the disjunction operator "$\vee$" in the logical formula $\sim(A \vee B)$. Following de Morgan's laws, a negated disjunction generates a conjunctive entailment: $(\sim A \ \& \sim B)$. Languages in which negation takes scope over disjunction include English, German, French, Greek, Romanian, Bulgarian, and Korean (Szabolcsi 2002). In Mandarin, disjunction has the other parameter value, OR = +PPI. Therefore, disjunction fails to generate a conjunctive entailment in negative sentences like (36). The logical formula corresponding to (36) is $(\sim A \vee \sim B)$. Languages in which disjunction takes scope over negation include Mandarin, Japanese, Hungarian, Russian, Serbo-Croatian, Slovak, and Polish (Szabolcsi 2002; Goro and Akiba 2004a,b).

## 10. Independent evidence for a scope analysis

We have used tests of polarity sensitivity to assess the viability of the Disjunction Parameter. More specifically, disjunction fails to "scope out" over negation in linguistic contexts that cancel the polarity sensitivity of PPIs. We will illustrate one such context using the English PPI *some*. First, let us establish that *some* is indeed a PPI. To this end, we would point to the difference in interpretation between sentence (38), with *some*, and sentence (39), with *any*. Assuming that both the PPI *some*, and the NPI *any* are instances of existential quantification, "∃", the difference between the meaning of (38) and the meaning of (39) is indicated alongside the examples: *some* is interpreted as taking scope over negation, ∃ > NOT, whereas *any* appears inside the scope of negation, NOT > ∃. So example (38) can be paraphrased as "There are kangaroos that Julia didn't chase," and example (39) can be paraphrased as "There do not exist kangaroos that Julia chased."

(38) Julia didn't chase **some** of the kangaroos. ∃ > NOT

(39) Julia didn't chase **any** of the kangaroos. NOT > ∃

### *10.1 Negation and disjunction in different clauses*

As Baker (1970) observed, the polarity sensitivity of English *some* is cancelled in sentences in which negation resides in a higher clause than the clause that contains *some*. Examples are given in (40) and (41). It is difficult to discern any difference in the interpretations of these two sentences. The existential *some* in (40) has the same meaning as *any* in (41). Both sentences are true if the speaker is **not** convinced that there **exist** kangaroos that Julia chased. That is, both examples receive the NOT > ∃ interpretation in which negation takes scope over the existential.

(40) They did**n't** convince me that Julia chased **some** of the kangaroos. NOT > ∃

(41) They did**n't** convince me that Julia chased **any** of the kangaroos. NOT > ∃

So, the English PPI *some* is interpreted inside the scope of negation in sentences where negation and *some* reside in different clauses.

We can apply the same test to disjunction words. If disjunction words are PPIs in some languages, as we have suggested, then negation will take scope over disjunction in sentences in which negation and disjunction are situated in different clauses, in these languages. Of course, in languages where disjunction is not a PPI, negation takes scope over disjunction regardless of whether these expressions are situated in the same clause, or in different clauses. But, the critical observation is that all human languages should converge on the same interpretation in structures where negation and disjunction reside in different clauses. A universal linguistic phenomenon is anticipated, and it turns out to be confirmed.

Examples (43–48) are translations of English (42) *John didn't see Ted order pasta or sushi*. The English example has been translated into Mandarin in (43), into Japanese in (44), into Dutch in (45), into Russian in (46), into Norwegian in (47), and into Hungarian in (48). Negation and disjunction are boldfaced in the examples. The interpretation of the corresponding sentence in each language is the same as for the English example. In all of them, disjunction generates a conjunctive entailment.

(42) John did**n't** see Ted order pasta **or** sushi.

(43) Yuehan **mei** kanjian Ted dian yidalimianshi **huozhe** shousi.

(44) John-wa Ted-ga sushi **ka** pasuta-o tanomu-no-o mi-**nakat**-ta.

(45) John zag Ted **niet** pasta **of** sushi bestellen.

(46) Dzhon **ne** videl/uvidel chto/kak Borja zakazal/zakazyval pastu **ili** sushi.

(47) Jon så **ikke** Ted bestille pasta **eller** sushi.

(48) János **nem** látta Edvardot tésztát **vagy** szusit rendelni.

## *10.2 Disjunction in the predicate phrase of focus operators*

There is another linguistic context in which the polarity sensitivity of disjunction words is canceled. This is when disjunction words appear in the predicate phrase of a focus operator (English *only*, Mandarin *zhiyou*). To see this, note that the English and the Mandarin sentences in (49a,b) have two meaning components, due to the focus operator. One meaning component is about the element in focus, which in these examples is the Subject NP, *John/Yuehan*. In this first meaning component, disjunction is interpreted as exclusive-*or*, in virtue of a scalar implicature. So, the assertion being made is that John/Yuehan brought wine or beer to the party, and (probably) not both. A second meaning component is contributed by the focus operators in (49a,b). This meaning component pertains to a presupposed set of individuals that are being contrasted with John/Yuehan. That is, it follows from the meaning of English *only* and Mandarin *zhiyou* that there are individuals being contrasted with the focus element, John/Yuehan, and that these individuals do not have the property being attributed to the focus element. This second meaning component is represented by a negated disjunction, as in (49c). We call this meaning component, the entailment.

(49) a. Only John brought wine or beer to the party.
b. Zhiyou Yuehan dai-le hongjiu huohze pijiu qu juhui.
Only John bring-ASP wine or beer go party
'Only John brought wine or beer to the party.'
c. Entailment: Everyone else did **not** bring wine or beer to the party.

Because negation is introduced "covertly," in the entailment, the negated disjunctions in (49a,b) do not license the inverse scope reading that is assigned to negation and disjunction in sentences without a focus operator. In sentences with a focus operator, like (49a,b), the PPI status of disjunction is expected to be cancelled in the entailment, even in languages like Mandarin. If so, then disjunction is expected to conform to one of de Morgan's laws. The entailment asserts that nobody in the contrast set brought either wine or beer.

It is anticipated that speakers of English and speakers of Mandarin, including children, should adhere to the laws of classical logic according to which disjunction is interpreted inside the scope of negation in sentences with focus operators, in the entailment. In short, there should be no cross-linguistic differences in the interpretation of disjunction in the predicate phrase of a focus operator in any human language. These predictions were recently tested using a Truth Value Judgment task (Crain and Thornton 1998). Twenty Mandarin-speaking children (mean 4;7, range 4;5 to 4;10) and 18 English-speaking children (mean age 4;3, range 3;5 to 5;1) were tested on their interpretation of sentences like (49a,b). In addition, 20 Mandarin-speaking adults and 13 English-speaking adults were tested as controls. As predicted, both adults and children in both languages rejected the assertions in (49a,b) if someone other than John either brought wine or beer (Mandarin-speaking children 70%, English-speaking children 90%, Mandarin-speaking and English-speaking adults 100%), but they accepted the assertions in (49a,b) if John alone brought either wine or beer (Mandarin-speaking children and adults 100%, English-speaking children 93%, English-speaking adults 100%). The findings show that focus operators successfully cancelled the polarity sensitivity of disjunction words in child language, and thereby permit us to witness the logical meanings that children assign to these expressions. Both English and Mandarin Chinese, including child language, adhere to the laws of classical logic, once the polarity sensitivity of disjunction is cancelled by focus operators (Crain 2012; Crain *et al.* 2012). The conjunctive entailment of disjunction in the scope of negation holds only if disjunction is interpreted as inclusive-*or*, as in classical logic. The findings from these experiments, along with many others like them, contribute additional evidence that disjunction is a polarity positive item in one class of human languages, as stated in the Disjunction Parameter.

## 11. Avoiding subset problems in language acquisition

Introducing the Disjunction Parameter raises new questions. One question is whether children are expected to adopt an initial, default setting of the Disjunction Parameter. Alternatively, children could be free to select either value. Following the line of reasoning first advanced in Berwick (1985), children are expected to initially adopt the same value for a certain class of parameters. The learning mechanism that determines the initial, default value for this class is called The Subset Principle. The Subset Principle orders parameter values according to the number of sentences and their corresponding meanings that can be assigned to linguistic expressions.

The Subset Principle is operative when the class of languages that adopts one setting of a parameter, P (call these P1 languages), generates fewer sentence/meaning pairs for a given type of expression than the class of languages that adopts the alternative setting of P (call these P2 languages). In such cases, the Subset Principle compels children learning P1 languages and children learning P2 languages to initially hypothesize that the local language is a P1 language, rather than a P2 language. Children learning P2 languages are therefore expected to speak a fragment of a 'foreign' language for a while. If it can be established that children differ from adults in this way, this would be strong presumptive evidence against the usage-based account of language development. Because the usage-based account is "input matching," these kinds of differences between child and adult languages are not anticipated.

The subset principle that is required to explain children's use of the Disjunction Parameter is a semantic version of the familiar subset principle described by Berwick (1985) and by Pinker (1984). Both of these researchers observed that a learnability problem could arise for children when one language generates a subset of the sentences generated by another language. In the absence of negative evidence, children are compelled to initially adopt the "subset" language. Since the early 1990s, it has been claimed, albeit controversially, that when children are presented with a semantic ambiguity, they are guided by a learnability constraint that compels them to initially adopt the subset interpretation in order to guarantee that the superset reading can be learned from positive evidence, if the superset interpretation is assigned by adult speakers of the local language (Crain *et al.* 1994). This constraint on semantic interpretation is sometimes called the Semantic Subset Principle or the Semantic Subset Maxim, to distinguish it from the (syntactic) Subset Principle proposed originally by Berwick and by Pinker. The Semantic Subset Principle has been critically discussed by Musolino (2006) and by Gualmini and Schwarz (2009). Responses to the criticism and new evidence in favor of this principle are provided in Notley, Thornton, and Crain (2012) and Notley *et al.* (2011). We offer additional evidence in Section 12.

The Semantic Subset Principle is expected to be operative in the case of the Disjunction Parameter. It can easily be verified that the circumstances in which sentences are true on the OR = +PPI value comprise a superset of those circumstances that make sentences true on the OR = −PPI value. In other words, the binary values are in a subset/superset relation. To see this, note that the OR = −PPI value yields a *neither* reading, whereas the OR = +PPI value yields a *not both* reading. A statement to the effect that *neither A nor B* is true in a subset of the circumstances corresponding to the statement endorsing *not both A and B*.

Based on learnability considerations (i.e., in the absence of negative evidence), Goro (2004, 2007) predicted that Mandarin- and Japanese-speaking children should adopt the OR = −PPI value of the Disjunction Parameter. If so, they would be expected to interpret sentences with negation and disjunction in the same way as English speakers, OR = −PPI, but not in the same way as adult speakers of Mandarin or Japanese. If children start with the subset language, OR = −PPI, this guarantees that there will be positive evidence to compel children to override their initial preferences for the scope relations between negation and disjunction, if these preferences are not exhibited by adult speakers of the local language. For disjunction, the positive evidence for Mandarin-speaking children will be sentence/meaning pairs exhibiting the preference by Mandarin-speaking adults for disjunction to take scope over negation. Because disjunction takes scope over negation, these sentences will typically engage a scalar implicature. This guarantees that negated disjunctions will be used by Mandarin and Japanese speakers in circumstances in which only one disjunct is false, not both. In Mandarin, then, the sentence corresponding to *Ted didn't order sushi or pasta* means that it is either sushi or pasta (but not both) that Ted didn't order. In contrast to adults, the same sentence is expected to be true for Mandarin and Japanese-speaking children only if both disjuncts are false, NOT > OR. So, the truth conditions assigned to negated disjunctions by adults are inconsistent with the truth conditions that correspond to children's initial interpretation. Assuming that scope preferences take time to reverse, a number of negated disjunctions must be encountered by children before they jettison their initial preference in favor of the adult parameter setting.

## 12. Experimental studies of the Disjunction Parameter

The predictions were confirmed in a series of experimental studies. The initial studies were conducted with Japanese-speaking children, by Goro and Akiba (2004a,b). The Goro and Akiba studies examined children's interpretation of Japanese negated disjunctions like (50). For adult speakers of Japanese, such negative sentences lack the conjunctive entailments associated with de Morgan's laws. Adult Japanese speakers interpret (50) to mean that the pig didn't eat the carrot or didn't eat the pepper. Despite the appearance of *ka* within the scope of sentential negation in surface syntax, *ka* is interpreted by adults as having scope over negation.

(50) Butasan-wa ninjin **ka** pi'iman-wo tabe-**nakat**-ta.
pig-TOP pepper or carrot-ACC eat-NEG-PAST
'It's the carrot or the pepper that the pig didn't eat.'

Thirty 3- to 6-year-old children's understanding of sentences like (50) was assessed using a version of the Truth Value Judgment task. On a typical trial, subjects were asked to judge whether or not (50) was an accurate description of a situation in which the pig had eaten the carrot but not the green pepper. The findings were as predicted by the Semantic Subset Principle. A control group of Japanese-speaking adults consistently accepted the target sentences, whereas children rejected them 75% of the time. The findings are even more compelling once the data from four children, who responded like adults, were set aside. The remaining 26 children rejected the target sentences 87% of the time.

Based on the findings of Goro and Akiba (2004a,b), and the observation that the Mandarin Chinese disjunction word *huozhe* is a positive polarity item, further evidence of a disjunction parameter was pursued. According to the Semantic Subset Principle, children acquiring Mandarin should initially interpret the disjunction operator *huozhe* in conformity with de Morgan's laws in simple negated sentences, despite the absence of this interpretation for Mandarin-speaking adults.

(51) Xiaozhu **meiyou** chi huluobo **huozhe** qingjiao.
Pig not eat carrot or pepper
'It's the carrot or the pepper that the pig didn't eat.'

Here are the main findings. In response to negated disjunctions, twenty Mandarin-speaking children (mean age 4;5) rejected the target "not … or" statements 97% of the time, as did English-speaking children and adults; by contrast Mandarin-speaking adults accepted them 95% of the time. To justify their rejections, Mandarin-speaking children pointed out the animals in question had only eaten one vegetable. This indicates that children had assigned the "neither" (OR = −PPI) reading, as in English (also see Jing *et al.* 2005).

It is worth pointing out that Chinese and Japanese differ in word order. In Japanese, the word for disjunction *ka* comes before negation *nakat*, as seen in example (50). In Chinese, the word for negation *meiyou* comes before the word for disjunction *huozhe*, as seen in example (51). We have seen also that adult speakers of both Chinese and Japanese interpret disjunction as having scope over negation (OR > NOT). Since the ordering of disjunction and negation is reversed in these languages, it follows that the interpretation assigned by adult speakers of both languages, according to which disjunction takes scope over negation, cannot be based on linear order. We also saw that children acquiring both Chinese and Japanese initially adopted the opposite scope relations, with negation taking scope over disjunction. It follows that children were not assigning this interpretation based on linear order, since the ordering of negation and disjunction differs across these languages. In short, no principle based on linear order could explain either the interpretation assigned by adults, or by children, across languages.

A parallel between Chinese and Japanese is the way in which adults generate the 'neither' reading. In both Japanese and Chinese, this reading is assigned to simple negative sentences with conjunction. For example, the Mandarin Chinese conjunction word *he* appears in the simple negated sentence in (52), which conveys the 'neither' interpretation. Notice that this interpretation of conjunction under negation is not consistent with de Morgan's laws, since 'not (A and B)' is logically equivalent to 'not A or not B', where (52) is interpreted as requiring both A and B to be false.

(52) Kermit **bu** hui yingwen **he** zhongwen.
Kermit not know English and Chinese
'Kermit does not know either English or Chinese.'

Disjunction is interpreted in the same way in human languages as it is in classical logic. But it would appear that this is done at the expense of conjunction, which appears to be non-Boolean in (52). Yet, again, appearances can be deceiving. It is also possible that conjunction is a PPI in languages like Mandarin. As we saw, this possibility can easily be verified by examining the scope relations between conjunction and negation when these operators appear in different clauses (see Crain 2012).

If scope parameters are based on subset/superset relations in logical entailments, as we have suggested, then we expect that both children's productions and their interpretations may be different from adults, depending on the default parameter setting, and the setting that is operative for adults. In further support of this view, it has been found that many English-speaking children produce the existential indefinite *some* in contexts where it is not licensed in the adult grammar. For adult English-speakers, *some* is a positive polarity item (PPI) and must take scope over local negation. For English-speaking children, however, it appears that *some* is not a PPI, and can be interpreted in the scope of negation. In fact, *some* can even be produced in the scope of local negation. Children have been found to use *some* or *something* in contexts where adults use *any* or *anything* to express the same message, e.g., *None of the people had some presents* (Musolino *et al.* 2000).

Negative polarity items, by contrast, are rarely, if ever, misunderstood or produced in the wrong linguistic environments by children at any age. Children adhere to the syntactic and semantic constraints on the use of negative polarity items from the earliest stages of language acquisition. Large-scale reviews of the spontaneous production data of both English-speaking children (aged 0;11–5;2) and Dutch-speaking children (aged 1;5–3;10) have revealed that children almost never produce negative polarity items without a downward-entailing licensor of some sort (Tieu 2010; Van der Wal 1996). In elicited production tasks, it has also been found that children do not produce negative polarity items in non-downward-entailing environments, while they do produce them in downward-entailing environments (Crain and Thornton 2006; O'Leary 1994; Van der Wal 1996). The fact that children produce negative polarity items in just the right contexts shows that they are sensitive to the difference between downward-entailing environments and non-downward-entailing environments.[1]

## 13. Conclusions

The model of the language apparatus proposed by Chierchia is innovative in several respects. Although the model is heavily influenced by Gricean principles, it clearly differs from the traditional Gricean account. Chierchia's model locates the computation of scalar implicatures within the semantic component of the language apparatus, rather than in the pragmatics, as on the Gricean approach. This reassessment of the semantics/pragmatics interface leads to expectation that young children, across the globe, should manifest adult-like abilities to produce and comprehend sentences with logical operators and quantificational expressions, including the computation and cancellation of scalar implicatures. We briefly reviewed progress that has been made on that front.

The model proposed by Chierchia has inspired cross-linguistic studies of child language, including investigations of children's knowledge of the licensing conditions of negative polarity items, and their interpretation of disjunction in different linguistic contexts. The findings of studies of children acquiring typologically distinct languages, including English and Mandarin Chinese, have verified that downward entailment is a unifying property in human languages, including child language. In conducting this research, we have uncovered several interesting and unexpected differences between child and adult languages. The observed discrepancies between child and adult language are difficult to explain on the usage-based account of children's emerging linguistic competence. The observed differences could be explained, however, by the theory of Universal Grammar, according to which child language is expected to differ from the local adult language along the natural seams of human languages, i.e., parameters. We discussed one "scope" parameter, the Disjunction Parameter. We saw that, across languages, children appear to initially favor the value of the Disjunction Parameter that generates scope relations that make sentences true in the narrowest range of circumstances.

This ensures that children will have access to positive evidence if the local language favors the alternative scope possibilities, those that make sentences true in a broader range of circumstances. This brings us back to the nature versus nurture debate. The research findings we have reviewed in this chapter are difficult to reconcile on a usage-based approach to language acquisition because the usage-based approach lacks the kinds of core principles, such as downward entailment, which underpin disparate linguistic phenomena that appear systematically in individual languages, and across human languages. The findings provide support for a theory of Universal Grammar that includes a computational system that expresses deep seated semantic regularities of the kinds anticipated on Chierchia's model, and which help explain children's rapid and uniform mastery of human languages

One last point. Nearly everyone admits that there are linguistic universals in some sense. At issue is whether the universals of human languages are specific to language, or whether cross-linguistic generalizations simply owe to the fact that humans are born with the "same basic conceptual apparatus" (Goldberg 2003: 16). In fact, there are compelling reasons for thinking that the interpretations generated by logical expressions in human languages are governed by principles that are specific to language, and are not simply a system of inferences that any rational system would make. Much previous research in child and adult language, and in the literature on reasoning, has emphasized differences between the meanings of expressions in classical logic and in human languages. Although there are some clear differences, we have offered some reasons to suppose that logic and human languages share some of the same basic meanings, including the meaning of disjunction. We began this chapter by citing some differences of opinion about the meaning of disjunction in human languages, as well as some observations about the nature of the input to children. Many scholars have reached the conclusion that disjunction is exclusive-*or* in human languages; the input to children is certainly consistent with this conclusion. However, the finding is that children, across languages, prefer to interpret disjunction as inclusive-*or* even in contexts in which adults prefer to interpret it as exclusive-*or*. This finding invites the inference that the inclusive-*or* meaning of disjunction is a contingent a priori fact about the minds/brains of human beings, and not a fact that is acquired by observing how others behave, or the meaning that any rational creature would adopt (for further discussion, see Crain 2012).

**Acknowledgments**

The research reported in this chapter was funded by an Australian Research Council (ARC) Discovery Grant (DP0879842) and further supported by the Australian Research Council Centre of Excellence for Cognition and its

Disorders (CE110001021). We would also like to acknowledge three anonymous reviewers whose thorough and very helpful comments made this a much better paper.

## NOTE

1. Our colleague Aijun Huang has conducted experiments assessing Mandarin-speaking children's comprehension of the NPI *renhe*, as well as experiments assessing children's comprehension of *wh*-words, which function like indefinites in downward-entailing contexts (also see Zhou and Crain 2011).

# 10 Acquisition meets comparison: an investigation of gradable adjectives

*Francesca Panzeri, Francesca Foppolo, and Maria Teresa Guasti*

## 1. Introduction

In this chapter, we review some works on the acquisition of adjectives and present novel experimental data on their interpretation. We interpret these data as suggesting that younger children start by interpreting relative gradable adjectives (GAs henceforth) like *tall* in a categorical way, i.e., as referring to sets of objects, and only at a later stage they switch to the comparative-like interpretation. We propose that this evolutionary trend can be easily explained within a semantic framework that assumes that relative GAs denote a partial function from individuals to truth-values. We further suggest a parallelism with the phenomenon of scalar implicature computation in children, a phenomenon that has been studied extensively by Gennaro Chierchia, whose valuable contribution extends from semantic theory (Chierchia 2006; Chierchia *et al.* 2012) to experimental investigation (Chierchia *et al.* 1998; Chierchia *et al.* 2001; Chierchia *et al.* 2004; Foppolo *et al.* 2012; Panizza *et al.* 2009). This chapter is organized as follows: after introducing the well-known distinction between intersective and relative adjectives (Section 1.1), we review the major findings in the literature on the acquisition of adjectives (Section 1.2); we then summarize the two major theoretical approaches that have been put forth to analyze the meaning of relative GAs, i.e., the degree-based analysis and the partial function account (Section 1.3). In Section 2, we present the experimental data of two studies and, in the final section, we discuss these results within the partial function approach.

### *1.1 The goals of this study*

Even if children's first vocabulary is overwhelmingly composed of nouns, around the age of 2 children start producing adjectives. In languages like English and Italian, adjectives can be identified by morphological cues (e.g., the suffix *–ish* in English, or *–oso* in Italian) and by their syntactic distribution (they can modify common nouns, as in "Leo is an *Italian/tall* man," and occur in copular constructions, as in "Leo is *Italian/tall*"). Nonetheless, their interpretation is not uniform. Some adjectives, such as *Italian*, *four-legged*, *wooden* are similar to common nouns, as they can be viewed as denoting sets of individuals that share a property. For example, the adjective *Italian* denotes the set of individuals that are Italian, just like the common noun *man* denotes the set of individuals that are men. These adjectives combine with the noun they modify *via* set intersection and for this reason have been labeled *intersective* adjectives (Partee 1995): e.g., "Italian man" refers to an individual that is both a man and an Italian. For other adjectives (like, e.g., *big, tall, intelligent*)[1] a different analysis is required: provided that, for instance, the very same individual can be judged *tall* as an Italian man but *non-tall* as a basketball player, it does not make sense to talk about the set of *big* or *tall* things in general. These adjectives have been labeled *relative*,[2] and exhibit two main characteristics: their interpretation is *context dependent* and is *vague*. As for context dependency, the interpretation of a sentence containing a relative adjective (and, eventually, its truth or falsity) depends on contextual factors that might set different standards of comparisons. For instance, consider (1):

(1) Leo is tall.

Assuming that Leo is 186 cm tall, we could be evaluating (1) in a situation in which we are talking about Italian men in general or basketball players: in this case, the truth of (1) would depend upon the intended normative class of comparison. Else, we could be looking at Leo standing close to Fred, who is 174 cm tall, or close to Max, who is 198 cm tall: in this case, the truth of (1) would depend upon perceptual considerations. Or, we could be trying to reach a cup on a shelf which is 195 cm or 250 cm high: in this case, the truth of (1) would depend upon functional considerations.

As for vagueness, the evaluation of a relative adjective admits borderline cases: even when the intended context of evaluation is set, there are cases for which we do not feel comfortable in attributing a truth-value to a sentence that contains a relative adjective like *tall*. This could happen, for instance, if we were to evaluate (1) in a situation in which Leo's height is too close to the average height of the class of comparison (e.g., if Leo were Dutch) or to a perceptually salient individual (e.g., if Leo were compared to Bart, who is 185 cm tall).

Relative adjectives have been investigated both from a developmental and a theoretical perspective. We will connect these two lines of research, by testing how children interpret relative adjectives and how experimental data can give us insights about their semantic analysis.

### *1.2 The acquisition of adjectives*

The acquisition of the meaning of adjectives takes a while and is marked by gradual achievements. Although morphological and syntactic cues can help children recognize novel words as adjectives, different experiments have shown that children up to age 3 need support from the context in order to acquire the meaning of a novel adjective, i.e., to understand that it refers to properties (and not categories) of objects. In particular, toddlers at around 11 months tend to interpret novel words presented as adjectives as referring to categories, and not to properties of objects (Waxman and Booth 2003). The link between adjectives and properties of objects emerges around 14 months, but just for color adjectives (Booth and Waxman 2003). Only around 36 months is it extended to another few properties, but just if the objects belong to the same basic category. For example, when 3-year-old children are presented with a rhinoceros labeled as *blickish*, they can correctly extend the relevant property to another rhino, but not to an elephant (Klibanoff and Waxman 2000). Similarly, Mintz and Gleitman (2002) have shown that 3-year-olds can use adjectives to qualify objects of different categories only if they are presented in combination with specific nouns ("This is a *stoof* horse"), but not when they are presented with the pro-form "one" or with the generic word "thing" ("This is a *stoof* one/thing"). Waxman and Klibanoff (2000) have shown that 3-year-old children can extend adjectives to objects of different categories only if they are provided the opportunity to make a comparison across objects.

The picture that emerges from these studies seems to suggest that children up to age 3 understand that adjectives apply to objects of different categories only if the linguistic or extralinguistic context is supportive. This fact should not be surprising, if we think that adjectives are parasitic on nouns. The gradual acquisition of the meaning of adjectives suggests that children proceed in steps in learning how to use and interpret them.

At the same time, children as young as 2 do produce some intersective adjectives. At this same age, they start using relative adjectives and, by the age of 3, they productively use adjectives such as *big/small(little)*, *tall/short*, *long/short*, *high/low*, *heavy/light*. As we have discussed above, the interpretation of relative adjectives requires a preliminary identification of the intended standard of comparison, which typically varies from situation to situation. The following developmental question thus arises: is children's understanding and use of these adjectives in fact adult-like, or do they develop the mastery of relative adjectives in different phases? With respect to this question, we conjecture that the meaning of adjectives proceeds stepwise. Therefore, we expect that at age 3 children's understanding of adjective meaning is not fully mastered. Findings in the literature are controversial on this matter.

On the one hand, a series of studies have shown that even 2-year-old children are able to retrieve the intended normative standard and use it to judge relative adjectives (Ebeling and Gelman 1988). For instance, they judge a given mitten as *big* (or *small*) "for being a mitten" and they make use of perceptual cues as well, judging a mitten as *big* (or *small*) compared to another physically present mitten. Pre-school aged children are also able to use functional standards, even if this ability seems to emerge later (Gelman and Ebeling 1989). At the same time, though, children are reported to make a consistent series of errors. In the first place, they seem reluctant to switch the contextual standard of comparison. For example, they refuse to re-label an object as *big* in the context of smaller objects if this same object was previously judged as *little* when compared to bigger objects, an ability that is attested only at age 4 (Sera and Smith 1987). Moreover, children exhibit extreme labeling: when they are asked to judge a series of objects decreasing along a relevant dimension (e.g., seven objects that decrease in height), younger children tend to apply the relative term only to the extremes of that series. For example, they consider only the first object as *tall* and only the last one as *short* (cf. Smith *et al.* 1986; Smith *et al.* 1988; Syrett 2007). Different studies also showed that children make substitution errors (E. Clark 1972; H. Clark 1973; Sera and Smith 1987). For example, they interpret the negative antonym of a pair as if it were the positive (e.g., they use *big* for *little* or *wide* for *narrow*) and use more general terms instead of specific ones (e.g., they use *big* instead of *long* or *tall*). Other studies documented problems with comparatives. For example, in a series of studies, children interpreted *less* as if it meant *more* (Donaldson and Balfour 1968; Palermo 1973; see also Gathercole 1979), and *before* as if it meant *after* (E. Clark 1971). More generally, the positive antonym of a relative adjective is understood sooner and better than its negative counterpart (cf. Donaldson and Wales 1970; Klatzky *et al.* 1973, on the following pairs: *big/small*, *tall/short*, *high/low*, *long/short*, *thick/thin* and *fat/thin*).

The picture that emerged from the acquisition field so far appears to lead to contrasting claims concerning children's comprehension and usage of relative terms: while children seem to exhibit an adult-like behavior in tasks in which the standard of comparison is easily identifiable, they also consistently make substitution errors and extreme labeling. In Section 2 we will report two experiments that we conducted in order to further investigate children's understanding of relative adjectives. In order to better detail our experimental hypotheses, we will first sketch the main theories that have been proposed to analyze the meaning of adjectives, i.e., the degree-based analysis and the partial function approach.

## *1.3 The semantics of adjectives*

As already alluded to, the class of adjectives is heterogeneous. Adopting a distributional criterion, a preliminary distinction can be drawn amongst those adjectives that can enter into comparative constructions and be modified by degree expression (i.e. GAs), and those that do not (i.e. non-GAs like *Italian*, *four-legged*, *vegetarian*). Semantically, non-GAs are intersective, whereas the class of GAs comprises relative GAs, that exhibit contextual variability and vagueness, and so-called absolute GAs, which are gradable according to the distributional criterion but whose interpretation appears to be independent from contextual considerations.[3] An absolute GA like *clean*, for instance, is gradable in that it can enter a comparative construction ("This cloth is clean*er* than that one") but its interpretation is not subject to the same kind of context variability as relative GAs. What counts as *clean* does not vary from situation to situation, but is equated with the presence of the absolute GA property to a maximum or minimum standard: something is *clean* if it has no dirt on it (maximum standard of cleanness), whereas it is *dirty* if it has at least some dirt on it (minimum standard of dirtiness).[4]

As for the semantic analysis, the most influential view assumes that the analysis of GAs crucially involves the notion of *degrees*, where degrees are abstract entities ordered along a scale associated with the dimension referred to by the adjective (Bierwisch 1989; Cresswell 1976; Kennedy 1999, 2007; Seuren 1973; Stechow 1984). Thus, for instance, the relative GA *tall* evokes a scale of ordered degrees of height, and it corresponds to a function that attributes to an individual the possession of the tallness property to a certain degree. When the GA is used in its bare form, as in (1), a null operator is assumed to introduce a contextual standard of comparison, and the sentence gets eventually interpreted as "Leo's height *exceeds that contextual standard of comparison for tallness*." Such an analysis handles in a very elegant and straightforward manner relative GAs' context dependency, since it assumes that the standard of comparison needs to be contextually retrieved. Different choices for setting the standard can lead to different interpretations and, eventually, to opposite truth-value assignments. As for the existence of borderline cases, Kennedy (2007) explicitly stipulates that the degree to which an individual possesses the gradable property (e.g., the degree to which Leo is tall) has to "stand out" with respect to the contextual standard of comparison. This is meant to account for the situations in which we do not feel comfortable in attributing, for instance, the tallness-property to a person whose height minimally exceeds the standard of comparison. Another desirable advantage of the degree-based analysis as proposed by Kennedy and McNally (2005) and Kennedy (2007) is the possibility of treating all GAs in a uniform way. Under this approach, all GAs would evoke scales of degrees with the difference that, while the scales associated to relative GAs like *tall* do not have linguistically identifiable lower or upper boundaries (e.g., there are no linguistic means to refer to an alleged minimum or maximum standard of height, as witnessed by the infelicity of the combinations "minimally/absolutely *tall*"), absolute GAs like *full* or *open* project on scales of degrees that do possess a "natural" boundary. For example, there is an upper limit to the fullness of a container (that can be judged as "absolutely *full*"); and there's a lower boundary to the openness of a door (that is equated with its maximal closeness). Kennedy (2007) proposes to reduce the difference between relative and absolute GAs to the way the standard of comparison is fixed: for relative GAs, the standard must be contextually retrieved; for absolute GAs, a principle of Interpretive Economy dictates to identify the standard of comparison with the GA's maximum or minimum standard (but see also McNally 2011; Toledo and Sassoon 2011 for a different approach).

A different perspective, though, might be assumed to deal with GAs, as we mentioned before. Klein (1980) claimed that the degree-based analysis is unnecessary complicated, because it postulates the existence of degrees as primitive entities; it assumes that a simple, bare form, such as "*a* is GA," is to be analyzed as a comparative form ("*a* has the GA property to a degree that exceeds a standard"); and it posits a radically different analysis for gradable and non-GAs. Klein defends an approach in which GAs are assigned a semantics that is simpler, closer to their surface syntax, and uniform: GAs are viewed as functions from individuals to truth-values, just like non-GAs. Differently from non-GAs, though, GAs correspond to *partial* functions. The interpretation of GAs requires a preliminary step that consists in the identification of the intended domain of application of the GA function,[5] and then the specific GA partitions this domain in three subsets: the set of individuals that possess the GA property, those that do not, and those individuals for which the function does not receive a value. Thus, relative GAs' context sensitivity is accounted for by assuming that the domain of application can be restricted to different comparison classes (in the normative interpretation) or to particular individuals (in the perceptual interpretation), and this corresponds to different outputs of the function. The partiality of the function, on the other hand, accounts for relative GAs' vagueness: for some borderline cases the function does not provide an output.

Although the proponents of these different theoretical approaches do not make explicit predictions about the way and timing in which children converge on adult-like interpretation of GAs, we will try to account for children's behavior reported in the previous section within a degree-based analysis or a partial function approach. While both of the theories sketched above can easily account for the fact that children exhibit an adult-like performance when the standard of comparison is easily retrievable or clearly identifiable in the context, they might diverge in explaining the origin and nature of the consistent errors that younger children make. For example, we reported above that children exhibit extreme labeling behavior, i.e., they tend to label only the extremes of a series as relative GA, and they refuse to label objects in the middle. This consistent behavior can be viewed as an overestimation of borderline cases. We believe that this tendency could straightforwardly be accounted for if relative GAs were interpreted as partial functions that assign a truth-value only to the most representative cases (corresponding to the extremes in the series) and leave a wide extension gap in-between (i.e., the set of individuals for which the function does not have an output). The developmental steps in this case would consist in a progressive narrowing of the partiality of the function.

In a degree-based approach, on the other hand, the tendency to extreme labeling could be accounted for in two different ways: either by assuming that children correctly identify the intended standard of comparison around the mid of a series, but, adopting Kennedy (2007)'s terminology, only consider the individuals that really "stand out" with respect to that property as being relative GA; or, children might settle the standard of comparison in a more extreme position, closer to the upper (or lower boundary) of a series, paralleling what happens for absolute GAs.

We intend to intervene with two experimental studies at this juncture, by testing children and adults in the interpretation of GAs in a situation in which the intended standard of comparison is not readily available. We will discuss the results of our studies within a partial function approach by proposing a novel hypothesis to explain children's behavior.

## 2. Testing GAs: non adult-like children and children-like adults

In a first experiment we investigated the interpretation of relative and absolute GAs in children and adults with the aim of attesting a difference within the class of GAs and, eventually, to identify a developmental trend between younger and older children in the comprehension of these adjectives (cf. also Foppolo and Panzeri in press). Relative and absolute GAs differ in the way the standard of comparison is set: relative GAs necessitate the retrieval of a contextual standard, whereas the interpretation of absolute GAs does not vary from situation to situation, since the standard is identified with the absolute GA's upper or lower boundary (i.e., its maximum or minimum standard). In our first study, we aimed at detecting whether children are aware of this difference in the first place,[6] and how they react when they are asked to evaluate a description such as "This is *relative GA*" when the standard of comparison is not retrievable from the context. In a second study, we employed similar material to test adults when considerations about informativeness were suspended.

### *2.1 Experiment 1: a developmental study on the interpretation of GAs*

*2.1.1 Participants, procedure, and materials of Experiment 1* We tested 3- and 5-year-old Italian speaking children (20 3-year-olds (3;0–3;11, MA=3;6) and 18 5-year-olds (5;0–6;1, MA=5;4)) and 23 adults that volunteered to participate. Participants were randomly assigned to one of two lists.

In a single experimental session, we administered a Truth Value Judgment Task followed by a Scalar Judgment Task. The participants were tested by two experimenters, one that manipulated a puppet and the other that showed the experimental objects and asked questions. As for the Truth Value Judgment Task, the procedure was as follows: the experimenter put a single object on the table in front of the participant. The puppet described that object by using an adjective (e.g., "This is tall"), and the participant had to evaluate the puppet's description by using one of three possible responses: "yes, correct," "no, incorrect," or "I can't tell, it depends." In order to familiarize the participants with this procedure, they were first given a training session in which different toys were presented and described by the puppet. In particular, a toy boy with a big hat was shown in the training session and described by the puppet as "This is blond." Given that the big hat covered the whole head of the boy, it was impossible to see what color his hair was. Thus, the response "I can't tell" was prompted.[7]

The second part of our experiment consisted of a Scalar Judgment Task like the one used by Syrett (2007); see also Syrett *et al.* (2010). In this task, the participants were presented with a series of seven objects and, for each of these items, they were asked "Is this *adjective*?" An option between "yes" and "no" was given in this case.

The experimental material for the Truth Value Judgment Task consisted of 6 pairs of positive/negative relative GA antonyms (*wide/narrow, heavy/light, fast/slow, big/small, tall/short(height), long/short(length)*))[8] and 6 pairs of absolute GA antonyms, classified as maximum standard (*clean, straight, dry, smooth, closed, full, empty*) and minimum standard adjectives (*dirty, bent, wet, rough, open*). Critical trials were interspersed with controls for a total of 24 items for each list. Besides the controls that prompted a genuine "yes" or "no" response (for example, participants were shown a blue object described as "This is yellow"), we inserted two trials that should prompt participants to answer "I don't know." In particular, a toy zebra was described as "This is obedient" and a toy man was described as "This is married."

In the Truth Value Judgment Task, we tested adjectives with respect to single objects that were as abstract as possible, i.e., not directly recognizable as having a specific function, so that they should not evoke any comparison class.[9] Each object was extracted from an ideal scale of seven objects decreasing along a relevant dimension. For example, for the scale of height we used seven different wooden rods ranging from the tallest (20 cm tall) to the shortest one (5 cm tall), with intervals of 2.5 cm between two consecutive elements in the series. We presented one object in isolation in the Truth Value Judgment Task and the whole series in the Scalar Judgment Task. In Figures 10.1–10.4 is a sample of the scales used in the Scalar Judgment Task for *tall/short* (Fig.10.1), *straight/bent* (Fig. 10.2), *full/empty* (Figs. 10.3 and 10.4), with the indication of which element(s) were used in isolation in the first part of the experiment.

We tested antonyms for relative GAs (e.g., *tall/short*) between lists with respect to the same type of object (e.g., a vertical wooden rod as in Fig. 10.1), but using different ends of the scale: in particular, we used the 2nd element from the left in the series of seven to test the positive antonym and the 6th element of the same series to test the negative antonym. We tested antonyms for the absolute GAs in which an abstract object was used between lists by using the same object in the series of seven: for example, the 2nd element from the left in Fig. 10.2 was used in List 2 to test *straight*, which is a maximum standard adjective, and in List 1 to test *bent*, which is its minimum standard counterpart. Finally, we tested *full/empty* and *open/closed* within lists but using different types of objects. In particular, two different series of objects were created for each pair of antonyms: seven bottles and seven paint-tubes ranging from being completely full to completely empty (Figs. 10.3–10.4), and seven purses with a zipper and a box with a lid ranging from being completely open to completely closed. As for the Scalar Judgment Task, a total of 9 scales were tested. Of these, 3 were series of "abstract" objects that were used to test couples of relative GAs antonyms (*big/small*, *long/short*, *wide/narrow*, *tall/short*), 2 were used to test absolute GAs with abstract objects (*clean/dirty*, *straight/bent*), and 3 were used to test *full/empty* and *open/closed*.

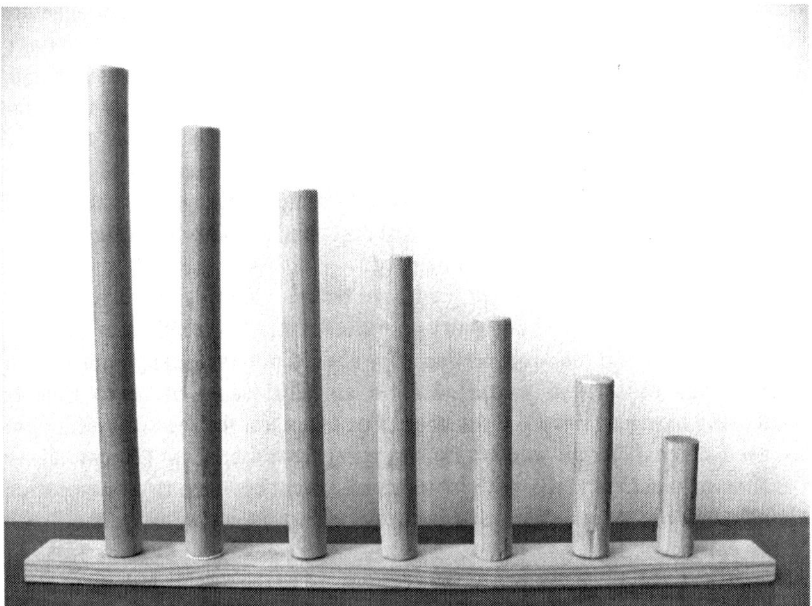

Figures 10.1–10.4 Sample of the material used to test relative and absolute GAs in the Truth Value Judgment Task and in the Scalar Judgment Task.

Figure 10.2 (cont.)

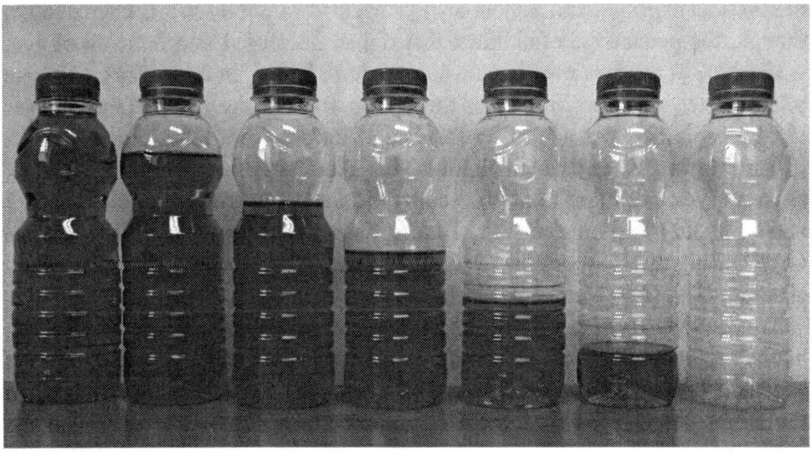

Figure 10.3 (cont.)

Again, antonyms were tested between lists, while the order of presentation was balanced across participants and lists: half of the participants in each list were shown a relative GA first, the other half encountered *full* as first item.[10] In testing antonyms across lists, we always started from the most representative element in

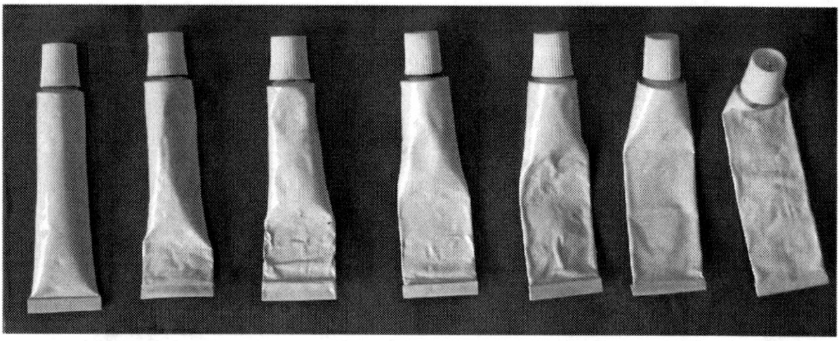

Figure 10.4 (cont.)

the series, which was crucially reversed across conditions: e.g., we started from the straightest rope when asking "Is this straight?" (1st element from the left in Fig. 10.2) and from the most bent rope when asking "Is this bent?" (7th element from the left in Fig. 10.2).

*2.1.2 Results of Experiment 1* As far as the controls are concerned, participants in each age group behaved almost at ceiling when asked to evaluate descriptions that were genuinely true or false with respect to the item shown. In case of the controls for which an "I don't know" response was expected, adults behaved as expected and almost always used this option (96%). Interestingly, though, the percentage of children that did so decreased as a function of age: while 40% of the 5-year-olds answered "I don't know" in these trials, only one of the 3-year-old children selected this option. Instead, the group of the younger children split between a "yes" (50%) and a "no" answer (48%).

Turning to the experimental trials, the distribution of the three types of answers (yes; no; I don't know) used by the three age groups (children aged 3 and 5; adults) is plotted in Fig. 10.5, differentiated by type of GA: relative GAs[11] (Rel); minimum standard absolute GAs (Abs Min); maximum standard absolute GAs (Abs Max).[12]

We can evince some very broad generalizations from the graph. First of all, adults' performance was at ceiling in case of absolute GAs: adults always accepted "This is *minimum standard absolute GA*" (e.g., "This is bent") when the target object possessed the GA property to a degree that exceeded the minimum standard degree (e.g., the minimally bent rope in Fig. 10.2) and they nearly always rejected the description "This is *maximum standard absolute GA*" (e.g., "This is straight") when the target object did not have the GA property to its maximum degree (e.g., the same minimally bent rope in Fig. 10.2). This behavior was predicted on the basis on Kennedy and McNally (2005). In case of relative GAs, adults answered "I don't know"

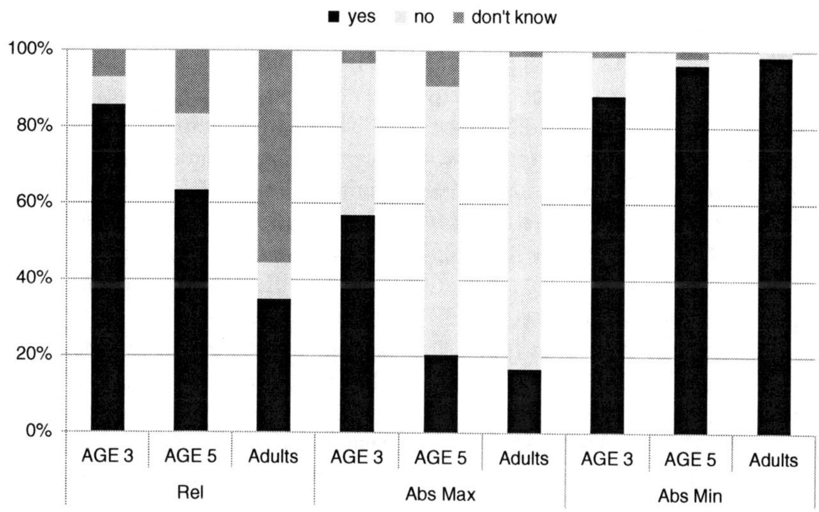


Figure 10.5 Answers' distribution per Age of participants and Type of GA.

60% of the time, and they accepted the description only 30% of the time. A high percentage of "I don't know" answers was predicted on the basis of the fact that we did not provide a contextual standard of comparison, and thus the description "This is *relative GA*" was not interpretable. On the basis of adults' performance, we can conclude that our experimental design can serve as a basis for distinguishing, experimentally, between these two classes of adjectives.

Turning to children, a difference emerged between 3- and 5-year-olds with respect to relative and maximum standard absolute GAs especially. First of all, in the case of absolute GAs, the performance of the 5-year-olds parallels that of adults: children aged 5 consistently rejected the description "This is *maximum standard absolute GA*" referred to an object that did not possess the property denoted by the adjective at a maximum degree (e.g. *straight* referred to the minimally bent rope), and consistently accepted the description "This is *minimum standard absolute GA*" even when referred to an object that possessed the property denoted by the adjective to a minimum degree (e.g., *bent* referred to the minimally bent rope). However, while the 3-year-old children did not differ from the older children and adults in this latter case (e.g., they accepted *bent* referred to a minimally bent rope), they also accepted the description "This is *maximum standard absolute GA*" referred to an object that did not possess the property denoted by the adjective at a maximum degree (e.g., they accepted *straight* referred to the minimally bent rope) more than the adults and the 5-year-olds. In the case of relative GAs, a developmental trend seems to emerge: while children at age 3 showed a prevalence of "yes" answers and adults a prevalence of "I don't know" answers, the distribution of the 5-year-old children's answers seems to lie in between.

Statistical comparisons by means of Fisher Exact Tests for count data revealed a significant general effect of Age in case of relative GAs ($p<.001$). A significant difference was attested in paired comparisons between the 3 and the 5-year-olds, between the 3-year-olds and the adults and between the 5-year-olds and the adults (all $ps<.001$). However, this effect might be partly due to the fact that children, in general, used the option "I don't know" much less than adults. Considering the incidence of "yes" answers over the total in case of relative GAs, the difference between the 3 and the 5-year-olds disappears ($p=.29$), while it does not comparing the 5-year-olds and the adults ($p<.01$). In case of minimum standard absolute GAs, a significant difference was observed between children aged 3 and adults ($p<.05$), but not between children of age 3 and 5 ($p=.14$), nor between children aged 5 and adults ($p=.53$). In case of maximum standard absolute GAs, a significant general effect of Age was revealed instead ($p<.001$). This difference was probably due to the fact that, differently from the older children and the adults, a lot of the 3-year-olds accepted the description "This is *maximum standard absolute GA*" referred to an object that did not possess the property denoted by the adjective at a maximum degree (all $ps<.001$). No statistical difference is revealed for maximum standard absolute GAs between the 5-year-olds and the adults instead ($p=.11$). Further statistical comparisons revealed that, like the adults, children at age 3 and 5 distinguished between relative and absolute GAs (minimum and maximum standard considered separately, all $ps<.001$), while children at age 3 distinguished relative GAs from maximum standard absolute GAs ($p<.001$) but not from minimum standard absolute GAs ($p=.29$). This was probably due to the fact that, while a "yes" answer was expected in case of minimum standard absolute GAs, the proportion of "yes" answers in the 3-year-old children was higher than expected in the case of relative GAs (more than 85%).

To better grasp children's behavior, we will first focus on their responses to relative GAs and then we will compare children's and adults' performance in the Scalar Judgment Task. As for children's behavior with relative GAs, we plotted in Fig. 10.6 the distribution of participants' "yes" answers (differentiated by Age) for each of the relative adjectives tested.

A very clear picture emerges: first of all, the incidence of "yes" responses in general is very high in children, in the younger group especially, where the rate of "yes" answers is always over 70%, reaching peaks of 90% and 100% in some cases. In the second place, except for the first two pairs of antonyms (*fast/slow*, *heavy/light*), the 5-year-old children seem to pattern more like the 3-year-olds than the adults, providing more than 60% of "yes" answers to the adjectives that presumably they are most familiar with (*big/small*, *tall/short*, *long/short*), and,

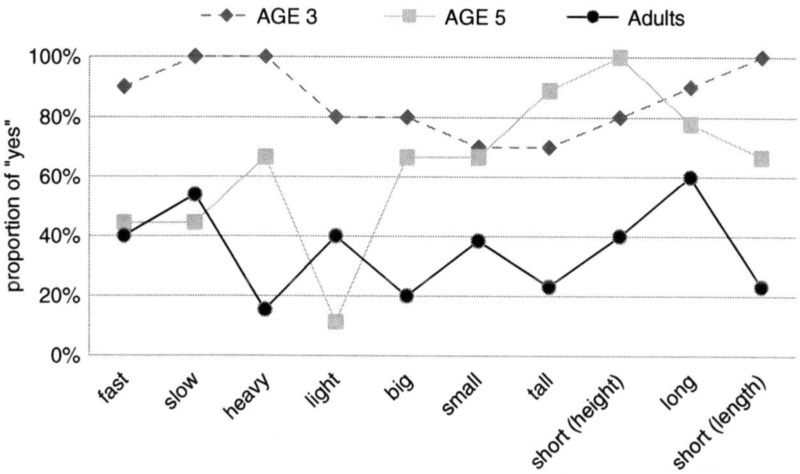


Figure 10.6 Relative-GAs: proportion of "yes" answers per Age and Adjective.

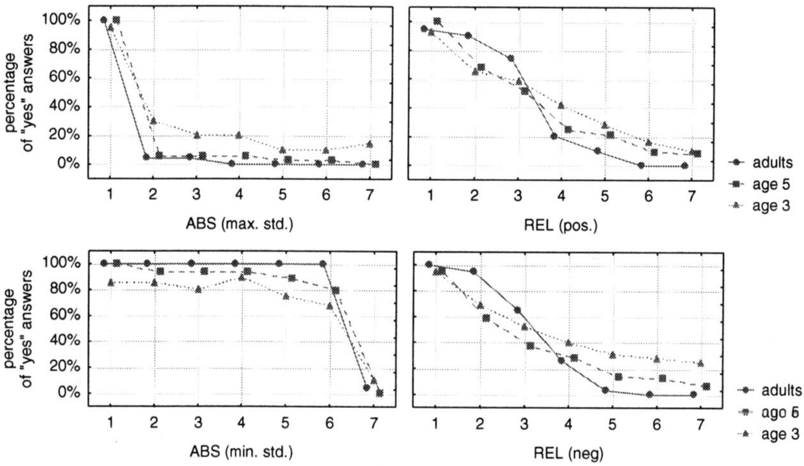


Figure 10.7 Percentage of "yes" by adults (solid line), 5-year-old children (dashed line) and 3-year-old children (dotted line) in the SJT, differentiated between max-std abs-GAs, positive rel-GAs (top panels), min-std abs-GAs and negative rel-GAs (bottom panels).

most importantly, not differentiating between antonyms. We will get back to this result in the discussion sessions of this paper.

Finally, we summarized the results of the Scalar Judgment Task in the graph in Fig. 10.7, in which the percentage of "yes" answers obtained for each of the seven items in the series are plotted for each age group separately, differentiating between antonyms. We report the percentage of "yes" answers by adults (solid line), 5-year-old children (dashed line), and 3-year-old children (dotted line) in the Scalar Judgment Task (SJT). Maximum standard absolute GAs, indicated as ABS (max. std.), and positive relative GAs, indicated as REL (pos.), are in the top panels. Minimum standard absolute GAs, indicated as ABS (min. std.), and negative relative GAs, indicated as REL (neg.), are in the bottom panels.

As is evident from the graphs, the pattern of response differs between the two conditions (relative vs. absolute) for all age groups: in general, participants were much more categorical in the absolute GAs condition (left panels)[13], independently of age. In particular, both adults and children drastically dropped their "yes" answers on item #2 in case of maximum standard absolute GAs but not in case of relative GAs, as expected and as already found by Syrett (2007): in case of relative GAs (right panels), adults' "yes" responses constantly decreased and dropped below 50% acceptance only on the 4th item and the same pattern is observable in children, even if the curve is smoother for the 5-year-old children, and even smoother for the 3-year-olds (cf. Foppolo and Panzeri in press for more details about the statistical comparisons for the Scalar Judgment Task).

## 2.2 *Interim discussion*

We believe that the results obtained in the first part of this study show that the methodology employed (i.e., the Truth Value Judgment Task, in which a description is evaluated with respect to a single object presented in isolation) constitutes a valid test for the interpretation of GAs in general. Taking the adults' results as a baseline, we can thus formulate some hypotheses to explain children's non adult-like behavior. We will focus in particular on the fact that children over-accepted the description "This is *relative GA*" in a situation in which it did not seem possible to evince any intended standard of comparison.

To make sense of this result, one might advocate a simple explanation that we intend to address first. One hypothesis would be that the younger children's preference for "yes" answers simply reflects their tendency to answer "yes" whenever they don't know what to do or are confused. As for this possibility, we believe it very unlikely that the 3-year-old children in our study did not know the meaning of adjectives like *long/short*, for which the percentage of "yes" answers was 90% and 100% respectively, and for two reasons mainly. First of all, there's ample evidence in the literature that children know how to use adjectives like *big/small*, *tall/short*, *long/short* from age 2 on (cf. the references in Syrett 2007). In the second place, we believe that the results obtained in the Scalar Judgment Task prove that the children tested in our study did in fact know the meaning of the adjectives used: almost all the 3-year-old children, in fact, gave opposite judgments to the objects that were at the extreme of the series, showing that they were not answering at random. More interestingly, while the percentage of children that judged the object presented in the Truth Value Judgment Task as *big* or *tall* was above 85%, it dropped to 60% in the Scalar Judgment Task when the same object was shown as part of a series of seven. The trend shown by the adults was the opposite: while only 20% of the adults judged the second object in the series as *big* in the Truth Value Judgment Task, around 90% of the adults did so when the same object was presented as part of a series of seven. We believe that the results of the Scalar Judgment Task not only tell us that children know the meaning of the adjectives tested, but the comparison between the two tasks also shows us something more interesting that needs to be accounted for.

There is a second hypothesis that might account for children's behavior in Experiment 1: children say "yes" whenever they can because, in general, they are more charitable or more tolerant than adults. With respect to this possibility, we believe a distinction should be made between the items described by relative GAs and the control items that should prompt an "I don't know" response. As we said above, in case of these control items, all children had the possibility to say "yes" (a man could well be married or a zebra obedient), but only half of them exploited this possibility and were "charitable." The other half, in fact, rejected the descriptions. At the same time, though, almost all the younger children accepted the descriptions with relative GAs. We believe that a more articulated hypothesis might be proposed to explain younger children's behavior with relative GAs in our first experiment. This will be addressed in the remaining part of this chapter.

## 2.3 *The nominal interpretation of relative GAs*

We propose to revitalize a hypothesis that was put forth by H. H. Clark (1970) in order to explain children's substitution errors in the interpretation of relative GAs in experimental settings. Clark first noted that the input to which children are exposed is in fact ambiguous, inasmuch as relative GAs may exhibit two distinct interpretations, as witnessed by (2) and (3):

(2) Silvio is 167 cm tall.

(3) Silvio is tall.

The adjective *tall* receives a neutral interpretation in (2): its function is simply to signal that the relevant dimension is height. Conversely, *tall* exhibits its comparative meaning in (3), implying that Silvio is judged tall*er* than a relevant standard of comparison. Clark then claims that children start by interpreting relative GAs in their neutral sense, as if they were "nominal," i.e., referring to individuals that share a property: according to this initial hypothesis, *tall* would simply identify the set of objects that have a vertical dimension. Only at a later stage, children would access the adult-like, comparative meaning. Notice that this hypothesis can immediately account for children's substitution of negative antonyms with their positive counterpart: if relative GAs were interpreted nominally, then both *tall* and *short* would target the same set of individuals (those that have a vertical dimension). This, in turn, would explain why negative antonyms are acquired later during acquisition and/or why they are first interpreted as their positive counterparts.

We borrow Clark's idea that children start by interpreting relative GAs nominally to make sense of 3-year-old children's over-acceptance of the description "This is *relative GA*" in our first experiment: if children interpreted "S is *tall*" or "S is *short*" as meaning "S has a vertical dimension," then they would accept this description to refer to objects that have a vertical dimension, such as the wooden rods targeted in Fig.10.1. The presence of a contextual standard of comparison, in fact, would only be required in the comparative reading. Building on this assumption, we further hypothesize that children switch to the comparative reading when they realize that the nominal interpretation is in fact underinformative in most situations, and thus they eventually arrive at computing the reading that requires the fixing of a contextual standard against which the adjective is evaluated.

We believe that 3-year-olds are in fact in the process of switching from the nominal interpretation to the comparative one, and are in a phase in which they are trying to set the standard of comparison. As is well-known from the literature, and as emerged from the Scalar Judgment Task, 3-year-olds exhibit extreme labeling, i.e. they apply the relative GA only to the extremes of a series while adults fix the crossover point around the mid of a series. Still, when the experimental task simply requires to identify one relative GA object among similar objects (e.g., a selection task in which subjects have to choose "the *big* S" among Ss), or to judge one particular item as being (or not being) relative GA (e.g., a Truth Value Judgment Task in which subjects have to say if a certain object is *big* or not), children successfully perform the task. In a task like ours, though, in which children were asked to accept or reject a description containing a relative GA in the absence of a relevant standard of comparison, either perceptual or normative, we believe that children resorted to a minimal, nominal like, interpretation. This would explain why, for instance, young children accepted the description "This is tall" or "This is short" referred to an object that had a vertical dimension, no matter how tall or short that object was.

Building on these assumptions, this is our proposal: in the process of language acquisition, the comparative interpretation of relative GAs evolves from the nominal interpretation for reasons of informativeness. If this were the case, then we should be able to detect the nominal interpretation of relative GAs also in adults, once we leave informativeness aside. We develop this prediction in a second experiment, that we report in the next section, in which we tried to turn adults into children.

## *2.4 Experiment 2: turning adults into children*

In a second study, we aim at prompting adults to accept a description like "This is *relative GA*" applied to an abstract object in isolation (i.e., when the standard of comparison was not retrievable from the context) by manipulating the experimental setting so as to instruct participants that informativeness was not at stake.

*2.4.1 Participants, procedure and materials of Experiment 2* A total of 73 Italian adults were tested, and randomly assigned to one of two lists. These were undergraduate students at the University of Milano-Bicocca that volunteered to participate.

The materials and procedure used were similar to the one used in the Truth Value Judgment Task in the first experiment, except for some crucial manipulations that we will describe in detail. Differently from the former study that involved children, in which the objects were physically presented to participants, items in this experiment were recorded in a sequence with a digital video camera and then were shown on a video. As before, two experimenters were involved: one introduced the study and provided instructions, and the other manipulated a puppet. As in the other study, the puppet provided a description for each of the items presented by using an adjective (e.g., "This is tall") and the participants were asked to express their judgment on a pre-compiled answer sheet. In this case, though, adults were given only two options of response: "yes" and "no." This solution was dictated by the fact that children in the first study did not use the option "I don't know."

First, we manipulated the procedure so that a training session was added, in which adults were asked to be as tolerant as they could with respect to the description provided by the puppet. To make sure that the participants understood what we meant by "being tolerant," we provided them with the following scenario. The puppet was introduced as being an alien on Earth. He was sent from his planet to test some hypotheses about the functioning of the languages spoken on Earth that his population had developed on the basis of fragments of conversations that they have been receiving from our planet. The participants were told that their aim was that of helping this alien in refining his hypotheses about Italian. In particular, they were instructed to be cautious in rejecting descriptions that, though not being optimal, could nevertheless apply to the situations presented. To this end, the participants were provided with some examples, to help them understand what they needed to do to solve this delicate task. In the first example, the puppet was asked to describe a situation in which a toy boy has four coins in his wallet. The puppet made a first guess by saying "The boy has seven coins." The experimenter warned the puppet that this description was not correct, and instructed the participants to straightforwardly reject incorrect descriptions of this sort. Then the puppet made a second guess by saying "The boy has three coins." At this point, the experimenter acknowledged the fact that the alien's description was not optimal, but at the same time she warned the participants that they might confuse the alien and prevent him from converging on the target language if they told him that "The boy has three coins" cannot be used to describe a situation in which the boy has four coins. To this aim, the experimenter suggested that the participants imagine a situation in which the toy boy wanted to buy an ice cream, and that the ice cream costs three coins. If the alien was told that it is not correct to say that the boy has three coins when he has four, then he would conclude that the boy could not buy an ice cream, which in fact is not true. By using a similar strategy, the experimenter instructed the participants to be cautious in rejecting the description "The boy pulled *some* of the flowers" in a situation in which the boy pulled *all* the flowers. By suggesting the scenario in which the boy was told "If you pull some of the flowers, you'll be punished," the experimenter aimed to convince the participants that the alien could be brought to an erroneous conclusion in this case too, if they were too strict in their evaluation. As before, if he were told that the description with *some* cannot be used in a situation in which *all* is at stake he will, erroneously, conclude that the boy wouldn't merit a punishment in case he pulled all the flowers.

As before, different classes of adjective were tested within subjects while antonyms of the same pair were presented between lists. Each list comprised a total of 29 items. Of these, 15 were controls: 6 were clearly true, 2 were clearly false and the remaining 7 were cases in which the adjective used was not applicable to the object, that should prompt a "no" response by the participants. For example, we tested adults with the description "This is vegetarian" referred to a toy plane and expected them to reject it on the basis that the property predicated by the adjective (i.e., "being vegetarian") cannot apply, under any circumstance, to a plane.

Of the critical items, 4 were pairs of absolute GA antonyms (*clean/dirty*, *straight/bent*, *open/closed*, and *full/empty*) and 4 were pairs of relative GAs (*fast/slow*, *big/small*, *tall/short*, *long/short*). These were tested using the same objects used in the former study, but with one crucial difference: in this study we did not pick objects from the different ends of the series to test antonyms. In particular, we always used the 6th element in the series, the one that was closer to the negative pole of the scale: for example, we used the 6th rod in Fig. 10.1 to test both *tall* and *short*.[14] This manipulation was dictated by the aim of this study: we wanted to prompt a "yes" answer from adults whenever the adjective could apply to a certain object. At the same time, though, we believed that it was too "easy" to prompt a yes answer to positive antonyms by using the element in the series that was the closest to the positive pole. In order to give more strength to our claim, we thus tried to make the task harder for the participants, who had to judge *tall* with respect to a pretty short item.

*2.4.2 Predictions* We predicted, in the first place, an increase of "yes" answers in case of relative GAs and maximum standard absolute GAs in this study compared to our previous study. For example, we expected more adults to accept the description "This is tall" referred to the short rod (item #6 in Fig. 10.1) on the hypothesis that the property predicated by the adjective (i.e., tallness) applies to any object that has some vertical dimension. Similarly, we expected more adults to accept the description "This is straight" referred to a minimally bent rope (item #2 in Fig. 10.2) on the hypothesis that the property predicated by the adjective (i.e., straightness) applies to any object that has some degree of straightness, even if this doesn't reach the maximum standard on the scale of straightness. At the same time, though, we expected adults to be tolerant with critical cases only and to reject the descriptions in case it was obviously false or when the adjective was not applicable to the object.

*2.4.3 Results of experiment 2* Our results confirmed our predictions. These are summarized in Fig. 10.8:

First of all, adults' performance with controls was at ceiling. In particular, they did not hesitate in rejecting a description when the adjective used was not applicable to the object (indicated as Contr-NA in Fig. 10.8) or when the

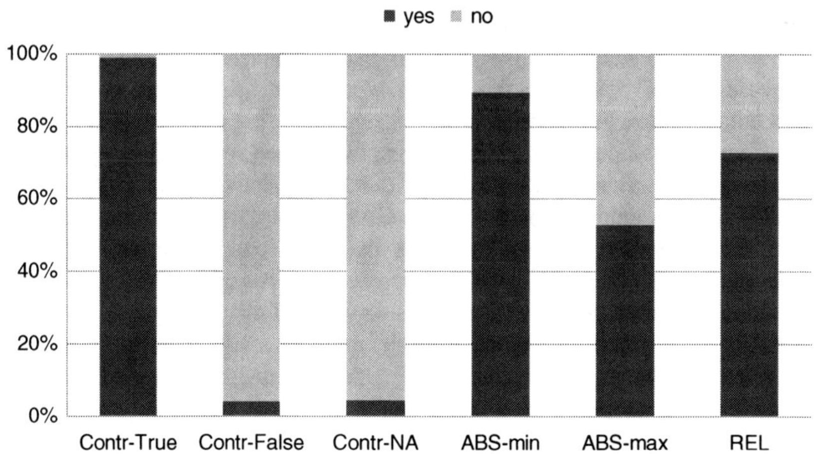


Figure 10.8 Distribution of adults' responses in Experiment 2.

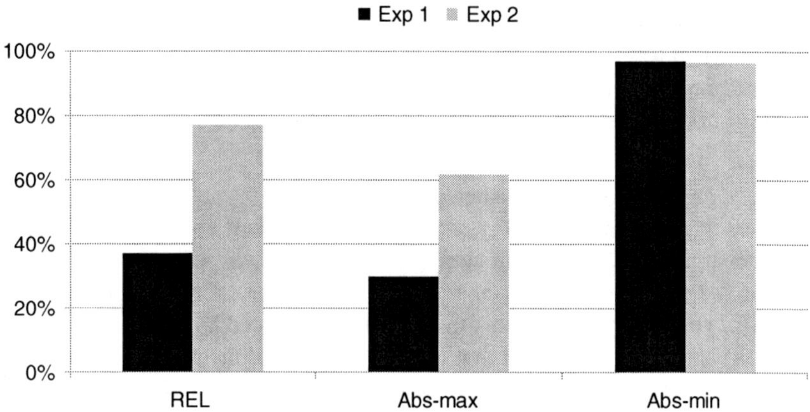


Figure 10.9 Distribution of adults' responses in Experiment 1 and 2.

description was false (indicated as Contr-False in Fig. 10.8). As we said, these controls were crucial for our experiment. As far as GAs are concerned, these gained a high percentage of "yes" answers from adults in all the categories considered: not only did the participants accept the description "This is *minimum standard absolute GA*" when the target object possessed the GA property to a degree that exceeded the minimum standard; half of the time, they also accepted the description "This is *maximum standard absolute GA*" referred to the same object. In case of relative GAs, adults accepted the description more than 70% of the time despite the fact that, as in the first experiment, no contextual or perceptual standard of comparison was provided.

Plotting the proportion of adults' "yes" responses in the two studies[15], the picture that emerged is shown in Fig. 10.9.

For what concerns relative and maximum standard absolute GAs, the increase of "yes" answers in this second experiment is significant, even taking into consideration the fact that in the second study the probability to answer "yes" was .50, while it was .33 in the first experiment, where three options of response were given ($\chi^2(2)=85.35$, $p<.0001$ for relative GAs; $\chi^2(2)=14.19$, $p<.001$ for maximum standard absolute GAs). In fact, for both types of adjective, the proportion of "yes" answers in the second study was different from chance ($\chi^2(1)=46.21$, $p<.0001$ for relative GAs; $\chi^2(1)=7.27$, $p<.01$ for maximum standard absolute GAs). This result is all the more surprising if we consider the fact that, differently from the previous study, here the "positive" relative adjective was referred to an object that had the property predicated by the adjective at a minimal degree (e.g., *tall* in this study was predicated of item #6 from the left in Fig. 10.1, while it was predicated of item #2 in the previous study) and the maximum standard absolute GAs *full* was referred to an object

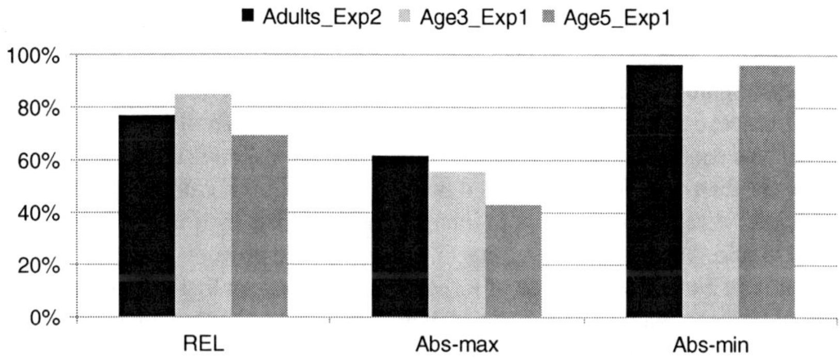


Figure 10.10 Proportion of "yes" answers by children and adults across studies, differentiated by Adjective type: relative (left), max-std abs-GAs (centre), min-std abs-GAs (right).

that had the property predicated by the adjective at a minimal degree (e.g., it was predicated of the almost empty bottle or paint tube in this study, while it was predicated of the almost full object in the previous study). Plotting adults' performance in the second study with children's performance in the first one, the picture that we get[16] is shown in Fig. 10.10.

As is evident from the graph, adults' performance in the case of relative and maximum standard absolute GAs did not differ from the younger children. Statistical comparisons by means of Fisher exact test confirmed that: (i) in the case of relative GAs, adults did not differ from 3-year-old and 5-year-old children ($\chi^2(1)=2.27$, $p=.13$; $\chi^2(1)=1.80$, $p=.18$ respectively); (ii) in the case of maximum standard absolute GAs, adults did not differ from the 3-year-olds ($\chi^2(1)=0.83$, $p=.36$) but, interestingly, they differed from the 5-year-olds ($\chi^2(1)=7.38$, $p<.01$).

*2.4.4 Discussion of Experiment 2* In this experiment, we aimed at turning adults into (young) children by banning informativeness considerations from the judgments of relative GA descriptions. We did so by training adults to be tolerant with respect to underinformative statements. For example, we asked them not to straightforwardly reject a description like "The boy pulled *some* of the flowers" in a situation in which the boy pulled *all* the flowers in consideration of the fact that, though not fully felicitous, that description was not logically wrong. This manipulation seemed to work, in the end: adults' acceptance rate of relative GA descriptions rose above 70% in Experiment 2. We interpreted this result as compatible with our hypothesis that relative GAs can be assigned a minimal, nominal-like interpretation when a comparison class or standard is not available in the context.

Within a degree-based semantic framework, one could explain adults' behavior in this second study by assuming that adults are in fact quantifying over possible contexts, and eventually, over possible standards of comparison. Under this assumption, adults would interpret "This is *relative GA*" not as meaning "This object can fall under the extension of GA" (as we maintain), but as "There could be a context *c* that sets a standard of comparison $d_c$ such that this object is more *GA* than $d_c$." We believe that, if this were the case, this would imply that, in principle, it would be possible to interpret relative GAs as if they were equivalent to minimum standard absolute GAs, i.e., as if an object is *relative GA* if it has at least a minimum degree of *relative GA*. We believe that this assumption would be less parsimonious because it would require two distinct interpretations for GAs: one in terms of degrees as abstract entities ordered along a scale (and, as Kennedy 2007 extensively argued, in this interpretation the scale of degrees evoked by relative GAs does not have a lower boundary that could constitute the minimum standard); the other interpretation would allow for the identification of a minimum standard for being *relative GA*, either by identifying an abstract degree that could serve as a lower boundary of the scale, or by assuming that relative GAs also evoke scales of individuals that are ordered along the relative GA dimension.

## 3. Conclusions

Our first study showed that 3-year-olds had a very high acceptance rate for relative GAs when the context did not supply a standard of comparison, and had a higher acceptance rate of maximum standard absolute GAs compared to adults' and 5-year-olds'. To explain this result, we hypothesized that, when they first encounter adjectives, children start by interpreting them as if they were common nouns, i.e., as denoting sets of individuals that share a property. Under this hypothesis, they would start by interpreting "S is long" as "S has a horizontal dimension" and "S is tall" as "S has a vertical dimension." This assumption is in line with the conceptual biases that have been suggested to explain infants' first acquisition of words (see Markman 1990) and with a series of studies that have further shown that even 4-year-olds tend to interpret a novel word that is distributionally and morphologically presented as an adjective as if it were a common noun, i.e., as referring to stable properties of objects (see Hall *et al.* 1993; Klibanoff and Waxman 2000; Mintz and Gleitman 2002; Waxman and Guasti 2009). Moreover, we think that this hypothesis would also account for children's systematic errors reported in the literature, substitution errors in particular, and for the fact that younger children did not seem to treat relative antonyms differently in our Experiment 1 (i.e., they accepted "This is long" as much as "This is short").

We further maintained that 3-year-old children are still in the process of switching from the nominal to the comparative interpretation. This would explain why they perform well in selection tasks in which they are asked to choose (or label) the unique (more) relative GA of a group on the one hand, and why they exhibit extreme labeling on the other, i.e., they attribute the relative GA property only to the extreme of a series. We proposed that this behavior ensues from the fact that children haven't reached the adult-like stage in the ability to retrieve the standard of comparison yet and thus stick to the nominal-like meaning first, when such a standard is not directly available. Building on the assumption that this ability undergoes development, we believe that a parallelism with the phenomenon of scalar implicature is worth exploring at this point. As has been attested in different studies (cf. Foppolo *et al.* 2012 for a recent overview), children tend to accept underinformative sentences like "Some Ss are P" in a situation in which "All Ss are P" would be more appropriate. Nonetheless, children have been shown to know that the description with "all" would be pragmatically more appropriate, and indeed choose that in a Felicity Judgment Task (a.o., cf. Experiment 5 in Foppolo *et al.* 2012). Also, they have shown sensitivity to pragmatic infelicity despite the fact that they were found to be more tolerant than adults in case of underinformative statements (Katsos and Bishop 2011). Analogously, we can view 3-year-old children's behavior with relative GAs as a hint that they are assigning them a minimal, nominal-like interpretation in the absence of a perceptual or a normative standard to exploit.

In Experiment 2 we tested whether this minimal, nominal-like interpretation was also detectable in adults. To this end, we tried to turn adults into children by manipulating the experimental setting so as to instruct them to be tolerant and accept underinformative descriptions, as long as they were true. In fact, the experimental manipulation was effective in prompting children-like responses in adults: adults accepted descriptions of the form "This is *relative GA*" in situations in which informativeness was left aside. We argue that, in such a situation, adults behaved as children resorting to the nominal interpretation of relative GAs.

At this point, we would like to speculate about how the semantic analysis of GAs could account for these facts. The main difference between the degree-based approach and the partial function perspective lies in the fact that the former assumes the existence of degrees as primitive entities, and associates scales of these abstract entities to GAs. According to this view, the GA *tall* evokes a scale of degrees of height. In order to understand a sentence containing a relative GA in its bare form, one needs first to evoke the scale of degrees associated to the relative GA dimension, then to identify the intended standard of comparison (by making reference to the normative class or perceptual cues for instance) and, finally, to compare the degree to which an individual possesses the relative GA to that standard. As we have seen, younger children accept "This is *relative GA*" even in the absence of a contextual standard of comparison.

The degree-based approach should assume that, in the absence of contextual cues, younger children posit a minimum standard of comparison for relative GAs ("S is tall" would mean "S has at least a minimum degree of height"), and thus accept the description. Even if this hypothesis could explain the results of the Truth Value Judgment Task, it would clash with the reports in the acquisition literature, and from the Scalar Judgment Task in Experiment 1: when presented with a series of objects, younger children tend to label only the extremes of a series, and this suggests that they posit the standard of comparison to the upper (and not lower) boundary of the series. Recall that in our first study, the 3-year-olds considered the same object to be *big* or *tall* in the Truth Value Judgment Task with a percentage of 85%; that dropped to 60% in the Scalar Judgment Task when the same object was shown as part of a series of seven.[17]

In the partial function analysis, on the other hand, the core meaning attributed to relative GAs is the same as that of common nouns: a function from individuals to truth-values, that is, a way to identify sets of individuals that share a property. The source of context-dependency of relative GAs lies in the identification of the intended domain of application of the function, and their vagueness is located in the partiality of the function, i.e., in the fact that for some individuals one could be unsure whether they belong to the extension of the relative GA predicate. The hypothesis that children start by interpreting GAs nominally can easily meet a partial function approach: they would first guess that GAs behave as common nouns, denoting total functions that identify sets of individuals, those that can in principle fall under the extension of the GA. The comparative interpretation, on the other hand, requires them to understand that different choices of the domain of application can lead to different outputs of the function, and this, in turn, would make the comparative interpretation more informative than the nominal one.

We believe that the 3-year-old children tested in Experiment 1 were in a phase in which they were switching to the comparative interpretation: when the intended normative class was not provided, as in our Truth Value Judgment Task in which the standard of comparison was not retrievable from the context, children would resort to the minimal, nominal-like interpretation (and behaved differently from the adults); when the normative class was explicitly presented to them, e.g. when a series of seven objects was given, as in the Scalar Judgment Task, they could switch to the comparative interpretation instead. Even in this case, though, they still had problems in partitioning the restricted domains, thus exhibiting extreme labeling, as attested also in the literature on the acquisition of adjectives summarized in the introduction. Observing the developmental trend in children in Experiment 1, we suggested a parallelism with the phenomenon of scalar implicature computation in children. In case of scalar implicatures, younger children are shown to be aware of the different informativeness status of scalar alternatives like "Some Ss are P" and "All Ss are P." Nonetheless, they have difficulties in retrieving the strong alternative with *all* (or rejecting the weak one with *some*) when the underinformative statements are given in isolation, as happens in a classical Sentence Evaluation Task (see Foppolo *et al.* 2012 for a recent overview). Conversely, when the scalar alternatives are provided, as in the Felicity Judgment Task, children have no difficulty in selecting the more appropriate description. Also, a recent study shows that children switch to the strengthened meaning of underinformative statements when they are made aware of the ambiguity associated with *some* (cf. Foppolo *et al.* 2012, Experiment 6). This seems analogous to what happens in case of relative GAs: children access the comparative reading of relative GAs when the comparison class is explicit (as in the studies in which a perceptual or a normative class is presented, or in the Scalar Judgment Task), while they accept the weaker, nominal reading of the relative GAs whenever the class of comparison, whether contextual, perceptual, or normative, is not explicitly provided.

## Acknowledgments

We are very honored and pleased to contribute to this volume that celebrates Gennaro Chierchia. We would like to offer Gennaro our paper as a warm hug for his birthday, in return for the many he has given us over the years. We also thank two anonymous reviewers for their valuable feedback and Ivano Caponigro and Carlo Cecchetto for their editorial help. For academic purposes, Francesca Panzeri is responsible for Sections 1.1, 1.3, 2.3, and 3; Francesca Foppolo for Sections 2.1, 2.2, and 2.4; and Maria Teresa Guasti for Section 1.2.

NOTES

1. In this chapter we will not take into consideration so-called intensional adjectives, such as *former* or *alleged*.
2. Partee (1995) coined the term *subsective*, since the denotation of *tall man* is equated with a subset of the denotation of the common noun *man*, i.e., the set of those men that count as tall.
3. The absolute/relative distinction within the class of GAs has also been labeled as total/partial, cf. Cruse (1980); Rotstein and Winter (2004); Yoon (1996).
4. Absolute GAs can exhibit some contextual variability too: the very same knife can be judged as *clean* for kitchen use, and as *not clean* for surgical use (Cruse 1980). However, given that the standard of what counts as clean cannot be shifted indefinitely, some authors maintained that the standard for *clean* is indeed absolute (and equated with the absence of any impurity), but pragmatic considerations can lead us to

be tolerant and accept a contextual loosening of the standard. For instance, Kennedy and McNally (2005) appeal to the notion of pragmatic halo (Lasersohn 1999).

5. The domain of individuals that fall under the extension of a GA is partially ordered along some dimension that makes reference to some notion of grading: e.g., height for the relative GA *tall*, cost for *expensive*, and so forth.
6. Syrett (2007) conducted a series of studies with the same goal, but she tested only two positive relative GAs (*big* and *long*), and, in two different experiments, two maximum standard absolute GAs (*full* and *straight*), and two minimum standard absolute GAs (*spotted* and *bumpy*). See also Syrett *et al.* (2010).
7. With respect to this manipulation, we are fully aware that the type of "I don't know" answer that was prompted in the training session might be of a different kind than the "I don't know" answer that was expected in the critical trials. The training, in fact, shows examples of epistemic uncertainty in which the answer is "I don't know" because we don't have access to what the relevant facts are (e.g., we don't see the boy's hair). Nonetheless, we didn't want to cue participants towards the scopes of our study by showing them a relative GA description during the training session. Also, we acknowledge the fact that the training worked well with the adults and the older children.
8. In Italian, there are two different adjectives corresponding to English "short": *basso*, antonym of *tall*, and *corto*, antonym of *long*.
9. This was not possible for the absolute GAs *full/empty* and *open/closed*, which were tested within lists with respect to two different "real life" objects (a plastic bottle and a paint tube for the first pair and a purse with zipper and a box with lid for the second pair).
10. This manipulation was meant to control for the order of presentation, a factor that might affect participants' responses on *full*, as observed by Syrett (2007).
11. Within the class of relative GAs, we excluded from this and further analyses the pair *wide/narrow* given that the object used to test these adjectives turned out to be inappropriate, as emerged from adults' behavior in the Scalar Judgment Task.
12. From this analysis we excluded the pair *full/empty* within the class of maximum standard absolute GAs, given that almost all the participants (not only children, as already found by Syrett 2007, but even adults) accepted "This is full" referred to a bottle (or paint tube) that was not completely full. This led us to hypothesize that the pair *full/empty* had a special status (see Foppolo and Panzeri in press for further details on this issue).
13. For example, participants correctly answered "no" to the question "Is this straight?" to all items with at least some (increasing) degree of inclination (items #2–7) and "yes" only to the completely straight item (item #1) – cf. Fig. 10.7, top-left panel; conversely, they correctly answered "yes" to the question "Is this bent?" to all items #1–6 (ranging from having degree 1 to degree 6 of inclination) and answered "no" only to the 7th item with 0 degree of inclination – cf. Fig. 10.7, bottom-left panel.
14. We applied the same manipulation to the pairs *open/closed* and *full/empty* that were tested using different items in Experiment 1. In this case, a box whose lid was minimally open was used to test for *open/closed* and an almost empty bottle or paint-tube was used to test for *full/empty*. This manipulation was made to render it more difficult to gain a "yes" response for maximum standard absolute GAs like "This is full" or "This is empty" referred to an almost empty container.

15. Please note that only those adjectives that were used in both studies are considered in this comparison.
16. As before, only the adjectives that were tested in both studies are plotted here, including *full/empty*.
17. Another objection that could be raised against the degree-based analysis underlying children's early usage of relative GAs is that it requires the mastering of scales of comparison. The evidence about children's comprehension of comparatives is controversial: some studies (Layton and Stick 1979) found a good understanding of comparative sentences (68% for 2½-year-olds and 84% for 3½-year-olds), but Bishop and Bourne (1985) argue that these results are artifactual, and that, as the results of the question about the understanding of a comparative construction in the Test for Reception of Grammar (TROG, Bishop 1993) also demonstrate, children encounter problems in the comprehension of comparative structures at least up to age 6.

# 11 Intervention in grammar and processing

*Adriana Belletti and Luigi Rizzi*

## 1. Introduction. The issue

It is a notorious fact that A′-dependencies with object gaps are mastered later in development than subject dependencies. In previous work in collaboration with Naama Friedmann (Friedmann *et al.* 2009) we have traced back this property to a particular implementation of the syntactic locality principle known as Relativized Minimality (Rizzi 1990, 2004): Object A′-dependencies inevitably cross the subject position, giving rise to an intervention configuration which is hard to compute for the child's system. This approach is supported by a rich array of experimental evidence showing that the difficulty that children experience with object A′-dependencies is modulated by the featural specification of the moved object and the intervening subject. The quoted chapter briefly hints at the possibility that the same explanatory scheme could be extended to account for the fact, familiar from the adult psycholinguistic experimentation, that object A′-dependencies are harder to process than subject dependencies also for adults. In the present chapter we would like to develop this insight further by reinterpreting some substantive results of psycholinguistic research (Gordon *et al.* 2001, 2004; Warren and Gibson 2002, 2005) in terms of our syntactic Relativized Minimality approach. This will lead us to propose a featural typology of nominal expressions inspired in part by Chierchia's influential work on nominals at the syntax–semantics interface (Chierchia 1998). We intend to show that a combination of the Relativized Minimality approach and a properly defined featural typology of nominal expressions provides a fine-grained system capable of predicting subtle gradations in intervention effects, such as those uncovered in the experimental work both with children and adults. The system thus provides a basis for a unified account of formal syntactic generalizations (e.g., the selectivity of weak islands), developmental facts, and results of real-time psycholinguistic experimentation in the adult.

## 2. Background

### *2.1 Selective intervention effects in syntax*

Intervention effects have been widely explored in formal syntax. A paradigmatic case is the unextractability from wh-islands and other weak islands in examples like (1) in English:

(1) *How do you wonder who behaved ___?

Intuitively, the wh-element *how* cannot be extracted across the other wh-element *who* introducing the embedded question. This constraint is explicitly expressed in terms of intervention by such principles as Relativized Minimality and its variants within the Minimalist framework (Minimal Link condition, Minimal Search etc., Chomsky 1995, 2000a). The principle has shown a wide empirical coverage and explanatory capacity in various domains, ranging from varieties of phrasal movement, to head movement (Roberts 2001), to semantically relevant intervention effects at the interface with syntax (as in Chierchia's to appear a approach to locality effects in scalar implicatures and the licensing of Negative Polarity Items).

Locality effects involving intervention are, however, modulated by a number of factors. Consider, as a classical illustration of the empirical intricacies of the effects, the following contrast in French:

(2) a. ? Combien de problèmes ne sais-tu pas comment résoudre ___?
how many of problems don't you know how to solve
b. *Combien ne sais-tu pas comment résoudre ___ de problèmes ?
how many don't you know how to solve of problems

(2b) illustrates an intervention violation. In terms of syntactic locality/Relativized Minimality the A′-dependency connecting *combien* to its trace is interrupted by the intervention of another wh-phrase, *comment*, in the embedded C-system. As the marginal acceptability of (2a) shows, this effect is selective. *Combien* has the capacity of both pied-piping the whole noun phrase it is part of, or else of being moved alone. It is only in the first case that extraction out of a weak island such as an indirect question is (marginally) acceptable, as in (2a). Among the various approaches to the asymmetries which have been proposed ever since Huang (1982), Rizzi (1990), and Cinque (1990), we would like to focus here on the featural approach to Relativized Minimality (Starke 2001; Rizzi 2004). According to this approach, intervention can be modulated by the featural constitution of the target and the intervener of the relevant dependency: if the target is more richly specified in morphosyntactic features than the potential intervener, the dependency can be established, otherwise it cannot. In more formal and general terms:

(3) *Relativized Minimality*
In the configuration [X Z Y], X and Y cannot be locally connected when Z intervenes between X and Y, and Z fully matches the relevant featural specification of X.

The "relevant featural specification" of X is the set of morphosyntactic features of X which trigger movement. So, if Z has a featural specification that does not (fully) match the specification of X (i.e., the featural specifications of X and Z are disjoint, or the featural specification of X is richer than the specification of Z, and properly includes it), then the local relation can be established.

In Friedmann *et al.* (2009), we have proposed that the relevant features in cases such as (2) are +Q and +NP, the former characterizing question operators, and the latter expressing the relevance of the presence of a lexical restriction in the target. In the chapter quoted, we also pointed out the existence of various types of evidence illustrating the fact that the presence/absence of a lexical restriction determines the landing site of wh-movement (see e.g., Munaro's 1999 description of certain North Eastern Italian dialects in which bare and restricted wh-elements target sharply different positions, and Rizzi 2011 for the discussion of various relevant cases); hence, the feature +NP, denoting selection of a lexical restriction by the wh-operator, can be counted among the attracting features determining movement. Under this set of assumptions, the sentences in (2) have the two types of representations indicated in (4):

(4) a. ? *Combien de problèmes* ne sais-tu pas *comment* résoudre ___ ?
[+Q, +NP] [+Q]
b. **Combien* ne sais-tu pas *comment* résoudre ___ de problèmes ?
[+Q] [+Q]

In (4b) the target and the intervener have the same relevant featural specification [+Q]; the intervener Z fully matches the specification of the target X, hence Relativized Minimality is violated. In (4a) instead, the target X is more richly specified than Z, as it contains also the relevant feature +NP, and it thus properly includes the featural specification of the intervener; therefore, the specification of Z does not fully match the specification of X, and the dependency can be established without violating featural Relativized Minimality.

## 2.2 *Selective intervention effects in acquisition*

It is a familiar observation from acquisition studies over a long period of time (e.g., Adams 1990; Adani *et al.* 2010; Arosio *et al.* 2009; Brown 1971; de Villiers *et al.* 1994; Friedmann and Novogrodsky 2004; Håkansson and Hansson 2000; McKee *et al.* 1998; Sheldon 1974; Tavakolian 1981) that there is an important temporal gap between the full mastery of certain types of A′-dependencies such as the relative clauses illustrated in (5):

(5) a. Show me *the boy that* __ *pushes the monkey* (Subject relative)
b. Show me *the boy that the monkey pushes* ___ (Object relative)

Whereas children can properly interpret and produce subject relatives already around the age of 3, they still have difficulties with object relatives at the age of 5 and later. This developmental fact has been shown to be quite robust and to hold cross-linguistically, as discussed in the quoted references (see a.o. Belletti and Contemori 2010, Contemori and Belletti 2011, Hamann and Tuller 2010 and the final report of Working Group 3 of COST Action 33, www.zas.gwz-berlin.de/cost/ for recent converging data on production).

In Friedmann *et al.* (2009) we have proposed that the observed asymmetry may be traced back to syntactic locality expressed through the Relativized Minimality system. The difficulty involves object relatives and not subject relatives because only in the former case does an element with certain crucial characteristics intervene in the dependency. We assumed the relevant property to be the presence of the lexical restriction, i.e., the feature +NP, in both the relative head and the intervening subject in cases like (5b). Based on experimental evidence from Hebrew-speaking children (age 3;7–5), we have shown that the difficulty with object relatives is in fact selective, as predicted by the Relativized Minimality approach. In particular, whereas lexically headed object relative clauses in which a lexically restricted subject is crossed as in (5b) are consistently problematic, if we eliminate the lexical restriction either on the lexical head of the relative clause (using a free relative, as in (6b)) or on the intervening subject (using a pronominal subject, as in (6c), where the subject position of the relative clause is *pro*) performance substantially improves. The following examples from the quoted chapter show the selectivity:

(6) a. tare li et *ha-pil* *she-ha-arie* martiv ___ (55% correct)
[+R+NP] [+NP]
show to-me ACC the-elephant that-the-lion wets
'Show me the elephant that the lion is wetting.'
b. tare li et *mi* *she-ha-yeled* menadned ___ (79% correct)
[+R] [+NP]
show to-me ACC who that-the-boy swings
'Show me the one that the boy is swinging.'
c. tare li et *ha-sus* she-mesarkim oto (83% correct)[1]
[+R +NP] pro
show to-me ACC the-horse that-brush.PL him
'Show me the horse that someone is brushing.'

In (6), +R designates the feature attracting the relative head to the initial periphery of the relative clause (in parallel with the Q feature for questions illustrated (4)). In our interpretation, it is the feature +NP, common to the relative head and the intervening subject which causes the problem in (6a); as soon as this common feature is removed, as in (6b–c), the child's system manages to properly interpret the structure.[2]

Adult speakers process sentences like (6a) unproblematically. Thus, there is a developmental effect. In the reference quoted, we proposed that children experience problems in dealing with configurations in which the featural specification of the target *properly includes* the specification of the intervener. So the configuration in (6a) is problematic as the feature specification of the intervening subject ([+NP]) is properly included in the specification of the relative head ([+R, +NP]). (6b) and (6c), we argued, are not problematic because they involve *disjoint* featural specifications in the potential intervener and the target. So the developmental effect is identified, in this approach, in the capacity of computing featural configurations of proper inclusion in Relativized Minimality contexts.[3]

Adult grammatical systems can compute object A′-dependencies such as the one in (6a) in an apparently unproblematic way. However, there is a consolidated array of empirical results from adult psycholinguistic experimentation showing that some types of object extracted constructions are in fact harder to process than others also for adults, when sophisticated experimental methods, both online and offline, are used to probe ease of processing. We now turn to a review of this distinct class of empirical results stemming from a different tradition from theoretical and developmental linguistics.

## 3. On some relevant psycholinguistic evidence

Object relatives such as (7a) are more difficult to process than subject relatives like (7b) for adult speakers:

(7) a. The reporter [ that the senator attacked ___ ] disliked the editor.
b. The reporter [ that ___ attacked the senator ] disliked the editor.

This type of contrast has been highlighted through very different psycholinguistic techniques, from phoneme monitoring, to response accuracy to probe questions, to self-paced reading times (Frauenfelder *et al.* 1980; King and Just 1991; Waters *et al.* 1987, etc.). A central idea in classical linguistically inspired psycholinguistic approaches is that the extra-complexity observable in object dependencies is linked to a structural cause (such as De Vincenzi's 1991 Minimal Chain Principle). The analysis we intend to explore closely follows this tradition.

We concentrate here on two major recently developed approaches, which we will refer to as:

A. *The similarity-based approach* (Gordon *et al.* 2001, 2004)
A dependency is hard to compute when an element intervenes which is similar to the target of the dependency.

B. *The increased referential processing approach* (Warren and Gibson 2002, 2005)
A dependency is hard to integrate when, in the course of the computation of the dependency, elements occur which require substantial referential processing.

The point of departure of the first approach is the observation due to Bever (1974) according to which double center embedded relative clauses which are completely unparsable when all noun phrases correspond to a lexical description (e.g., *the reporter*), become much easier to understand if the noun phrases are sufficiently different, and do not all correspond to lexical descriptions. The contrast presented in the references quoted is given in (8) vs. (9):

(8) The reporter the politician the commentator met trusts said the president won't resign. (unparsable)

(9) The reporter everyone I met trusts said the president won't resign. (parsable)

Bever's original idea was that somehow a crucial role in the amelioration should be attributed to the difference among the three noun phrases, which should be submitted to different types of "rules" in the assignment of their grammatical roles. In other words, the embryo of a similarity-based type of account. The specific version that Gordon *et al.* (2001) assume is in terms of storage in working memory during processing: in object relatives, two noun phrases (the relative head and the subject) must be stored in working memory before the A′-dependency is resolved and the appropriate thematic roles are assigned, and this temporary storage is facilitated if the two noun phrases are sufficiently different along dimensions to be made precise. Gordon *et al.* (2001) contrast an approach inspired by Bever's idea with Gibson's (1998) original account of the processing of complex sentences, the source of Warren and Gibson (2002, 2005, to be discussed below), according to which the difficulty involved in dependency resolution is a function of the processing cost for the assignment of discourse referents to nominals occurring while the dependency is computed.

Let us discuss the two approaches in turn. A fundamental insight of Gordon *et al.* (2001) has been to manipulate the intervening subject in object relatives and test how this could affect processing. In a series of reading time and comprehension experiments devoted to the comparison between the processing of subject vs. object relative clauses, the authors have shown that in object relative clauses whose head is a lexically restricted noun phrase in our terminology, manipulating the nature of the subject of the relative clauses as in (10) has clear effects in reducing the reading time and improving the accuracy in the comprehension of the structure. In two distinct experiments the authors have compared the case of lexically restricted subjects with proper names and pronominal subjects, as in the following pairs:

(10) a. The barber that *the lawyer/you* admired climbed the mountain.
b. The barber that *the lawyer /Joe* admired climbed the mountain.

What emerged from these experiments was that the intervention of the lexically restricted subject determined a difficulty both in terms of reading times at the critical words (the verb of the relative clause and the main clause verb) and in terms of accuracy of comprehension, in comparison to the case of an intervening (1st or 2nd) pronominal or proper name subject. As Gordon *et al.* (2001) pointed out, the amelioration effect brought about by a pronominal or a proper name subject is expected under a similarity-based approach of the kind inspired by Bever's (1974) original insight. The authors have also tested the processing of subject relatives under comparable experimental conditions (with a lexically restricted relative clause head and the object argument either a lexically restricted noun phrase or a pronominal or a proper name) and have found no comparable effect in reading time at the critical words or in comprehension accuracy. In line with the authors' account, we can then draw the conclusion that similarity-based effects only arise in the case of object dependencies.

Gordon *et al.* (2001) have also tested object extracted clefts, comparing cases in which the extracted object was a lexically restricted noun phrase with cases in which it was a proper name, with the subject of the cleft sentence also varying in the same way. The relevant material in the object extracted cleft experiment is constituted by sentences like (11):

(11) It was the barber/John that *the lawyer/Bill* saw in the parking lot.

The reason for using clefts to test a further case of object extracted construction is that with clefts the comparison between the two relevant noun phrases, i.e., the object extracted phrase and the subject of the cleft sentence, can be directly performed in all conditions relevant for the similarity account, a possibility which is precluded in relative clauses since a proper name cannot be a (restrictive) relative head (except in special cases such as *The Paris I love*). The result of the cleft experiment is particularly revealing: the cases in which the object extracted noun phrase and the subject of the cleft sentences were both of the same type, i.e., both a proper name or both a lexically restricted noun phrase, were the hardest cases (e.g., *It was John that Bill saw in the parking lot*); when there was mismatch, lexically restricted/name or name/lexically restricted (e.g., *It was the barber that Bill saw in the parking lot*), the object extracted clefts were both read faster at the critical words and the sentences were more accurately comprehended (the difference was particularly strong in the comprehension test).

The general conclusion that Gordon *et al.* (2001) drew from their studies is that a similarity-based account which takes into consideration the nature of *both* relevant noun phrases – the head and the subject of the relative clause in the case of object relatives, the extracted object and the subject of the cleft sentence in the case of clefts – and their (dis-)similarity can explain their results better than competing theories. In particular, these authors argue that the similarity-based account fares better than a discourse integration account *à la* Gibson, in which the crucial role in affecting performance is solely played by the nature of the subject of the object relative clause, or of the subject of the cleft sentence in object extracted clefts.[4] This is so because, in a discourse integration account, the more or less complex computation of the referential properties of the subject of the relative/cleft is the only relevant factor, while the (dis-)similarity between the two noun phrases is not expected to affect the computation of an A′-dependency with an object gap.

Gordon *et al.*'s (2001) similarity approach is essentially cast in the same mould as our syntactic and developmental analysis based on Relativized Minimality, reviewed in Sections 2.1, 2.2. The crucial questions are: how is similarity determined? And, is there any added value if we can derive the (dis-) similarity effect from a formal syntactic principle, rather than solely ascribing it to the functioning of the processing system?

Before addressing these points, let us turn to the second approach, the increased referential processing approach, repeated here for convenience:

B. *The increased referential processing approach* (Warren and Gibson 2002, 2005)
A dependency is hard to integrate when, in the course of the computation of the dependency, elements occur which require substantial referential processing.

According to this approach, an object relative like (7a) is harder to process than a subject relative like (7b) because the lexically restricted noun phrase in subject position, *the senator* (a kind of expression requiring substantial processing to establish its referent in the discourse context) occurs while the A′-dependency is being resolved between the head of the relative, *the reporter*, and the gap in the object position of *attack*. In (7b), nothing involving significant referential processing occurs in the dependency between the relative head and the subject gap, which is therefore easier to process.

This theory makes more refined predictions if coupled with an independent ranking of nominal expressions along a hierarchy of referential accessibility. Consider such a theory stating that first and second person pronouns are ranked as the most accessible, since they have their referents immediately given by the speech act (speaker and hearer); proper names are intermediate, and definite descriptions are the hardest in referent accessibility (the authors quote Ariel 1990; Gundel *et al.* 1993 in this connection). The approach then predicts an increasing processing difficulty to resolve the dependency in the following cases of object relatives, as Warren and Gibson (2005) discuss in detail:

(12) a. The reporter [ that you attacked ___ ] disliked the editor.
b. The reporter [ that Bill attacked ___ ] disliked the editor.
c. The reporter [ that the senator attacked ___ ] disliked the editor.

This prediction is borne out: Warren and Gibson (2005) report a series of experiments in which sentences like (12a) are on average 30 ms faster to read at the critical word (the embedded verb *attacked*, at which the A′-dependency must be resolved) than sentences like (12b), which are in turn on average 28 ms faster to read at the critical word than sentences like (12c). The gradation of the reading times of *attacked* in these examples is, in this approach, a symptom of the increasing referential processing load required by the subject noun phrase intervening in the object dependency, hence a consequence of the increased referential processing approach, in combination with a reasonable hierarchy of referential accessibility, or givenness.

Notice that also the similarity-based approach is consistent with Warren and Gibson's observation that (12c) involves the slowest reading time at the critical word *attacked*. On the other hand, as Warren and Gibson observe, the similarity-based approach does not immediately predict that reading time at the critical word is faster with the intervening pronoun (12a) than with the intervening proper name (12b). It should be noticed in this connection that the similarity-based approach can be made consistent with this observation if it can be supplemented by a precise theory of structural similarity from which it can be derived that a proper name is more similar to a definite description than a pronoun is (on this, see below). In that case, the similarity-based approach could also predict the experimental finding reported above from Warren and Gibson (2005).

More experimental work has been brought to bear on adjudicating between the two hypotheses. Recall that Gordon *et al.* (2001) compared subject and object clefts with either proper names or definite descriptions in clefted and subject position; here we only report the relevant object clefts in better detail (definite description = DefD, i.e., a lexically restricted noun phrase in our terms, proper name = PropN):

(13) a. It was the barber that the lawyer saw ___ in the parking lot. DefD – DefD
b. It was the barber that John saw ___ in the parking lot. DefD – PropN
c. It was Bill that the lawyer saw ___ in the parking lot. PropN – DefD
d. It was Bill that John saw ___ in the parking lot. PropN – PropN

The similarity-based approach predicts that (13a) and (13d), involving the intervention of a structurally identical subject in the object dependency, should be harder to process than (13b–c), involving structurally distinct elements. The prediction is borne out, as Gordon *et al.* (2001) have shown. This effect is not predicted under the increased referential processing approach, according to which the only relevant factor should be the referential accessibility of the intervening subject. So, the increased referential processing approach correctly predicts that (13a) should be harder to process than (13b), but incorrectly expects that (13c) should be harder than (13d) because the referential processing involved by the definite description *the lawyer* in (13c) should be higher than the referential processing cost involved by the proper name *John* in (13d), while the empirical evidence shows the opposite. So, this appears to be critical evidence in favor of the similarity-based approach, which makes the right prediction on (13).

Warren and Gibson (2005) responded to this critique by introducing into the picture also the case of pronominals, both in clefted and in subject position. They thus considered the following sentence type, involving 9 possible combinations:

(14) It was (the lawyer/Bill/you) that (the businessman/Dan/we) avoided at the party.

Warren and Gibson (2005) studied the processing of such sentences through different online and offline measures, but the most relevant result for the comparison between the two hypotheses is that the pronoun – pronoun condition (15a) showed a very fast reading time at the critical verb *avoided*, while both the PropN – PropN (15b) and the DefD – DefD (15c) conditions were much slower, with reading at the critical verb involving about 50 extra ms:

(15) a. It was you that we *avoided* __ at the party. Pron – Pron: fast
b. It was Bill that Dan *avoided* __ at the party. PropN – PropN: slow
c. It was the lawyer that the businessman *avoided* __ at the party. DefD – DefD: slow

The authors have pointed out that the fast reading time at the critical verb in (15a) is unexpected under a similarity-based approach, as the pronominal nature of both the clefted element and of the intervening subject should cause about as much difficulty as the two other cases with match (PropN – PropN, DefD – DefD), contrary to fact.[5]

So, the very fast reading at the critical verb in the Pron – Pron condition (15a) is a problem for the similarity-based approach. However, it seems to us that this very same set of data related to object extraction in clefts also raises a question for the increased referential processing approach. As we reported above, Gordon *et al.* (2001) observed a similarity effect in cases like (11)/(13): object extraction across a subject matching its status of definite description or proper name gives rise to a detectable difficulty at the critical verb, clearly a similarity-based effect. Figure 3 of Warren and Gibson (2005) seems to confirm such an effect. Relevant examples are the following, in which the intervening subject is always a PropN:

(16) a. It was the lawyer that Dan avoided ___ at the party. DefD – PropN
b. It was Bill that Dan avoided ___ at the party . PropN – PropN
c. It was you that Dan avoided ___ at the party . Pron – PropN

If we compare reading times of the three cases of (16) (see Warren and Gibson 2005, Figure 3), a substantially higher reading time is found at the critical word for the match condition (16b) compared to the two mismatch conditions (16a) and (16c). This is unexpected under the increased referential processing approach, according to which the crucial factor is the referential accessibility of the intervening subject (which is held constant in (16a–c)); on the other hand, the slower reading time at the critical word in (16b) is what is predicted by the similarity-based account, as in that approach what counts is the similarity of the two noun phrases, the target and the intervener, hence a slowing effect is expected in the match condition (16b), but not in the two mismatch conditions, as observed by Gordon *et al.* (2001) in connection with (11)/(13).

In conclusion, this array of experimental evidence raises at least one empirical problem for each approach:

(17) i. *Problem for the similarity-based approach:*
Why is the reading time at the critical word so fast in the match Pron – Pron condition (15a)?
ii. *Problem for the increased referential processing approach:*
Why is the reading time at the critical word slower in the match PropN – PropN condition (16b) with respect to the two mismatch conditions (16a-c) (see also the discussion of (11)/(13))?

## 4. Back to syntactic locality: selective intervention effects in psycholinguistics

In this Section we would like to show that the approach developed in Section 2.2 to the difficulties children experience with object relatives and based on syntactic locality as presented in Section 2.1, can offer some insight on how to address the similarity issue and the results on adults from the psycholinguistic literature just reviewed, specifically the questions raised in (17).

Clearly, our approach has much in common with Gordon *et al.* (2001): both approaches attribute a crucial role to the similarity between, in our terms, the target and the intervener of the local dependency. The two approaches differ in that for Gordon *et al.* similarity solely affects the processing system by conditioning the operation of working memory, to the effect that the temporary storage required for dependency resolution is facilitated if the target and the intervener are sufficiently dissimilar, whereas our approach directly appeals to a formal grammatical principle.

A question that is central to both accounts is: how is similarity determined? Various refinements in the Relativized Minimality tradition, in particular featural Relativized Minimality, represent an attempt to make the relevant dimension of similarity precise. For us, the expression of the operative distinctions is in terms of the specifications of morphosyntactic features triggering syntactic movement, while other imaginable dimensions of similarity – i.e., purely semantic, purely phonological, etc. – are not relevant.

Gordon *et al.* (2004), a follow up of the original study of Gordon *et al.* (2001), provide strong empirical evidence for the conclusion that only morphosyntactic features define the relevant dimension of similarity causing the effect in adult reading time. Thus there is strong converging evidence with the conclusion we reached on the basis of the syntactic and developmental facts.

Specifically, Gordon *et al.* (2004) showed that, given lexically headed object relatives (e.g., *the salesman*), manipulation of the definite, indefinite, or generic nature of the subject of the relative clause (e.g., *The salesman that the accountant* vs. *an accountant* vs. *accountants contacted spoke very quickly*) does not ameliorate the reading time and accuracy in comprehension, nor is there any amelioration if the subject of the relative clause is impoverished in its lexical descriptive content (e.g., *The salesman that the accountant* vs. *the person contacted spoke very quickly*).[6] In contrast, the authors found a strong amelioration in cases in which the subject of the relative clause was a quantified expression like *everyone*. The relevant contrast is given in (18)–(19):

(18) The salesman that *the accountant* contacted spoke very quickly.

(19) The salesman that *everyone* contacted spoke very quickly.

The reading time difference at the critical word, the verb *contacted*, was quite robust (736 vs. 487 ms, respectively). Also the accuracy in answering the comprehension question reached ceiling in cases like (19), while it was lower in (18). The amelioration with *everyone* is coherent with the amelioration found in the previous study from Gordon *et al.* (2001), brought about by a (1st and 2nd person) pronominal subject in object relatives as in the relevant case of (10). In our terms the amelioration effect in (19) relates to the lack of a lexical restriction in the quantified expression *everyone.*[7]

It is natural to explore the hypothesis that the developmental effects illustrated in Section 2.2 and the processing effects with adults addressed in this Section have a common explanation. Since for us the developmental effects are a consequence of the operation of the formal syntactic principle Relativized Minimality, the natural next step is to make the proposal that the processing asymmetries between subject and object A′-dependencies in adults can be ascribed to the same theoretical construct. In fact, the generalization arrived at empirically by Gordon *et al.* (2004) is precisely what is expected under our assumption that a formal syntactic principle is involved in the processing asymmetries: the fact that only morphosyntactic features are relevant in the computation of similarity follows from the fact that the causal operative principle is syntactic in nature.[8]

We see this convergence as a welcome outcome, one that goes in the direction of looking at processing and grammar as tightly integrated systems which operate with the same computational ingredients. We take up this point again in the conclusions.

Let us now go back to the problems in (17i) and (17ii), respectively left open by the competing processing accounts considered. In order to deal with them, we have to sharpen our assumptions on the featural system involved in nominal expressions.

Starting from (17ii), a major finding of the Gordon *et al.* (2001) paper is that a similarity effect is found in (13), repeated in (20) for convenience, in which (20a) and (20d), involving the crossing of the same kind of nominal expression, show a significant slowing down in the reading time of the critical verb:

(20) a. It was the barber that the lawyer saw ___ in the parking lot. DefD – DefD
b. It was the barber that John saw ___ in the parking lot. DefD – PropN
c. It was Bill that the lawyer saw ___ in the parking lot. PropN – DefD
d. It was Bill that John saw ___ in the parking lot. PropN – PropN

How can this effect be captured by our syntactic approach? We assume that proper names always involve an N component which must be somehow specified in the lexicon as expressing singularity (Chierchia 1998), hence they form a special class of nouns, stored as such in the lexicon. Let us refer to this class as $N_{proper}$ as opposed to $N_{common}$. This featural distinction is clearly morphosyntactic in nature as it triggers different kinds of syntactic behaviors; e.g., in various Romance languages an $N_{proper}$ requires obligatory movement to D, a movement motivated by the need of acquiring argument status (Longobardi 1994, Chierchia 1998). Since $N_{proper}$ and $N_{common}$ have distinct morphosyntactic status, we expect that they will give rise to selective intervention effects, with $N_{proper}$ being a stronger intervener in an $N_{proper}$ dependency, and similarly for $N_{common}$ in an $N_{common}$ dependency. Remember that cases like (20a) and (20d) are well-formed under featural Relativized Minimality because the target has a featural specification richer than the intervener, as it also contains the feature attracting the noun phrase to the left periphery, presumably +Focus in the case of a cleft (Belletti 2008, 2009). So, for instance the noun phrase *Bill* in (20d) is specified [+Foc, +NP, $+N_{proper}$ ], a specification that properly includes the one of the intervening subject, which is just [+NP, $+N_{proper}$ ], a permissible configuration under Relativized Minimality.

All the examples of (20) are thus well-formed and accessible to the adult grammatical system. Nevertheless, the complexity of the computation of the inclusion relation is detectable through the slowing effect in reading time and the decreased accuracy in comprehension.[9] So, the difficulty with the computation of featural inclusion, insurmountable for young children, persists in adults in a subtler form, which is highlighted through the sophisticated techniques of experimental psycholinguistics.

Consider now problem (17i), illustrated by the fact that a pronoun crossing another pronoun does not give rise to a similarity-based effect, i.e., (21a) is characterized by a fast reading time at the critical verb, even though two nominal expressions in the crossing configuration are present which belong to the same syntactic category. Why is this case different from the cases in (21b) and (21c)?

(21) a. It was you that we *avoided* ___ at the party. Pron – Pron: fast
b. It was Bill that Dan *avoided* ___ at the party. PropN – PropN: slow
c. It was the lawyer that the businessman *avoided* ___ at the party. DefD – DefD: slow

Here we want to capitalize on the fact that pronominals lack a lexical restriction. We suggest that this can be expressed in featural terms by assuming that they lack the feature +NP altogether. So, the A′-dependencies in (21b) and (21c) involve a target and an intervener both specified with the feature +NP, whereas (21a) does not involve any such feature. Of course the two pronominals will share the category label, presumably D; however, in this system shared categorial features do not necessarily imply membership to the same class for intervention: only features triggering movement play a role (see also note 8). What are such features? On the one hand we have criterial features such as Q(uestion), R(elative), Foc(us), Top(ic), etc. If Rizzi and Shlonsky (2007) are on the right track, +N also is the attracting feature involved in the Subject Criterion, the principle capturing the EPP and accounting for the attraction of a nominal expression to the canonical subject position. Some ϕ-features (e.g., Case, Person, Number…) also presumably function as attractors, as in the standard minimalist analysis of A-movement, or in cliticization. Other features may have a morphological realization and may enter into the labeling of expressions; however, they may be inert for triggering movement. We assume that this is precisely the case for the categorial feature D. Again this discussion reiterates the point that what is relevant for triggering minimality effects is not a generic notion of similarity: not only purely semantic similarity, but also categorial identity may be uninfluential if the relevant features are not movement related.[10]

Under this set of assumptions, it is expected that a pronominal crossing another pronominal, as in (21a), will not give rise to an increase of complexity analogous to the cases in which a proper name or a definite description cross a nominal of the same kind, as in (21b–c).

An alternative that comes to mind to account for the ease of processing characterizing examples like (21a) would be to appeal to the difference in person between the two pronouns. This could also be the source of the observation reported above that 1st and 2nd person pronouns never give rise to interfering effects with 3rd person definite descriptions. This alternative would predict that 3rd person pronouns should give rise to interference among themselves and with definite descriptions, which are inherently 3rd person. While we do not know of adult psycholinguistic evidence bearing on this prediction, we would like to go back to acquisition and report on some elicited production data with children, showing that children from very young ages are able to produce the difficult headed object relatives when a third person (null) pronominal subject is crossed in Italian, in examples like (22) (from Belletti and Contemori to appear):

(22) Quello che ha fatto __ E.D. (4;3)
The_one that *pro* has prepared __
'The one that he prepared.'

Already the youngest group tested (3;4–3;11) was able to produce target sentences of the type in (22) in 94% of the cases. If the person feature was (solely) responsible for the facilitating effect in (21a) one would not expect a 3rd person subject pronoun to determine any facilitating effect for children in an object relative with a 3rd person relative head. The acquisition data suggest that the facilitation with pronominals holds independently of the person mismatch; hence, as we have suggested above, there is something inherent in the pronoun inducing the facilitation effect: in our terms, the lack of a lexical restriction (see also Belletti and Contemori to appear for relevant discussion).

## 5. Concluding remarks

Formal linguistic research has elaborated a detailed theory of locality based on the notion of intervention. In previous work we have proposed that linguistic locality can play an explanatory role in accounting for developmental effects such as the delay in acquisition of certain object A′-dependencies. In this chapter we have proposed that the same theoretical apparatus can successfully address the important empirical results arrived at in the experimental studies of adult processing that have been reviewed here. Psycholinguistic research has observed that there are robust asymmetries in reading times and accuracy to probe questions between subject relatives and subject extracted clefts on the one hand and object relatives and object extracted clefts on the other. Moreover, such effects are modulated by the similarity of the target with the intervening subject in the case of object A′-dependencies, as explicitly claimed by Gordon *et al.* (2001). We have explored the natural hypothesis that such asymmetries stem from the same source as intervention effects analyzed in syntactic theory and in the study of development. We have proposed a unified account of the empirically distinct manifestations of the intervention effects through featural Relativized Minimality. The unification is supported, among other considerations, by Gordon *et al.*'s (2004) results that among the imaginable dimensions of similarity (purely semantic, purely phonological, morphosyntactic, etc.) only certain morphosyntactic featural distinctions are relevant. The highly selective nature of the effect strongly suggests that the locus of interference is not "general working memory," which would lead us to expect unselective similarity effects, but rather the computational devices specifically dedicated to syntactic computations. This is precisely what is expected under the assumption that a formal syntactic principle like Relativized Minimality plays a causal role here: only featural specifications involved in the triggering of movement operations are taken into account in the computation of the locality principle in (movement-related) syntactic dependencies.

We may think of the relevant morphosyntactic features as instructions for movement, and of Relativized Minimality as a principle requiring distinctness in potentially ambiguous situations arising from intervention: when an intervener is not distinct from the target, the system blocks; when the intervener is disjoint with respect to the target, the system works smoothly; when the intervener is only partially distinct from the target (inclusion in the relevant feature specification; on intersection see note 9) the system has to cope with a more complex computation which is inaccessible in early stages of development, and which gives rise to the persistent complexity effects uncovered in the adult psycholinguistic research that we have reviewed.

We take the conclusion that syntactic locality enters in a unified manner into the explanation of development and of adult parsing as a welcome result, as it goes in the direction of a substantial unification of grammar and processing, taking them as systems operating with largely overlapping ingredients and in tightly integrated manners.

## Acknowledgments

We are indebted to Daniele Panizza for insightful comments on an earlier draft of this article. We take the opportunity to also thank our dear friend Gennaro for his long lasting friendship, scientific and otherwise. We look forward to his illuminating contributions to come.

NOTES

1. The percentages indicate correct picture selection in a picture matching task. Example (6c) involves a resumptive pronoun. Resumption, a productive relativization strategy in Hebrew, is normally optional, but it is required in the adult grammar in this particular kind of example. We showed in the paper (Experiment 2) that the resumptive strategy does not improve children's performance in examples like (6a); hence, (6c) remains relevant to prove our point.
2. It has been observed (Carlo Cecchetto, talk, CISCL/University of Siena, June 2011) that in configurations like those in (6a) the lexical restriction is embedded within the subject DP; if intervention is expressed in terms of c-command, then the presence of a lexical NP within the subject should not be relevant for the calculation of locality which should only "see" the maximal DP node. But notice that the highest head that labels the nominal expression, D in the case of (6a), must carry a feature indicating that it selects a lexical restriction, NP. This is the specification +NP that we are assuming. So, when D and NP are merged together, if the label of the newly created category is inherited from the selecting category (D), its featural specification +NP will be expressed in the label of the whole phrase, hence it will be accessible for the computation of intervention (on the labeling algorithm see Chomsky 2008, and Donati and Cecchetto 2011). DPs have a rich cartographic structure (Cinque 2002) and various complications arise when more complex DPs are taken into account. We will not try to address more complex cases here.
3. This version of the Relativized Minimality related account differs from the original formulation of the principle (Rizzi 1990) in that it permits an A position, the subject, to act as an intervener in an A′-dependency, the one involved in the relative clause. In fact, this is expected under the adopted featural approach to Relativized Minimality, which does not refer to a broad typology of positions, such as A/A′, but to a finer grained typology, based on morphosyntactic features (Rizzi 2004; Starke 2001).

   In a similar vein, variants of this approach have been appealed to, to account for amelioration effects induced by other kinds of featural mismatch between the target and the intervener: the comprehension of lexically headed relative clauses has been shown to improve with number mismatch with an intervening lexical subject in child Italian (Adani *et al.* 2010), Case mismatch in Greek (Guasti *et al.* 2008), and gender mismatch in child Hebrew, in contrast to child Italian (Belletti *et al.* 2012). The cross-linguistic difference in the latter case is related in Belletti *et al.*, to the different morphosyntactic status of gender in Italian and Hebrew.
4. See Friedmann *et al.* (2009: fn. 11) where this point is explicitly addressed.
5. Warren and Gibson (2005) do not deny that a similarity-based effect is found through offline measures, but dispute the claim that it is also operative online. Nevertheless, as discussed below, there seems to be a similarity effect detectable online.
6. A reviewer points out the relevance in this connection of the children data mentioned in Goodluck (2010) showing an amelioration of the comprehension of *which* questions in which the extracted object is the descriptively impoverished noun *animal* compared to a descriptively rich noun like *lion*, i.e. *Which animal/lion did the zebra kiss?* Gordon *et al.* (2004) observe no amelioration effect with adults in relatives when a descriptively impoverished noun is the intervener. It would be interesting to find out whether a minimal contrast holds for children depending on the position of the impoverished noun as either target or intervener. We leave this issue open for future work.

7. An immediate prediction in this case is that if the quantifier *every* was associated with a lexical restriction, i.e., *every accountant* the slowing down effect should be strong again.
8. In fact the principle is not activated by morphosyntactic features in general, but only by those morphosyntactic features which trigger movement: the rationale is that the minimality effect is relativized to the particular kind of dependency on which locality is checked, and to the features that trigger it. As the dependencies involved in the A′-constructions discussed here are movement dependencies triggered by morphosyntactic features, it is expected that only such features will be taken into account in computing intervention.
9. Notice that, whereas the more difficult structures (20a) and (20d) involve an inclusion configuration (in (20a) X = [+Foc, +NP, + $N_{common}$], Z = [+NP, + $N_{common}$]; in (20d) X = [+Foc, +NP, + $N_{proper}$], Z = [+NP, + $N_{proper}$]), the easier structures (20b) and (20c), involving different types of nominal expressions, instantiate an intersection configuration (in (20b) X = [+Foc, +NP, + $N_{common}$], Z = [+NP, + $N_{proper}$]; in (20c) X = [+Foc, +NP, + $N_{proper}$], Z = [+NP, +$N_{common}$]). Consistently with this observation, Belletti *et al.* (2012) found out that intersection configurations (involving gender mismatch in Modern Hebrew) improve children's comprehension of object relatives, compared to inclusion configurations. As far as we know, comprehension with match/mismatch configurations with proper and common nouns has not been tested yet with children.

   One may wonder whether it is the movement of N to D (whatever morphosyntactic feature implements that operation) that is the critical property distinguishing common and proper nominal expressions, or whether the distinction of the classes $N_{proper}$ and $N_{common}$ is sufficient, as we have assumed in the text. The two alternatives may be distinguishable empirically and testable experimentally. One relevant empirical domain to look at would be the case of languages in which proper names co-occur with the definite determiner (as in e.g. *la Maria* 'the Maria' in many Italian varieties), and in which the proper name does not overtly raise to D. Would such cases pattern with definite descriptions or with proper names in the contexts discussed? Other interesting issues arise in languages in which also common nouns raise to some definite determiners (e.g., Romanian, Scandinavian, etc.), which we will leave open for further analysis.
10. The proposed feature system also offers a natural basis to interpret Warren and Gibson's result on the increasing complexity of examples (12a), (12b), and (12c). Lexically restricted descriptions have "more in common" with proper names than with pronouns under our analysis, as common and proper nominal expressions share feature +NP (while differing with respect to the further specification $N_{proper}$ and $N_{common}$), which pronominals lack. So, if the degree of interference depends in part on the number of relevant features shared by target and intervener, we expect that (12b) (where target and intervener share feature +NP) will give rise to a degree of interference intermediate between (12a) (no relevant feature in common) and (12c) (target and intervener share features +NP and $N_{common}$). Further predictions are generated by the proposed system.

    In some cases, pronouns can be accompanied by a lexical restriction, e.g. in examples like "we linguists." Thus, the prediction that our system makes is that in a case like (i), we should observe the delay in reading time at the critical word that is characteristic of the lexically restricted target and intervener configurations.

    (i) It was you philosophers that we linguists *avoided* ___ at the party

# Appendix A Gennaro Chierchia's list of publications

## I. Theoretical work

"Usi metalinguistici riflessivi nei sistemi formali e nelle lingue naturali." In Daniele Gambarara (ed.), *Linguaggi e Formalizzazioni. Atti dell'Incontro Annuale della Società di Linguistica Italiana*, 73–77. Roma: Bulzoni, 1979.

"An autosegmental theory of Raddoppiamento." In James Pustejovsky and Peter Sells (eds.), *Proceedings of the XIIth Meeting of the North Eastern Linguistic Society (NELS 12)*, 49–62. Amherst, MA: Graduate Linguistic Student Association, University of Massachusetts (GLSA), 1982.

"English bare plurals, mass nouns and nominalization." In Daniel Flickinger, Marlys Macken, and Nancy Wiegand (eds.), *Proceedings of the First West Coast Conference on Formal Linguistics (WCCFL 1)*, 243–255. Stanford, CA: Stanford Linguistic Association, 1982.

"Nominalization and Montague Grammar. A semantics without types for natural languages." *Linguistics and Philosophy* 5: 303–354, 1982.

"On plural and mass nominals and the structure of the world." In Toni Borowski and Dan Finer (eds.), *University of Massachusetts Occasional Papers in Linguistics*, Vol. VIII, 17–45. Amherst, MA: Graduate Linguistic Student Association, University of Massachusetts (GLSA), 1983.

"Outline of a semantic theory of (Obligatory) Control." In Michael Barlow, Daniel Flickinger, and Michael Wescoat (eds.), *Proceedings of the Second West Coast Conference on Formal Linguistics (WCCFL 2)*, 19–31. Stanford, CA: Stanford Linguistic Association, 1983.

"Anaphoric properties of infinitives and gerunds." In Mark Cobler, Susannah MacKaye, and Michael Wescoat (eds.), *Proceedings of the Third West Coast Conference on Formal Linguistics (WCCFL 3)*, 28–47. Stanford, CA: Stanford Linguistic Association, 1984.

"Configurational notions in Discourse Representation Theory." In Charles Jones and Peter Sells (eds.), *Proceedings of the XIVth Meeting of the North Eastern Linguistic Society (NELS 14)*, 49–63. Amherst, MA: Graduate

Linguistic Student Association, University of Massachusetts (GLSA), 1984. With Mats Rooth.

"Topics in the syntax and semantics of infinitives and gerunds," Ph.D. thesis. University of Massachusetts at Amherst, 1984. Also published by Garland, New York and London, 1988.

"Formal semantics and the grammar of predication." *Linguistic Inquiry* 16: 417–443, 1985.

"Length, syllabification and the phonological cycle in Italian." *Journal of Italian Linguistics* 8: 5–34, 1986.

"Local and long distance Control." In Stephen Berman, Jae-Woong Choe and Joyce M. McDonough, (eds.), *Proceedings of the XVIth Meeting of the North Eastern Linguistic Society (NELS 16)*, 57–74. Amherst, MA: Graduate Linguistic Student Association, University of Massachusetts (GLSA), 1986. With Pauline Jacobson.

"Semantics and Property Theory." *Linguistics and Philosophy* 11: 261–302, 1988. With Raymond Turner.

"Aspects of a categorial theory of Binding." In Richard Oehrle, Emmon Bach, and Deidre Wheeler (eds.), *Categorial Grammar and Natural Language Structures*, 125–152. Dordrecht: Kluwer/Reidel, 1988.

"Dynamic Generalized Quantifiers and donkey anaphora." In Manfred Krifka (ed.), *Genericity in Natural Language*, 53–84. Tuebingen: Seminar fur Natuerlich Sprachliche Systeme, 1988.

*Properties, Types and Meaning. Volume I: Foundational Issues. Volume II: Semantic Issues*, edited with Barbara H. Partee and Raymond Turner, Dordrecht: Kluwer/Reidel, 1989.

"Introduction." In Gennaro Chierchia, Barbara H. Partee and Raymond Turner (eds.), *Properties, Types and Meaning*, Vol. I, 1–16. Dordrecht: Kluwer/Reidel, 1989. With Barbara H. Partee and Raymond Turner.

"Introduction." In Gennaro Chierchia, Barbara H. Partee and Raymond Turner (eds.), *Properties, Types and Meaning*, Vol. II, 1–20. Dordrecht: Kluwer/Reidel, 1989. With Barbara H. Partee and Raymond Turner.

"Structured meanings, thematic roles and control." In Gennaro Chierchia, Barbara H. Partee and Raymond Turner (eds.), *Properties, Types and Meaning*, Vol. II, 131–166. Dordrecht: Kluwer/Reidel, 1989.

"Anaphora and attitudes *de se*." In Renate Bartsch, Johan van Benthem and Peter van Emde Boas (eds.), *Semantics and Contextual Expression*, 1–31. Dordrecht: Foris, 1989.

"Anaphora and Dynamic Logic." In Jeroen Groenendijk and Martin Stokhof (eds.), *Quantification and Anaphora I*, Esprit Basic Research Action BR 3175, Deliverable R2.2.A, 1990.

*Meaning and Grammar. An Introduction to Semantics*. Cambridge, MA: MIT Press, 1990 With Sally McConnell-Ginet.

– Second Edition (substantially revised) 2000.
– Italian Edition, translated and edited by Walter Castelnovo, Muzzio Editore, Padua, 1993.
– Korean Edition, translated and edited by Ik-Hwan Lee, Kyoung-Won Kwon, and In-Young Jhee, Hankook Publishing Co., Seoul, 2004.

"Functional WH and weak crossover." In Daun Bates (ed.), *Proceedings of the Tenth West Coast Conference on Formal Linguistics (WCCFL 10)*, 75–90. Stanford, CA: CSLI, 1991.

"Anaphora and Dynamic Binding." *Linguistics and Philosophy* 15: 111–183, 1992.

"Logica e linguistica. Il contributo di Montague." In Marco Santambrogio (ed.), *La Filosofia Analitica del Linguaggio*, 287–359. Bari: Laterza, 1993.

"Questions with quantifiers." *Natural Language Semantics* 1: 181–234, 1993.

"Intensionality and context change." *Journal of Logic, Language and Information* 3: 141–168, 1994.

"A note on the stage-level vs. individual-level contrast and German subjects." In Pier Marco Bertinetto, Valentina Bianchi, and James Higginbotham (eds.), *Proceedings of the Cortona Meeting on Tense and Aspect.* Turin: Rosenberg & Sellier, 1995.

*Dynamics of Meaning. Anaphora, Presupposition and the Theory of Grammar.* Chicago, IL: University of Chicago Press, 1995.

"Individual-level predicates as inherent generics." In Gregory N. Carlson and Francis Jeffry Pelletier (eds.), *The Generic Book*, 176–223. Chicago, IL: University of Chicago Press, 1995.

"Genericity: An introduction." In Gregory N. Carlson and Francis Jeffry Pelletier (eds.), *The Generic Book*, 1–124. Chicago, IL: University of Chicago Press, 1995. With Manfred Krifka, Francis Jeffry Pelletier, Gregory N. Carlson, Alice ter Meulen, and Godehard Link.

"Variability of impersonal subjects." In Emmon Bach, Angelika Kratzer, Eloise Jelinek, and Barbara H. Partee (eds.), *Quantification in Natural Languages*, 107–144. Dordrecht: Kluwer, 1995.

"Sulla distinzione tra nomi massa e nomi contabili." In Tullio De Mauro e Vincenzo Lo Cascio (eds.), *Lessico e Grammatica*. Roma: Bulzoni, 1997.

"A note on the syntax-semantics interface in current linguistic theories." In Gabriela Matos, Mafilde Miguel, Ines Duarte, and Isabel Faria (eds.), *Interfaces in Linguistic Theory*. Lisbon: Linguistic Society of Portugal, 1997.

"Nota informale sui rapporti fra sintassi e semantica formale." In Renato Arena Maria Patrizia Bologna, Maria Luisa Meyer Modena, and Alessandro Passi (eds.), *Bandhu. Studi in Onore di Carlo Della Casa*, Alessandria, Italy: Dell'Orso, 1997.

"Partitives, reference to kinds and semantic variation." In Aaron Lawson (ed.), *Proceedings from Semantics and Linguistic Theory (SALT 7)*, 73–98. Ithaca, N.Y.: CLC Publications – Cornell University, 1997.

*Semantica. Le Strutture del Linguaggio*, Bologna, Italy: Il Mulino, 1997. Portuguese Edition edited by Rodolfo Ilari, Editora Unicamp, Campinas, Brasil, 2004.

"Plurality of mass nouns and the notion of 'Semantic Parameter'." In Susan Rothstein (ed.), *Events in Grammar*. 53–103. Dordrecht: Kluwer, 1998.

"Reconstruction in dislocation constructions and the syntax/semantics interface." In Kimary N. Shahin, Susan Blake, and Eun-Sook Kim (eds.), *Proceedings of the Seventeenth West Coast Conference on Formal Linguistics (WCCFL 17)*, 132–146. Stanford, CA: CSLI, 1998. With Carlo Cecchetto.

"Reference to kinds across languages." *Natural Language Semantics* 6: 339–405, 1998.

"Linguistics and languages." In Robert A. Wilson and Frank C. Keil (eds.), *MIT Encyclopedia of the Cognitive Sciences*, xci-cx. Cambridge, MA: MIT Press, 1999.

"Syntax-semantics interface." In Robert A. Wilson and Frank C. Keil (eds.), *MIT Encyclopedia of the Cognitive Sciences*, 824–826. Cambridge, MA: MIT Press, 1999.

"Chinese conditionals and the theory of conditionals." *Journal of East Asian Linguistics* 9: 1–54, 2000.

"A puzzle about indefinites." In Carlo Cecchetto, Gennaro Chierchia, and Maria Teresa Guasti (eds.), *Semantic Interfaces: Reference, Anaphora and Aspect*, 51–89. Stanford, CA: CSLI, 2001.

*Semantic Interfaces: Reference, Anaphora and Aspect*. Stanford, CA: CSLI, 2001. With Carlo Cecchetto and Maria Teresa Guasti (eds.).

"A semantics for unaccusatives and its syntactic consequences." In Artemis Alexiadou, Elena Anagnostopoulou, and Martin Everaert (eds.), *The Unaccusativity Puzzle: Studies on the Syntax-Lexicon Interface*, 60–84. Oxford University Press, 2003 [Written in 1989; published in the original form with a postscript.]

"Scalar implicatures, polarity phenomena and the syntax/pragmatics interface." In Adriana Belletti (ed.), *Structures and Beyond: The Cartography of Syntactic Structures*, Volume 3, 39–103. Oxford University Press, 2004. [The manuscript began circulating in 2001].

"Formal semantics." In Keith Brown (ed.), *Encyclopedia of Language and Linguistics*, 564–579. Oxford: Elsevier, 2005. doi: http://dx.doi.org/10.1016/B0-08-044854-2/01114-7.

"Broaden your views. Implicatures of domain widening and the 'logicality' of language." *Linguistic Inquiry* 37: 535–590, 2006.

"Definites, locality, and intentional identity." In Gregory N. Carlson and Francis Jeffry Pelletier (eds.), *Reference and Quantification: The Partee Effect*, 143–178. Stanford, CA: CSLI, 2006.

"Langage, pensée et réalité à la suite de Chomsky." In Jean Bricmont and Julie Frank (eds.) *Chomsky*, 129–147. Paris : Cahiers de L'Herne 88, 2007.

"Hurtford's Constraint and the theory of scalar implicatures: Evidence for embedded implicatures." In Paul Egré and Giorgio Magri (eds.), *Presuppositions and Implicatures. Proceedings of the MIT-Paris Workshop*, 47–62. Cambridge, MA: MIT Working Papers in Linguistics 60, 2009. With Danny Fox and Benjamin Spector.

"Mass nouns, vagueness and semantic variation." *Synthese* 174: 99–149, 2010.

"The grammatical view of scalar implicatures and the relationship between semantics and pragmatics." In Claudia Maienborn, Klaus von Heusinger, and Paul Portner (eds.), *Semantics: An International Handbook of Natural Language Meaning*, Vol. III. Berlin: Mouton de Gruyter, 2012. With Danny Fox and Benjamin Spector.

"Free choice nominals and free choice disjunction: The identity thesis." In Anamaria Fălăuş (ed.) *Alternatives in Semantics*. London: Palgrave Macmillan. to appear.

*Logic in Grammar: Polarity, Free choice, and Intervention*. Oxford University Press, to appear.

"Where do Chinese wh-items fit?" In Luis Alonso-Ovalle and Paula Menendez-Benito (eds.), *Epistemic Indefinites*. Oxford University Press, to appear. With Hsiu-Chen Daphne Liao.

*Semantic Inquiries*. Cambridge University Press, in preparation.

## II. Experimental work

"Syntactic bootstrapping and the acquisition of noun meanings: The mass/count issue." In Barbara Lust, Margarita Suñer, and John Whitman (eds.), *Syntactic Theory and Language Acquisition*, Vol. I. Princeton, NJ: Erlbaum Associates, 1994.

"*Some* and *or*: A study on the emergence of logical form." In Annabel Greenhill, Mary Hughes, Heather Littlefield, and Hugh Walsh (eds.), *Proceedings of the 22nd Annual Boston University Conference on Language Development*, 97–108. Somerville, MA: Cascadilla Press, 1998. With Stephen Crain, Maria Teresa Guasti, and Rosalind Thornton.

"Backward versus forward anaphora: Reconstruction in child language." *Language Acquisition* 8: 129–170, 1999/2000. With Maria Teresa Guasti.

"The acquisition of disjunction: Evidence for a grammatical view of scalar implicatures." In Anna H.-J. Do, Laura Domínguez, and Aimee Johansen (eds.), *Proceedings of the 25th Annual Boston University Conference on*

*Language Development*, 157–168. Somerville, MA: Cascadilla Press, 2001. With Stephen Crain, Maria Teresa Guasti, Andrea Gualmini, and Luisa Meroni.

"On the nature of selective deficits involving nouns and verbs." *Rivista di Linguistica* 14: 43–71, 2002. With Claudio Luzzatti.

"Linguistic-pragmatic factors in interpreting disjunctions." *Thinking and Reasoning* 8: 297–326, 2002. With Ira A. Noveck, Florelle Chevaux, Raphaelle Guelminger, and Emmanuel Sylvestre.

"Semantic and pragmatic competence in children's and adults' comprehension of *or*." In Ira Noveck and Dan Sperber (eds.), *Experimental Pragmatics*, 283–300. New York: Palgrave Macmillan, 2004. With Maria Teresa Guasti, Andrea Gualmini, Luisa Meroni, Stephen Crain, and Francesca Foppolo.

"Why children and adults sometimes (but not always) compute implicatures." *Language and Cognitive Processes* 20: 667–696, 2005. With Maria Teresa Guasti, Stephen Crain, Francesca Foppolo, Andrea Gualmini, and Luisa Meron.

"Noun-verb dissociation in aphasia: The role of imageability and functional locus of the lesion." *Neuropsychologia* 44: 73–89, 2006. With Davide Crepaldi, Silvia Aggujaro, Lisa Saskia Arduino, Giusy Zonca, Graziella Ghirardi, Maria Grazia Inzaghi, Mariarosa Colombo, and Claudio Luzzatti.

"On the role of entailment patterns and scalar implicatures in the processing of numerals." *Journal of Language and Memory* 61: 503–518, 2009. With Daniele Panizza and Charles Clifton.

"Relevance of polarity for the online interpretation of scalar terms." In Ed Cormany, Satoshi Ito, and David Lutz (eds.), *Proceedings from Semantics and Linguistic Theory 19 (SALT 19)*, 360–378, 2009. With Daniele Panizza, Yi-ting Huang, and Jesse Snedeker. http://elanguage.net/journals/salt/article/view/19.21/1880.

"Scalar implicatures in child language: Give children a chance." *Language Learning and Development* 8: 365–394, 2012. With Francesca Foppolo and Maria Teresa Guasti.

# Appendix B Logic and Linguistics: A Marriage of Inconvenience

A play by
*Raymond Turner and Kathy*

Amherst, Massachusetts
1984

## LOGIC AND LINGUISTICS:
## A MARRIAGE OF INCONVENIENCE.

THE PLAYERS: Linguist (G), Logician (R), Computer Scientist (B). The first act takes place outdoors. The background is a palatial Californian estate. This is a true story, only the names have been changed to protect the innocent.

ACT I

Entering stage right:

G: Hi R

Sitting in a lounge chair on the patio:

R: Hello G, what have you been doing since we last met; are you still trying to prop-up C's theory of properties?

G: Not exactly, C himself has been doing that. I have been using his theory of properties as a basis for Natural Language semantics.

R: Does he still have that dreadful notion of stratification at the heart of his theory? As I understand it only wff which are in some sense 'stratified' denote properties.

G: That's correct. (walking slowly across the stage) Basically, a wff $\phi$ is <u>stratified</u>, if there exists a function f: Variables of $\phi \longrightarrow \mathbb{N}$, such that for each atomic wff of $\phi$ of the form $X(x_0,\ldots,x_{n-1})$, $f(X) = 1 + f(x_0) = 1 + f(x_1) = \ldots$ .

R: (sitting up straight) This notion seems so ad-hoc; it really lack any intuitive motivation. What intuitions about properties and predication could ever lead one to adopt such a notion???

G: (abruptly stopping his pacing) The intuitions are those which stem from Russell's theory of types.

R: I thought you were trying to get away from all that. In your thesis you introduced several quite convincing arguments to establish that type-theory will not work, as a foundation for NL-semantics.

G: (walking quickly to R and towering over him) I still believe that my arguments are basically sound. C's theory is meant to be a second-order analogue of Russell's type-theory. You can do everything you want to do with type-theory and more. Why do logicians not like stratification anyway?

R: (leaning back in lounge chair and crossing arms) First, it does not get you very much more than type-theory. The only cases of self-application it sanctions are quite uninteresting. Secondly and more importantly, I am not at all convinced that stratification is so easily motivated by type-theoretic considerations. The intuitions which underly type-theory are essentially semantic. There is a clear intuitive picture of what is going on, in terms of objects, properties of objects, properties of such properties, etc. In the case of stratified theories we have no notion of what the intended models look like. We have nothing like such a clear intuitive picture. Moreover, (waggling his finger) Jenson's consistency proof is no help: one has to trace the model construction throught the whole regime of model-theoretic forcing, (now talking with both hands in motion) and, no matter how ingenious the construction, it cannot be taken as a formalization

R cont: of the intended models of a theory of properties. Such a model can serve only as a metamathematical device to establish consistency relative to ZF. 2

G: (continuing slow pacing with arms behind back) In essence I agree with all this, but (arms brought forward) do you have something better to offer?

R: Would I (pointing at himself) be raising such objections if I did not?

G: (pointing and gesturing) Knowing you, YES. You raise objections just for the hell of it. So what is this theory you have to offer. Is it the one based upon domain theory? (smirk on face)

I had a great deal of difficulty with your L&P paper. Moreover, what I was able to grasp I did not like much. Why, for example, should all the functions, we are permitted to employ in NL-semantics, be in some sense continuous. Is this not a REAL constraint????

R: (sitting up) I thought linguists liked constraints. This is a 'computational' constraint on NL-semantics. Is that not an (standing up) interesting thing to explore?

G: (walking over to patio table, turning to face R) Not if it constrains things too much. Can we really do semantics with so 'few' functions?

R: (begins pacing - G sit on edge of table) Well, that is a hard question. It certainly looks as if the constraint bites too hard. The underlying mathematical theory is quite weak. I still have some hopes of amending the theory, but there are some rather (waving hands around a bit) serious and difficult issues to deal with. It's a shame, because it is such a beautiful theory of functionality, with much computational and epistemological appeal.

G: (noticing an empty glass near lounge - eyes search area to find out where drink came from) A beautiful theory of functionality it might be, (frantically looking for the bar and trying not to be obvious) but its not obviously a theory of properties. That's the trouble with you logicians and mathematicians you get carried away with the beauty of your theories and forget about the applications. We linguists deal in ugliness. We cannot afford to get carried away contemplating beauty and the like. We have to deal with the world, as it is, not how you logicians would like it to be. Can you tell me where to get a drink?

(Enter B carrying radio)

B: Do you guys mind if I play some music?

R: No

G: Well, where did you get your drink from?

R: What are you talking about?

G: I asked where I could get a drink.

R: Over there (pointing). (G walking in direction of bar mumbling to himself) Something ugly.

G: (stopping & turning) What?

R: The world.

G: So you have, for the moment at least, given-up domain theory. What do you now advocate? (continuing trip to bar)

R: Did you read my "3-Theories" paper?

G: Yes - (pouring stronger drink than he originally wanted)

R: (returning to lounge and sitting) Did you understand it?

G: (drink in hand, walks to table and sits in chair) I only understood the prose. Could you explain it to me.

R: (grinning broadly - so broadly he can barely speak) I thought you would never ask. Here goes. (leaning back in lounge and closing eyes) Imagine that we have the first-order predicate calculus where there is just one basic relation, p, -a binary predication relation. The atomic wff are thus all of the form $p(t_1,t_2)$ where $t_1,t_2$ are terms. Moreover, all expressions of the form $\lambda x.\phi(x,y_1,...y_n)$ are terms, where $\phi$ is any wff. Such $\lambda$ -abstracts denote the properties of the theory. Obviously, we must impose (G looks down and stirs drink with finger) some constraints upon the interpretation of such $\lambda$-abstracts and such constraints really constitute the theory. Perhaps the most natural theory is the one where (R begins to write in air with finger)

(1) $P(\lambda x\cdot \phi(x,y_1,...,y_n),\ t) \leftrightarrow \phi(t).$

(G takes long drink) Under such circumstances the $\lambda$ -abstracts denote the properties we intended them to. Unfortunately, (1) cannot be true in general; Russell's paradox can be constructed within such a theory, using only minimal logic. C & Q's theory restricts (1) to wff which are stratified. We must, no doubt, restrict the truth of (1) to 'harmless' cases but we must do it in a philosophically well-motivated way. (G deep in though about the contents of his drink) I should say, to begin with, (R looking very pleased with himself) that the theory I will now present is not my latest theory. I have already developed several extensions and modifications, which are a vast improvement on this basic theory. In this regard, I am in line with the way research in situation semantics is going.

G: (studying fingernails) Is that meant to be some sort of recommendation for your theory?

R: (scowling - sitting up) Please don't interrupt unless you have something constructive to add.

G: (hand over heart, trying to look sincere, not succeeding) I'll try.

R: (leaning back in lounge and watching G to make sure he pays attention) One rather influential approach to the semantic paradoxes has employed partial predicates and some form of 3V-logic. Kripke, for example, employs Kleene's strong 3V-logic to develop a theory of truth for a language which contains its own truth-predicate. I shall NOT employ 3V-logic, but I shall provide (emphasis with hands) a theory of properties and predication which is motivated by those intuitions which demand that certain instances of predication be deemed problematic or ill-defined. (R closes eyes - G turns attention to fly in drink) Basically, the theory admits equivalences of the form

$$P(\lambda x.\ \phi(x,\bar{y}),t) \leftrightarrow \phi^+(t,\bar{y})$$

where $\phi^+$ is, in a sense to be made precise, an "approximation" to $\phi$. There is a certain residue (G deciding to pour drink into plant but save ice to chew on) of the 3V-approach, in that, in order to state the theory, we must extend our language by the addition of a (negative) predication operator $\bar{p}$, which satisfies: (R beginning to write in air again)

$$\sim(p(x,y)\ \&\ \bar{p}(x,y))\ \ldots \quad \text{(Dis)}$$

In other words, $p(x,y)$ and $\bar{p}(x,y)$ cannot both be true, but they can both be false. We can then define $\phi^+$ by first pushing all the negations in $\phi$ inward. As a consequence they only apply to atomic wff. We then replace each occurrence of $\sim p(t_1,t_2)$ by $\bar{p}(t_1,t_2)$ and each occurrence of $\sim\bar{p}(t_1,t_2)$ by $p(t_1,t_2)$. We then put $\phi^- = (\sim\phi)^+$. We can now state the theory:

$$(2) \quad P(\lambda x\cdot\phi(x,\bar{y}),\ t) \leftrightarrow \phi^+(t,\bar{y})$$

$$P(\lambda x\cdot\sim\phi(x,\bar{y}),t) \leftrightarrow \phi^-(t,\bar{y})$$

G: (showing polite interest) O.K. I get the rough picture. But what do the models of the theory look like? You made all that fuss about C's theory having no intuitive models, so you are under some obligation to provide one. Are there any potato chips?

R: I was just coming to that.

G: Chips???

R: It would help if you were a little more patient and sympathetic. To begin with, we need to say, in general, what the models look like. They have the form:

$$\mathfrak{M} = \langle D,\ p,\ \bar{p}\rangle$$

where D is a non-empty domain of individuals and $p$, $\bar{p}$ are binary relations which satisfy

$$\bar{p}(e,d) = \begin{cases} p(\lambda x\cdot\sim\phi(x,\bar{c}),\ d) & \text{if} \quad e = \lambda x\cdot\phi(x,\bar{c}) \\ \sim p(e,d) & \text{if} \quad e \neq \lambda x\cdot\phi(x,\bar{c}),\ \text{some } \phi \end{cases}$$

We must construct such a model in which each instance (2) is true. We proceed via an inductive construction similar to those used in Generalized Recursion Theory and the theory of Inductive Definability. There are no chips.

G: I have no idea what all that means. Cut out all the fancy stuff and just give me the guts of the argument.

R: Basically, we construct an ordinal sequence of models,

$$\mathfrak{M}_0,\ \mathfrak{M}_1,\ \mathfrak{M}_2,\ldots,\ \mathfrak{M}_\alpha,\ \ldots$$

in which the relation of predication is continually modified. As the construction proceeds more and more instances of predication are rendered true and more and more instances of (2) are validated. At a certain stage a 'fixed-point' is reached where all instances of (2) are validated. We can think of the process as an investigative procedure, whereby more and more facts get validated, until at the 'fixed-point' we have exhausted all that can be uncovered via the procedure. Much more can be said about 'Grounded' and Ungrounded' instances of predication and about extensions to the theory but this is all contained in My Amsterdam Paper. (R looking quite smug) In any case, I have said enough to convince you of the intrinsic beauty of the theory.

G: (taking off his shoes) Hmmm! I am not sure.

R: (leaping out of lounge chair and heading towards table) God, you Linguists are never satisfied.

G: (head held high) Non siamo qui per accettare tutte le cazzate che voi logici tirate fuori

R: (wind taken out of his sail) Pardon.

G: (with a flip of the hand) Nothing, I have a question and a possible objection. First the question. Do you have extensionality i.e. can two properties have the same extension without being the same property?

R: (regaining composure & beginning to speak a little louder) Of course, but I assume we want this. After all, we are after a theory of properties and not a set-theory.

G: (leaning back in chair and putting feet on table) I agree we don't want extensionality. That was the question, here comes the objection. Your theory does not (leaning forward - hands in motion) discriminate between predicates when they occur in their primary linguistic role (i.e. their predicative role) and when they themselves (or deformations of them) become the object of predication (their nominalized role). For example, consider the sentences

(1) John runs
(2) To run is fun.

In (1), <u>runs</u> functions semantically as a predicate but in (2) its nominalization <u>To run</u> functions semantically as an object. Surely, any semantic theory of NL must reflect such intuitions. I believe that this cannot be done, in a natural way, within a first-order framework such as the one you advocate.

R: (sitting on edge of table) Well, it can be done. One way is to employ a many-sorted theory.

G: Is that not going to be messy?

R: Perhaps, but it can be done. You linguists are here to make life inconvenient. (standing up)

G: We are after truth not esoteric dreams.

R: I thought we logicians and philosophers were seeking truth.

G: (grinning knowingly) You only THINK you are.

(B who has been in the background the whole time - walks to the table )

B: Would you guys like some dinner.

G: I will make some pasta.

END OF ACT I

ACT II

Setting: Formal Dining Room - table set with fine china and crystal. Players are seated around the table - and are quite involved in eating pasta.

G: (without looking up from his plate) O.K. it seems as if I must say something more about my basic ontological position.

R: (with a mouthful) If you must.

G: (gesturing with a forkful of pasta) At heart I am a Fregean. For me properties and objects are fundamentally different. Properties are 'unsaturated entities'; objects are not. Properties have to be supplied with objects to be 'completed'; in themselves they are 'incomplete'. (G eats some pasta) Moreover, the nominalized forms of predicative expressions, do not denote the same thing as the expressions denote in their primary linguistic role. Rather, they denote objects which are somehow correlated with properties . I believe it to be in harmony with how, predicative expressions and their nominalizations, function in NL. (G eats some pasta) Moreover, I believe that these intuitions cannot be formalized directly in a first-order framework. One must employ second-order logic.

R: (trying to squeeze the last drop from the wine bottle) I under stand your position and I am not unsympathetic, but what is the axiomatic theory you are advocating? All I know, so far, is that it is a second-order theory and that it must reflect the Fregean traditions on properties and objects, but Frege's own theory was inconsistent.

G: (waving a piece of bread) The stratified theory of C reflects the Fregean tradition and is consistent.

R: (drains wine from glass before he speaks) I have already outlined my arguments against C's theory and I do not have the stamina to recite them again. (eyeing B's glass of wine which apparently has remained untouched) Non siamo qui per accettare tutte le cazzate che voi linguisti tirate fuori.

G: What?

R: My grandfather was an italian car thief.

G: (surveying table with thoughts of a second helping in mind) O.K., so can you develop a theory like yours, directly, within the Fregean perspective?

R: (folding napkin, then leaning back in chair) I guess so, but first I need to know a little more about the role model-theory plays in your theory. Suppose we adope C's second order language, and admit , as terms of the language, all expressions of the form $^\wedge(\lambda x \cdot \phi(x,\bar{y}))$. Intuitively, $^\wedge(\lambda x \cdot \phi(x,\bar{y}))$ denotes the nominalized form of the predicative expression $\lambda x \cdot \phi(x,\bar{y})$. Is that correct?

G: (with mouthful) Yes.

R: What do models of the theory look like?

G: (finishing last little bit, putting down his fork and pushing his chair back from the table)

G: Well, basically they are a direct formalization of my intuitive Fregean picture. There is, however, something that I should add to my informal statement. I take sentences to describe or refer to propositions - at least directly. It is propositions which have truth-values. This may or may not be at odds with a pure Fregean view but I am not too disturbed by that, either way. Propositions can be given various intuitive interpretations including thinking of them as structured objects of some type. One might even employ the theology of situations and situation types to furnish an interpretation. For neutrality, however, I shall not commit myself to any particular interpretation; just select your favorite notion of proposition and stick it in.
(G stands and starts pacing the length of the table)
A Fregean-Frame $F = \langle U, \langle X_n \rangle_{n \in \omega}, f, h \rangle$ where U is the domain of individuals, $X_0$ the domain of 'propositions', $X_n \subseteq U^n \rightarrow X_0$ is the domain of n-place propositional functions ($n \geq 1$) and $f : X_n \rightarrow U$ the Fregean 'correlate" function. The function h assigns a truth-value to each proposition. As regards the interpretation of terms of the form $^\wedge(\lambda x \cdot \phi(x))$, we employ the Fregean correlate function:

$$[[^\wedge(\lambda x \cdot \phi(x))]] = f([[\lambda x \cdot \phi(x)]]).$$

B: (Standing up) Would anyone like coffee?

G: No thanks.

R: Why not?

G: I don't drink coffee in the evening. (B forgotten... leaves the room)

R: No - I meant... O.K. I understand all that. So to placate the Fregean Linguist I need to reproduce my theory within a second-order regime, where the interpretation of the theory is to be given via these Fregean Frames. Is that about it?

G: Yes (taking his seat at the table again)

R: (leaning forward and putting elbows on table) I am sure this can be done but first I want to raise an issue which I think needs some thought.

G: Go ahead.

R: I am not clear about the role of model theory in a theory of properties or sets or indeed, more generally, in the semantic analysis of natural language. So that I can get my ideas straight, indulge me a little?

G: How do you want to be indulged?

R: Consider Modal Logic.

G: (studying pattern of tablecloth) I am considering it.

R: (with hands in motion) In the semantic analysis of modal notions, possible worlds, and various functions and relations between them, play a central role. We have some pre-theoretical intuitions concerning the nature of possible worlds, and although we may not all agree about their exact metaphysical or ontological status, there is a sufficient general measure of agreement to enable formalization. The actual representation of possible worlds, within ZF are of course not the worlds themselves. The intended interpretation can only be the pre-theoretical one.

G: (looking up from intensive tablecloth study) Can one not tell a similar story about set and property theory? Do we not have an intuitive picture of the notion of set or property?

R: Several. (flipping bread crumbs around on tablecloth) For example, the pre-theoretical picture of ZF is based upon the intuitive notion of the cumulative hierarchy of sets. Sets are constructed, layer by layer, (R. tries to pile-up crumbs) built up from the empty set by applying the pre-theoretical operation of collecting things together in groups. This much is common to both areas. But there is more going on here: the formalization of the cumulative hierarchy is carried out within set-theory itself.

G: The moral you should draw from this is that the axiomatization itself should define the theory.

R: That is one moral.

G: (hands in the air) What else is there?

R: (brushing crumbs from hands, leaning forward and putting elbows on table)
Two issues are of some concern.
Firstly, what role are models of one set or property theory meant to play, when constructed inside a second? For example, my intuitive picture of the investigative procedure, which resulted in the stage-by-stage revision of the predication relation, was the intended interpretation of my theory of properties and predication. It was formalized inside ZF - why?

G: (sarcastically) Hey, you did it, so you should know.
(little more politely) One obvious remark concerns consistency. Given a theory as powerful as yours, the best one can do is to establish its consistency relative to ZF. For this you must construct models inside ZF.

(B: peeks in door - listens for a second - retreats)

R: I AM aware of that. (pointing at himself) I AM THE LOGICIAN HERE.

G: THEN WHAT ARE YOU SAYING?

R: (starting to fold and refold napkin) I'm not sure. I am groping in the dark. The need to establish consistency, although absolutely essential, cannot, it seems to me, be the complete story. Consistency can be established by building any old model; models, which in no way reflect the intended interpretation. For example, stratified theories have no clear intended interpretation, yet relative consistency can be established, for some variants, by building any model of the axioms inside ZF.

G: (looking totally confused) I still don't take your point.

R: (getting upset with G) You placed a great deal of emphasis upon the Fregean perspective. Your notion of Fregean frame was meant to reflect that perspective. The only reason, I can see, for the introduction of a replica of that perspective, inside ZF, is one of convenience. It is easier to establish consistency, with a representation of the intended model, inside ZF. But even this is not obviously always the case.

G: (humoring R) I sort-of understood your concern. You're asking about the conceptual role played by building models of the interpretation of one theory inside a second.

R: (not catching on that G has had it) I think so. One thing that occurs to me relates to the role played by topological models of intuitionistic logic. They are meant as an aid to the realist logician not the constructivist. She presumably has an intuitive picture of intutitionistic logic and no formalization within the world of sets will ever do justice to it.

B: (returns and makes his presence known) Is this discussion getting you guys anywhere?

G: (grateful for the interruption) B's right, we have only one week left. (Stands up and starts clearing the table)

R: (still not wanting to give up the ship) Don't rush me. Let me just make One More Point and then I will get on. (Looking crushed, G sits down again) In your thesis you provide an interpretation of a NL-fragment whose semantics is ultimately given in terms of Fregean Frames. The latter are formalized inside ZF. There is something quite curious about this. We are proposing to replace ZF by property theory as a foundation for semantics, yet our basic model-theoretic structures (i.e. Fregean Frames)are still being formalized in ZF. Should the semantics not be given directly in terms of structures formalized within our property theory. There is yet another analogy here. (G fidgets and groans) In 3VL the semantics is always given in classical terms - the model theoretic structures are formalized in ZF and the logic of the metatheory is classical. This seems like cheating. If one really believes in 3VL the semantics ought to be given in such terms. The same is true of property theory. If we are really advocating such a major foundational shift, we ought to develop the semantics directly in terms of property theory.

G: (in his most sincere voice) I think that I agree. (R believes that G agrees) But perhaps we ought to develop the theory first.

R: (happily) O.K.

The three player begin to clear the table.
Curtain closes

END OF ACT II

FINAL ACT

Two days later. It's morning and the setting is a formal breakfast nook. All three players are in their underware, milling around the room, trying to wake up. They are fairly civil to another, initially.

R: Good morning, B. (smiling but eyes only half open)

G: B, is there any milk? could you pass it to me please?

B: I could do. Do you wish me to? (smiling)

G: Why does he always ignore Gricean maxims? (puzzled)

R: (already gearing up for a day of theory in the sun) He thinks about the nature of metaphor too much. He no longer believes in the difference between literal and metaphorical truth.

G: (it's still too early for this state of mind) Is that true B?

B: (most cooperatively) I am not certain that I understand what it would mean for it to be true.

G: (still trying to make conversation) R, have you reconstructed your theory in Fregean terms?

R: (trying to decide between CocoPuffs and Frosted Flakes) Yes, the idea is pretty much the same as the original theory (deciding to try the Grape-Nuts) but recast within your second-order language. The basic axioms of the theory, (walking to the table with his bowl of cereal) are those of standard-second order logic (roughly) extended to this new language, plus

$$\lambda \bar{x} \cdot \phi(\bar{x})(t) \leftrightarrow \phi^{+}(\bar{t})$$

$$\lambda \bar{x} \cdot \sim \phi(\bar{x})(t) \leftrightarrow \phi^{-}(\bar{t})$$

Consistency is established pretty much as before via a fixed-point construction.

G: (trying to take pits out of the OJ) What about the models? How is $\lambda \bar{x} \cdot \phi(\bar{x})$ to be interpreted in Fregean frames?

(B is in the background, toaster is smoking, sugar bowl is knocked over and B is opening window then working on getting english muffin out of toaster with butter knife.)

R: (crunching on the Grape-Nuts) Well, that's easy. We associate with each $\lambda \bar{x} \cdot \phi(\bar{x})$ an element $r_{\phi} \in X_n$ and then construct a model, $\mathfrak{J}^*$ such that (waiving his spoon around)

$$h_{\mathfrak{J}^*}(r_{\phi}(\bar{d})) = h_{\mathfrak{J}^*}([\![\phi^{+}(\bar{d})]\!]).$$

This is achieved via the fixed-point construction. Looks good. (taking another mouthful) HuH?

G: (eyes watering from smoking toaster, and really not wanting to start <u>this</u> again)
Not Really. (turns his attention to a grapefruit)

R: What the hell is wrong now?

B: (returning to table triumphantly carrying english muffin) Are we going to CSLI?

G: (glaring at R) You have lost COMPOSITIONALITY.

R: (taken back) What do you mean?

G: (explaining with all the patience he can muster in the morning) Consider your proposed interpretation of $\lambda\bar{x}\cdot\phi$. According to you, it gets associated with some arbitrary element of $X_n$. It get's the right truth-value under h but surely we really want more; we require: (getting another cup of coffee):

$$[\![\lambda\bar{x}\cdot\phi]\!] = \lambda d\cdot[\![\phi^+(d)]\!].$$

R: What's so great about compositionality? (standing and starting to pick up his breakfast dishes) Situation Semantics is not compositional.

G: (patiently pointing out what should be obvious) That's just another thing wrong with it. No, (banging hand on table) we must have compositionality. (composing himself) Let's go back and see what we can do with C's theory.

R: I need to go to the bathroom.

B: Where shall we have lunch?

R: (yelling thru bathroom door) O.K., I think I can see how to amend the construction.
Here's how it goes. We construct the function

$$r : \text{wffs} \longrightarrow \bigcup_{n\in\omega} X_n.$$

step by step, through the construction of $\mathcal{L}_\omega = \bigcup_{n\in\omega}\mathcal{L}_n$.
The sublanguage $\mathcal{L}_n$ contains at most n-nested abstraction operators. We then Gödel number all the wffs of $\mathcal{L}_\omega$. We put $X_n^m = \{P_{gn(\phi)} : \phi\in\mathcal{L}_m\}$ where $\langle P_i\rangle_{i\in\omega}$ is an enumeration of a denumerable subset of $X_n$. We then let $r^0 : \mathcal{L}_0 \to X_n^0$ be any mapping such that if, $\lambda\bar{d}\cdot[\![\phi^+(d)]\!] = \lambda\bar{d}\cdot[\![\psi^+(d)]\!]$ then $r^0(\phi) = r^0(\psi)$. This is always possible since the Godel numbering associates distinct elements of $X_n^0$ with distinct wff. Now assume we have (R starts writing in the air) $r^m : \mathcal{L}_m \to X_n^m$ which satisfies: $\lambda\bar{d}\cdot[\![\phi^+(\bar{d})]\!]_{r^{m-1}} = \lambda\bar{d}\cdot[\![\psi^+(\bar{d})]\!]_{r^{m-1}}$ $\Rightarrow r^m(\phi) = r^m(\psi)$. Now extend $r^m$ to $r^{m+1} : \mathcal{L}_{m+1} \to X_n^{m+1}$ so that if $\lambda\bar{d}\cdot[\![\phi^+(\bar{d})]\!]_{r^m} = \lambda\bar{d}\cdot[\![\psi^+(\bar{d})]\!]_{r^m}$, then $r^{m+1}(\phi) = r^{m+1}(\psi)$, for $\phi,\psi\in\mathcal{L}_{m+1}-\mathcal{L}_m$. Again this is possible by the Gödel numbering. Now amend $r^{m+1}$ so that if $\phi\in\mathcal{L}_{m+1}\setminus\mathcal{L}_m$ and $\psi\in\mathcal{L}_m$ satisfy $\lambda\bar{d}\cdot[\![\phi^+(\bar{d})]\!]_{r^m} = \lambda\bar{d}\cdot[\![\psi^+(\bar{d})]\!]_{r^{m-1}}$ then put

$\rho^{m+1}(\phi) = \rho^m(\psi)$. The upshot of all this is a sequence of functions

$$\rho^0, \rho^1, \rho^2, \ldots$$

such that $\rho^m\ \mathcal{L}_m \to X_n^m$ and $\rho^{m+1} \restriction \mathcal{L}_m = \rho^m$.

Let $\rho^\omega = \bigcup_{m \in \omega} \rho^m$. Now observe that for $\phi, \psi \in \mathcal{L}_\omega$ there is an $m$ such that $\rho^\omega(\varphi) = \rho^m(\varphi)$ and $\rho^\omega(\chi) = \rho^m(\psi)$ — since for $m$ large enough $\phi, \psi \in \mathcal{L}_m$.

Now suppose $\lambda\bar{d} \cdot [\![\varphi^+(\bar{a})]\!]_{\rho\omega} = \lambda\bar{d} \cdot [\![\psi^+(\bar{d})]\!]_{\rho\omega}$.

Then $\lambda\bar{d} \cdot [\![\varphi^+(\bar{d})]\!]_{\rho m} = \lambda\bar{a} \cdot [\![\psi^+(\bar{d})]\!]_{\rho m}$. Hence, $\rho^m(\varphi) = \rho^m(\psi)$ & so $\rho^\omega(\varphi) = \rho^\omega(\psi)$. Hence we have a frame

$$F = \langle U, \langle X_n \rangle_{n \in \omega}, f, h, \rho^\omega \rangle$$

such that if $\lambda\bar{d} \cdot [\![\varphi^+(\bar{a})]\!]_{\rho\omega} = \lambda\bar{a} \cdot [\![\psi^+(\bar{a})]\!]_{\rho\omega}$ then $\rho^\omega(\varphi) = \rho^\omega(\psi)$. We can now use the fixed point construction for $h$, on top of this, to obtain

$$\mathcal{F} = \langle U, \langle X_n \rangle_{n \in \omega}, f, h, \rho \rangle$$

such that

$$h(r_\varphi(\bar{a})) = h([\![\varphi^+(\bar{a})]\!])$$

& if $\lambda\bar{d}.\ [\![\varphi^+(\bar{a})]\!] = \lambda\bar{d} \cdot [\![\psi^+(\bar{a})]\!]$ then $r_\varphi = r_\psi$. (*)

We can now define $\alpha : \{\lambda\bar{d} \cdot [\![\varphi^+(\bar{a})]\!] : \varphi \in \mathcal{I}\} \to X_n$ by $\alpha(\lambda\bar{a}\ [\![\varphi^+(\bar{a})]\!]) = r_\varphi$. By (*) $\alpha$ is well-defined (& 1-1)

Now extend $\mathcal{F}$ to $\mathcal{F}' = \langle U, \langle Y_n \rangle_{n \in \omega}, f^*, h \rangle$ where $Y_n = X_n \cup \{\lambda\bar{d} \cdot [\![\varphi^+(\bar{a})]\!] : \varphi \in \mathcal{L}\}$ and

$$f^*(a) = f(a) \text{ for } a \in X_n$$
$$f^*(\lambda\bar{d} \cdot [\![\varphi^+(\bar{a})]\!]) = f(\alpha(\lambda\bar{d} \cdot [\![\varphi^+\bar{d}]\!])$$

QED.

R returns to the breakfast nook a little bit horse from yelling thru the bathroom door but quite satisfied with his little lecture.

G: Did you think all this up in the bathroom?

R: There's no window - nothing to look at so I might as well think.

B: Is it safe to go in the bathroom now?

G: Good, now we can write up the paper.

Players stand and bow.

FINAL CURTAIN

Great round of applause.

Players come out for another bow.

Standing ovation continues for several minutes

Players return and promise another performance next Thursday.

# References

Abrusán, Marta (2011). "Predicting the presuppositions of soft triggers." *Linguistics and Philosophy* 34: 491–535.
Abrusán, Marta and Benjamin Spector (2011). "A semantics for degree questions based on intervals: negative islands and their obviation." *Journal of Semantics* 28: 107–147.
Abusch, Dorit (2010). "Presupposition triggering from alternatives." *Journal of Semantics* 27: 37–80.
Adams, Catherine (1990). "Syntactic comprehension in children with expressive language impairment." *British Journal of Disorders of Communication* 25: 149–171.
Adani, Flavia, Heather van der Lely, Matteo Forgiarini, and Maria Teresa Guasti (2010). "Grammatical feature dissimilarities make relative clauses easier: a comprehension study with Italian children." *Lingua* 120: 2148–2166.
Aloni, Maria (2001). "Quantification under conceptual covers." Ph.D. thesis. University of Amsterdam.
(2007a). "Expressing ignorance or indifference. Modal implicatures in BiOT." In Balder David ten Cate and Henk Zeevat, eds., *Proceedings of the Sixth International Tbilisi Symposium on Language, Logic and Computation (TbiLLC)*, 1–20. Batumi, Georgia.
(2007b). "Free choice, modals and imperatives." *Natural Language Semantics* 15: 65–94.
(2012). "On epistemic indefinites: a note on emphatic free choice uses." In Ana Aguilar Guevara, Anna Chernilovskaya, and Rick Nouwen, eds., *Proceedings of Sinn und Bedeutung (SuB) 16*. Cambridge, MA: MIT Working Papers in Linguistics.
Aloni, Maria and Angelika Port (2010). "Epistemic indefinites crosslinguistically." In Lena Fainleib, Nicholas LaCara, and Yangsook Park, eds., *Proceedings of the North East Linguistic Society (NELS) 41*. Philadelphia, PA: University of Pennsylvania.
(2011). "On epistemic indefinites." Talk given at *Sinn und Bedeutung 16*, University of Utrecht, September 6.
Aloni, Maria and Floris Roelofsen (2011). "Indefinites in comparatives." In Neil Ashton, Anca Chereches, and David Lutz, eds., *Proceedings from Semantics and Linguistic Theory (SALT) 21*, 19–38. Ithaca, NY: Department of Linguistics, Cornell University.
Aloni, Maria and Robert van Rooij (2004). "Free choice items and alternatives." In Gerlof Bouma, Irene Krämer, and Joost Zwarts, eds., *Proceedings of the KNAW Academy Colloquium: Cognitive Foundations of Interpretation (KNAW)*, 5–26. Amsterdam: Royal Netherlands Academy of Arts and Sciences.

Alonso-Ovalle, Luis (2009). "Even and biased questions: the case of Spanish *siquiera*." In Ed Cormany, Satoshi Ito, and David Lutz, eds., *Proceedings from Semantics and Linguistic Theory (SALT) 19*, 1–18. eLanguage.

Alonso-Ovalle, Luis and Paula Menéndez-Benito (2008). "Minimal domain widening." In Natasha Abner and Jason Bishop, eds., *Proceedings of the 27th West Coast Conference on Formal Linguistics (WCCFL 27)*, 36–44. Somerville, MA: Cascadilla Proceedings Project.

(2010). "Modal indefinites." *Natural Language Semantics* 18: 1–31.

(2011). "Expressing indifference: Spanish *un NP cualquiera*." In Neil Ashton, Anca Chereches, and David Lutz, eds., *Proceedings from Semantics and Linguistic Theory (SALT) 21*, 333–352. Ithaca, NY: Department of Linguistics, Cornell University.

Ariel, Mira (1990). *Accessing Noun Phrase Antecedents*. London: Routledge.

Arosio, Fabrizio, Flavia Adani, and Maria Teresa Guasti (2009). "Grammatical features in the comprehension of Italian relative clauses by children." In José Brucart, Anna Gavarrò, and Jaune Sola, eds., *Merging Features: Computation, Interpretation and Acquisition*, 138–158. Oxford University Press.

Bach, Emmon (1989). *Informal Lectures on Formal Semantics*. New York, NY: State University of New York Press.

Bach, Emmon and Barbara H. Partee (1980). "Anaphora and semantic structure." In Jody Kreiman and Alerindo Ojeda, eds., *Papers from the Parasession on Pronouns and Anaphora*, 1–28. Chicago, IL: Chicago Linguistic Society. Reprinted in Barbara H. Partee (2004). *Compositionality in Formal Semantics: Selected Papers by Barbara H. Partee*, 122–152. Oxford: Blackwell.

Baker, Carl L. (1970). "Double negatives." *Linguistic Inquiry* 1: 169–186.

Barker, Chris (2011). "Free choice permission as resource sensitive reasoning." *Semantics and Pragmatics* 3: 1–38.

Barner, David and Asaf Bachrach (2009). "Inference and exact numerical representation in early language development." *Cognitive Psychology* 60: 40–62.

Barrett, Robert B. and Roger Gibson, eds. (1990). *Perspectives on Quine*. Oxford: Blackwell.

Barwise, Jon (1981). "Scenes and other situations." *Journal of Philosophy* 78: 369–397.

Barwise, Jon and Robin Cooper (1981). "Generalized quantifiers and natural language." *Linguistics and Philosophy* 4: 159–219.

Barwise, Jon and John Perry (1981). "Situations and attitudes." *Journal of Philosophy* 78: 668–691.

(1983). *Situations and Attitudes*. Cambridge, MA: MIT Press.

Beaver, David (1994). "When variables don't vary enough." In Mandy Harvey and Lynn Santelmann, eds., *Proceedings from Semantics and Linguistic Theory (SALT) 4*, 35–60. Department of Modern Languages and Linguistics, Cornell University.

(1999). "Presupposition accommodation: a plea for common sense." In Lawrence Moss, Jonathan Ginzburg, and Maarten de Rijke, eds., *Logic, Language, and Computation, Volume 2*, 21–44. Stanford, CA: CSLI Publications.

(2001). *Presupposition and Assertion in Dynamic Semantics*. Stanford, CA: CSLI Publications.

(2006). "The proviso problem: comments on von Fintel." Paper presented at *Workshop On Presupposition Accommodation*, Ohio State University, Columbus, OH, October 14.

Beaver, David and Bart Geurts (2011). "Presupposition." In Edward Zalta, ed., *Stanford Encyclopedia of Philosophy (Summer 2011 Edition)*. http://plato.stanford.edu/archives/sum2011/entries/presupposition/.

Beaver, David and Emiel Krahmer (2001). "A partial account of presupposition projection." *Journal of Logic, Language and Information* 10: 147–182.

Beck, Sigrid. (2006). "Intervention effects follow from focus interpretation." *Natural Language Semantics* 14: 1–56.

Belletti, Adriana (2008). "The CP of clefts." *Rivista di Grammatica Generativa* 33: 191–204.

(2009). *Structures and Strategies*. London: Routledge.

Belletti, Adriana and Carla Contemori (2010). "Intervention and attraction. On the production of subject and object relatives by Italian (young) children and adults." In João Costa, Ana Castro, Maria Lobo, and Fernanda Pratas, eds., *Language Acquisition and Development, 3. Proceedings of Gala 2009*, 39–52. Cambridge Scholars Publishing (CSP).

(to appear). "Subjects in children's object relatives." *Revue Roumaine de Linguistique*.

Belletti, Adriana, Naama Friedmann, Dominique Brunato, and Luigi Rizzi (2012). "Does gender make a difference? Comparing the effect of gender on children's comprehension of relative clauses in Hebrew and Italian." *Lingua* 122: 1053–1069.

Berwick, Robert C. (1985). *The Acquisition of Syntactic Knowledge*. Cambridge, MA: MIT Press.

Bever, Thomas G. (1974). "The ascent of the specious, or there is a lot we don't know about mirrors." In David Cohen, ed., *Explaining Linguistic Phenomena*, 173–200. Washington, DC: Hemisphere.

Bhatt, Rajesh and Roumyana Pancheva (2004). "Late merger of degree clauses." *Linguistic Inquiry* 35: 1–46.

Bierwisch, Manfred (1989). "The semantics of gradation." In Manfred Bierwisch and Ewald Lang, eds., *Dimensional Adjectives*, 71–262. Berlin: Springer.

Bishop, Dorothy V. M. (1993). Test for Reception of Grammar. Test available from the author at the University of Manchester.

Bishop, Dorothy V. M. and Elizabeth Bourne (1985). "Do young children understand comparatives?" *British Journal of Developmental Psychology* 3: 123–132.

Booth, Amy E. and Sandra Waxman (2003). "Mapping words to the world in infancy: infants' expectations for count nouns and adjectives." *Journal of Cognition and Development* 4: 357–381.

Boster, Carole and Stephen Crain (1993). "On children's understanding of *Every* and *Or*." *Proceedings of Early Cognition and Transition to Language*, University of Texas at Austin.

Braine, Martin D. S., and Barbara Rumain (1981). "Development of comprehension of 'or': evidence for a sequence of competencies." *Journal of Experimental Child Psychology* 31: 46–70.

Breheny, Richard (2008). "A new look at the semantics and pragmatics of numerically quantified noun phrases." *Journal of Semantics* 25: 93–139.

Brisson, Christine (1998). "*Distributivity, maximality, and floating quantifiers*." Ph.D. thesis. Rutgers University.

Brown, H. Douglas (1971). "Children's comprehension of relativized English sentences." *Child Development* 42: 1923–1936.

Brown, Roger W. (1958). *Words and Things: an Introduction to Language*. New York, NY: Simon & Schuster.

(1973). *A First Language: The Early Stages*. Cambridge, MA: Harvard University Press.

Bultinck, Bert (2005). *Numerous Meanings: The Meaning of English Cardinals and the Legacy of Paul Grice*. Amsterdam: Elsevier.

Büring, Daniel (2007). "More or less." In Malcolm Elliott, James Kirby, Osamu Sawada, Eleni Staraki, and Suwon Yoon, eds., *Papers from the 43rd Annual Meeting of the Chicago Linguistic Society (CLS). Volume 1: The Main Session*. Chicago Linguistic Society.

Carlson, Gregory N. (1977). "*Reference to kinds in English*." Ph.D. thesis. University of Massachusetts, Amherst.

(1989). "The semantic contribution of English generic sentences." In Gennaro Chierchia, Barbara H. Partee, and Raymond Turner, eds., *Properties, Types and Meaning*, Vol. II, 167–192. Dordrecht: Kluwer.

Carlson, Gregory N. and Francis Jeffry Pelletier, eds. (1995). *The Generic Book*. University of Chicago Press.

Carston, Robyn (1988). "Implicature, explicature and truth-theoretic semantics." In Ruth Kempson, ed., *Mental Representations: The Interface Between Language and Reality*, 155–181. Cambridge University Press.

(1998). "Informativeness, relevance and scalar implicature." In Robyn Carston and Seiji Uchida, eds., *Relevance Theory: Applications and Implications*, 179–236. Amsterdam: John Benjamins.

Charlow, Simon (2009). "'Strong' predicative presuppositional objects." In Nathan Klinedinst and Daniel Rothschild, eds., *Proceedings of the 2009 European Summer School of Logic, Language, and Information (ESSLLI) Workshop: New Directions in the Theory of Presupposition*.

Chemla, Emmanuel (2009a). "Presuppositions of quantified sentences: experimental data." *Natural Language Semantics* 17: 299–340.

(2009b). "Universal implicatures and free choice effects: experimental data." *Semantics and Pragmatics* 2: 1–33.

Chemla, Emmanuel and Philippe Schlenker (in press). "Incremental vs. symmetric accounts of presupposition projection: an experimental approach." *Natural Language Semantics*.

Chierchia, Gennaro (1982a). "English bare plurals, mass nouns, and nominalization." In Daniel Flickinger, Marlys Macken and Nancy Wiegand, eds., *Proceedings of the First West Coast Conference on Formal Linguistics (WCCFL 1)*, 243–255. Stanford, CA: Stanford Linguistics Association, Stanford University.

(1982b). "Nominalization and Montague Grammar. A semantics without types for natural languages." *Linguistics and Philosophy* 5: 303–354.

(1983a). "On plural and mass nominals and the structure of the world." In Toni Borowski and Daniel Finer, eds., *University of Massachusetts Occasional Papers in Linguistics VIII*, 17–45. Amherst, MA: Graduate Linguistic Student Association, University of Massachusetts (GLSA).

(1983b). "Outline of a semantic theory of (Obligatory) Control." In Michael Barlow, Daniel Flickinger, and Michael Wescoat, eds., *Proceedings of the Second West Coast Conference on Formal Linguistics (WCCFL 2)*, 19–31. Stanford, CA: Stanford Linguistics Association, Stanford University.

(1984a). "Topics in the syntax and semantics of infinitives and gerunds." Ph.D. thesis. University of Massachusetts, Amherst. [Also published by Garland Publishing Inc., New York and London, 1988]

(1984b). "Anaphoric properties of infinitives and gerunds." In Mark Cobler, Susanna MacKaye, and Michael Wescoat, eds., *Proceedings of the Third West Coast Conference on Formal Linguistics (WCCFL 3)*, 28–39. Stanford, CA: Stanford Linguistic Association.

(1985). "Formal semantics and the grammar of predication." *Linguistic Inquiry* 16: 417–443.

(1988a). "Aspects of a categorial theory of Binding." In Richard Oehrle, Emmon Bach, and Deirdre Wheeler, eds., *Categorial Grammar and Natural Language Structures*, 125–152. Dordrecht: Kluwer/Reidel.

(1988b). "Dynamic Generalized Quantifiers and donkey anaphora." In Manfred Krifka, ed., *Genericity in Natural Language*, 53–84. University of Tübingen.

(1989). "Anaphora and attitudes *de se*." In Renate Bartsch, Johan van Benthem, and Peter van Emde Boas, eds., *Semantics and Contextual Expression*, 1–31. Dordrecht: Foris.

(1995). *Dynamics of Meaning: Anaphora, Presupposition, and the Theory of Grammar.* Chicago, IL: University of Chicago Press.

(1998). "Reference to kinds across languages." *Natural Language Semantics* 6, 339–405

(2004). "Scalar implicatures, polarity phenomena, and the syntax/pragmatics interface." In Adriana Belletti, ed., *Structures and Beyond: The Cartography of Syntactic Structures*, Volume 3, 39–103. Oxford University Press.

(2006). "Broaden your views: implicatures of domain widening and the 'logicality' of language." *Linguistic Inquiry* 37: 535–590.

(2010). "Mass nouns, vagueness and semantic variation." *Synthese* 174: 99–149.

(to appear a). "Logic in grammar: polarity, free choice, and intervention." Oxford University Press.

(to appear b). "Free choice nominals and free choice disjunction: the identity thesis." In Anamaria Fălăuş, ed., *Alternatives in Semantics*. London: Palgrave Macmillan.

Chierchia, Gennaro, Stephen Crain, Maria Teresa Guasti, Andrea Gualmini, and Luisa Meroni (2001). "The acquisition of disjunction: evidence for a grammatical view of scalar implicatures." In Anna H.-J. Do, Laura Domínguez, and Aimee Johansen, eds., *Proceedings of the 25th Annual Boston University Conference on Language Development*, 157–168. Somerville, MA: Cascadilla Press.

Chierchia, Gennaro, Stephen Crain, Maria Teresa Guasti, and Rosalind Thornton (1998). "'Some' and 'or': a study on the emergence of logical form." In Annabel Greenhill, Mary Hughes, Heather Littlefield, and Hugh Walsh, eds., *Proceedings of the 22nd Annual Boston University Conference on Language Development*, 97–108. Somerville, MA: Cascadilla Press.

Chierchia, Gennaro, Danny Fox, and Benjamin Spector (2012). "The grammatical view of scalar implicatures and the relationship between semantics and pragmatics." In Claudia Maienborn, Klaus von Heusinger, and Paul Portner, eds., *Semantics: An International Handbook of Natural Language Meaning* Vol. III. Berlin: Mouton de Gruyter.

Chierchia, Gennaro, Maria Teresa Guasti, Andrea Gualmini, Luisa Meroni, Stephen Crain, and Francesca Foppolo (2004). "Semantic and pragmatic competence in children's and adults' comprehension of *or*." In Ira Noveck and Dan Sperber, eds., *Experimental Pragmatics*, 283–300. New York, NY: Palgrave Macmillan.

Chierchia, Gennaro and Pauline Jacobson (1986). "Local and long distance Control." In Stephen Berman, Jae-Woong Choe, and Joyce McDonough, eds., *Proceedings of the XVIth Annual Meeting of the North Eastern Linguistic Society (NELS 16)*, 57–74. Amherst, MA: Graduate Linguistic Student Association, University of Massachusetts (GLSA).

Chierchia, Gennaro and Sally McConnell-Ginet (1990). *Meaning and Grammar: An Introduction to Semantics*. Cambridge, MA: MIT Press. [substantially revised second edition: 2000]

Chierchia, Gennaro, Barbara H. Partee, and Raymond Turner (1989a). "Introduction." In Gennaro Chierchia, Barbara H. Partee, and Raymond Turner, eds., *Properties, Types and Meaning. Volume I: Foundational Issues*, 1–16. Dordrecht: Kluwer.

eds. (1989b). *Properties, Types and Meaning. Volume I: Foundational Issues. Volume II: Semantic Issues*. Dordrecht: Kluwer.

Chierchia, Gennaro and Mats Rooth (1984). "Configurational notions in Discourse Representation Theory." In Charles Jones and Peter Sells, eds., *Proceedings of the XIVth Meeting of the North Eastern Linguistic Society (NELS 14)*, 49–63. Amherst, MA: Graduate Linguistic Student Association, University of Massachusetts (GLSA).

Chierchia, Gennaro and Raymond Turner (1988). "Semantics and property theory." *Linguistics and Philosophy* 11: 261–302.

Chomsky, Noam (1965). *Aspects of the Theory of Syntax*. Cambridge, MA: MIT Press.

(1966). *Cartesian Linguistics*. New York, NY: Harper & Row.

(1975). *Reflections on Language*. New York, NY: Pantheon Books.

(1995). *The Minimalist Program*. Cambridge, MA: MIT Press.

(1996). *Powers and Prospects: Reflections on Human Nature and the Social Order*. London: Pluto Press.

(2000a). "Minimalist inquiries: the framework." In Roger Martin, David Michaels, and Juan Uriagereka, eds., *Step by Step – Essays in Minimalist Syntax in Honor of Howard Lasnik*, 89–156. Cambridge, MA: MIT Press.

(2000b). *New Horizons in the Study of Language and Mind*. Cambridge University Press.

(2001). "Derivation by phase." In Michael Kenstowicz, ed., *Ken Hale: A Life in Language*, 1–52. Cambridge, MA: MIT Press.

(2008). "On phases." In Robert Freidin, Carlos Otero, and Maria Luisa Zubizarreta, eds., *Foundational Issues in Linguistic Theory: Essays in Honor of Jean Roger Vergnaud*, 133–166. Cambridge, MA: MIT Press.

Cinque, Guglielmo (1990). *Types of A′ Dependencies*. Cambridge, MA: MIT Press.

ed. (2002). *Functional Structure in CP and IP. The Cartography of Syntactic Structures*, Vol. I. Oxford University Press.

Clark, Eve V. (1971). "On the acquisition of the meaning of *before* and *after*." *Journal of Verbal Learning and Verbal Behavior* 10: 266–275.

(1972). "On the child's acquisition of antonyms in two semantic fields." *Journal of Verbal Learning and Verbal Behavior* 11: 750–758.

Clark, Herbert H. (1970). "The primitive nature of children's relational concepts." In John Hayes, ed., *Cognition and the Development of Language*, 269–278. New York, NY: Wiley.

(1973). "Space, time, semantics, and the child." In Timothy Moore, ed., *Cognitive Development and the Acquisition of Language*, 27–63. New York, NY: Academic Press.

Condoravdi, Cleo (1997). *Descriptions in Context*. New York, NY: Garland Publishing.

Contemori, Carla and Adriana Belletti (2011). "Relatives and passive object relatives in Italian speaking children and adults: intervention in production and comprehension." Manuscript, University of Siena.

Crain, Stephen (2008). "The interpretation of disjunction in universal grammar." *Language and Speech* 51: 151–169.

(2012). *The Emergence of Meaning*. Cambridge University Press.

Crain, Stephen, Takuya Goro, and Utako Minai (2007). "Hidden units in child language." In Andrea C. Schalley and Drew Khlentzos, eds., *Mental States Evolution, Function and Nature*, 275–294. Amsterdam: John Benjamins.

Crain, Stephen, Takuya Goro, and Rosalind Thornton (2006). "Language acquisition is language change." *Journal of Psycholinguistic Research* 35: 31–49.

Crain, Stephen, Takuya Goro, Peng Zhou, and Anna Notley (2012). "Polarity meets focus in child language." Presented at the Linguistic Society of America's Eighty-Sixth Annual Meeting, Portland, OR, USA, January 5–8.

Crain, Stephen, Andrea Gualmini, and Paul Pietroski (2005). "Brass tacks in linguistic theory: innate grammatical principles." In Peter Carruthers, Stephen Laurence, and Stephen Stich, eds., *The Innate Mind: Structure and Contents*, 175–197. Oxford University Press.

Crain, Stephen and Drew Khlentzos (2008). "Is logic innate?" *Biolinguistics* 2: 24–56.

(2010). "The Logic instinct." *Mind and Language* 25: 30–65.

Crain, Stephen, Weija Ni, and Laura Conway (1994). "Learning, parsing and modularity." In Chuck Clifton, Lyn Frazier and Keith Rayner, eds., *Perspectives on Sentence Processing*, 443–468. Hillsdale, NJ: Lawrence Erlbaum.

Crain, Stephen, and Rosalind Thornton (1998). *Investigations in Universal Grammar: A Guide to Experiments on the Acquisition of Syntax and Semantics*. Cambridge, MA: MIT Press.

(2006). "Acquisition of syntax and semantics." In Matthew Traxler and Morton Gernsbacher, eds., *Handbook of Psycholinguistics*, 2nd edition, 1073–1110. London: Elsevier.

Cresswell, Maxwell J. (1973). *Logics and Languages*. London: Methuen.

(1976). "The semantics of degree." In Barbara H. Partee, ed., *Montague Grammar*, 261–292. New York, NY: Academic Press.

Crnič, Luka (2011a). "Getting even." Ph.D. thesis. Massachusetts Institute of Technology, Cambridge, MA.

(2011b). "On the meaning and distribution of concessive scalar particles." In Lena Fainleib, Nick LaCara, and Tangsook Park, eds., *Proceedings of the 41st Annual Meeting of the North East Linguistic Society (NELS 41)*. Philadelphia, PA: University of Pennsylvania.

Cruse, David Alan (1980). "Antonyms and gradable complementaries." *Perspektiven der Lexikalischen Semantik: Beitrage zum Wuppertaler Semantikkolloquium vom* 2–3: 14–25.

Dalrymple, Mary Makoto, Kanazawa, Yookyung Kim, Sam Mchombo, and Stanley Peters (1998). "Reciprocal expressions and the concept of reciprocity." *Linguistics and Philosophy* 21: 159–210.

Dayal, Veneeta (1992). "The singular-plural distinction in Hindi generics." In Chris Barker and David Dowty, eds., *Proceedings from Semantics and Linguistic Theory (SALT 2)*, OSU Working Papers in Linguistics 40, 39–58. Columbus, OH: Ohio State University.

(1996). *Locality in Wh Quantification: Questions and Relative Clauses in Hindi.* Dodrecht: Kluwer.

(1997). "Free relatives and *ever:* identity and free choice readings." In Aaron Lawson, ed., *Proceedings from Semantics and Linguistic Theory (SALT 7)*, 99–116. Ithaca, NY: CLC Publications.

(1999). "Bare NP's, reference to kinds, and incorporation." In Tanya Matthews and Devon Strolovitch, eds., *Proceedings from Semantics and Linguistic Theory (SALT 9)*, 34–51. Ithaca, NY: Cornell University.

(2004). "Number marking and (in)definiteness in kind terms." *Linguistics and Philosophy* 27: 393–450.

(2009). "Variation in English free choice items." In Rajat Mohanty and Mythili Menon, eds., *Universals and Variation: Proceedings of GLOW in Asia VII*, 237–256.

(2011a). "Bare noun phrases." In Claudia Maeinborn, Klaus von Heusinger, and Paul Portner, eds., *Semantics: An International Handbook of Natural Language Meaning*, Vol. II, 1087–1108. Berlin: Mouton de Gruyter.

(2011b). "Hindi pseudo incorporation." *Natural Language and Linguistic Theory* 29: 123–167.

(in prep). *Bare Noun Phrases, Genericity and (In)definiteness: A Cross-linguistic Perspective.* Oxford: Blackwell.

Dennett, Daniel (2012). "Sakes and dints, and other definitions that philosophers really need not seek." *Times Literary Supplement*, March 2, 12–14.

De Villiers, Jilles, Peter De Villiers, and Esme Hoban (1994). "The central problem of functional categories in the English syntax of oral deaf children." In Helen Tager-Flusberg, ed., *Constraints on Language Acquisition: Studies of Atypical Children*, 9–47. Hillsdale, NJ: Lawrence Erlbaum.

De Vincenzi, Marica (1991). *Syntactic Parsing Strategies in Italian: The Minimal Chain Principle.* Dordrecht: Kluwer.

Diesing, Molly (1992). *Indefinites.* Cambridge, MA: MIT Press.

Donaldson, Margaret and George Balfour (1968). "Less is more: a study of language comprehension in children." *British Journal of Psychology* 59: 461–471.

Donaldson, Margaret and Roger Wales (1970). "On the acquisition of some relational terms." In John Hayes, ed., *Cognition and the Development of Language*, 235–268. New York, NY: Wiley.

Donati, Caterina and Carlo Cecchetto (2011). "Relabeling heads: a unified account for relativization structures." *Linguistic Inquiry* 42: 519–560.

Dowty, David (1987). "Collective predicates, distributive predicates and *all*." In Fred Marshall, Ann Miller, and Zheng-sheng Zhang, eds., *Proceedings of Third ESCOL Meeting*, 97–125. Columbus, OH: Ohio State University.

Dummett, Michael (1978). *Truth and Other Enigmas*. Cambridge, MA: Harvard University Press.

Ebeling, Karen S. and Susan Gelman (1988). "Coordination of size standards by young children." *Child Development* 59: 888–896.

Eckardt, Regine (2007). "Licensing *or*." In Uli Sauerland and Penka Stateva, eds., *Presupposition and Implicature in Compositional Semantics*, 34–70. London: Palgrave Macmillan.

Elbourne, Paul (2011). *Meaning: A Slim Guide to Semantics*. Oxford University Press.

Enç, Mürvet M. (1981). "Tense without scope: an analysis of nouns as indexicals." Ph.D. thesis. University of Wisconsin, Madison.

(1987). "Anchoring conditions for tense." *Linguistic Inquiry* 18: 633–657.

Fălăuş, Anamaria (2009). "Polarity items and dependent indefinites in Romanian." Ph.D. thesis. University of Nantes.

(2011). "Alternatives as sources of semantic dependency." In Nan Li and David Lutz, eds., *Proceedings from Semantics and Linguistic Theory (SALT 20)*, 406–427. eLanguage.

(2012). "(Partially) free choice of alternatives." Manuscript, University of the Basque Country (UPV/EHU).

Farkas, Donka (2002). "Extreme non-specificity in Romanian." In Claire Beyssade, Reineke Bok-Bennema, Frank Drijkoningen, and Paola Monachesi, eds., *Romance Languages and Linguistic Theory 2000*, 127–151. Amsterdam/Philadelphia: John Benjamins.

(2006). "Free choice in Romanian." In Betty Birner and Gregory Ward, eds., *Drawing the Boundaries of Meaning: Neo-Gricean Studies in Pragmatics and Semantics in Honor of Laurence R. Horn*, 71–94. Amsterdam/Philadelphia: John Benjamins.

Fauconnier, Gilles (1975). "Pragmatic scales and logical structure." *Linguistic Inquiry* 6: 353–375.

Feferman, Solomon (1985). "Intensionality in mathematics." *Journal of Philosophical Logic* 14: 41–55.

Fintel, Kai von (2000a). "Singleton indefinites (re. Schwarzschild 2000)." Handout from a talk to MIT Syntax-Semantics Reading Group. http://web.mit.edu/fintel/fintel-2000-singleton.pdf.

(2000b). "What is presupposition accommodation?" Manuscript, Massachusetts Institute of Technology. http://mit.edu/fintel/fintel-2000-accomm.pdf.

(2000c). "Whatever." In Brendan Jackson and Tanya Matthews, eds., *Proceedings from Semantics and Linguistic Theory (SALT 10)*, 27–39. Ithaca, NY: Cornell University. http://elanguage.net/journals/salt/article/view/10.27/1708

(2008). "What is presupposition accommodation, again?" *Philosophical Perspectives* 22: 137–170.

Føllesdal, Dagfinn (1990). "Indeterminacy and mental states." In Robert Barrett and Roger Gibson, eds., *Perspectives on Quine*, 98–109. Oxford, UK: Blackwell.

Foppolo, Francesca, Maria Teresa Guasti, and Gennaro Chierchia (2012). "Scalar implicatures in child language: give children a chance." *Language Learning and Development* 8: 365–395.

Foppolo, Francesca and Francesca Panzeri (in press). "Do children know when their room counts as clean?" In *Proceedings of the 40th Annual Meeting of the North East Linguistics Society (NELS 40)*. Amherst, MA: Graduate Linguistic Student Association, University of Massachusetts (GLSA).

Fox, Danny (2007a). "Free choice disjunction and the theory of scalar implicatures." In Uli Sauerland and Penka Stateva, eds., *Presupposition and Implicature in Compositional Semantics*, 71–120. New York: Palgrave Macmillan.

(2007b). "Too many alternatives: density, symmetry and other predicaments." In Masayuki Gibson and Tova Friedman, eds., *Proceedings from Semantics and Linguistic Theory (SALT 17)*, 89–111. Ithaca, NY: Cornell University.

(2008). "Two short notes on Schlenker's theory of presupposition projection." *Theoretical Linguistics* 34: 237–252.

(2011). "Presupposition projection, trivalence and relevance." HUJI / TAU Syntax Semantics Reading Group, November/December 2011. http://pluto.huji.ac.il/~dfox/Talks_files/presup%20and%20rel-new.pdf.

Fox, Danny, and Martin Hackl (2006). "The universal density of measurement." *Linguistics and Philosophy* 29: 537–586.

Fox, Danny, and Roni Katzir (2011). "On the characterization of alternatives." *Natural Language Semantics* 19: 87–107.

Franke, Michael (2009). "Signal to act: game theory in pragmatics." Ph.D. thesis. University of Amsterdam.

(2011). "Quantity implicatures, exhaustive interpretation, and rational conversation." *Semantics and Pragmatics* 4: 1–82.

Frauenfelder, Ulrich, Jacques Mehler, and Juan Segui (1980). "Monitoring around the relative clause." *Journal of Memory and Language* 19: 328–337.

Frege, Gottlob (1884). *Die Grundlagen der Arithmetik*. Translated into English as *The Foundations of Arithmetic*. Evanston, IL: Northwestern University Press, 1980.

Friedman, Joyce, Douglas Moran, and David Warren (1978a). "An interpretation system for Montague grammar." *American Journal of Computational Linguistics* microfiche 74: 23–96. acl.ldc.upenn.edu/J/J79/J79–1074.pdf.

(1978b). "Explicit finite intensional models for PTQ." *American Journal of Computational Linguistics* microfiche 74:3–22. acl.ldc.upenn.edu/J/J79/J79–1074.pdf.

Friedmann, Naama and Rama Novogrodsky (2004). "The acquisition of relative clause comprehension in Hebrew: a study of SLI and normal development." *Journal of Child Language* 31: 661–681.

Friedmann, Naama, Adriana Belletti, and Luigi Rizzi (2009). "Relativized relatives: types of intervention in the acquisition of A-bar dependencies." *Lingua* 119: 67–88.

Gallistel, Charles R. (1990). "Representations in animal cognition: an introduction." *Cognition* 37:1–22. Reprinted in Charles Gallistel, ed. (1991). *Animal Cognition*. Cambridge, MA: MIT Press.

Gajewski, Jon (2002). "L-Analyticity and natural language." Manuscript, Massachusetts Institute of Technology.

Gathercole, Virginia C. (1979). "The acquisition of *more* and *less*. A critical review." In Geoffrey Gathercole and Kurt Godden, eds., *Kansas Working Papers in Linguistics Vol. 4 No. 2*. Lawrence, KS: Linguistics Department, University of Kansas.

Gazdar, Gerald J. (1979). *Pragmatics: Implicature, Presupposition, and Logical Form*. New York, NY: Academic Press.

(1982). "Phrase structure grammar." In Pauline Jacobson and Geoffrey Pullum, eds., *The Nature of Syntactic Representation*, 131–186. Dordrecht: Reidel.

Gazdar, Gerald, Ewan Klein, Geoffrey Pullum, and Ivan Sag (1985). *Generalized Phrase Structure Grammar.* Oxford, UK: Blackwell.

George, Benjamin R. (2008). "Predicting presupposition projection: some alternatives in the strong Kleene tradition." Manuscript, University of California, Los Angeles. http://semanticsarchive.net/Archive/DY0YTgxN/.

(2010). "A new case for an old logic: reviving strong Kleene approaches to presupposition projection." Manuscript, University of California, Los Angeles.

Gelman, Susan A., and Karen Ebeling (1989). "Children's use of nonegocentric standards in judgments of functional size." *Child Development* 60: 920–932.

Gentner, Dedre and Laura Namy (2006). "Analogical processes in language learning." *Current Directions in Psychological Science* 15: 297–301.

Gerstner-Link, Claudia and Manfred Krifka (1993). "Genericity." In Joachim Jacobs, Arnim von Stechow, Wolfgang Sternefeld, and Theo Vennemann, eds., *Handbuch der Syntax*, 966–978. Berlin: de Gruyter.

Geurts, Bart (1996). "Local satisfaction guaranteed: a presupposition theory and its problems." *Linguistics and Philosophy* 19: 259–294.

(2006). "Take 'five': the meaning and use of a number word." In Svetlana Vogeleer and Liliane Tasmowski, eds., *Non-definiteness and Plurality*, 311–329. Amsterdam: John Benjamins.

(2011). *Quantity Implicatures*. Cambridge University Press.

Geurts, Bart and Rick Nouwen (2007). "*At least* et al.: the semantics of scalar modifiers." *Language* 83: 533–559.

Geurts, Bart and Nausicaa Pouscoulous (2009). "Free choice for all: a response to Emmanuel Chemla." *Semantics and Pragmatics* 2: 1–10.

Giannakidou, Anastasia (2007). "The landscape of *even*." *Natural Language and Linguistic Theory* 25: 39–81.

Giannakidou, Anastasia and Josep Quer (2011). "Against universal free choice: free choice and referentially vague indefinites in Greek, Catalan, and Spanish." Manuscript, University of Chicago and Universitat Pompeu Fabra.

Gibson, Edward (1998). "Linguistic complexity: locality of syntactic dependencies." *Cognition* 68: 1–76.

Gillies, Anthony S. (2004). "Epistemic conditionals and conditional epistemics." *Noûs* 38: 585–616.

Gleitman, Lila R., and Barbara Landau (2012). "Every child an isolate: nature's experiments in language learning." In Massimo Piattelli-Palmarini and Robert Berwick, eds., *Rich Languages from Poor Inputs*. Oxford University Press.

Goetz, Stewart, and Charles Taliaferro (2011). *A Brief History of the Soul*. Oxford: Wiley-Blackwell.

Goldberg, Adele (2003). "Constructions: a new theoretical approach to language." *Trends in Cognitive Science* 7: 219–224.

(2006). *Constructions at Work: The Nature of Generalizations in Language*. Oxford University Press.

Goodluck, Helen (2010). "Object extraction is not subject to child relativized minimality." *Lingua* 120: 1516–1521.

Gordon, Peter C., Randall Hendrick, and Marcus Johnson (2001). "Memory interference during language processing." *Journal of Experimental Psychology: Learning, Memory and Cognition* 27: 1411–1423.

(2004). "Effects of noun phrase type on sentence complexity." *Journal of Memory and Language* 51: 97–114.

Goro, Takuya (2004). "The emergence of universal grammar in the emergence of language: the acquisition of Japanese logical connectives and positive polarity." Manuscript, University of Maryland at College Park.

(2007). "Language-specific constraints on scope interpretation in first language acquisition." Ph.D. Thesis. University of Maryland at College Park.

Goro, Takuya and Sachie Akiba (2004a). "The acquisition of disjunction and positive polarity in Japanese." In Vineeta Chand, Ann Kelleher, Angelo Rodríguez, and Benjamin Schmeiser, eds., *Proceedings of the 23rd West Coast Conference on Formal Linguistics (WCCFL 23)*, 251–264. Somerville, MA: Cascadilla Press.

(2004b). "Japanese disjunction and the acquisition of positive polarity." In Yukio Otsu, ed., *Proceedings of the 5th Tokyo Conference on Psycholinguistics (TCP)*, 243–254. Tokyo: Hituzi Syobo.

Grice, H. Paul (1975). "Logic and conversation." In Peter Cole and Jerry Morgan, eds., *Syntax and Semantics, Vol. III: Speech Acts*, 41–58. New York, NY: Academic Press.

Groenendijk, Jeroen and Martin Stokhof (1984). "Studies on the semantics of questions and the pragmatics of answers." Ph.D. thesis. University of Amsterdam.

Gualmini, Andrea, Stephen Crain, and Luisa Meroni (2000). "Acquisition of disjunction in conditional sentences." In S. Catherine Howell, Sarah Fish, and Thea Keith-Lucas, eds., *Proceedings of the 24th Annual Boston University Conference on Language Development*, 367–378. Somerville, MA: Cascadilla Press.

Gualmini, Andrea, Luisa Meroni, and Stephen Crain (2003). "An asymmetric universal in child language." In Matthias Weisgerber, ed., *Proceedings of Sinn und Bedeutung (SuB) 7*, 136–148. Arbeitspapiere des Fachbereichs Sprachwissenschaft (Konstanz linguistics working papers), vol. 114. Universität Konstanz, Germany.

Gualmini, Andrea and Bernard Schwarz (2009). "Solving learnability problems in the acquisition of semantics." *Journal of Semantics* 26: 185–215.

Guasti, Maria Teresa, Gennaro Cherchia, Stephen Crain, Francesca Foppolo, Andrea Gualmini, and Luisa Meroni (2005). "Why children and adults sometimes (but not always) compute implicatures." *Language and Cognitive Processes* 20: 667–696.

Guasti, Maria Teresa, Stavroula Stavrakaki, and Fabrizio Arosio (2008). "Number and case in the comprehension of relative clauses: evidence from Italian and Greek." In Anna Gavarró and M. João Freitas, eds., *Language Acquisition and Development*, 230–240. Cambridge Scholars Publishing (CSP).

Guerzoni, Elena (2008). "Even-NPIs in *yes/no* questions." *Natural Language Semantics* 12: 319–343.

Gundel, Jeanette K., Nancy Hedberg, and Ron Zacharski (1993). "Cognitive status and the form of referring expressions in discourse." *Language* 69: 274–307.

Hackl, Martin (2000). "Comparative quantifiers." Ph.D. thesis. Massachusetts Institute of Technology, Cambridge, MA.

Håkansson, Gisela and Kristina Hansson (2000). "Comprehension and production of relative clauses: a comparison between Swedish impaired and unimpaired children." *Journal of Child Language* 27: 313–333.

Hall, D. Geoffrey, Sandra Waxman, and Wendy Hurwitz (1993). "How two- and four-year-old children interpret adjectives and count nouns." *Child Development* 64: 1651–1664.

Hamann, Cornelia, and Laurie Tuller (2010). "Relative clause production in French children and adolescents." Manuscript, University of Oldenburg-Université de Tours.

Haspelmath, Martin (1997). *Indefinite Pronouns*. Oxford University Press.

Heim, Irene (1982). "The semantics of definite and indefinite NP's." Ph.D. thesis. University of Massachusetts, Amherst.

(1983a). "File Change Semantics and the Familiarity Theory of Definiteness". In Rainer Bäuerle, Christoph Schwarze, and Arnim von Stechow, eds., *Meaning, Use, and Interpretation of Language*, 164–189. Berlin: de Gruyter.

(1983b). "On the projection problem for presuppositions." In Michael Barlow, Daniel Flickinger, and Michael Wescoat, eds., *Proceedings of the Second West Coast Conference on Formal Linguistics (WCCFL 2)*, 114–125. Stanford, CA: Stanford Linguistics Association, Stanford University.

(1992). "Presupposition projection and the semantics of attitude verbs." *Journal of Semantics* 9: 183–221.

(2000). "Degree operators and scope." In Brendan Jackson and Tanya Matthews, eds., *Semantics and Linguistic Theory 10*, 40–64. Ithaca, NY: CLC Publications.

(2006). "A note on the proviso problem." Handout from 2006 Milan Meeting, Gargnano.

Heim, Irene and Angelika Kratzer (1998). *Semantics in Generative Grammar*. Oxford, UK: Blackwell.

Heller, Daphna and Linsey Wolter (2011). "On identification and transworld identity in natural language: the case of *–ever* free relatives." *Linguistics and Philosophy* 34: 169–199.

Hopper, Paul and Elizabeth Traugott (1993). *Grammaticalization*. Cambridge University Press.

Horn, Laurence R. (1972). "On the semantic properties of logical operators in English." Ph.D. thesis. University of California Los Angeles.

(1989). *A Natural History of Negation*. Chicago, IL: University of Chicago Press.

(1992) "The said and the unsaid." In Chris Barker and David Dowty, eds., *Proceedings from Semantics and Linguistic Theory (SALT) 2*, 163–192. Columbus, OH: OSU Working Papers in Linguistics.

(1996a). "Exclusive company: only and the dynamics of vertical inference." *Journal of Semantics* 13: 1–40.

(1996b). "Presupposition and implicature." In Shalom Lappin, ed., *The Handbook of Contemporary Semantic Theory*, 299–319. Oxford, UK: Blackwell.

Huang, James (1982). "Logical relations in Chinese and the theory of grammar." Ph.D. thesis. Massachusetts Institute of Technology, Cambridge, MA.

Huang, Yi Ting, and Jesse Snedeker (2009). "From meaning to inference: Evidence for the distinction between lexical semantics and scalar implicature in online processing and development." Manuscript, Harvard University.

Huang, Yi Ting, Jesse Snedeker, and Elizabeth Spelke (2009). "What exactly do numbers mean?" Manuscript, Harvard University.

Hurewitz, Felicia, Anna Papafragou, Lila Gleitman, and Rochel Gelman (2007). "Asymmetries in the acquisition of numbers and quantifiers." *Language Learning and Development* 2: 77–96.

Ionin, Tania and Ora Matushansky (2006). "The composition of complex cardinals." *Journal of Semantics* 23: 315–360.

Jayez, Jacques and Lucia Tovena (2006). "Epistemic determiners." *Journal of Semantics*, 23: 217–250.

(2008). "Evidentiality and determination." In Atle Grønn, ed., *Proceedings of Sinn und Bedeutung (SuB) 12*, 271–286. Oslo: Department of Literature, Area Studies and European Languages, University of Oslo.

Jing, Chunyuan, Stephen Crain, and Ching-Fen Hsu (2005). "Interpretation of focus in Chinese: child and adult language." In Yukio Otsu, ed., *Proceedings of the Sixth Tokyo Conference on Psycholinguistics*, 165–190. Tokyo: Hituzi Syobo.

Jubien, Michael (1989). "On properties and property theory." In Gennaro Chierchia, Barbara Partee, and Raymond Turner, eds., *Properties, Types and Meanings. Vol. I: Foundational Issues*, 159–176. Dordrecht: Kluwer.

Kadmon, Nirit and Fred Landman (1993). "Any." *Linguistics and Philosophy* 16: 353–422.

Kamp, Hans (1973). "Free choice permission." *Proceedings of the Aristotelian Society* 74: 57–74.

(1981). "A theory of truth and semantic representation." In Jeroen Groenendijk, Theo Janssen, and Martin Stokhof, eds., *Formal Methods in the Study of Language; Mathematical Centre Tracts 135*, 277–322. Amsterdam: Mathematical Centre. Reprinted in Jeroen Groenendijk, Theo Janssen, and Martin Stokhof, eds. (1984). *Truth, Interpretation, Information GRASS 2*, 1–41. Dordrecht: Foris. Reprinted in Paul Portner and Barbara Partee, eds. (2002). *Formal Semantics: The Essential Readings*, 189–222. Oxford: Blackwell.

Kamp, Hans and Barbara Partee (1995). "Prototype theory and compositionality." *Cognition* 57: 129–191.

Kamp, Hans and Uwe Reyle (1993). *From Discourse to Logic*. Dordrecht: Kluwer.

Karttunen, Lauri (1974). "Presupposition and linguistic context." *Theoretical Linguistics* 1: 181–193.

Katsos, Napoleon and Dorothy Bishop (2011). "Pragmatic tolerance: implications for the acquisition of informativeness and implicature." *Cognition* 120: 67–81.

Katzir, Roni and Ray Singh (2010). "A note on presupposition accommodation." Manuscript, Cornell University and Carleton University.

Kaufmann, Magdalena (2012). *Interpreting Imperatives*. Berlin: Springer.

Keenan, Edward L., and Jonathan Stavi (1986). "A semantic characterization of natural language determiners." *Linguistics and Philosophy* 9: 253–326.

Kegley, Charles W., and Jacquelyn Kegley (1978). *Introduction to Logic*. Lanham, MD: University Press.

Kennedy, Christopher (1999). *Projecting the Adjective: The Syntax and Semantics of Gradability and Comparison*. New York, NY: Garland Press. [Also Ph.D. thesis, University of California, Santa Cruz, 1997]

(2007). "Vagueness and grammar: the semantics of relative and absolute gradable adjectives." *Linguistics and Philosophy* 30: 1–45.

(2011). "A neo-Fregean semantics for number words." Paper presented at Semantics and Linguistic Theory (SALT 24), Rutgers University, New Brunswick, NJ, May 20–22.

Kennedy, Christopher and Louise McNally (2005). "Scale structure, degree modification, and the semantics of gradable predicates." *Language* 81: 345–381.

Kennedy, Christopher and Jason Stanley (2009). "On *average*." *Mind* 118: 583–646.

King, Jonathan and Marcel Adam Just (1991). "Individual differences in syntactic processing: the role of working memory." *Journal of Memory and Language* 30: 580–602.

Klatzky, Roberta L., Eve Clark, and Marlys Macken (1973). "Asymmetries in the acquisition of polar adjectives: linguistic or conceptual?" *Journal of Experimental Child Psychology* 16: 32–46.

Klein, Ewan (1980). "A semantics for positive and comparative adjectives." *Linguistics and Philosophy* 41–45.

(1991). "Comparatives." In Arnim von Stechow and Dieter Wunderlich, eds., *Semantics: An International Handbook of Contemporary Research*, 673–691. Berlin: de Gruyter.

Klibanoff, Raquel S. and Sandra Waxman (2000). "Basic level object categories support the acquisition of novel adjectives: evidence from preschool-aged children." *Child Development* 71: 649–659.

Klinedinst, Nathan (2006). "Plurality and possibility." Ph.D. thesis. University of California, Los Angeles.

Koenig, Jean-Pierre (1991). "Scalar predicates and negation: punctual semantics and interval interpretations." In Lise Dobrin, Lynn Nichols, and Rosa Rodriguez, eds., *Proceedings of Chicago Linguistic Society (CLS) 27*, 140–155. Chicago Linguistic Society.

Krahmer, Emiel (1998). *Presupposition and Anaphora.* Stanford, CA: CSLI Publications.

Kratzer, Angelika (1979). "Conditional necessity and possibility." In Rainer Bäuerle, Urs Egli and Arnim von Stechow, eds., *Semantics from Different Points of View*, 117–147. Dordrecht: Springer.

(1986). "Conditionals." In Anne M. Farley, Peter Farley and Karl-Erik McCollough, eds., *Papers from the Parasession on Pragmatics and Grammatical Theory*, 115–135. Chicago Linguistics Society.

(1995). "Stage-level and individual-level predicates." In Gregory N. Carlson and Francis Jeffrey Pelletier, eds., *The Generic Book*, 125–175. University of Chicago Press. Reprinted in Paul Portner and Barbara Partee, eds. (2002). *Formal Semantics: The Essential Readings*, 289–323. Oxford: Blackwell.

(2005). "Indefinites and the operators they depend on: from Japanese to Salish." In Gregory N. Carlson and Francis Jeffry Pelletier, eds., *Reference and Quantification. The Partee Effect*, 113–142. Stanford, CA: CSLI Publications.

(2011). "Situations in natural language semantics." In Edward Zalta, ed., *The Stanford Encyclopedia of Philosophy (Fall 2011 Edition)*. http://plato.stanford.edu/archives/fall2011/entries/situations-semantics/.

Kratzer, Angelika and Junko Shimoyama (2002). "Indeterminate pronouns: the view from Japanese." In Yukio Otsu, ed., *The Proceedings of the Third Tokyo Conference on Psycholinguistics*, 1–25. Tokyo: Hituzi.

Krifka, Manfred (1989). "Nominal reference, temporal constitution and quantification in event semantics." In Renate Bartsch, Johann van Benthem, and Peter van Emde Boas, eds., *Semantics and Contextual Expression*, 75–115. Stanford, CA: CSLI Publications.

(1995). "The Semantics and pragmatics of polarity items." *Linguistic Analysis* 25: 209–257.

(1999). "At least some determiners aren't determiners." In Ken Turner, ed., *The Semantics/Pragmatics Interface from Different Points of View*, 257–291. Amsterdam: Elsevier Science B.V.

Krifka, Manfred, Francis Jeffry Pelletier, Gregory Carlson, Alice ter Meulen, Gennaro Chierchia, and Godehard Link (1995). "Genericity: an introduction." In Gregory Carlson and Francis Jeffry Pelletier, eds., *The Generic Book*, 1–124. University of Chicago Press.

Kripke, Saul (1979). "A puzzle about belief." In Avishai Margalit, ed., *Meaning and Use*, 239–283. Dordrecht: Reidel.

Kroch, Anthony (1972). "Lexical and inferred meanings for some time adverbs." *Quarterly Progress Report of the Research Laboratory of Electronics 104*, Massachusetts Institute of Technology, Cambridge, MA.

(1974). "The semantics of scope in English." Ph.D. thesis. Massachusetts Institute of Technology, Cambridge, MA.

Ladusaw, William (1979). "Polarity sensitivity as inherent scope relations." Ph.D. thesis. University of Texas, Austin.

Lahiri, Uptal (1998). "Focus and negative polarity in Hindi." *Natural Language Semantics*, 6: 57–123.

(2010). "Some *evens* are "*even if. . . only*": The concessive *even* in Spanish." Manuscript. Universidad del País Vasco, Vitoria-Gasteiz, Spain.

Landau, Barbara and Lila Gleitman (1985). *Language and Experience: Evidence from the Blind Child*. Cambridge, MA: Harvard University Press.

Landman, Fred (1986). "Pegs and alecs." In Joseph Y. Halpern, ed., *TARK '86 Proceedings of the 1986 Conference on Theoretical Aspects of Reasoning about Knowledge*, 45–61. Los Altos, CA: Morgan Kaufmann. Longer version in Fred Landman (1986). *Towards a Theory of Information. The Status of Partial Objects in Semantics*, 97–155. Dordrecht: Foris.

(2003). "Predicate argument mismatches and the adjectival theory of indefinites." In Martine Coene and Yves d'Hulst, eds., *From NP to DP Volume*, 211–238. Amsterdam: John Benjamins.

(2004). *Indefinites and the Type of Sets*. Oxford: Blackwell.

Lasersohn, Peter N. (1995). *Plurality, Conjunction and Events*. Dordrecht: Kluwer.

(1999). "Pragmatic halos." *Language* 75: 522–551.

Lassiter, Daniel (to appear). "Quantificational and modal interveners in degree constructions." In *Proceedings from Semantics and Linguistic Theory (SALT 24)*.

Lauer, Sven (2010). "Some news on *irgendein* and *algún*." Talk given at the *Workshop on Epistemic Indefinites*, University of Göttingen, June 10–12.

Layton, Thomas L., and Sheldon Stick (1979). "Comprehension and production of comparatives and superlatives." *Journal of Child Language* 6: 511–527.

Levinson, Stephen C. (1983). *Pragmatics*. Cambridge University Press.

Lewis, David (1970). "General semantics." *Synthese* 22: 18–67. Reprinted in Donald Davidson and Gilbert Harman, eds. (1972). *Semantics of Natural Language*, 169–218. Dordrecht: Reidel and in Barbara H. Partee, ed., (1976). *Montague Grammar*, 1–50. New York, NY: Academic Press.

(1975). "Adverbs of quantification." In Edward Keenan, ed., *Formal Semantics of Natural Languages*, 3–15. Cambridge University Press.

(1979a). "Attitudes de dicto and de se." *The Philosophical Review* 88: 513–543. Reprinted (with postscripts) in David Lewis (1983). *Philosophical Papers. Volume I*, 131–159. Oxford University Press.

(1979b). "Scorekeeping in a language game." *Journal of Philosophical Logic* 8: 339–359. Reprinted in Paul Portner and Barbara Partee, eds. (2002). *Formal Semantics: The Essential Readings*, 162–177. Oxford: Blackwell.

Liao, Hsiu-Chen (2011). "Alternatives and exhaustification: non-interrogative uses of Chinese Wh-words." Ph.D. thesis. Harvard University, Cambridge, MA.

Lieven, Elena V. M., Julian Pine, and Gillian Baldwin (1997). "Lexically-based learning and early grammatical development." *Journal of Child Language* 24: 187–219.

Link, Godehard (1983). "The logical analysis of plural and mass terms: a lattice-theoretical approach." In Rainer Bäuerle, Christoph Schwarze, and Arnim von Stechow, eds., *Meaning, Use and the Interpretation of Language*, 302–323. Berlin: de Gruyter. Reprinted in Paul Portner and Barbara Partee, eds., (2002). *Formal Semantics: The Essential Readings*, 127–146. Oxford: Blackwell.

Löbner, Sebastian (1985). "Definites." *Journal of Semantics* 4: 279–326.

Longobardi, Giuseppe (1994). "Reference and proper names." *Linguistic Inquiry* 25: 609–665.

Ludlow, Peter (2003). "Referential semantics for I-languages?" In Louise Antony and Norbert Hornstein, eds., *Chomsky and His Critics*, 140–162. Oxford: Blackwell.

MacWhinney, Brian (2002). "The gradual emergence of language." In Talmi Givón and Bertram Malle, eds., *The Evolution of Language Out of Pre-language*, 231–263. Philadelphia, PA: John Benjamins.

Magri, Giorgio (2011). "Another argument for embedded scalar implicatures based on oddness in downward entailing environments." *Semantics and Pragmatics* 4: 1–51.

Malamud, Sophia Alexandra (forthcoming). "The meaning of plural definites: a decision-theoretic approach." *Semantics and Pragmatics*.

Markman, Ellen M. (1990). "Constraints children place on word meanings." *Cognitive Science* 14: 57–77.

Matsumoto, Yo (1995). "The conversational condition on Horn scales." *Linguistics and Philosophy* 18: 21–60.

Mayr, Clemens, and Benjamin Spector (2011). "Not too strong! Generalizing the scope economy condition." In Martin Prinzhorn, Viola Schmitt, and Sarah Zobel, eds., *Proceedings of Sinn und Bedeutung (SuB) 14*, 305–321. Vienna. www.univie.ac.at/sub14/proc/mayr-spector.pdf

McGilvray, James (2003). "Introduction." In Noam Chomsky, *Cartesian Linguistics*, 3rd edition., 1–52. Cambridge University Press.

McKee, Cecile, Dana McDaniel, and Jesse Snedeker (1998). "Relatives children say." *Journal of Psycholinguistic Research* 27: 573–596.

McNally, Louise (2011). "The relative role of property type and scale structure in explaining the behavior of GAs." In Rick Nouwen, Robert van Rooij,

Uli Sauerland, and Hans-Christian Schmitz, eds., *ViC 2009 (Papers from the ESSLLI 2009 Workshop on Vagueness in Communication). Lecture Notes in Artificial Intelligence 6517*, 151–168. Berlin: Springer.

Medina, Tamara N., Jesse Snedeker, John Trueswell, and Lila Gleitman (2011). "How words can and cannot be learned by observation." *Proceedings of the National Academy of Sciences* 108: 9014–9019.

Meroni, Luisa, and Andrea Gualmini (2012). "Do you know all SI? I know some: give children a reason to compute SI." Presented at the 13th Tokyo Conference on Psycholinguistics.

Meroni, Luisa, Andrea Gualmini, and Stephen Crain (2006). "Everybody knows." In Veerle van Geenhoven, ed., *Semantics in Acquisition*, 89–114. Dordrecht: Springer.

Mintz, Toben H., and Lila Gleitman (2002). "Adjectives really do modify nouns: the incremental and restricted nature of early adjective acquisition." *Cognition* 84: 267–293.

Montague, Richard (1970). "Universal grammar." *Theoria* 36: 373–398. Reprinted in Richmond Thomason, ed. (1974). *Formal Philosophy. Selected Papers of Richard Montague*, 222–246. New Haven, CT/London: Yale University Press.

Moravcsik, Julius (1975). "Aitia as generative factor in Aristotle's philosophy of language." *Dialogue* 14: 622–636.

Morris, Bradley J. (2008). "Logically speaking: evidence for item-based acquisition of the connectives AND & OR." *Journal of Cognition and Development* 9: 67–88.

Munaro, Nicola (1999). *Sintagmi Interrogativi nei Dialetti Italiani Settentrionali*. Padua, Italy: Unipress.

Murphy, M. Lynne (1997). "Why adjectives occur (or don't) in measure phrases." Paper presented at the Annual Meeting of the Linguistics Society of America, Chicago, IL.

Muskens, Reinhard (1994). "A compositional Discourse Representation Theory." In Paul Dekker and Martin Stokhof, eds., *Proceedings of the 9th Amsterdam Colloquium*, 467–486. Institute for Logic, Language and Computation, University of Amsterdam (ILLC).

Musolino, Julien (2004). "The semantics and acquisition of number words: integrating linguistic and developmental perspectives." *Cognition* 93: 1–41.

(2006). "On the semantics of the subset principle." *Language Learning and Development* 2: 195–218.

Musolino, Julien, Stephen Crain, and Rosalind Thornton (2000). "Navigating negative quantificational space." *Linguistics* 38: 1–32.

Notley, Anna, Rosalind Thornton, and Stephen Crain (2012). "English-speaking children's interpretation of disjunction in the scope of 'not every'." *Biolinguistics* 6: 32–69.

Notley, Anna, Peng Zhou, Britta Jensen, and Stephen Crain (2011). "Children's interpretation of disjunction in the scope of 'before': a comparison of English and Mandarin." *Journal of Child Language* 39: 482–522.

Nouwen, Rick (2008). "Upper-bound *no more:* the exhaustive interpretation of non-strict comparison." *Natural Language Semantics* 16: 271–295.

(2010). "Two kinds of modified numerals." *Semantics and Pragmatics* 3: 1–41.

Noveck, Ira A. (2001). "When children are more logical than adults: experimental investigations of scalar implicatures." *Cognition* 78: 165–188.

O'Leary, Carrie A. (1994). "Children's awareness of polarity sensitivity." M.A. Thesis. University of Connecticut, Storr, CO.

Palermo, David S. (1973). "More about less: a study of language comprehension." *Journal of Verbal Learning and Verbal Behavior* 12: 211–221.

Panizza, Daniele, Gennaro Chierchia, and Charles Clifton Jr. (2009). "On the role of entailment patterns and scalar implicatures in the processing of numerals." *Journal of Memory and Language*, 61: 503–518.

Papafragou, Anna and Julien Musolino (2003). "Scalar implicatures at the semantics-pragmatics interface." *Cognition* 80: 253–282.

Papafragou, Anna and Niki Tantalou (2004). "Children's computation of implicatures." *Language Acquisition* 12: 71–82.

Partee, Barbara H. (1973). "Some transformational extensions of Montague grammar." *Journal of Philosophical Logic* 2: 509–534. Reprinted in Barbara H. Partee, ed., (1976). *Montague Grammar*, 51–76. New York, NY: Academic Press.

(1979). "Semantics – mathematics or psychology?" In Rainer Bäuerle, Urs Egli, and Arnim von Stechow, eds., *Semantics from Different Points of View*, 1–14. Berlin: Springer-Verlag.

(1986a). "Ambiguous pseudoclefts with unambiguous *be*". In Stephen Berman, Jae-Woong Choe, and Joyce McDonough, eds., *Proceedings of the 16th Annual Meeting of the North East Linguistics Society (NELS l6)*, 354–366. Amherst, MA: University of Massachusetts, Amherst. Reprinted in Barbara H. Partee (2004). *Compositionality in Formal Semantics: Selected Papers by Barbara H. Partee*, 190–202. Oxford: Blackwell.

(1986b). "Noun phrase interpretation and type-shifting principles." In Jeroen Groenendijk, Theo Janssen, and Martin Stokhof, eds., *Studies in Discourse Representation Theory and the Theory of Generalized Quantifiers, GRASS 8*, 115–143. Dordrecht: Foris. Reprinted in Paul Portner and Barbara H. Partee, eds. (2002). *Formal Semantics: The Essential Readings*, 357–381. Oxford: Blackwell. Reprinted in Barbara H. Partee (2004). *Compositionality in Formal Semantics: Selected Papers by Barbara Partee*, 203–230. Oxford: Blackwell.

(1995). "Lexical semantics and compositionality." In Lila Gleitman and Mark Liberman, eds., *Invitation to Cognitive Science Vol. I*, 311–360. Cambridge, MA: MIT Press.

(2005). "Reflections of a formal semanticist as of Feb 2005." Manuscript. University of Massachusetts, Amherst, MA. http://people.umass.edu/partee/docs/BHP_Essay_Feb05.pdf. [A shorter version was published as: Partee, Barbara H. (2004). *Compositionality in Formal Semantics: Selected Papers of Barbara Partee*, 1–15. Oxford Blackwell.]

(2011). "Formal semantics: Origins, issues, early impact." In Barbara H. Partee, Michael Glanzberg, and Jurģis Šķilters, eds., *Formal Semantics and Pragmatics. Discourse, Context, and Models. The Baltic Yearbook of Cognition, Logic, and Communication*. Vol. VI. Lawrence, KS: New Prairie Press. http://dx.doi.org/10.4148/biyclc.v6i0.1580

Partee, Barbara H. and Mats Rooth (1983). "Generalized conjunction and type ambiguity." In Rainer Bäuerle, Christoph Schwarze, and Arnim von Stechow, eds., *Meaning, Use, and Interpretation of Language*, 361–383. Berlin: de Gruyter. Reprinted in Paul Portner and Barbara H. Partee, eds. (2002). *Formal Semantics: The Essential Readings*, 334–356. Oxford: Blackwell.

Pérez Carballo, Alejandro (2007). "A first shot at the proviso problem." Manuscript. Massachusetts Institute of Technology, Cambridge, MA.

(2009). "Toward a dissolution of the proviso problem." In Paul Egré and Giorgio Magri, eds., *Presuppositions and Implicatures: Proceedings of the MIT-Paris Workshop, volume 60*. Cambridge, MA: MIT Working Papers in Linguistics.

Peters, Stanley (1979). "A truth-conditional formulation of Karttunen's account of presupposition." *Synthese* 40: 301–316.

Pinker, Steven (1984). *Language Learnability and Language Development*. Cambridge, MA: MIT Press.

Porterfield, Leslie and Veneeta Srivastav (1988). "(In)definiteness in the absence of articles: evidence for Hindi and Indonesian." In Hagit Borer, ed., *Proceedings of the Seventh West Coast Conference on Formal Linguistics (WCCFL) 7*, 265–276. Stanford, CA: Stanford Linguistics Associations, Stanford University.

Pouscoulous, Nausicaa, Ira Noveck, Guy Politzer, and Anne Bastide (2007). "A developmental investigation of processing costs in implicature production." *Language Acquisition* 14: 347–375.

Quine, Willard V. O. (1960). *Word and Object*. Cambridge, MA: MIT Press.

(1992). *Pursuit of Truth*. Cambridge, MA: Harvard University Press.

Rawlins, Kyle (2008). "(Un)conditionals: an investigation in the syntax and semantics of conditional structures." Ph.D. thesis. University of California, Santa Cruz.

Richards, Thomas J. (1978). *The Language of Reason*. Rushcutters Bay, Australia: Pergamon Press.

Rizzi, Luigi (1990). *Relativized Minimality*. Cambridge, MA: MIT Press.

(2004). "Locality and the left periphery." In Adriana Belletti, ed., *Structures and Beyond: The Cartography of Syntactic Structures*, Vol. III, 223–251. Oxford University Press.

(2011). "Some locality principles in Italian syntax." Manuscript, University of Siena.

Rizzi, Luigi, and Ur Shlonsky (2007). "Strategies of subject extraction." In Uli Sauerland and Hans-Martin Gärtner, eds., *Interfaces + Recursion = Language?*, 115–160. Berlin: Mouton de Gruyter.

Roberts, Ian (2001). "Head movement." In Mark Baltin and Chris Collins, eds., *The Handbook of Contemporary Syntactic Theory*, 113–147. Oxford: Blackwell.

Romero, Maribel and Chung-hye Han (2004). "On negative *yes/no* questions." *Linguistics and Philosophy* 27: 609–658.

Romoli, Jacopo (2012). "Presupposition wipe-out can't be all or nothing: a note on conflicting presuppositions." *Snippets* 25. www.ledonline.it/snippets/allegati/snippets25004.pdf

Rooij, Robert van (2000). "Permission to change." *Journal of Semantics* 17: 119–143.

Rooij, Robert van and Katrin Schulz (2004). "Exhaustive interpretation of complex sentences." *Journal of Logic, Language and Information* 13: 491–519.

Rooth, Mats (1992). "A theory of focus interpretation." *Natural Language Semantics* 1: 75–116.

Rothstein, Susan (2011). "Counting, measuring and the semantics of classifiers." In Barbara H. Partee, Michael Glanzberg, and Jurģis Šķilters, eds., *Formal Semantics and Pragmatics. Discourse, Context, and Models. The Baltic International Yearbook of Cognition, Logic and Communication*. Vol. VI. Lawrence, KS: New Prairie Press. http://dx.doi.org/10.4148/biyclc.v6i0.1582

Rotstein, Carmen and Yoad Winter (2004). "Total adjectives vs. partial adjectives: scale structure and higher-order modifiers." *Natural Language Semantics* 12: 259–288.

Sadock, Jerrold (1984). "Whither radical pragmatics." In Deborah Schiffren, ed., *Meaning, Form, and Use in Context: Linguistic Applications*, 139–149. Washington, DC: Georgetown University Press.

Salmon, Nathan (1997). "Wholes, parts, and numbers." *Noûs Supplement: Philosophical Perspectives, 11, Mind, Causation and World* 31: 1–15.

Sandt, Rob van der (1989). "Presupposition and discourse structure." In Renate Bartsch, Johan van Benthem, and Peter van Emde Boas, eds., *Semantics and Contextual Expression*, 267–294. Dordrecht: Foris.

Sauerland, Uli (2004). "Scalar implicatures in complex sentences." *Linguistics and Philosophy* 27: 367–391.

(2012). "The computation of scalar implicatures: pragmatic, lexical or grammatical." *Language and Linguistics Compass* 6: 36–49.

Săvescu-Ciucivara, Oana (2007). "*Oarecare* indefinites are not just any indefinites." In Gabriela Alboiu, Larisa Avram, Andrei Avram, and Daniela Isac, eds., *Pitar Moş: A Building with a View. Papers in Honor of Alexandra Cornilescu*, 205–225. Bucharest: Editura Universităţii din Bucureşti.

Scharten, Rosemarijn (1997). "Exhaustive interpretation: a discourse-semantic account." Ph.D. thesis. Katholieke Universiteit Nijmegen.

Schlenker, Philippe (2008a). "Be articulate: a pragmatic theory of presupposition projection." *Theoretical Linguistics* 34: 157–212.

(2008b). "Presupposition projection: the new debate." In Tova Friedman and Satoshi Ito, eds., *Proceedings from Semantics and Linguistic Theory (SALT 18)*, 655–693. http://elanguage.net/journals/salt/article/view/18.655/1924

(2008c). "Local contexts" (pre-published version). http://files.nyu.edu/pds4/public/Local_Contexts_Old.pdf.

(2009). "Local contexts". *Semantics and Pragmatics* 2: 1–74.

(2011). "The proviso problem: a note." *Natural Language Semantics* 19: 395–422.

Schulz, Katrin (2005). "A pragmatic solution for the paradox of free choice permission." *Synthese* 142: 343–377.

Schulz, Katrin and Robert van Rooij (2006). "Pragmatic meaning and non-monotonic reasoning: the case of exhaustive interpretation." *Linguistics and Philosophy* 29: 205–250.

Schwarzschild, Roger (2002). "Singleton indefinites." *Journal of Semantics* 19: 289–314.

Sera, Maria and Linda Smith (1987). "Big and little: 'Nominal' and relative uses." *Cognitive Development* 2: 89–111.

Seuren, Pieter A. M. (1973). "The comparative." In Ferenç Kiefer and Nicolas Ruwet, eds., *Generative Grammar in Europe*, 528–564. Dordrecht: Reidel.

Sharvy, Richard (1980). "A more general theory of definite descriptions." *The Philosophical Review* 89: 607–624.

Sheldon, Amy (1974). "The role of parallel function in the acquisition of relative clauses in English." *Journal of Verbal Learning and Verbal Behavior* 13: 272–281.

Singh, Raj R. (2007). "Formal alternatives as a solution to the proviso problem." In Tova Friedman and Masayuki Gibson, eds., *Proceedings from Semantics and*

*Linguistic Theory (SALT 17)*, 264–281. http://elanguage.net/journals/salt/article/view/17.264/1854

(2008). "Modularity and locality in interpretation." Ph.D. thesis. Massachusetts Institute of Technology, Cambridge, MA.

(2009). "Symmetric and interacting alternatives for implicature and accommodation." In Nathan Klinedinst and Daniel Rothschild, eds., *Proceedings of the 2009 European Summer School of Logic, Language, and Information (ESSLLI) Workshop: New Directions in the Theory of Presupposition.*

(2010). "On the structure sensitivity of the alternatives for accommodation." Manuscript, Carlton University, Ottawa.

Smith, Carol L. (1980). "Quantifier and question answering in young children." *Journal of Experimental Child Psychology* 30: 191–205.

Smith, Linda B., Nancy Cooney, and Carol McCord (1986). "What is 'high'? The development of reference points for 'high' and 'low.' *Child Development* 57: 583–602.

Smith, Linda B., Mary Jo Rattermann, and Maria Sera (1988). "'Higher' and 'lower': Comparative and categorical interpretations by children." *Cognitive Development* 3: 341–357.

Spector, Benjamin (2005). "Aspects de la pragmatique des opérateurs logiques." Ph.D. thesis. Université Paris 7.

Stalnaker, Robert C. (1975). "Indicative conditionals." *Philosophia* 5: 269–286.

(1978). "Assertion." In Peter Cole, ed., *Syntax and Semantics 9*, 315–322. New York, NY: Academic Press.

Starke, Michal (2001). "Move dissolves into merge: a theory of locality." Ph.D. thesis. University of Geneva.

Stechow, Arnim von (1984). "Comparing semantic theories of comparison." *Journal of Semantics* 3: 1–77.

Stoy, Joseph (1977). *Denotational Semantics: The Scott-Strachey Approach to Programming Language Theory.* Cambridge, MA: MIT Press.

Strawson, Peter F. (1950). "On referring." *Mind* 59: 320–344.

Su, Esther (2011). "Disjunction and downward entailment in child Mandarin: An experimental investigation into the acquisition of semantic universals." Ph.D. Thesis. Macquarie University, Sydney.

Sudo, Yasutada Y. (2012). "On the semantics of phi features on pronouns." Ph.D. thesis. Massachusetts Institute of Technology, Cambridge, MA.

Sudo, Yasutada Y., Jacopo Romoli, Martin Hackl, and Danny Fox (2012). "Presupposition projection out of quantified sentences: strengthening, local accommodation and inter-speaker variation." In Maria Aloni, Vadim Kimmelman, Floris Roelofsen, Galit W. Sassoon, Katrin Schulz, and Matthijs Westera, eds., *Logic, Language and Meaning. 18th Amsterdam Colloquium. Revised Selected Papers.* Lecture Notes in Computer Science Volume 7218, 210–219. Berlin: Springer.

Syrett, Kristen (2007). "Learning about the structure of scales: adverbial modification and the acquisition of the semantics of gradable adjectives." Ph.D. thesis. Northwestern University, Evanston, Illinois.

Syrett, Kristen, Christopher Kennedy, and Jeffrey Lidz (2010). "Meaning and context in children's understanding of GAs." *Journal of Semantics* 27: 1–35.

Szabolcsi, Anna (2002). "Hungarian disjunctions and positive polarity." In István Kenesei and Peter Siptar, eds., *Approaches to Hungarian*, Volume 8, 217–241. Budapest: Akadémiai Kiadó.

(2004). "Positive polarity – negative polarity." *Natural Language and Linguistic Theory* 22: 409–452.

Takahashi, Shoichi (2006). "More than two quantifiers." *Natural Language Semantics* 14: 57–101.

Tavakolian, Susan L. (1981). "The conjoined-clause analysis of relative clauses." In Susan Tavakolian, ed., *Language Acquisition and Linguistic Theory*, 167–187. Cambridge, MA: MIT Press.

Taub, Alison (1989). "Collective predicates, Aktionsarten and *all*" in Emmon Bach, Angelika Kratzer, and Barbara H. Partee, eds., *Papers on Quantification*. Amherst, MA: Graduate Linguistic Student Association, University of Massachusetts (GLSA).

Tiel, Bob van (2011). "Universal free choice?" Talk held at *Sinn und Bedeutung (SuB) 16*, University of Utrecht, September 6–8.

Tieu, Lyn (2010). "On the tri-ambiguous status of *any*: the view from child language." Handout from talk at *Generative Approaches to Language Acquisition North America (GALANA) 4*, University of Toronto, September 1.

Toledo, Assaf and Galit Sassoon (2011). "Absolute vs. relative adjectives – Variance within vs. between individuals." In Neil Ashton, Anca Chereches, and David Lutz, eds., *Proceedings from Semantics and Linguistic Theory (SALT 21)*, 135–154. http://elanguage.net/journals/salt/article/view/21.135/2396

Tomasello, Michael (2003). *Constructing a Language: A Usage-based Theory of Language Acquisition*. Cambridge, MA: Harvard University Press.

Trinh, Tue (2011). "Nominal reference in two classifier languages." Ingo Reich, Eva Horch, and Dennis Pauly, eds., *Proceedings of Sinn und Bedeutung (SuB) 15*, 1–16. Saarbrücken, Germany: Universität des Saarlandes. http://universaar.uni-saarland.de/monographien/volltexte/2011/30/pdf/SinnUndBedeutung15.pdf

Turner, Raymond (1989). "Two issues in the foundations of semantic theory." In Gennaro Chierchia, Barbara H. Partee, and Raymond Turner, eds., *Properties, Types and Meaning. Vol. I: Foundational Issues*, 63–84. Dordrecht: Kluwer.

Turner, Raymond and Kathleen Adamczyk (1984). *Logic and Linguistics: A Marriage of Inconvenience*. Manuscript. Amherst, MA. [Published in Appendix B in this volume.]

Van Geenhoven, Veerle (1998). *Semantic Incorporation and Indefinite Descriptions*. Stanford, CA: CSLI.

(1999). "Pro properties, contra generalized kinds." In Brendan Jackson and Tanya Matthews, eds., *Proceedings from Semantics and Linguistic Theory (SALT) 10*, 221–238. Ithaca, NY: CLC Publications. Also available on eLanguage: http://elanguage.net/journals/salt/article/view/10.221/1730

(2004). "For-adverbials, frequentative aspect and pluractionality." *Natural Language Semantics* 12: 135–190.

Veltman, Frank (1996). "Defaults in update semantics." *Journal of Philosophical Logic* 25: 22–261.

Wal, Sjoukje van der (1996). "Negative Polarity Items and Negation: Tandem Acquisition." Ph.D. thesis. University of Groningen. (Groningen Dissertations in Linguistics 17)

Warren, Tessa and Edward Gibson (2002). "The influence of referential processing on sentence complexity." *Cognition* 85: 79–112.

(2005). "Effects of NP-type on reading English clefts." *Language and Cognitive Processes* 20: 751–767.

Waters, Gloria S., David Caplan, and Nancy Hildebrandt (1987). "Working memory and written sentence comprehension." In Max Coltheart, ed., *Attention and Performance XII: The Psychology of Reading*, 531–555. Hove: Lawrence Erlbaum.

Waxman, Sandra R. and Amy Booth (2003). "The origins and evolution of links between word learning and conceptual organization: new evidence from 11-month-olds." *Developmental Science* 6: 128–135.

Waxman, Sandra R., and Maria Teresa Guasti (2009). "Nouns, adjectives, and the acquisition of meaning: new evidence from Italian-acquiring children." *Language Learning and Development* 5: 50–68.

Waxman, Sandra R., and Raquel Klibanoff (2000). "The role of comparison in the extension of novel adjectives." *Developmental Psychology* 36: 571–581.

Wilkinson, Karina (1991). "Studies in the semantics of generic NP's." Ph.D. thesis. University of Massachusetts, Amherst.

Williams, Edwin (1980). "Predication." *Linguistic Inquiry* 11: 203–238.

Yalcin, Seth (2007). "Epistemic modals." *Mind* 116: 983–1026.

Yang, Rong (2001) "Common nouns, classifiers, and quantification in Chinese." Ph.D. thesis. Rutgers University, New Brunswick, NJ.

Yoon, Youngeun (1996). "Total and partial predicates and the weak and strong interpretations." *Natural Language Semantics* 4: 217–236.

Zamparelli, Roberto (2007). "On singular existential quantifiers in Italian." In Ileana Comorovski and Klaus von Heusinger, eds., *Existence: Semantics and Syntax*, 293–328. Dordrecht: Springer.

Zeevat, Henk (1989). "A compositional approach to discourse representation theory." *Linguistics and Philosophy* 12: 95–131.

(1994). "Questions and exhaustivity in update semantics." In Harry Bunt, Leen Kievit, Reinhard Muskens, and Margriet Verlinden, eds., *Proceedings of the First International Workshop on Computational Semantics (IWCS-1)*. Tilburg: Institute for Language Technology and Artificial Intelligence.

Zhou, Peng and Stephen Crain (2011). "Children's knowledge of the quantifier *dou* in Mandarin Chinese." *Journal of Psycholinguistic Research* 40: 155–176.

Zimmermann, Ede (2000). "Free choice disjunction and epistemic possibility." *Natural Language Semantics* 8: 255–290.

Zondervan, Arjen (2006). "The question under discussion focus condition for scalar implicatures." M.A. Thesis. University of Utrecht.

Zucchi, Alessandro and Michael White (2001). "Twigs, sequences and temporal sequences of predicates." *Linguistics and Philosophy* 24: 223–270.

# Index of names

# Index of subjects

Lightning Source UK Ltd.
Milton Keynes UK
UKOW05n2303230514

232235UK00003B/78/P